Authoritarian Police in Democracy

In countries around the world, from the United States to the Philippines to Chile, police forces are at the center of social unrest and debates about democracy and rule of law. This book examines the persistence of authoritarian policing in Latin America to explain why police violence and malfeasance remain pervasive decades after democratization. It also examines the conditions under which reform can occur. Drawing on rich comparative analysis and evidence from Brazil, Argentina, and Colombia, the book opens up the "black box" of police bureaucracies to show how police forces exert power and cultivate relationships with politicians, as well as how social inequality impedes change. González shows that authoritarian policing persists not in spite of democracy but in part because of democratic processes and public demand. When societal preferences over the distribution of security and coercion are fragmented along existing social cleavages, politicians possess few incentives to enact reform.

Yanilda María González is Assistant Professor of Public Policy at Harvard Kennedy School. She holds a PhD in Politics and Social Policy from Princeton University and was a postdoctoral fellow at the Ash Center for Democratic Governance and Innovation at Harvard Kennedy School.

Cambridge Studies in Comparative Politics

General Editors
Kathleen Thelen   *Massachusetts Institute of Technology*

Associate Editors
Catherine Boone   *London School of Economics*
Thad Dunning   *University of California, Berkeley*
Anna Grzymala-Busse   *Stanford University*
Torben Iversen   *Harvard University*
Stathis Kalyvas   *University of Oxford*
Margaret Levi   *Stanford University*
Melanie Manion   *Duke University*
Helen Milner   *Princeton University*
Frances Rosenbluth   *Yale University*
Susan Stokes   *Yale University*
Tariq Thachil   *University of Pennsylvania*
Erik Wibbels   *Duke University*

Series Founder
Peter Lange   *Duke University*

Other Books in the Series

Continued after the Index

Authoritarian Police in Democracy

Contested Security in Latin America

YANILDA MARÍA GONZÁLEZ

Harvard Kennedy School

 CAMBRIDGE
UNIVERSITY PRESS

CAMBRIDGE
UNIVERSITY PRESS

University Printing House, Cambridge CB2 8BS, United Kingdom

One Liberty Plaza, 20th Floor, New York, NY 10006, USA

477 Williamstown Road, Port Melbourne, VIC 3207, Australia

314–321, 3rd Floor, Plot 3, Splendor Forum, Jasola District Centre, New Delhi – 110025, India

79 Anson Road, #06–04/06, Singapore 079906

Cambridge University Press is part of the University of Cambridge.

It furthers the University's mission by disseminating knowledge in the pursuit of education, learning, and research at the highest international levels of excellence.

www.cambridge.org
Information on this title: www.cambridge.org/9781108830393
DOI: 10.1017/9781108907330

First published 2021

A catalogue record for this publication is available from the British Library.

Library of Congress Cataloging-in-Publication Data
NAMES: González, Yanilda Mariá, author.
TITLE: Authoritarian Police in Democracy : contested security in Latin America / Yanilda Mariá González.
DESCRIPTION: Cambridge, United Kingdom ; New York, NY : Cambridge University Press, 2021. | Includes bibliographical references and index.
IDENTIFIERS: LCCN 2020024237 (print) | LCCN 2020024238 (ebook) | ISBN 9781108830393 (hardback) | ISBN 9781108907330 (ebook)
SUBJECTS: LCSH: Police – Latin America. | Police misconduct – Latin America. | Democracy – Latin America. | Violent crime – Latin America. | Internal security – Latin America. | Latin America – Politics and government.
CLASSIFICATION: LCC HV8160.5.A2 G66 2021 (print) | LCC HV8160.5.A2 (ebook) | DDC 363.2098–dc23
LC record available at https://lccn.loc.gov/2020024237
LC ebook record available at https://lccn.loc.gov/2020024238

ISBN 978-1-108-83039-3 Hardback
ISBN 978-1-108-82074-5 Paperback

Contents

Figures

Tables

List of Tables

Acknowledgments

Many of us who study the police have likely come across a phrase written by veteran police scholar David Bayley: "A scholar who studies the police must be willing to do extensive fieldwork in unprepossessing surroundings, to brave bureaucratic intransigence, and to become politically suspect and socially déclassé." Over the course of two-and -a-half years of field research for this project, I can attest to the particular challenges of studying the police, from the discomfort of officers candidly recounting their own abuses and of ordinary citizens gleefully celebrating torture and police killings to concerns for one's own safety. But this work has also shed light on the urgency of studying the police in order to understand how police constitute the palpable gap between formal democratic rights and lived experience.

The tensions between policing and democracy have long been evident to me. As an immigrant child growing up in New York City during the 1990s, my sisters and I watched the local news religiously (we didn't have cable), which seemed to be equally inundated with, on the one hand, a racialized discourse of panic over out-of-control crime and, on the other, stories of similarly racialized police violence, from the Central Park Five to Abner Louima, Nicholas Heyward Jr, and Amadou Diallo. The 9/11 attacks and their aftermath were similarly instructive. At the age of nineteen I began working at the New York Civil Liberties Union on a grassroots campaign focused on public education and mobilization around the threat of post-9/11 anti-terrorism policies to civil rights and civil liberties. Through this work I encountered many New Yorkers who defended racial and religious profiling, surveillance, and detentions without due process, insisting that the threat of terrorism necessitated that we restrict some rights in the name of security. A few years later, I encountered similar contradictions upon arriving in Argentina as a Fulbright fellow in 2006 – the thirty-year anniversary of the military coup that gave rise to Argentina's infamously repressive dictatorship. In my interviews and everyday contexts I spoke with many Argentines who reminisced fondly about the dictatorship period, reasoning that at least back then crime wasn't a problem and they felt safe. Others commemorated the victims of state violence under the dictatorship and celebrated hard-won gains in human rights under democracy, while saying little about rampant police violence and its many victims under democracy.

These early experiences taught me invaluable lessons about the interdependence of and tensions between security and democracy that I sought to explore in this book. Security is a basic human right, without which the enjoyment of other rights and democratic citizenship become impossible. But security is not merely a public good: it is a site of contestation about the distribution of protection and repression, and the nature of that distribution can pose fundamental challenges for democracy. This book is an effort to grapple with this tension and elucidate some of its causes – and will hopefully contribute to debates about its solutions.

I am deeply indebted to Deborah Yashar, who provided much meaningful support and guidance throughout my academic career and the development of this project and who had an immeasurable impact on my identity as a scholar and educator. I'm also thankful for the support and guidance of Mark Beissinger and Evan Lieberman, whose early encouragement to focus on the politics of policing was essential for this project and for developing my own approach to political science.

During graduate school, I had the privilege of being part of the Drugs, Security, and Democracy Program (Social Science Research Council/Open Society Foundations), which not only provided generous funding for my dissertation fieldwork but also enabled me to take part in an amazing interdisciplinary network of scholars focused on violence, drugs, and security in Latin America. I cannot say enough praise about the DSD network and about the incredible scholars who constitute it, from whom I've learned so much, including Angelica Duran-Martinez, Lina Britto, Ana Villarreal, Ana Arjona, Benjamin Lessing, Jose Miguel Cruz, Eduardo Moncada, and Desmond Arias. Similarly, my time as a postdoctoral democracy fellow at the Ash Center for Democratic

Governance and Innovation at the Harvard Kennedy School was a formative and transformative experience, where conversations with Archon Fung, Quinton Mayne, Candelaria Garay, and other democracy fellows profoundly shaped my thinking about policing and democracy. This book benefited immensely from conversations with a range of scholars whose work I deeply admire, including Daniel Brinks, Beatriz Magaloni, Lisa Miller, Richard Snyder, and Vesla Weaver, who generously provided careful feedback on different sections and versions of this book. Other conversations were more informal but no less impactful. I often look back to a conversation at a coffee shop in São Paulo with Daniel Brinks and Tianna Paschel about identity, police, and democracy during the start of my fieldwork that continues to shape my thinking a decade later.

In addition to the generous mentorship from senior scholars, I'm also grateful for various spaces of peer mentorship. Throughout graduate school and since, Sarah El-Kazaz and Sharece Thrower have been friends and scholarly interlocutors, without whom I would not have been able to navigate generals, thesis prospectus, fieldwork, thesis writing, and the job market. I've also been incredibly fortunate to be part of writing groups with Emily Clough, Sheena Greitens, Alisha Holland, Kyle Jaros, Lauren McCarthy, Brian Palmer-Rubin, Suzanne Scoggins, and Nicholas Smith, who read countless pages of this book and greatly helped to improve its ideas and analysis. Conversations with wonderful friends and colleagues including Janice Gallagher, Lindsay Mayka, and Jessica Rich also helped strengthen this book and the field research that informs it.

I am indebted to the research assistants whose hard work, interest, and commitment helped make this book a lot better: Ignacio Claut, Santiago Battezzati, Carol Schlitter, Tatiana Machulis, Thaisa Ferreira, Jaime Landínez Aceros, Celina Doria, and Anne Ruelle.

I would like to thank the dozens of community leaders, human rights activists, researchers, police officers, and government officials in Buenos Aires City and Province, São Paulo, and Bogotá who welcomed me into their homes and places of work, took time out of their days to show me around their communities, invited me to their meetings and events, and shared their stories and experiences with me. I hope that in this work I was able to do justice to the lessons you taught me. I am especially grateful for the guidance of Débora Maria da Silva, whose words begin this book and whose life, struggle, and vision exemplify the challenges at its heart.

My deepest gratitude goes to my parents and their vision and hope for a better life. Before I learned English, my father translated my third-grade math word problems after a sixteen-hour workday so that I could do my homework. Their many years of sacrifice and struggle has made all things possible. Finally, I thank Juwendo Denis for helping me get this book past the finish line.

Police

Authoritarian Enclaves in Democratic States

"I looked [then] President Dilma [Rousseff] in the eyes and told her she is the hope of more than 60,000 'Mothers of May' produced by my country. [But] she should stop celebrating the end of the dictatorship, because we live in a false democracy, a democracy that kills tens, scores, hundreds."[1] Débora Maria da Silva – the mother of a young black man killed by São Paulo's police in May 2006 and founder of Mães de Maio (Mothers of May), an organization of similarly afflicted mothers – routinely denounces what she calls the "democracy of massacres" (*democracia das chacinas*) meticulously executed by Brazil's Military Police forces. For da Silva, who lost her brother to state security forces under the military dictatorship and her son to police under democracy, Brazil's much-celebrated democratic transition did little to curtail the routine torture, extrajudicial killings, and massacres at the hands of the state.

Nora Cortiñas, a member of Argentina's Mothers of Plaza de Mayo whose son was disappeared under the military dictatorship, similarly reflected on the continuity of authoritarian coercive practices in democracy, observing that "the dictatorship ended and the military had to go back to the barracks." But, she noted, "the security forces have continuity. There is a long list of *desaparecidos* (disappeared) during constitutional governments ... [Meanwhile] *gatillo fácil* ('trigger-happy' killings) increased because the police forces have more permissiveness – they're given carte blanche to act."[2]

---

[1] Remarks by Débora Maria da Silva at the event "Fue el estado: An International Call Against Impunity," New York City, June 1, 2016.
[2] Author interview with Nora Cortiñas, Castelar, Buenos Aires Province, August 29, 2017.

The manifest contradictions between well-documented patterns of police violence in Latin America and the promise of democracy to constrain the exercise of the state's monopoly of legitimate force within the bounds of the rule of law have been a compelling rallying cry for human rights activists in the region. Like Mães de Maio's memorial for "the invisible victims of democracy" (Movimento Mães de Maio 2019), Argentina's anti-police-violence group CORREPI keeps a running tally of what they call "the invisible repression of democracy" (Verdú 2009) – a count that intentionally begins in 1983, the year of Argentina's transition to democratic rule.

Long after the onset of the "third wave" of democratization (Huntington 1991), police institutions in many Latin American countries have constituted stubborn pockets of authoritarianism. Even as formal national democratic institutions flourished, patterns of coercion in many Latin American democracies have been characterized by widespread extralegal use of lethal force, arbitrary and discriminatory enforcement of the law, rampant corruption and predation, and weak or nonexistent external accountability. While many observers and scholars (e.g., Hite & Cesarini 2004; Pinheiro 1994) situate these patterns of violence within the history and legacy of the police forces' relationship to previous military dictatorships (as well as older historical processes), this book elucidates the ways in which such patterns of coercion are firmly rooted in democratic processes.

This book examines the politics of continuity and reform among coercive institutions under democracy. It asks why police forces in what are otherwise healthy democracies often exhibit sustained patterns of violence and corruption that are incompatible with democracy, and it investigates why these patterns persist and the conditions under which politicians choose to undertake reform.

The book draws on comparative analysis of periods of continuity and reform among police forces in Buenos Aires Province, Argentina; in São Paulo State, Brazil; and in Colombia, to demonstrate that the persistence of authoritarian coercive institutions is not the result of a failure of democratic processes, nor is it merely a set of structures and practices inherited from a previous period of authoritarian rule. Instead, police forces may emerge as authoritarian enclaves within otherwise democratic states as a result of ordinary democratic politics – citizens' claims-making and expression of demands for protection, as well as politicians assessing electoral incentives based on societal demands and political competition. As I argue in Chapter 2, when societal preferences over policing and security are fragmented, irrespective of political competition, reform brings little electoral gain and carries the risk of alienating a powerful bureaucracy whose cooperation politicians need. Preference fragmentation thus favors the persistence of authoritarian coercive practices. Reform becomes likely, however, when societal preferences converge and incumbents face a robust political opposition, because politicians now face an electoral counterweight to the structural power of police. Paradoxically, then, even as coercive institutions in Latin America (and beyond) constitute an enduring blight on democracy in the region, democracy, too, may pose an important challenge for reforming coercive institutions.

THE PERSISTENCE OF AUTHORITARIAN POLICING AND ITS RENEWAL UNDER DEMOCRATIC RULE

The chapters that follow provide detailed accounts of the seamless continuity of police practices, structures, and personnel from authoritarian periods to democratic rule. While democratization brought considerable institutional change – including the enactment of significant military reforms and new constitutions – Latin America's transitions to democratic rule left police institutions largely intact.

But the remarkable persistence of police institutions in the face of regime change – from formal institutions such as rank structures and disciplinary systems to informal ones such as torture practices – should not be seen as an oversight, nor as vestigial remnants of previous authoritarian periods. Instead, this book demonstrates that the persistence of authoritarian modes of coercion in democracies results from a strictly democratic political logic. While previous periods of dictatorship gave birth to many current authoritarian coercive structures and practices of the region's police forces, they have been subjected to reproduction and renewal through ordinary democratic politics.

Accounting for the persistence of decidedly authoritarian modes of coercion in democracies requires understanding policing as a political resource that can be distributed toward electoral ends. Politicians' incentives to use the distribution of protection and repression to achieve political objectives in turn endow police forces with considerable agency to defend institutional prerogatives. As the primary entity to which the state delegates its monopoly of the legitimate use of force, police control a fundamental instrument of state making. This control over coercion endows the police with considerable structural power, enabling police to constrain the policy options available to politicians and raise the threshold for reform. Absent an electoral threat, politicians are unlikely to undertake the risks of reforming, and potentially alienating, the police forces they ostensibly control. The problem for would-be police reformers in Latin America is that such electoral threats to political leaders that neglect to rein in violent, corrupt, and unaccountable police forces have, more often than not, failed to materialize.

A key reason that authoritarian coercive structures and practices are reproduced under democracy is that they are often the result of citizens' demands. Indeed, the challenge of reforming the police is that the types of police violence denounced by Débora Maria da Silva are actively demanded by many of her fellow citizens who, in their minds, are simply seeking protection from the state. Such demands are common throughout the region. Residents at a community security meeting in a low-income neighborhood in São Paulo, for instance, responded to an announcement by the local police commander that police had shot and killed a criminal suspect with applause and cries of "Thank God" (*Graças a Deus*).[3] Residents of Santo Domingo, Dominican Republic, meanwhile, are – according to the leader of a human rights organization – "tired of seeing so many muggings, so much robbery, [such that] you can't even go outside ... People wish that human rights didn't exist here, and we recognize that. If you were to do a survey, they would say, 'Kill all the delinquents'."[4] Such societal contestation over the distribution of protection and repression results in the formation of fragmented preferences and demands that may render reforming the police electorally disadvantageous.

The enduring authoritarian patterns of coercion prevalent in many democracies – from extrajudicial killings and torture to politicized repression – thus cannot be attributed solely to the legacies of previous periods of authoritarian rule. While the failure to reform police at the time of transitions was an oversight of many Latin American democracies, policing in democracy can create electoral incentives and generate patterns of demand-making that reproduce authoritarian coercion irrespective of these legacies. As a reformist Brazilian police official remarked incredulously after the Constituent Assembly voted to maintain police structures intact during the transition to democracy, "the dictatorship

---

[3] A meeting of the local Community Security Council (CONSEG, Conselho Comunitário de Segurança) attended by the author in a low-income neighborhood in the northern zone of São Paulo in 2012.

[4] Author interview with anonymous leader of human rights NGO, Santo Domingo, Dominican Republic, January 14, 2015.

militarized the police and now democracy has consecrated this"[5] (see Chapter 3).

THE CENTRALITY – AND DISSONANCE – OF POLICE IN DEMOCRACY

Making democracy real entails the provision of meaningful security to citizens. As the entity to which the state delegates its coercive authority, police are central to this task. Policing shapes the construction of democratic citizenship through the distribution of protection and repression (González 2017). Deficient security provision results in constrained citizenship, wherein citizens lack the security necessary to engage in the basic political, social, and economic activities that are constitutive of citizenship. Unequal security provision, meanwhile, results in stratified citizenship, where access to security and protection from state repression are determined by existing societal hierarchies, such as race, class, and geography. The ways in which police perform their central task are thus highly consequential for democracy. As the veteran police scholar David Bayley put it, "a government that cannot provide minimal safety to its citizens cannot be called a government, let alone a democratic one" (Bayley 2006, 22).

Meaningful security, however, has proven elusive for much of democratic Latin America. Homicide rates in post-civil-war El Salvador exceeded the average annual deaths during the civil war, becoming the second highest in the world in 1996 (Call 2003, 840). Colombia's homicide rate, meanwhile, skyrocketed from 32 per 100,000 inhabitants in 1980 to 86 in 1992 and 127 in 1994 (Franco Agudelo 1997, 95). Even countries with relatively low homicide rates by regional standards saw a rise in crime and violence. Argentina saw its violent crime rate increase fivefold during the 1980s and 1990s (Ungar 2002, 259), while Costa Rica saw its homicide rate double from 5.3 in the mid-1990s to 10 in 2011 (UNODC 2013). Despite considerable variation across countries, Latin America remains the most violent region in the world, with a homicide rate that is four times the global average (UNODC 2013, 23).

In the context of the high rates of crime and violence that have characterized Latin America since transitions to democracy in the preceding decades, citizens' demands for improved protection have become increasingly urgent. Indeed, it would be difficult to overstate the significance of crime and violence for Latin America's citizens and democratic governments.

---

[5] "Polícia Civil perde a função preventiva," *Correio Brasiliense*, November 7, 1987, p. 5.

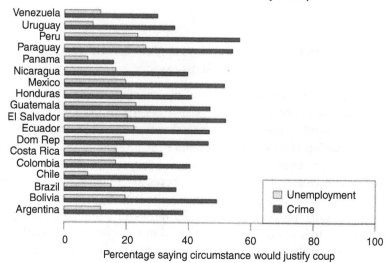

FIGURE 1.1 Comparison of the percentage of respondents expressing the opinion that high crime and high unemployment would justify "a military takeover over the state"
AmericasBarometer Survey 2012, Latin American Public Opinion Project (LAPOP)

Regional surveys such as the Latinobarometer and the AmericasBarometer have documented the growing concern of the region's citizens with crime and insecurity over the last two decades, in some instances overtaking every other issue identified by citizens as the most important problem facing their countries (Zechmeister 2014).

Just as urgent as citizens' demand for security, however, is the risk it poses for democratic stability. Indeed, many citizens appear to be highly skeptical about the ability of democratic governments to protect them and keep crime under control. In particular, a large proportion of citizens in the region seemingly believe that the military regimes of previous eras might be better suited for addressing the region's crime problem. Figure 1.1 shows responses to two survey questions asking respondents in Latin American countries about conditions that would justify "a military takeover of the state."[6] As we can observe from the chart, large groups of citizens – ranging from one-

---

[6] The questions are from the 2012 wave of the AmericasBarometer survey. The survey question asked, "Some people say that under some circumstances it would be justified for the military of this country to take power by a coup d'état (military coup). In your opinion would a coup be justified under the following circumstances?" For each circumstance (high unemployment,

quarter to more than half – in nearly all countries agree that "a lot of crime" would justify a military coup.[7] In comparison, far fewer citizens believe that high unemployment would justify a coup. Rather than a wholesale rejection of democracy, citizens in much of Latin America appear to doubt that democracy can keep them safe from crime and seem particularly willing to turn to undemocratic responses to address this problem.

This dilemma is not merely abstract. Scholars have provided ample evidence of how the failure to provide adequate protection for citizens undermines the broader quality of democracy and, potentially, its long-term stability. Davis (2006) and Call (2003) have provided compelling analyses of the challenges of reforming coercive institutions and providing security for citizens, as well as the threat the failure to do so poses for the durability of new democratic institutions in Mexico and El Salvador, respectively. Scholars working in Central America – which has the highest rates of violence in the region – have found that crime victimization and fear of crime lead citizens to express lower support for democracy and increased support for military coups (Carreras 2013; Cruz 2003; Pérez 2003, 2009). Moreover, recent work by Cruz (2015) found that police corruption, abuse, and outright criminality can decrease support for the incumbent administration and for the democratic regime overall.

Coercion, and the state institution primarily charged with exercising it, are thus fundamental components of democracy. Indeed, as Guillermo O'Donnell told us decades ago, "a state that is unable to enforce its legality supports a democracy of low-intensity citizenship" (O'Donnell 1993, 1361). Thus, in instances where "what citizens can see of the state" (González 2017) is a police force that not only neglects to protect them but is also unconstrained by the rule of law and accountability, democratic citizenship, as well as the quality and stability of democracy, are at risk of being severely eroded.

HOW TRANSITIONS TO DEMOCRACY LEFT POLICE BEHIND

Despite the importance of policing for democracy, Latin America's democratic governments have focused remarkably little on reforming the police, even as they prioritized overhauling other institutions. As I lay

---

a lot of crime, a lot of corruption), respondents had to agree or disagree with the statements that a military takeover of the state would be justified.

[7] This is a fairly consistent finding. For instance, since 2004, between 40 percent and 50 percent of respondents of each wave of the AmericasBarometer survey have declared that high crime would justify a military coup.

out in the chapters that follow, the decades following democratic transitions in Latin America saw political leaders enact new constitutions, reform militaries and court systems, and pass transformative policies in a range of policy areas. Police institutions, however, rarely underwent such processes of legislative reform. Venezuela's comprehensive police reform begun in 2006, for instance, was the first such effort in nearly 100 years (Gabaldón & Antillano 2007, 9). Similarly, the ambitious police reforms adopted in Buenos Aires Province in the late 1990s (discussed in Chapter 7) was only the second reform effort in a century (Barreneche 2007). Meanwhile, Colombian President César Gaviria's *"revolcón institucional"* (institutional shakeup), a transformative agenda to remake the Colombian state and rebuild its legitimacy through radical institutional changes, excluded the National Police (see Chapter 5). Finally, São Paulo's Military Police, one of the most lethal police forces in the Americas, has yet to undergo comprehensive structural reform more than three decades after the return to democratic rule (see Chapters 3 and 6). With the exception of Central American countries such as El Salvador and Guatemala, whose transitions to democracy saw the creation of entirely new police forces as part of peace agreements (Call 2003), police reform did not appear to be a priority for the region's democratic leaders.

The lack of urgency in reforming police following transitions to democracy stands in sharp contrast to the priority given to reforming another coercive institution – the military. Democratic leaders throughout the region sought to dismantle the political power, financial resources, coercive capacity, and intelligence apparatus of the armed forces that previously ruled over their countries (Diamint 1999; Pion-Berlin 1997). These essential reforms accompanied transitions to democracy or followed shortly thereafter. In some cases, the imposition of civilian rule over the once-dominant National Security Doctrine (Buitrago 2003; Pion-Berlin 1988) was itself the product of the political incentives created by democratization (Hunter 1997). While this emphasis on reforming militaries was wholly appropriate, the lack of reform of police institutions following transitions to democracy remains puzzling. As Chapter 3 on São Paulo State and Chapter 4 on Buenos Aires Province demonstrate, police forces were fundamental components of the machinery of repression under military dictatorships. While soldiers returned to the barracks following transitions to democracy, police officers returned to the streets, with their legal structures, repertoires of repression, and personnel left largely intact.

It is little wonder, then, that police forces throughout Latin America often bear little semblance to democratic ideals. Following the dramatic increases in crime and violence that accompanied the transition to democracy in many countries (Yashar 2019), police forces previously dedicated to political repression were ill-equipped to carry out their formal tasks of preventing and investigating crimes, a common pattern in new democracies (Tanner 2000). But police forces didn't only perform poorly at protecting citizens from criminal violence: they also remained a significant source of violence against citizens, largely unconstrained by the rule of law and accountability mechanisms. In Argentina and Brazil, the years following the end of military rule saw instruments of torture common under each country's dictatorship – the *picana eléctrica* (electric shock device) and *pau de arara* (a pole on which individuals are hanged upside down), respectively – become routine tools at the hands of police (Chevigny 1995). Killings carried out by police in Brazil each year not only exceed the total number of deaths at the hands of the state during the twenty years of military rule (Arias & Goldstein 2010, 2; Pereira 2005), but they also constitute a significant proportion of all homicides to this day (see Chapter 3). Even in less well-known cases, the numbers of citizens dying at the hands of police are staggering. In the Dominican Republic, human rights NGOs denounced in 2010 the killing of nearly 500 people by police, many of them summarily executed after they had already been detained.[8]

These extraordinarily high levels of police violence are exacerbated by the fact that, as the cases of São Paulo State, Buenos Aires Province, and Colombia show, characteristics such as race, class, or where one happens to reside are often stronger predictors of being subject to police action than is actual involvement in criminal activity. Rather than the rule of law, Latin American police forces seemingly adhere to the view attributed to patrolmen in various US cities in the 1970s by Wilson (1978): "What they deserve depends on what they *are*" (36). Moreover, the case studies also attest to the failure of other institutions of democracy to intervene to curtail these arbitrary and discriminatory policing practices. As was thoroughly researched by Brinks (2008), the Latin American police forces that most contravened the rule of law in their deployment of coercion were also the least likely to be held accountable by the judiciary. Chevigny (1999) argues further that opaque and weak disciplinary systems and nearly nonexistent oversight by executives and legislatures also serve to undermine accountability.

---

[8] "CNDH afirma van 478 caídos en 'intercambios de disparos'," *Hoy*, December 11, 2010.

Thus, even as democratic rule has taken hold throughout Latin America and endured far longer than previous democratic episodes, police bureaucracies continue to function as authoritarian enclaves. But while these practices and structures were honed under authoritarian rule, they are sustained and reproduced by democratic processes, as I argue in Chapter 2.

UNDERSTANDING COERCION: BEYOND REGIME TYPE

The experiences of Latin America's democratic governments thus demonstrate that regime type and police force characteristics don't always correspond in the ways we might expect. Indeed, democratic governments in Latin America (and elsewhere) have long struggled to organize police institutions such that they address citizens' demands for order and security and so that the deployment of coercion against citizens is applied equitably and constrained by law and external accountability. Security and policing in the region exemplify what Holston and Caldeira (1998) call "disjunctive democratization," which is characterized by the contradictions inherent in the institutionalization of national-level democratic politics, juxtaposed with the "privatization of justice, escalation of both violent crime and police abuse, criminalization of the poor, and massive support for illegal and/or authoritarian measures of control" (265).

Indeed, the empirical chapters in this book attest to a range of coercive patterns and practices that defy notions of the rule of law and democratic citizenship. In São Paulo and elsewhere in Brazil, police officers routinely operate death squads responsible for the off-duty killing of hundreds of citizens, in addition to hundreds of extrajudicial on-duty killings. In Buenos Aires Province, police officials of all ranks have operated a lucrative criminal enterprise based upon extensive predation of the citizenry. In Colombia, the police force was profoundly infiltrated by and complicit with drug-trafficking organizations, leading to rampant violence against the population. And throughout the region, police routinely deploy coercion in the service of political and private interests.

Because of the clear mismatch between the formal democratic institutions that have taken root in most of the region and the ways in which the region's police forces exercise the state's coercive authority, it is essential to develop a theoretical framework about coercion that is distinct from regime type. Such theorizing can help us better understand the choices of democratic political leaders and the great variation in the deployment of coercion among the police forces they ostensibly control. After all, to paraphrase Linz (2000) as he contemplated his typology of authoritarian regimes, we all know that police forces are different and that it is not the same thing to be subject to one or another police force, *especially* in matters of daily life (49).[9]

In order to conceptualize the seeming mismatch between regime type and the patterns of coercion prevalent throughout Latin America (and beyond), I begin by considering the implications of democratic institutions for the deployment of coercion in the pursuit of order and security. As the preceding discussion on Latin America illustrates, democratic governments face a twofold challenge in the provision of order and security. They must not only address urgent societal demands for improved security for the sake of democratic responsiveness and winning elections: they must also strive to do so in accordance with democratic principles.

Whether one subscribes to minimalist definitions of democracy or broader conceptions, democratic theorists offer valuable insights about what the state's exercise of coercion ought to look like under formal democratic rule. Classic theories conceived of democracy as a primarily electoral endeavor for selecting who will govern; they were fundamentally concerned with identifying an "institutional arrangement for arriving at political decisions" (Schumpeter 1942, 269), one "which permits the largest possible part of the population to influence these decisions" (Lipset 1959, 71). Dahl (1971) extends the focus on citizens' ability to influence governance, emphasizing participation and contestation, while Schmitter and Karl (1991) cite "channels for the expression of interests and values" (81).

What we can derive from these theories is that, as with many other actions taken by the state, citizens in democracies ought to be able to influence the exercise of coercion to ensure that it serves their interests. This represents a stark departure from the traditional role of coercion in state building, which was exercised primarily in the interest of consolidating leaders' hold on power (Bayley 1975; Tilly 1985). Given the impossibility of exercising the rights of democratic citizenship in the context of a "war of every man against every man" (Hobbes [1651] 1996), democratic coercion must instead have as its primary function the protection of citizens.

But democracy does not only require that coercion be exercised in the interest of citizens and with their input: it also requires that the exercise

---

[9] "We all know that governments are different and that it is not the same thing to be the citizen or subject of one or another country, even in matters of daily life" (Linz 2000, 49).

~~of coercion adhere to the rule of law.~~ The implications of the rule of law for how democracies ought to deploy coercion are clear, whether understood through its standard features of predictability and equality (Holmes 2003), a "democratic rule of law" conceptualized as "fairness, access, universality, and legality" (Holston & Caldeira 1998, 283), or the more expansive view of "a truly democratic rule of law that ensures political rights, civil liberties, and mechanisms of accountability which in turn affirm the political equality of all citizens and constrain potential abuses of state power" (O'Donnell 2004, 32). Coercion exercised in accordance with the rule of law thus entails limits on police authority to provide protection and exert repression, based not only on the law but also on the premise of equal treatment of all citizens.

Finally, just as some prominent definitions of democracy require that "rulers are held accountable for their actions" (Schmitter & Karl 1991, 78), "democratic coercion" also requires that it be subject to external accountability. Per Schedler (1999), accountability entails "subjecting power to the threat of sanctions; obliging it to be exercised in transparent ways; and forcing it to justify its acts" (14). O'Donnell (1998) argues – with respect to executives – that such accountability ought to be imposed by other state entities, though Schmitter (1999) counters that horizontal accountability can also be exercised by non-state actors. Applied to police forces exercising the state's coercive power, we ought to expect democracies to create formal *external* mechanisms by which civilian (i.e., non-police and non-military) state actors can monitor the use of coercion, conduct oversight in practice, and employ sanctions when such use of coercion falls outside the bounds of the law.

Nevertheless, one of the central arguments of this book is that the coercive structures and practices described here, and illustrated in greater detail in Chapters 3–5, are not simply undemocratic: they are unequivocally authoritarian. Understanding this characterization requires a definition of authoritarian coercion. Much of the literature on authoritarianism follows the reasoning that "one of the easiest ways to define a concept is to say what it is not" (Linz 2000, 50),[10] defining authoritarianism by "the absence of democratic processes" (Brownlee 2010). A shortcoming of this approach, as has been highlighted by a number of

---

[10] Glasius (2018) develops an extensive critique of this scholarly practice to define authoritarianism by the absence of the defining features of democracy.

scholars, is that "it does not consider the possibility of authoritarianism occurring within a democratic regime."[11]

In theorizing about the relationship between regime type and modes of policing and coercion, it is similarly important to avoid definitions of authoritarian policing simply by the absence of democratic coercion. Instead, I look to the literature on coercive institutions in authoritarian regimes to conceptualize authoritarian coercion. While political science has traditionally ignored the police as an object of study, a small but robust literature on coercion and policing in autocracies has emerged in recent years, offering invaluable insights on how authoritarian rulers organize police institutions and how, as well as to what ends, they deploy coercion. As I argue, police may emerge and persist as authoritarian enclaves within otherwise democratic states, not simply due to the absence of the features of democratic coercion already described but due to structures and practices that resemble those of coercive institutions in authoritarian regimes.

Under authoritarian rule, the primary function of coercive institutions and the deployment of coercion is to keep the leader in power. Coercive institutions are organized with the objective of neutralizing or eliminating threats to the ruler – including from within coercive institutions themselves (Policzer 2009) – and the nature of those threats will shape institutional design and the deployment of coercion (Greitens 2016). Irrespective of institutional variation, however, authoritarian regimes have long deployed coercion to repress political adversaries and consolidate power, whether in Argentina in the 1930s (Kalmanowiecki 2000) or in Russia under Vladimir Putin in the early twenty-first century (Taylor 2011). Authoritarian rulers are invariably concerned with their own political survival, such that Greitens (2016), in her study of institutional variation in the design of coercive institutions and patterns of repression, finds that rulers organize coercive institutions and deploy coercion to achieve one of two objectives – "coup-proofing" and quelling popular unrest – in order to neutralize threats to the leader's hold on power (4). The argument here is not that police forces in authoritarian settings do not offer protection from crime. Instead, what we can learn from the literature on authoritarian coercion is that leaders' choices about the design and organization of coercive institutions, and about how coercion is deployed,

---

[11] Beetham 2015, 2. Other scholars featured in the symposium raised similar critiques of standard approaches to theorizing authoritarianism from the perspective of democracy studies.

are oriented not toward protecting citizens from crime but rather toward
their own political survival.

Another feature of coercion in authoritarian settings is that its usage is
not based on or bound by law. In autocracies, Maravall and Przeworski
(2003) tell us, "the law is the instrument of the sovereign, who, by
definition of sovereignty, is not bound by it"; as a result, "extralegal
commands are as forceful as those dressed as law" (3). This characterization resembles Taylor's account of the "new regime of repression" used by
Vladimir Putin to consolidate political and economic power in Russia:
building the capacity of coercive institutions to enforce what he calls
"exceptional decisions," based on "specific circumstances that may be
discretionary, or even potentially unlawful, under existing rules," rather
than "routine decisions" based on existing laws and procedures (Taylor
2011, 16). It would be reductive to say that there is no place for law under
authoritarian regimes, and scholars such as Pereira (2005) would likely
caution us to take "authoritarian legality" seriously. Yet, even in Pereira's
careful study of the use of laws and courts by Southern Cone authoritarian
regimes, coercion was not bounded by law. Instead, the law was used as
a means of legitimizing each regime's preferred mode of coercion. In
authoritarian regimes, interpretation of the law is left "to the rulers
themselves, rather than to independent objective bodies, and [applied]
with a wide range of discretion" (Linz 2000, 59). Thus, if a defining
feature of democratic coercion is that it ought to be based on the rule of
law, the exercise of authoritarian coercion is instead exceptional or arbitrary, systematically deployed beyond what is in the law and unconstrained by rights and limits defined by law. The notion of
"exceptional" coercion is based on the concept of "state of exception,"
a legal condition in which executives grant themselves the authority to
govern outside the bounds of the law, typically in times of crisis or
existential threats, but which has come to be used in more expansive
ways by contemporary democratic governments (Agamben 2005).
Exceptional or arbitrary coercion thus describes generalized structures
or practices, rather than individual agents (sometimes characterized as
"bad apples") or sporadic actions that transgress the rule of law.

From this we can derive a third feature of coercion in authoritarian
settings: the extent to which its use is subject to external accountability. As
Policzer (2009) observes in his study of authoritarian coercion in
Pinochet's Chile, "secrecy is the norm" (4), serving as "a basic tool of
unconstrained power" (16). Although external monitoring of coercion
and coercive institutions is not absent in authoritarian regimes, it does not

TABLE 1.1 *A continuum of coercion*

	Authoritarian	Democratic
Primary function	Serves interests of leaders	Protects citizens from crime
Legal basis	Arbitrary/exceptional	Based on rule of law
External accountability	Weak	Robust

entail accountability. Indeed, as Policzer notes, "If these [accountability] institutions existed, and if they were truly free, the regime in question would not be authoritarian" (Policzer 2009, 18). Thus, while foreign governments and human rights groups may monitor the use of coercion in authoritarian settings and attempt to sanction abuses through "shaming" and other mechanisms, the absence of formal, systematic mechanisms of transparency and sanctions means that, in autocracies, "nothing compels the sovereign to rule by law" (Maravall & Przeworski 2003, 3).

Based on the preceding discussion, we can develop a continuum of coercion (see Table 1.1). We can distinguish between the two ideal types along three dimensions: (1) whether coercion is used primarily to serve the interests of the leader or to protect citizens from crime and violence; (2) the extent to which the use of coercion is governed by law or is exceptional; and (3) the existence of meaningful formal external accountability mechanisms for the deployment of coercion. Democratic coercion is defined by the deployment of coercion for the purpose of protecting citizens from crime, based on the rule of law, and subjected to robust external accountability. Authoritarian coercion, meanwhile, is defined by the deployment of coercion whose primary function is to serve the interests of the leader to remain in power, is exceptional rather than based on law, and is subjected to weak or nonexistent external accountability mechanisms.

While there are certainly some police forces that neatly fit one of these two ideal types, the dichotomy should instead be conceived of as a continuum, with most police forces falling somewhere in between authoritarian and democratic coercion and potentially shifting between them over time.[12] Indeed, as I discuss in Chapter 2, the chief undertaking of this book will be to explain why police forces in democracies may

[12] Since the classification is based on three dimensions, one might similarly envision additional types based on different configurations of the three dimensions. Such differentiation, however, is beyond the scope of this book.

remain closer to the authoritarian end of the continuum, as well as the conditions under which political leaders choose to enact reforms to shift coercive institutions toward the democratic end.

Conceptualizing coercion in this way is conducive to understanding the contradictions between patterns of police violence in Latin America and democratic principles. This framework decouples the type of coercion from the type of regime, allowing us to contemplate the persistence of authoritarian modes of coercion in democracies and democratic modes of coercion in authoritarian or semi-authoritarian countries. Evidence of the former abounds in Latin America (and elsewhere), and recent research has analyzed efforts to introduce forms of what I call democratic coercion in an electoral authoritarian regime (Light 2016). Accordingly, a focus on coercive structures and practices "allows a shift away from only designating 'regimes' as authoritarian, recognizing that in contemporary politics, governance arrangements can be more fluid" (Glasius 2018, 523).

This framework also underscores that "authoritarian enclaves" are not only territorial or subnational jurisdictions (Gibson 2013; Giraudy 2015; Mickey 2015); they can also encompass state bureaucracies. This framework thus helps to elucidate the notion that democracies can sustain authoritarian institutions, just as they can permit "authoritarian enclaves" to flourish within their territory. Elucidating these political choices about the design of coercive institutions and the deployment of coercion will demonstrate that, as with the "persistence of local authoritarianism," the persistence of authoritarian coercion – and the decision to reform – are "part and parcel of everyday politics within the modern nation-state" (Gibson 2013, 4).

THE STRUCTURAL POWER OF POLICE AND THE POLITICS OF COERCION IN DEMOCRACY

As the empirical chapters in this book demonstrate, the coercive structures and practices of many Latin American police forces following transitions to democracy have been decidedly authoritarian. But why do democracies continue to sustain police forces that systematically exercise authoritarian coercion? In the chapters that follow, I demonstrate how police forces exercise a form of "boundary control" (Gibson 2013). By virtue of their structural power, police organizations can induce political leaders to engage in accommodation, mutually beneficial exchange relationships wherein leaders grant police greater autonomy in exchange for cooperation.

In order to understand the persistence of these authoritarian coercive structures and practices in otherwise democratic states, it is essential to understand the relationship between coercion and democratic politics and, crucially, the structural power of the entity that exercises the state's coercive authority. Coercion is a defining feature of the state (Tilly 1993; Weber 2009), and it is also a defining feature of police. Despite this, even theorists who understand state capacity in terms of the state's ability to control and enforce its laws throughout its territory (e.g., Mann 1984, 189; Soifer 2015, 9) nevertheless overlook the actual entity to which the state delegates its monopoly of the legitimate use of force. Indeed, for scholars of policing, the authorization to use force is the core of the policing role (Bayley 1985; Bittner 1970; Goldstein 1977). It is little wonder, then, that leaders across a range of regime types have historically undertaken state-building efforts by "enlarging, professionalizing, and ultimately arming the police" (Wilson 1978, 32). Police had a central role in early state formation in Europe (Bayley 1975; Reiner 1998; Tilly 1985) and in Latin America during the twentieth century (Barreneche & Galeano 2008; Camacho 1993; Kalmanowiecki 2000). But rather than serving as a response to objective conditions of criminality, these efforts are better understood as a response to political threats (Bayley 1975, 357; Kalmanowiecki 2000, 48). According to these accounts, then, this building up of the police as a means of building the state followed a strictly political logic.

As with these early – largely authoritarian – states, coercion and coercive institutions play a central role in state building in contemporary democracies. While militaries may be more prominent under some authoritarian regimes, police are primarily charged with the maintenance of order in democracies (Bayley 1985; Goldstein 1977).[13] As crime and violence reached historically high levels in many Latin American countries in recent decades, order and security have been among citizens' most urgent demands (Zechmeister 2014), placing police at the center of democratic politics in the region. But police institutions are not only the entity to which the state delegates its monopoly of the legitimate use of force. They are also a key instrument of the state's infrastructural power, "the capacity of the state to actually penetrate civil society, and to implement logistically political decisions throughout the realm" (Mann 1984, 189).

---

[13] Bayley (1985) cites the authorization to use force internally as the unique competence of police, clarifying that "when military formations are used for order maintenance within a society, they should be regarded as acting as police" (8).

As such, for the great majority of citizens – as a former commander of the Colombian National Police told me in an interview – police officers are "the materialization of the state, what [citizens] can see of the state."[14]

Through their control of a vital policy area – order and security – police constitute the "nerve center of the state" (Ungar 2002). Order and security are essential for any society to flourish and constitute a particularly urgent question for Latin America's "violent democracies" (Arias & Goldstein 2010). Where citizens must endure "continual fear and danger of violent death" (Hobbes [1651] 1996), they have little possibility of enjoying what T. H. Marshall calls the "social component" of citizenship – guaranteeing the "right to share to the full in the social heritage and to live the life of a civilized being according to the standards prevailing in the society" (Marshall 1950, 11) – nor what Holston and Caldeira (1998) call the "civil component," which entails the "rights to associate, assemble, and communicate among private individuals who thus become associated individuals and who thereby create the public sphere of society" (264). Whether or not states – and, specifically, the police – effectively provide order and security is a key determinant of the extent to which formal democratic institutions translate into the ability to engage in everyday political, economic, and social activities that are constitutive of democratic citizenship in practice (Brysk 2012; González 2017; Yashar 2012).

Because police are charged with providing a service that is essential for the functioning of society, police forces also serve as an essential instrument of political power. If the police force were to withdraw its service, it would prove to be politically catastrophic for elected leaders. Moreover, because police protection is so highly valued by citizens, police forces provide a service that can be distributed in politically beneficial ways. Indeed, even in present-day democracies, politicians have used police forces to serve their political interests and consolidate power, by selectively providing protection for favored constituents (Wilkinson 2004), shielding them from unfavorable enforcement of the law (Davis 2006; Holland 2015), punishing political opponents (Saín 2006), and raising revenue (Sances & You 2017).

This structural position of police – as a political resource and a purveyor of an essential condition of governance – means that, as Lindblom (1977) argued about business leaders, police occupy a "privileged position," given their role as "functionaries performing

---

[14] Author interview with the former director of the Colombian National Police, General (ret.) Miguel Ángel Gómez Padilla, October 12, 2013.

functions that government officials regard as indispensable" (175). Just as with the business sector in market-oriented societies, police bureaucracies can be formidable assets for politicians. But they also present important constraints. By commission or omission, police forces can create politically uncomfortable situations for elected officials. For instance, apparent work slowdowns by police in cities such as New York,[15] Baltimore,[16] and São Paulo[17] – during which police officers scaled back patrols and arrests, in some cases leading to increased violence – proved to be deeply embarrassing for their respective mayors. Just as Lindblom warned that "depression, inflation, or other economic distress can bring down a government" (172–173), a former secretary of security in Buenos Aires Province issued a similar warning regarding the risks posed by police: "Any governor or president knows that insecurity events can corrode an administration. You can build a lot of roads, a lot of public works, but these events can undermine your administration."[18]

As a result of the opportunities and risks posed by the police's control of coercion, politicians have strong incentives to engage police forces in accommodation, a mutually beneficial exchange relationship in which politicians grant police autonomy in exchange for the organization's cooperation in pursuing political objectives. Police forces not only have an interest in maximizing autonomy, a standard bureaucratic prerogative (Lipsky 2010, 14): they are also uniquely situated among state bureaucracies to achieve autonomy and defend institutional interests, in no small part due to a hierarchical, often-militarized structure that facilitates coordination and makes credible the threat of withdrawal of service. Indeed, scholars have noted that police can successfully resist incursions on their "turf," exhibiting hesitation to adopt new tasks (Wilson 1989, 107), rejecting mechanisms of accountability to outside actors (Alpert & Dunham 2004, 9), and weakening of reforms even after they are adopted (Ungar 2002; Hinton 2006; Goldstein 1977).

---

[15] See "For Second Week, Arrests Plunge in New York City," *New York Times* January 5, 2015; "In Police Rift, Mayor de Blasio's Missteps Included Thinking It Would Pass," *New York Times*, January 11, 2015.

[16] "With Killings Rising in Baltimore, Mayor 'Examining' Decrease in Arrests," *Baltimore Sun*, May 27, 2015.

[17] Wanderley Preite Sobrinho and Ricardo Galhardo, "Prefeitura de São Paulo tenta despolitizar violência na Virada Cultural," IG São Paulo, May 20, 2013, http://ultimosegundo.ig .com.br/brasil/sp/2013-05-20/prefeitura-de-sao-paulo-tenta-despolitizar-violencia-na-vir ada-cultural.html.

[18] Author interview with Alberto Piotti, Buenos Aires, November 2, 2011.

In order to understand the nature of the police's agency and the patterns of accommodation that emerge between politicians and police, Taylor's distinction between the police's "routine" (formal, defined by law) and "exceptional" (informal, possibly extralegal) tasks may prove helpful (Taylor 2011, 16). These two sets of tasks may operate as distinctly separate dimensions, such that police forces may possess capacity in performing exceptional tasks but institutional weakness in their formal role, as Taylor shows was the case in Putin's Russia. Police may also exchange cooperation in one dimension for autonomy in another. In Buenos Aires Province, for instance, police cultivated considerable autonomy in their routine task of security provision in exchange for cooperation with politicians and political parties in an expansive network of illicit political financing (Chapter 4). The Colombian police, meanwhile, faced little civilian intervention despite widespread extralegal violence and corruption in exchange for continued cooperation with the government's policy priority, the war against drug cartels (Chapter 5). As these examples suggest, there is variation in the specific forms of police–politician accommodation; but, as with business, their relationship is defined by "reciprocal dependence" (Culpepper 2015). Police forces are a political instrument utilized by politicians in some dimensions; but they are also a political actor, successfully exercising agency in pursuit of their own prerogatives in other dimensions.

Thus, while police forces are a potent political instrument utilized by politicians, they are also a formidable political actor, endowed with structural power due to their control of coercion. Indeed, police institutions exercise power in all its "faces," as conceptualized by scholars such as Gaventa (1980) and Lukes (1974). As evidenced in the cases analyzed in this book, police forces routinely prevail in specific contests, as occurred often when police commanders in Buenos Aires Province leveraged their political relationships to prevent reformist security officials from removing them from their posts due to corruption (Chapter 4). They also succeed in keeping certain issues off the agenda, as exemplified by the shelving of a police reform bill in the Colombian congress due, according to the minister of defense at the time, to opposition from the National Police (Chapter 7). Finally, police also shape discourses and understandings of the problem of crime and security, as occurred when São Paulo's police forces convinced politicians and a majority of citizens that the governor's reform attempts were a threat to security (Chapter 6).

The police's structural power is key to understanding the persistence of authoritarian coercion in democracies. Rather than constituting an oversight by political leaders or a view that reforming the police was less consequential than reforming militaries – as one Argentine official argues in Chapter 4 – the police's ability to leverage its structural power to constrain the policy agenda and thwart reform is an essential driver of its institutional persistence. The book's main argument, developed further in Chapter 2, elucidates how ordinary democratic processes reinforce, rather than challenge, this persistence of authoritarian coercion.

THE STRUGGLE FOR DEMOCRATIC COERCION

This book demonstrates that, because ordinary democratic politics can reproduce and sustain authoritarian coercion, a shift toward democratic coercion requires intentional comprehensive structural police reforms. But under what conditions do such reform processes emerge? Based on two-and-a-half years of qualitative fieldwork in Argentina, Brazil, and Colombia, this book shows that ordinary democratic politics can be both a barrier to and a catalyst for democratic coercion. I argue that electoral incentives are central to politicians' decision to maintain the status quo of authoritarian coercion or to enact police reform to promote democratic coercion. When societal preferences over policing and security are fragmented, politicians will see little electoral gain in enacting reform and a substantial risk of alienating a powerful bureaucracy whose cooperation they need. In contrast, when politicians observe preference convergence through a scandal and face a robust political opposition, reform becomes more likely, since they now face an electoral counterweight to the police's structural power.

As the empirical chapters illustrate, understanding the structural role and structural power of police institutions is essential for explaining why eradicating decidedly authoritarian coercive structures and practices within police forces has proven to be so challenging for democracies. Because of their control over coercion, police organizations are uniquely positioned to resist reform efforts. At the same time, politicians may be especially reluctant to place constraints on their ability to use police toward their own political ends. These forces are not deterministic (as is also true for the structural power of business, per Culpepper (2015)) but instead create a set of entrenched interests that raise the stakes (and risks) of reform. To a much greater extent than other policy areas, where politicians may seek to be "policy entrepreneurs" or simply act out of an adherence to democratic principles, executives seeking to reform authoritarian coercive practices and structures among the police forces under their control must contend with the likely resistance from a powerful bureaucracy whose actions, and inaction, have the potential to "corrode" their administrations. The largely failed efforts of then São Paulo governor André Franco Montoro to reform his state's police forces in the years after the transition to democracy (Chapter 6) illustrate the challenges inherent in such reform attempts. Police forces routinely and successfully leverage their structural power to achieve considerable autonomy from the elected leaders to whom they are ostensibly accountable. It is unsurprising, then, that in much of Latin America, as in much of the United States, "police now actually have greater autonomy than other agencies of government that exercise much less authority" (Goldstein 1977, 134).

The implication of this framework, developed further in the next chapter, is that politicians will be unlikely to incur the costs of attempting to reform the police unless not doing so poses an electoral threat. Because of their structural power, police forces can successfully leverage their control of coercion to constrain the policy options available to politicians and raise the threshold for reform. Within this constrained policy space, whether authoritarian modes of coercion persist or are subjected to reform processes is a function of how societal preferences and demands, as well as political competition, shape the electoral incentives of politicians when choosing between the status quo and reform. In this context, the emergence of police as authoritarian enclaves within the state results from the nature of ordinary democratic politics. Thus, what appears to be a failure of democratic processes to address coercive institutions that routinely and fundamentally contravene democratic principles may instead be an exercise of democratic responsiveness to the preferences and demands of large and powerful sectors of the citizenry who – like the São Paulo residents who applauded a police killing of their fellow citizen – may view such practices as necessary for their own protection.

THEORETICAL CONTRIBUTIONS

In 2016 Darrell Cannon stood in front of dozens of college students and recounted his harrowing experience with torture at the hands of officers from the Chicago Police Department, remarking that it must have seemed "like something out of a Third World dictatorship."[19] Yet, what Cannon

---

[19] Chicago Torture Archive launch event, University of Chicago, October 18, 2016. Public event attended by the author.

endured took place not under an authoritarian regime but rather in the context of a consolidated democracy. Cannon was one of over 100 men – mostly Black and poor – tortured by the Chicago police to extract false confessions, a practice that went on for nearly two decades with little to no intervention from the courts or elected officials (Ralph 2020).

This book is part of a growing literature on the limitations of democracy and the potential for democratic processes to produce undemocratic outcomes. Scholars such as Achen and Bartels (2016) have demonstrated how ordinary democratic politics may actually undermine government responsiveness, while Gilens (2014) examines how democratic processes can reproduce societal inequalities, with important implications for representation. Recent studies have also examined the susceptibility of democracy to extremism, norm erosion, and authoritarian political movements that may ultimately bring about its downfall (Levitsky & Ziblatt 2018), a concern that has long been the focus of democratic theorists (Loewenstein 1937). The analysis presented here draws on these insights to explore the tensions that policing and coercion pose for democracy, emerging as authoritarian enclaves due to many of the same factors identified by these scholars.

Elucidating the processes through which patently authoritarian coercive practices can become a routine tool of policing in democracies is the central task of this book. Recent scholarship has advanced our understanding of how authoritarian leaders make choices regarding the organization and deployment of coercion to remain in power (Greitens 2016; Policzer 2009; Taylor 2011). Yet, we still know relatively little about the role of coercion in democracies, despite the fact that coercion – and the primary institution charged with exercising it – may be highly consequential for the everyday lives of citizens and democratic governance. This book seeks to contribute to this new and important literature by investigating how leaders – and citizens – in established and developing democracies alike make choices about how to organize, deploy, and control coercive institutions. It demonstrates that police in democracies are also instruments of power. Far from the conventional notion of security as a public good, police provide a highly coveted and contested service that politicians can distribute selectively to pursue their political objectives, a condition police forces skillfully leverage toward their own ends. This book therefore theorizes about the agency and structural power of a bureaucracy that leverages its control of coercion to selectively provide its service in the interests of elected leaders but can also threaten leaders by withdrawing its service of providing order and security. This analysis allows us to better understand the conditions under which police bolster – or threaten – leaders' hold on power, as well as governability and the rule of law.

In doing so, this book also adds important insights to recent scholarship exploring the contours, causes, and consequences of racialized policing and abuses in the United States in the post-Ferguson era. While much of this work probes the consequences of racialized policing for the relationship between communities of color and the state (Laniyonu 2018; Soss & Weaver 2017), and shows how political underrepresentation of Black Americans leads to unequal policing (Eckhouse 2019), police institutions remain a "black box" in these analyses. Yet police forces are the only institution of the state legally empowered to use violence against its own citizens, making police distinct from other types of bureaucracies. This book theorizes police as political actors, elucidating how police successfully exercise agency in pursuit of their own prerogatives and act as a veto player, setting the bounds of policy options available to politicians choosing between continuity and reform. A key takeaway from the book's analysis for observers of the challenges posed by unequal policing in the United States is that reforms that fail to contend with the police's structural power will likely do little to address patterns of racialized policing and other abuses.

This book also joins a long line of scholarship exploring the endurance of police violence in established and developing democracies alike (Ahnen 2007; Bonner, Seri & Kubal 2018; Caldeira & Holston 1999; Smith 2019; Wahl 2018). Yet, even as scholars have consistently demonstrated that democratic institutions have failed to prevent the types of extrajudicial violence employed by the authoritarian regimes that preceded them, this book unpacks the mechanisms by which ordinary democratic politics may alternately reinforce such patterns and practices – or create conditions that make reform possible.

The book also develops and tests a nuanced theory of institutional persistence and change, demonstrating that societal pressures and mobilization as well as political competition can produce both continuity and reform. The analysis presented in this book demonstrates that the emergence and persistence of police forces as authoritarian enclaves are not merely the consequence of incomplete transitions from dictatorship nor of the failure of democratic institutions. Instead, this institutional persistence is sustained and reproduced by democratic processes of citizen contestation and demand-making, as well as leaders' responsiveness based on electoral incentives. As the case studies show, these democratic processes may serve alternately as impediments to building state capacity and distinctly democratic forms of coercion or as key levers for change.

The analysis presented here also provides important insights into other prominent cases where policing, and the provision of security more broadly, comes into sharp tension with democracy. In the Philippines, President Rodrigo Duterte carried out a concerted campaign of thousands of extrajudicial killings under the pretense of a drug war, with massive popular support.[20] In South Africa, a robust human rights regime has come to be viewed by ordinary citizens as an impediment to security, leading to increased support for vigilantism and extrajudicial state violence (Smith 2015). Meanwhile, even consolidated democracies have not been immune from persistent authoritarian coercive practices, as evidenced by the enduring contestation over extrajudicial killings of unarmed Black men in the United States. This analysis thus sheds light not only on why democratic governments in Latin America and elsewhere have been deficient in performing the defining task of the state but also on why their police forces have in many ways continued to operate as authoritarian enclaves.

PLAN OF THE BOOK

The chapters that follow develop and test a theoretical framework that builds on the central argument presented in this chapter: that democratic processes often sustain and reproduce authoritarian police. Chapter 2 presents the book's theoretical framework, unpacking the dependent variable – the persistence of authoritarian coercive institutions or reform to promote democratic coercion – and laying out the argument that the fragmentation of societal preferences over police reform and patterns of political competition shape the incentives of political leaders choosing between the status quo and reform.

The empirical chapters are organized around variation in the dependent variable, leveraging change over time across the case studies. Part I of the book examines the persistence of authoritarian coercion among police forces in São Paulo State, Buenos Aires Province, and Colombia. In each of Chapters 3, 4, and 5, I explore entrenched authoritarian coercive structures and practices, as well as the failure of democratic institutions to constrain them. I then lay out how the police force in each case leveraged

---

[20] Regine Cabato, "Thousands Dead. Police Accused of Criminal Acts. Yet Duterte's Drug War Is Wildly Popular," *Washington Post*, October 23, 2019.

its structural power to constrain policy agendas to maintain the status quo of authoritarian coercion, and I demonstrate how fragmentation of societal preferences and contestation reinforced institutional persistence, thereby reproducing authoritarian patterns of coercion in each setting.

Part II of the book focuses on reform efforts to promote democratic coercion. Chapter 6 examines a series of failed efforts to enact structural police reform in São Paulo State, leading to the persistence of a police force that serves the political interests of leaders, exercises rampant violence outside the bounds of the law, and faces little external accountability – more than three decades after the return to democratic rule in Brazil. The chapter elucidates how the structural power of police constrains policy agendas and how societal preference fragmentation – and, crucially, weak political competition – can block efforts to enact police reforms to promote democratic coercion. Chapter 7, meanwhile, jointly considers the comprehensive and ambitious reform processes of the police forces of Buenos Aires Province and Colombia, demonstrating how shifts in societal preferences and political competition change politicians' incentives in favor of reform.

The concluding chapter considers the implications of the persistence of authoritarian coercion for democracy and reflects upon the empirical analysis to consider the ways in which high levels of violence and inequality exacerbate these processes. Chapter 8 also sketches out how the argument might extend to other democracies, particularly those afflicted by violence and inequality.

2

Ordinary Democratic Politics and the Challenge of Police Reform

In November 1982, on the eve of São Paulo State's first democratic elections after nearly twenty years of military rule, then-governor José Maria Marin made strong declarations about rampant violence by the state's Military Police, which had already killed hundreds of people that year: "I want to let the people [of São Paulo] know that I will not have the slightest doubt in going to the final consequences to ensure those cases do not repeat themselves. May it hurt whomever it may hurt. The people need to be able to trust in the power of authority, which should be exercised to preserve their tranquility ... I will go to the final consequences to contain police violence."[1] That same day, a high-ranking Civil Police official also spoke out emphatically about the need for police reform, namely by demilitarizing the Military Police and integrating the state's two police forces.

After three decades of democracy – and despite Marin's adamant call for, in essence, democratic coercion – relatively little has changed. São Paulo State's Military Police continues to kill hundreds of people each year, with the number of civilians killed by police exceeding 800 in 2016, according to official figures, the equivalent of 23 percent of homicides reported that same year.[2] In recent years, with levels of police violence rising once again, prominent security and police officials cited demilitarization and unification of the Civil and Military police forces as

---

[1] "Marin promete fim da violência da polícia" and "E o delegado faz suggestões," *O Estado de São Paulo*, November 2, 1982.

[2] Estatísticas Trimestrais, Secretaria de Segurança Pública do Estado de São Paulo. Available at www.ssp.sp.gov.br/Estatistica/Trimestrais.aspx.

the key to getting police violence under control, just as they had thirty years earlier.[3]

In the years following Argentina's transition to democracy, meanwhile, the Police of Buenos Aires Province suffered from similar institutional deficiencies. By the mid-1990s, the *Bonaerense* (the provincial police) had come to be known as the *"maldita policía"* (damned police), due to its routine involvement in extensive corruption and human rights violations and its participation in many of the criminal acts it was formally tasked with preventing and repressing.[4]

In both settings, authoritarian coercive practices and structures flourished, with police forces routinely deployed in exceptional ways, with negligible external accountability and in the service of political leaders' interests. As the empirical chapters demonstrate, these modes of policing persisted for many years following the end of authoritarian rule, not as mere vestigial legacies of military dictatorships but sustained by ordinary democratic politics. In Buenos Aires Province, however, political leaders eventually chose to enact comprehensive structural reform in an effort to promote democratic coercion by the provincial police. In São Paulo State, meanwhile, democratic politics has, in many ways, acted as an obstacle to reform, thereby serving to reproduce authoritarian coercion three decades after the formal end of the military dictatorship.

São Paulo State and Buenos Aires Province, and their respective police forces, share a number of structural characteristics. Each is the largest, most populous, and most economically powerful unit in a federal structure in which the state/province is charged with security provision and overseeing the police. They experienced contemporaneous transitions to democracy that left intact police institutions that had been integral to the repressive apparatus under military rule. And both societies largely failed to contain authoritarian coercion by their police forces in the context of historically high rates of crime and violence.

Yet the *Bonaerense* has by now been subjected to highly ambitious structural reforms, while reform of the Military Police of São Paulo State has been restricted to marginal reforms, with broader structural reform largely off the table. Instead, despite constituting, in many ways, the structural opposite of Buenos Aires Province (see Table 2.2), it was

---

[3] "Os policiais brasileiros querem desmilitarizar a instituição," *El País*, July 29, 2014; Luiz Eduardo Soares, "Desmilitarização e reforma do modelo policial," *Le Monde Diplomatique Brasil*, November 1, 2013.

[4] See Carlos Dutil and Ricardo Ragendorfer, "Maldita Policía," *Noticias*, August 10, 1996.

Colombia that enacted a comprehensive reform of its National Police that was remarkably similar to that passed in Buenos Aires Province. In Colombia, as in Buenos Aires Province, democratic police reform came after more than a decade of state inaction in the face of authoritarian coercive practices – including extrajudicial killings, torture, and disappearances – as well as institutional decay, extensive involvement in criminal activity, and incompetence in the face of rising crime and violence. Political leaders in both settings sought to address these urgent problems by demilitarizing, decentralizing, and professionalizing their police forces, changing rank structures, raising recruitment standards, modernizing training, overhauling disciplinary systems and internal oversight mechanisms, creating structures for civilian oversight and citizen participation, and improving social welfare for police officers.

Thus, while Colombia, Buenos Aires Province, and São Paulo State have all grappled with the stubborn persistence of authoritarian coercion among their police forces, leaders in Buenos Aires Province and Colombia would eventually, and rather abruptly, change course toward a set of comprehensive reforms, while their counterparts in São Paulo State have yet to undertake such reforms after nearly four decades of democratic rule.

I argue that politicians choosing between the status quo of authoritarian coercive institutions and reform to promote democratic coercion assess the electoral risks and benefits of each, based on electoral competition and societal contestation over the distribution of protection and repression. Drawing on the concept of structural power (Lindblom 1977) discussed in Chapter 1, I demonstrate how police forces leverage their control of coercion to constrain the policy options available to politicians, raising the threshold for reform. Within this constrained policy space, politicians choose between continuity and reform by looking to societal preferences and political competition. When societal preferences over policing are fragmented, politicians are likely to conclude that police reforms are not electorally advantageous. When societal preferences converge and politicians face a robust political opposition, incumbents will be more likely to enact police reform, since they face an electoral counterweight to the structural power of police.

Authoritarian coercive institutions may thus be sustained and reproduced by ordinary democratic politics – citizen contestation and politicians' electoral incentives – long after the end of military dictatorships. In the discussion that follows, I present a theoretical framework to understand when societal contestation over the distribution of protection and repression and political competition favor the continuity of authoritarian coercion, as well as the conditions under which shifting electoral incentives and societal demands can bring about police reforms to promote democratic coercion.

EXPLAINING INSTITUTIONAL CONTINUITY AND CHANGE

The scholarly literature on institutional change generally and police reform specifically yield conflicting predictions about institutional persistence and reform. In many ways, observing police bureaucracies that endure for decades without meaningful reform is consistent with the expectations of much of the literature on institutions, which predict institutional persistence (Mahoney 2000, 507; North 1990) or, at most, institutional change that is gradual, incremental, and endogenous (Greif & Laitin 2004; Mahoney & Thelen 2009). Other scholars, meanwhile, predict rapid institutional change and instability in weak institutional contexts (Levitsky & Murillo 2014) or offer dynamic theories to account for "dramatic and discontinuous" institutional change, characterizing crisis as a key driver of rare ambitious reforms (Weyland 2008). Crisis-based explanations are common in the policing literature, as scholars have cited it as an explanation of reform in contexts as diverse as Latin America, England, and the United States, arguing that egregious scandals and "things going wrong" lead politicians to reform police because they fear being punished (Savage 2007; Sherman 1978; Ungar 2002).

Yet both sets of theories fall short when it comes to patterns of continuity and change among police institutions. Theories of gradual, endogenous institutional change tell us little about the conditions under which we can expect institutional stasis to give way to dramatic reform measures. A focus on crisis, meanwhile, is likely to overpredict reform. As the case studies demonstrate, Latin America's police forces often appear to be in a race to the bottom, making clear that crisis is often poorly defined conceptually and difficult to identify empirically. Indeed, the cases analyzed in this book – from the seemingly permanent crisis of the Colombian National Police in the 1980s and early 1990s to the incessant cases of police violence by the Buenos Aires provincial police and the Military Police of São Paulo State during the 1990s – underscore the point that, at least in the case of police, scandals and crises are more likely to result in symbolic or individualized responses than they are in reform.

Social scientists have also identified other political conditions that may serve as catalysts for reform, particularly in Latin America. Scholars have written about how transitions to democracy (Hunter 1997; Waylen 2007) and the drafting of new constitutions (Paschel, 2010) created political openings and changed incentives that led to the reform of powerful institutions or the creation of new institutions. While transitions to democracy and constitutional conventions undoubtedly shifted political opportunity structures in favor of a range of policy and institutional transformations in Argentina, Brazil, and Colombia, the empirical chapters that follow demonstrate that these processes nonetheless left police structures and practices largely unchanged.

Scholars of police reform, meanwhile, have identified additional political and structural conditions that can serve as catalysts or obstacles to reform. Several scholars, for instance, highlight the role of societal pressure in bringing about police reform, from widespread public concern with insecurity (Bailey & Dammert 2005) and institutional malfunction (Ungar 2002) to the mobilization of organized civil society (Fuentes 2005). Yet, many of these studies select on the dependent variable, ignoring the more common outcome of profound and prolonged police malfeasance and societal pressure: continuity. As the case studies that follow demonstrate, police reform is far from "the most frequent first response to perceptions of increased insecurity" (Bailey & Dammert, 2005, 2). A more common subject of analysis in the police literature in political science is not what leads to the onset of reform but rather what factors lead to its demise (Ungar 2002; Hinton 2006; Ruiz Vasquez, Illera Correal & Manrique 2006; Eaton 2008; Saín 2015). Ungar (2002) examines how the relationship between executives and police and judicial bureaucracies acts as a hindrance to reforms. Eaton (2008) and Hinton (2006), meanwhile, show how federalism and partisan competition impeded reforms from becoming firmly rooted and functioning as intended in Argentina and Brazil, in contrast with the broader literature on institutional change, which views these factors as conducive to reform (Falleti 2010; Geddes 1994; Grzymala-Busse 2007; Heilmann 2008; Oates 1999).

Many prominent theories of institutional change thus do little to advance our understanding of both the endurance of authoritarian police institutions within democratic states and important political shifts such as the highly ambitious, comprehensive police reforms that are often adopted to promote democratic coercive institutions after long periods of institutional stasis, as occurred in Buenos Aires Province and Colombia. In this chapter I lay out a nuanced theory of institutional change, arguing that, because the police's structural power enables them to constrain policy agendas, societal pressures and political competition can produce both the persistence of authoritarian coercive structures and practices under democratic rule *and* reform toward democratic coercion. By examining police reform more closely, we can thus refine theories of institutional change by considering the ability of police bureaucracies to constrain policy options or block reforms. Such insights, in turn, may help elucidate other policy areas where reform appears to be particularly challenging.

THE DEPENDENT VARIABLE: INSTITUTIONAL PERSISTENCE OR REFORM

The question at the heart of this book concerns the persistence or reform of police forces that exercise authoritarian coercion in democracies. Its central concern is the decision-making of elected officials when faced with police forces that are useful tools for achieving political objectives yet routinely fail to protect citizens from crime, engage in extrajudicial killings and torture, act outside the scope of the rule of law, and are unaccountable to civilian authorities. Indeed, Latin America's police forces in democracy have largely been characterized by poor training, low levels of specialization, insufficient resources, inefficacy in crime prevention and investigation, weak oversight mechanisms, rampant corruption and extralegal violence, and, consequently, high levels of societal distrust (Macaulay 2012; Ungar 2002). Because police forces are part of the executive branch, executives typically exercise considerable control over police – whether directly or through designated ministries – and are the key actors in decisions to undertake reform or maintain the status quo. Such decisions, meanwhile, are shaped by the demands executives consistently receive from citizens and organizations engaged in contestation over the distribution of protection and repression. Despite no shortage of programmatic motive, however, broad citizen pressure for and politicians' decision to enact police reforms have been relatively rare.

Accordingly, the key dependent variable for this study is whether, when faced with these conditions, political leaders choose to pursue reforms to promote democratic coercion or to maintain the status quo of authoritarian coercion. I define police reform as the successful enactment of a written policy intended to permanently change internal structures, rules, and practices within the organization as a whole. Such written policies may take the form of laws passed by the legislature, executive orders or decrees, or administrative directives. Reform as defined here is thus internal, permanent, and structural, leaving out many common policy responses to citizen demands for improved security. Politicians have, for instance, established stiffer penalties for certain crimes, created prosecutor's offices, or reformed the courts; such policies, however, leave internal police structures, rules, and practices intact. Politicians have also taken actions to address allegations of widespread corruption among their police forces, including special authorization to carry out mass purges of the organization and firing high-ranking police officials amid scandals. These measures, however, constitute one-time ad hoc actions rather than formal policy changes intended to be permanent.

The dependent variable in this theoretical framework is thus dichotomous: the maintenance of the status quo of authoritarian coercion or the enactment of police reform to promote democratic coercion. But police reform can take varied forms and can have varied objectives beyond promoting democratic coercion. Thus, while the outcome of interest of this analysis is procedural – a political decision to enact police reform – it is also a question about the substance and depth of such reform.

I therefore introduce an index of democratic police reform that outlines a number of indicators of the substance and depth of reforms (Table 2.1). Drawing on the continuum of coercion I developed in Chapter 1, policies promote democratic coercion if they bolster the police force's focus on protecting citizens from crime with citizens' input, strengthen adherence to the rule of law, and/or create mechanisms for robust external accountability.

But policies that seek to achieve these objectives may nonetheless differ in their depth and, accordingly, the extent to which they constitute police reform as defined here. Policies may involve changes to external entities alone (marginal), police practices (operational), organizational systems and rules (structural), and the creation of external authority mechanisms that in turn require changes to internal structures and practices (external control). Leaders may thus opt for marginal reforms, creating a Police Ombudsman's Office where citizens may bring complaints of police abuse or corruption, or neighborhood security councils for community participation, as occurred in São Paulo. I characterize such reforms as marginal because they are external to the police organization, leave internal practices and structures intact, and grant external actors no formal authority over police. Alternatively, police may adopt operational policies, such as community policing, which change police practices and tasks but otherwise leave internal rules and structures unchanged. Politicians may also opt for structural reforms, which are policies that change internal structures of the organization, such as disciplinary systems, promotion standards, and internal oversight. Finally, leaders may choose to grant external entities formal control and oversight of internal police practices and structures, such as Colombia's short-lived commissioner and Buenos Aires Province's Ministry of Security (Chapter 7).

Table 2.1 details an index of democratic police reform, enabling us to assess policies that seek to promote democratic coercion by whether their institutional target is marginal, operational, structural, or external control. This index elucidates consequential differences across common policies enacted in the wake of broad societal discontent with policing. Participatory security institutions, such as São Paulo's community security councils (CONSEGs) or Chicago's CAPS program (Fung 2004), create formal spaces for citizen input in local policing, but they are marginal reforms, leaving internal police rules and structures intact. The same holds for body-worn cameras, which became widespread among US police departments following social unrest in 2014, an operational change that enables the collection and dissemination of video of police encounters with citizens. Because of their limited depth, marginal and operational reforms are scored as "Low" in the index of democratic police reform. Such policies indeed seek to promote democratic coercion, but they fall short of the definition of police reform if they do not also change police rules and structures.

The police reforms analyzed in this book therefore encompass deeper structural and external control reforms, scored as "Moderate" and "High," respectively in the index of democratic police reforms. Such policies seek to promote democratic coercion by enacting changes that are internal, permanent, and structural. Structural reforms target the rules and systems of police bureaucracies, including rank structures, promotion standards, and disciplinary regimes, a more robust set of institutional instruments for achieving programmatic security provision with citizen input, adherence to the rule of law, and external accountability. External control reforms, meanwhile, link *internal* structural reforms to authority granted to *external* entities to govern security policy, ensure police compliance with the rule of law, and, in its absence, enforce sanctions. The cases of police reform analyzed in this book exemplify these models of democratic police reforms. The reform undertaken in Buenos Aires Province in 1998, for instance, eliminated the previous police leadership structure, created a civilian Ministry of Security to govern security policy and receive citizen input through neighborhood security forums, and endowed the ministry with authority to determine promotions, sanctions, and removal of police officials.

TABLE 2.1 *Index of Democratic Police Reforms (DPR)*

	Protect citizens/citizen input	Adherence to rule of law	Robust external accountability	DPR score
Marginal	External institution to cooperate with security policy/promote citizen participation (e.g., participatory security)	Legal constraints on police action (e.g., prohibition of torture)	External entity to collect and publicize data on police actions (e.g., São Paulo's Police Ombudsman's Office)	Low
Operational	Police initiative to build capacity in security provision/strengthen proximity to communities (e.g., community policing)	Internal guidelines and processes outlining police actions (e.g., use-of-force rules)	Police-driven initiative to collect and publicize data on police actions (e.g., body-worn cameras)	Low
Structural	Specialization of organization and governance for security tasks and citizen proximity (e.g., specialized units, programmatic promotion standards)	Independent internal disciplinary institutions	Internal institutions mandating transparency and cooperation with external entities	Moderate
External control	Civilian programmatic governance of security policy with mechanisms for compliance (e.g., Buenos Aires Province's Ministry of Security)	Executive/legislative/judicial mechanisms to ensure compliance with constraints on police action	Executive/legislative/ judicial investigation and sanction of police actions (e.g., Colombia's police commissioner)	High

The argument presented in the next section thus seeks to explain the conditions under which politicians choose to maintain the status quo or to enact structural and external oversight police reforms that promote democratic coercion. A theoretical framework focused on a dichotomous dependent variable – the enactment of a formal policy or the decision to maintain the status quo – is not without its limitations. It leaves unaddressed other important dimensions of institutional change, including the implementation, effectiveness, outputs, and durability of these policies. Yet, this approach presents a number of strengths and may be preferable for understanding the causes of institutional change. Other outcomes, such as the implementation of such policies, may be shaped by processes that not only are more difficult to identify than the adoption of a formal written policy but also may differ greatly from the processes that led to its adoption, as well as being longer in duration. Meanwhile, potential "outputs" of police reform, such as crime rates or numbers of police killings, while profoundly important, may also complicate our analysis, since their causes are varied and depend on far more than the political decision that led to the adoption of a particular policy.

Despite its limits, the seemingly procedural binary outcome nevertheless represents a highly consequential political choice. Citizen contestation and executive policy choices over policing often favor the persistence of authoritarian coercion. Indeed, as discussed in Chapter 1, the choice to undertake police reform in response to these conditions has been relatively rare, particularly in relation to the magnitude and salience of the problem. This framework, moreover, enables us to understand how political decision-making takes place under the constrained policy space generated by police. It demonstrates how police act as veto players and identifies the substantial barriers to getting police reform enacted, as well as the conditions under which it becomes more likely. Police reform thus emerges as an important political decision that signals a "dramatic and discontinuous" (Weyland 2008) political and societal shift intended to dismantle authoritarian coercive institutions.

How, then, do we account for this political decision to either maintain the status quo of authoritarian coercion or undertake institutional reform to promote democratic coercion? In the section that follows I present a theoretical framework that accounts for both long periods of persistence of authoritarian coercive institutions and the relatively rare onset of police reform by looking to how societal preferences and political competition shape the incentives of politicians.

THE ARGUMENT: SOCIETAL PREFERENCES AS DRIVERS
OF CONTINUITY AND REFORM

When discussing the structural power of business, Lindblom (1977) posits that its "privileged position" creates incentives that put political leaders at odds with majoritarian interests, since the business sector can pressure politicians to enact policies favoring its own interests rather than those of the broader electorate. If we were to look at the structural power of police through this lens, we might similarly explain the remarkable continuity of police institutions as the result of a lack of responsiveness of elected leaders to citizens' demands for improved security and for less violent, less corrupt police. Indeed, as discussed in Chapter 1, police forces similarly possess such structural power because, by virtue of controlling coercion, they can both serve as a valuable asset that can advance political objectives and pose a formidable threat if they withdraw their service. Police can therefore pressure politicians to engage in accommodation, a mutually beneficial exchange relationship in which politicians grant police autonomy in exchange for cooperation in pursuing political interests. Through such accommodation, police can successfully constrain the policy options available to politicians to address citizens' demands for improved security.

I argue, however, that the patterns of authoritarian coercion among police forces in many Latin American democracies do not persist because police forces subvert democratic responsiveness. Instead, both the persistence of these institutional structures and practices and the political decision to reform result from ordinary democratic processes of citizen demand-making and partisan competition.

Facing bureaucracies they formally control but which can withdraw cooperation, politicians choosing between reform and the status quo navigate a constrained policy space. Because the police's structural power raises the threshold for reform, executives choose between the status quo and reform by determining whether policing poses an electoral threat – that is, whether they observe a coherent societal demand for police reform, and whether they face a robust political opposition (Figure 2.1). When societal preferences over policing are fragmented, irrespective of political competition, reform brings little electoral gain and risks alienating a powerful bureaucracy whose cooperation politicians need. Preference fragmentation thus leads executives to choose continuity, favoring the persistence of authoritarian coercive institutions. Societal preference convergence and a robust opposition, however, constitute an electoral counterweight to the police's structural power, thereby making reform likely.

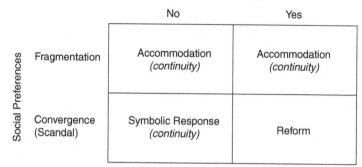

FIGURE 2.1 Determinants of politicians' choices between police continuity and reform

This theoretical framework expands upon an extensive scholarship on state–society relations and policy outcomes (Amengual 2014; Falleti 2010; Fox 1992; Rich 2019). Beyond constituting isolated instances of "societal accountability" (Peruzzotti & Smulovitz 2006), these studies show how state–society interactions drive policy outcomes and institutional change through a mutually reinforcing "opening from above" and "pressure from below" (Fox 2015). My theory contributes to this literature, disaggregating both state and societal actors. It elucidates how executives and a powerful bureaucracy reconcile divergent interests and how this accommodation constrains policy options available to politicians to address citizen demands. It also highlights societal fragmentation and conflicting demands, showing that societal pressure need not always move in the direction of policy change. Rather than promoting policy change that improves state capacity, as in the aforementioned studies, I argue that societal pressure sometimes works in the opposite direction, reinforcing authoritarian practices and structures among police.

Societal Structures and the Distribution of Protection and Repression

Far from constituting a public good, security and policing are subject to distributive contestation and selective provision by politicians for electoral gain. Rather than being determined by solely programmatic reasons, the distribution of protection and repression quite often corresponds to existing social cleavages and inequalities. Policing practices and structures come to reflect patterns of social stratification through two mechanisms. The first is the process of demand formation, wherein relatively privileged citizens facing crime and violence articulate demands for protection via the repression of citizens disadvantaged by class, race, and spatial status. The second mechanism is the process by which these conditions determine whose demands for protection state officials prioritize – and whose they ignore.

The literature on policing and criminal justice in Latin America and beyond provides ample evidence of such unequal provision of security and treatment by police and other rule-of-law institutions. Whether in the newer democracies of Latin America or in more established ones such as the United States and Canada, scholars have repeatedly found disparities along race, class, and geography in the extent to which citizens have been subjected to police stops (Barros 2008; Najdowski, Bottoms & Goff 2015), protest repression (Davenport, Soule & Armstrong 2011), arrests (Sinhoretto, Silvestre & Schlitter 2014), and extrajudicial violence (Brinks 2008), as well as the quality of police services (Fruhling 2009, 71; Pinheiro, Izumino & Fernandes 1991). Such findings have not been limited to academic studies. Government-appointed commissions investigating wrongdoing by police departments in advanced democracies – from Chicago to London – have found important racial disparities in who is granted protection by police and who is subject to repression.[5] In the case of the London Metropolitan Police, the commission's report famously declared that the police force was "institutionally racist." Moreover, though we have less evidence about the impact of these disparities in Latin America, scholars in North America have found that these race, class, and geographic disparities are similarly reflected in citizens' attitudes toward the police (Cao 2011; Prowse, Weaver & Meares 2019; Weitzer & Tuch 2004), which in turn result from personal experiences with police (Skogan 2006; Weitzer & Tuch 2005).

While explaining the formation of citizen preferences is outside the scope of this book, the distribution of protection and repression along prominent social cleavages and inequalities suggests that different societal groups may have vastly different experiences with the state's coercive apparatus, leading to fragmented understandings and preferences toward

---

[5] See Police Accountability Task Force (2016), "Recommendations for Reform: Restoring Trust between the Chicago Police and the Communities they Serve." Available at https:// chicagopatf.org/.

"The Stephen Lawrence Inquiry: Report of an Inquiry by Sir William MacPherson of Cluny," presented to Parliament by the Secretary of State for the Home Department by Command of Her Majesty, February 1999. Available at https://assets.publishing.service.gov .uk/government/uploads/system/uploads/attachment_data/file/277111/4262.pdf.

policing and security. Part I of this book, focused on institutional persistence, shows how a range of social and political processes shape preference formation over policing and security, exacerbating existing societal inequalities. In São Paulo State (Chapter 3) and Buenos Aires Province (Chapter 4), rising crime and social unrest resulting from economic crisis drove support for authoritarian coercive practices against marginalized communities. In Colombia (Chapter 5), widespread guerrilla and drug violence similarly helped sustain a constituency for authoritarian coercion. Scholars of Latin America have more broadly documented the rise of "punitive populism," demonstrating how media coverage and political campaigns can shape societal preferences and demands in favor of "iron fist" policing and even extrajudicial practices (Bonner 2018; Fernandez Roich 2017; Krause 2014).

How Preference Fragmentation Promotes Institutional Persistence

Scholars have characterized Latin Americans' conflicting demands over policing as "schizophrenic" (Ungar 2002) or "paradox[ical]" (Caldeira 2002). We should instead understand such conflicting demands as fragmentation, wherein attitudes and preferences regarding police and security are divided among considerable segments of society, typically along existing societal cleavages, such that there may not be a clear majority position. Consider, for instance, the findings of a 2013 poll that asked Venezuelans about recent police reforms; 45 percent viewed the reform positively and 43 percent viewed it negatively, a division that aligned with support for or opposition to Chavismo.[6] Such findings would signal to politicians that citizens' preferences over police reform are divided – and that continuing to deepen police reforms may be electorally disadvantageous.

A key question that emerges from this framework, however, is *how* politicians learn about preferences and discern between fragmentation and convergence. Elected leaders learn about the preferences held by different groups of citizens toward policing and security from a range of sources. In addition to using public opinion polls, demonstrations, media reports, and direct contact, citizens also form organizations, networks,

---

[6] Survey data from Rebecca Hanson and David Smilde, "Police Reform on a Political Tightrope: Citizen Security and Public Perceptions," *Venezuelan Politics and Human Rights Blog*, November 21, 2013. Available at http://venezuelablog.tumblr.com/post/67701053085/police-reform-on-a-political-tightrope-citizen.

and social movements that convey specific demands to politicians and police. These groups – often organized around class, race, and other social cleavages – routinely meet with politicians and security officials, make statements in the media, and mobilize protests around specific cases or general demands for security. Scholars have amply documented the efforts of such organized citizens to influence policing and security policy, from "pro-order" and "civil rights" coalitions mobilizing in Argentina and Chile (Fuentes 2005) and the influence of business groups on security policies in Colombian cities (Moncada 2016) to Black middle-class organizations pressuring for harsh anti-crime policies in New York during the 1970s (Fortner 2015) and mass protests demanding greater security in Mexico and Argentina (Davis 2006; Eaton 2008; Peruzzotti & Smulovitz 2000).

Indeed, over the course of my fieldwork in Argentina, Brazil, and Colombia, I encountered countless efforts by organized groups of citizens to influence government officials over local security conditions. Such organization at times takes place on a small scale, such as the human rights organizations that attend São Paulo's CONSEG meetings with the hope of shaping local policing and security (see Chapter 3). In other instances, organizations seek to influence security policy on a larger scale, such as the sophisticated work of the Bogotá Chamber of Commerce to provide its own crime statistics (including a victimization survey) and make policy recommendations, after realizing that "obviously, [economic] competitiveness and development are associated with a series of variables that relate directly to the conditions of the city ... [including] citizen security."[7]

Politicians, then, consistently receive demands from different groups of citizens attempting to influence the distribution of protection and repression, whether through collective action, media statements, public opinion surveys, or direct contacts. Such signals are likely to reflect fragmentation under the status quo, such that politicians will perceive conflicting demands from different sectors of society. Given existing inequalities and power imbalances in society, however, politicians are not likely to grant equal weight and attention to the preferences and demands of all social groups. Instead, in light of preference fragmentation over policing and security, politicians are likely to side with those higher up in the social hierarchy.

---

[7] Author interview with Jairo García, director of security for the Bogotá Chamber of Commerce, Bogotá, July 23, 2012.

Importantly, the role of social stratification in shaping the distribution of protection and repression can be observed even in communities that may overall be classified as low-income or otherwise disadvantaged within the broader social structure. The accounts of communities located in São Paulo's periphery (Chapter 3), for instance, illustrate how the demands of relatively privileged citizens, such as small business owners, favored the repression of those that are relatively disadvantaged. This "paradox" was widely documented by Caldeira (2000, 2002), who found some support for police violence among those who are themselves poor, black, and from the periphery, even though they belong to the population most likely to suffer police violence in Brazil. Fragmented preferences can thus also be found even within marginalized communities, where the distribution of protection and repression leaves these citizens more likely to suffer both crime victimization and police violence. As Chapter 3 suggests, marginalized citizens' vulnerability in the face of the former may lead many to demand more of the latter as a solution, a view reinforced by media and political discourses favoring "iron fist" policies as the only option.

Politicians deciding whether to undertake reform or maintain the status quo assess societal preferences over policing to determine whether there is a broadly shared societal demand for police reform. Ordinary citizens, however, may not hold articulable preferences for or against police reform or even specific policies. Nonetheless, while ordinary citizens may lack clear preferences on specific security policies, they do express identifiable views about policing that serve as information cues for politicians. When hundreds of residents of a wealthy São Paulo neighborhood call government officials to praise an operation in which police killed 10 alleged burglars,[8] and hundreds of citizens experiencing homelessness protest a police killing of a man experiencing homelessness,[9] politicians draw inferences about the distribution of preferences over police use of lethal force across different societal groups.

I therefore use a number of proxies for preferences in favor of or against police reform that correspond to how ordinary citizens experience policing, which they regularly convey to government officials: citizens' trust in police, assessment of police performance, and views about police

---

[8] Author interview with anonymous official at Police Ombudsman's Office (Ouvidoria da Polícia), São Paulo, September 15, 2017.

[9] Author interview with anonymous leader of organization for the rights of the population experiencing homelessness in São Paulo State, São Paulo, September 16, 2017.

discretion and authority. These are basic elements of policing over which citizens can reasonably be expected to have direct experience and articulable opinions and that serve as proxies for specific preferences regarding distinct policies on civilian oversight, militarization, lethal force, accountability, etc. As discussed, politicians learn about these preferences from various sources – including surveys, direct contacts, media statements, protests, and societal organizations and networks – that convey specific demands to politicians to influence policing.

Politicians draw on these information cues to assess the first key explanatory variable, the degree of preference fragmentation. I operationalize fragmentation as whether there is a clear majority view on the three proxies or whether they are divided among substantial segments of the population, as well as the extent to which such divisions fall along social cleavages such as race, class, and geography. Under high fragmentation, or simply fragmentation, executives and other politicians receive information from surveys, media reporting, protests, or meetings with organizations, indicating that trust in police, assessments of police performance, and views on police discretion and authority are divided among considerable segments of the population, such that there is no clear majority opinion (see Figure 2.2), and that such divisions correspond to relevant social cleavages. Importantly, I argue that preference fragmentation holds when fragmentation is high on any of these three dimensions, even if there appears to be consensus on one or more of the others. While it makes intuitive sense that these three dimensions would vary together, they actually convey different views that

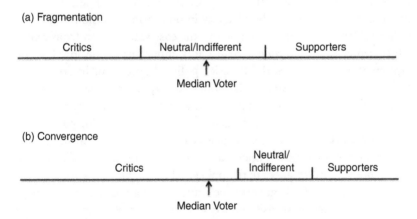

FIGURE 2.2 Hypothesized shift in societal preferences over policing under fragmentation and convergence

may well contradict one another. Scholars and security officials alike have drawn attention to this contradiction. Teresa Caldeira, for instance, identified the "paradox" that shows broad distrust in police but also considerable support for greater police authority to kill (Caldeira 2002). Meanwhile, public officials such as former Buenos Aires security minister León Arslanian and former Colombian inspector general Carlos Gustavo Arrieta similarly characterized societal opinions and demands as "erratic" (see Chapters 4 and 5, respectively). These contradictions, I argue, are a manifestation of fragmentation and have important policy implications. In contrast, under low fragmentation – which I call convergence – politicians receive information about shared discontent along these dimensions across race, class, and geographic cleavages (see next subsection).

In the context of fragmentation, politicians are unlikely to see police reform as electorally advantageous. Per Luna's work on political parties' "segmented representation," a unified programmatic policy approach is untenable for winning elections in high-inequality settings, where class preferences likely conflict (Luna 2014, 21). Instead, parties adopt a "segmented" strategy, pursuing programmatic appeals with middle-class constituents and clientelistic linkages in low-income constituencies, with policy being "significantly biased" in favor of the former. A similar dynamic occurs with policing. Executives perceiving fragmented preferences over policing are unlikely to pursue reform if discontent is concentrated in low-income sectors, reproducing a pattern of inequality shown by work on the judiciary's treatment of police killings (Brinks 2008).

In light of the fact that police violence and ineffectiveness in fighting crime disproportionately affect the poor and working classes, it is worth discussing the role played by ideology in politicians' decision-making on police reform. While the executives in the case studies span from center-left to center-right (González 2019b), it is important to consider how the argument applies across the broader political spectrum. In contrast to Garay's findings regarding social policy (Garay 2017), I argue that even leftist politicians who cater to poor and working-class voters are unlikely to pursue police reform under fragmentation. While left-wing parties with poor and working-class constituencies can afford to antagonize business groups in pursuing social policies in the face of opposition, leftist leaders can seldom afford to alienate the police, who can withdraw their service and put order and basic governance – and therefore their or their party's electoral fortunes – at risk. Police leverage their structural power to restrict the policy options even of politicians who ideologically favor reform, as the case of São Paulo's Governor Montoro illustrates

(Chapter 6). Scholars have shown that, even when leftist executives take power, they often not only fail to enact reforms but also pursue accommodation with police, as occurred in Mexico City (Müller 2017) and Bahia, Brazil (Durazo Hermann 2017). Thus, politicians – even those whose core constituencies suffer the brunt of police violence and malfeasance – across the ideological spectrum are susceptible to the constraints posed by the structural power of police and are unlikely to enact police reform under preference fragmentation. Under such conditions, leaders would likely choose to satisfy their constituents through less divisive policies that entail fewer electoral risks.

How Preference Convergence Shifts Incentives toward Reform

Politicians' electoral calculations change when societal preferences shift from fragmentation toward convergence. Figure 2.2 summarizes the hypothesized shift in the distribution of preferences, from fragmentation (a) to convergence (b). A helpful heuristic is to consider where the median voter might lie under fragmented preferences and under convergence. Under the condition of fragmentation, the median voter likely lies in the neutral or supporter category, leading politicians to infer that most voters do not prefer police reform. Under convergence, however, the median voter moves into the critics' camp, such that leaders infer that a majority comes to demand police reform. Rather than pursuing a "segmented" strategy as they would in a context of divergent preferences, political leaders observing this broadly shared discontent will be more likely to address policing deficiencies. Consider, for instance, the findings of a survey conducted in Buenos Aires in the late 1990s, discussed in Chapter 4, which found that 45 percent of respondents favored expanding police authorities, while the remainder opposed it; by contrast, 84 percent supported increasing penalties and sentences for certain crimes (Fraga 1998). Politicians observing such results are likely to see the latter as cutting across social cleavages, making them more inclined to pursue higher criminal penalties as a response, rather than police reform. Preference convergence, of course, does not guarantee policy enactment, as illustrated by the failure to enact gun control measures in the United States despite near-consensus support for policies such as universal background checks. But in contrast to fragmentation, convergence provides an incentive to politicians to take action on a broadly shared demand.

While issue preferences can shift gradually toward convergence, scandals are a useful methodological tool for identifying convergence and assessing its impact on politicians' strategies over a short period. Scandals, defined as high-profile acts of police deviance that generate broad societal outrage, mobilize groups that are typically critical of police – such as leftists, human rights activists, and sectors that are routinely subjected to police abuse – and move sectors of society, typically the middle class, that previously supported, tolerated, or were indifferent toward certain police behaviors into the ranks of critics.

Scandals lead to a change in the types of signals that politicians receive about the preferences of different societal groups toward police reform. Whereas under the status quo politicians perceive preference fragmentation in citizens' contacts, surveys, media reports, and collective action, these same types of actions come to convey preference convergence and shared views toward the police in the context of a scandal, as the chapters that follow demonstrate. In São Paulo, televised acts of police violence led to survey results showing an increase in the number of *paulistanos* (São Paulo residents) viewing the police as too violent from 44 percent to 73 percent, as well as protests by low-income residents and denouncements by business leaders (Chapter 6). In Colombia, following the rape and murder of a little girl in a police station, even the National Federation of Commerce began calling for police reform, an unusual position for the business sector in Colombia, which traditionally relied on selective protection from police (Chapter 7). In Argentina, a broad range of middle-class sectors engaged in mass protest in response to an egregious act of police violence, whereas such protests had previously been more common in low-income communities (Chapter 7). Scandals thus focus societal and political attention on points of consensus about policing, incorporating broad sectors beyond groups that are typically critical of police.

Politicians know, however, that scandals fade and that convergence is temporary. In the absence of a political opposition that poses an electoral threat, politicians may prefer to pursue symbolic responses, such as firing a high-ranking official, to address broadly shared societal discontent. For instance, Governor Eduardo Duhalde's firing of his long-time police chief following a long list of acts of misconduct among the Buenos Aires provincial police force (Chapter 4) and Governor Mário Covas's formal apology in the wake of a televised act of police violence by the São Paulo Military Police (Chapter 6) were important gestures, but neither resulted in actual police reform.

Reform becomes likely when preferences converge and incumbents face a robust opposition that "comprise(s) a daunting threat of replacement" (Grzymala-Busse 2007). A strong opposition party might view the broadly shared discontent and criticism of police as a profitable avenue for threatening the incumbent's electoral success. The larger the majority represented in the convergence of pro-reform preferences, the greater the likelihood that a strong opposition party can successfully mobilize voters against the incumbent in the next elections. I identify five indicators to measure the strength of an opposition party to pose an electoral threat: party vote shares; holding executive office at other levels of government; opposition to the executive's legislative agenda;[10] incumbent's approval ratings;[11] and proximity to elections. These characteristics indicate whether an opposition party has access to, and ability to marshal, institutional resources – hearings, investigations, or legislation – and media attention to mobilize the scandal (Sherman 1978) by strategically employing and keeping it on the agenda to attack the incumbent. The latter two indicators in particular also provide additional incentive to mobilize media and public attention around the scandal strategically to attack the incumbent. Thus, while police induce executives to pursue accommodation, convergence and a robust opposition provide an electoral counterweight to the police's structural power, shifting politicians' strategy toward reform.

Politicians from the opposition will also be well situated to broaden the scope of the scandal. When a scandal is only mobilized by societal actors (community groups, NGOs, etc.), we are likely to see not reform but instead an individualized institutional response to the specific case. For instance, as in the case of José Luis Cabezas discussed in Chapter 7, societal mobilization may lead a police killing to be investigated and prosecuted rather than what routinely happens in these cases throughout much of Latin America (Brinks 2008) and the United States: nothing.[12] When a scandal is mobilized by leaders of a robust political opposition, however, they can use it as a platform to attack the incumbent by making it into a broader institutional issue rather than an isolated case.

But while opposition politicians and parties will use police scandals to their advantage, they may well be unlikely to make police reform a priority in the absence of such a convergence of preferences. On the

---

[10] In Latin America, legislative proposals typically originate with the executive, reducing the legislature to a reactive role, amending, approving, or rejecting bills (Cox & Morgenstern 2001).

[11] Scholars have shown the importance of presidents' approval ratings for getting their legislative agendas passed (see Rivers & Rose 1985; Canes-Wrone 2010).

[12] Kimberly Kindy and Kimbriell Kelly, "Thousands Dead, Few Prosecuted," *Washington Post*, April 11, 2015.

one hand, opposition politicians will similarly observe fragmentation and contradictory demands from different societal groups, making such an approach electorally disadvantageous. On the other, politicians from the ruling party and the opposition alike may engage in accommodation with the police. For instance, as will be discussed in the São Paulo case (Chapter 6), a mayoral candidate for the opposition in the city of São Paulo culti- vated political support from the police and ran on a platform that was highly critical of, and helped sink, the governor's reformist agenda. I observed a similar exchange in 2011 in a municipality of Buenos Aires Province, during which a provincial legislator who was a candidate for mayor met with four high-ranking police officers (*comisarios*) to discuss how they could help the politician get votes, as well as the type of support they could count on the politician to provide – both in the present, as a legislator, and potentially as mayor – for said votes.[13]

Politicians from the opposition may therefore be equally unlikely as those in the ruling party to call for police reform when societal preferences are fragmented because they will see little electoral benefit, while risking mutually beneficial relationships with the police. For this reason, an observable implication of the theoretical framework presented here is that police reform will be unlikely in the absence of a scandal or the convergence of societal preferences, even if there is a robust political opposition. The Colombian context during the early 1990s provides an example of the failure of an increasingly robust opposition to push for police reform in the absence of societal preference convergence. It was the subsequent combination of these two factors that shifted the calculations of political leaders in favor of reform.

Police, meanwhile, are more likely to accept reform because such a prolonged scandal places pressure on political leaders to intervene in police structures and activity, constituting a threat to their autonomy. In order to minimize the loss of institutional autonomy, police organizations cooperate (to varying degrees) with reform in order to ensure that the reform reflects their preferences, as occurs with other organized interests (Carpenter & Sin 2007, 155). Though police institutions can act as barriers to reform, the police leadership's reading of broad societal dis- content and the electoral pressure facing the executive will lead it to get behind the reform effort so as to advocate for the policies that are most favorable to the organization. This "daunting threat of replacement"

---

[13] Date and location of meeting withheld to preserve anonymity of the legislator and police officials.

(Grzymala-Busse 2007) faced by the incumbent executive, alongside preference convergence, thus serves as an electoral counterweight to structural power of the police, changing the political calculus in favor of reforms to address authoritarian modes of coercion.

Unpacking Scandals

Given the role of scandals as instances of temporary convergence of societal preferences and demands, it is worth unpacking the concept further in order to better understand the causal process by which scandal, alongside a robust political opposition, can increase the likelihood of police reform. Crucially, I argue that scandals are not a function of the quality of a particular police force or of the level of police violence. I argue instead that the process by which a deviant act becomes a scandal – that is, the process by which a deviant event (1) occurs, (2) becomes known, (3) receives media coverage, and (4) generates a strong negative reaction from a broad swath of society is plausibly exogenous.

While individual steps in the process may be endogenous – more corrupt and low-capacity police forces may have a higher incidence of deviant acts, increasing the likelihood that they may become public (or not), societies with more sophisticated or independent media outlets may be more likely to unearth and report on such acts, etc. – it is difficult, if not nearly impossible, to predict ex ante which of these acts that become known and are reported on by the media will resonate with public opinion in such a way that they lead to protests, petitions, broad reach on social media, critical reports, condemnation from prominent leaders, and countless other expressions of societal outrage.

It is also difficult to predict ex ante whether characteristics of the victim, including those that may make the victim more sympathetic to the middle class, or of the event – or the availability of video – will result in a scandal, let alone police reform. Even a cursory comparison of prominent and relatively unknown cases shows that such features are far from deterministic and, therefore, are unlikely predictors of when an act of police malfeasance will bring about the convergence of preferences. In the United States, social protest became widespread across the country – and racialized police violence a central component of the public agenda – following the killing of nineteen-year-old Michael Brown at the hands of police in Ferguson, Missouri, in August 2014. But while that killing of an unarmed young Black man by police became widely known and a source of broad protest, the killing of another unarmed young Black man four days prior to the killing of Michael Brown – twenty-two-year-old John Crawford III by police in Beavercreek, Ohio – did not cause a similar degree of outrage, despite a video showing that police shot and killed the young father within seconds of entering a Walmart store while he was holding a toy gun sold at the store.[14] The comparison of Michael Brown and John Crawford III underscores that neither the purported mainstream sympathy of the victim nor the availability of video footage can predict which cases of police deviance will become a scandal. Although media are an essential technology of scandal – as Lawson (2002) showed in the case of Mexico – and the rise of social media may increase our knowledge of extrajudicial police killings and malfeasance, it's not clear that this would affect the likelihood that any individual act would generate broad societal outrage.

The frequency of acts of police malfeasance is also not necessarily a predictor of which cases will become scandals. For instance, the disappearance of Amarildo de Souza from a favela in Rio de Janeiro after being in police custody became a cause for ongoing protests and outrage within and outside of Rio, while other cases of disappearance of individuals while in police custody before and after the case of de Souza remain ignored by the media and the public alike,[15] despite evidence that such disappearances have increased in some favelas after the installation of Pacification Police Units (UPP).[16] Moreover, virtually all police forces include some members that engage in deviant acts, and – while the characteristics of the deviance may vary – scandals can occur in nearly all societies. Police killings have caused scandals in London,[17] New York City,[18] the Netherlands,[19] and Bogotá[20] at times when their

[14] "Ohio Wal-Mart Surveillance Video Shows Police Shooting and Killing John Crawford III," *Washington Post*, September 25, 2014.
[15] "À procura de outros Amarildos," *O Dia*, August 4, 2014. Available at http://odia.ig.com.br/noticia/rio-de-janeiro/2013-08-04/a-procura-de-outros-amarildos.html.
[16] "Desaparecimentos em favelas do Rio aumentam após início das UPP," UOL 3, August 2014. Available at http://noticias.uol.com.br/cotidiano/ultimas-noticias/2013/08/03/desaparecimentos-aumentaram-em-favelas-do-rio-apos-inicio-das-upps.htm.
[17] "Britain Says Man Killed by Police Had No Tie to Bombings," *New York Times*, July 24, 2005.
[18] "Safer Era Tests Wisdom of 'Broken Windows' Focus on Minor Crime," *New York Times*, July 24, 2014.
[19] Marc Krupanski, "A Death in Police Custody, an Outpouring of Anger in the Netherlands," Open Society Foundations, July 8, 2015. Available at www.opensocietyfoundations.org/voices/death-police-custody-outpouring-anger-netherlands.
[20] "Lo que se sabe de la muerte de Diego Felipe," *El Tiempo*, September 4, 2013.

respective police forces enjoyed broad approval and were widely seen as models for other institutions. Even the police force of Finland, which enjoys remarkably high levels of trust (Kääriäinen 2008) – according to polls, the percentage of respondents expressing "much or very much" trust in the Finnish police reached 96 percent in 2016[21] – faced a massive scandal when the head of the agency's anti-drug unit was found to have engaged in widespread drug smuggling.[22] The events that resonate with broad sectors of society and lead to shared expressions of outrage are largely exogenous to level of development, state capacity, institutional quality of the police force, or other characteristics.

These examples illustrate the relative nature of scandal. It is possible that what shocked in London would not shock in New York, that what caused a scandal in Finland would not have the same result in Colombia. Or, for that matter, that what shocked in Colombia in 2011 would not have caused a similar scandal in Colombia in 1993 (see Chapter 7). But within each specific context, the process by which a deviant act occurs, becomes visible, appears in the media, and shocks public opinion is essentially random. Deviant acts can occur in just about any institutional setting. Whether that act of deviance results in a scandal can be the result of the characteristics of the victim (such as the case of Sandra Catalina, a young girl raped and killed in a police station in Bogotá), the availability of video (particularly with violent acts, such as the televised rampage by Military Police officers against residents in Favela Naval in São Paulo), the official police reaction (such as the case of Diego Felipe Becerra in Bogotá), contemporaneous social and political developments (as in the case of Amarildo de Souza already described), or more ineffable reasons such as the way an event reflects or interacts with societal values, suggesting "that the society itself is deviant from its own standards of conduct" (Sherman 1978, 61). The process by which this occurs does not depend on the institutional strength or quality of the police. An event can become a scandal in a police force that is seen as being in a long period of decline as well as in a police force that is seen as functioning well and highly capable. A scandal cannot be reduced to being the culmination of a series of bad actions or to the crossing of a threshold of deviance. A scandal may follow a stream of similarly

---

[21] "Majority Finns Trust Police: Survey," *Finland Times*, October 6, 2016. Available at www.finlandtimes.fi/national/2016/10/06/30644/Majority-Finns-trust-police:-Survey.
[22] "Finland Unnerved by Trial of Police Detective on Drug Charges," *New York Times*, August 2, 2015.

egregious deviant acts that were publicly reported but did not result in societal outrage; it may also come after years of relative quiet or minor acts of deviance.

A scandal also cannot be reduced to the strategic behavior of politicians and officials, as argued by Balán (2011), particularly those in the opposition. Police scandals are no more likely to occur in settings with significant political competition than they are in settings that are dominated by a single political party with a weak opposition. While a robust political opposition plays a key role in driving police reform following the onset of a scandal, it is not, according to the framework presented here, a cause of scandal. Consider the example of the Carandiru prison massacre in São Paulo in 1992 (Chapter 6). Despite this being a case of police violence that became internationally infamous, a robust opposition did not strategically mobilize the issue – even in the context of an electoral campaign – because the Carandiru massacre did not lead to the convergence of preferences.

A final point worth clarifying is that the discussion about scandal as a "plausibly exogenous" occurrence refers only to the initial societal reaction to an act of police deviance. Scandals can, of course, be mobilized in multiple ways to meet the strategic ends of multiple actors. The initial convergence of opinion may well give way to the usual fragmentation. Indeed, as I discuss in Chapter 7, even after hard-fought reform is enacted, societal preferences often shift back to fragmentation, leading to important reversals of police reform (Casas Dupuy 2005; Saín 2015). Thus, while scandals can produce abrupt shifts in societal preferences and demands that shape the incentives of elected officials toward reform, they raise questions about the sustainability of convergence on such a highly contested issue area.

ORDINARY DEMOCRATIC POLITICS AND THE PERSISTENCE OF AUTHORITARIAN COERCION

The argument presented thus far situates policing within extensive social science scholarship on citizen–state linkages and policy change. Although there are important distinctions across these theoretical frameworks, taken together they define a set of processes that constitute ordinary democratic politics: the varied ways in which citizens – whether through mass public opinion, organizations, social movements, and other forms of collective action – influence public policies by shaping the electoral incentives of political leaders. The implication of my argument is that the policy choices that have favored the persistence of authoritarian coercion among many police forces in Latin America (and elsewhere) are not merely the legacy of authoritarian rule but a product of ordinary democratic processes.

Over the last several decades, for instance, political scientists have studied the extent of policy congruence in democracies, examining the relationship between mass public opinion and policy. Scholars have shown that changes in public opinion can drive changes in public policy across a range of issue areas (Hill & Hinton-Anderson 1995; Lax & Phillips 2009; Page & Shapiro 1983). While such a correspondence between what citizens want and what their elected representatives do is precisely what we ought to expect in a democracy, such responsiveness should not be taken for granted, particularly since it can be undermined by conditions such as high inequality (Gilens & Page 2014). The theoretical framework developed here is consistent with these insights from the policy congruence literature, predicting that political leaders will be responsive to demands for police reform when mass public opinion reflects convergence of preferences and will maintain the status quo when they observe fragmentation of public opinion. My argument, however, adds two important caveats to the policy congruence literature. First, police forces leverage their structural power to constrain the policy agenda, limiting the scope of policy options available to politicians to respond to citizens' demands. Second, such responsiveness to the convergence of preferences over police reform is most likely to occur if incumbents face a robust political opposition.

Another model of democratic politics views public policy not as a result of public opinion but rather as the product of contestation between different sets of organized interests representing existing social cleavages. Foundational political science scholars have debated whether such contestation produced healthy democratic outcomes through an exercise of pluralism (Dahl 1961) or systematically unequal outcomes biased toward more powerful actors and groups (Bachrach & Baratz 1962). The framework presented here argues that politicians' decision-making regarding the distribution of protection and repression indeed results from ordinary contestation between different groups of citizens, with politicians' choices reflecting societal inequalities and power structures. Policing is thus a key example of how democratic governments may function as "potential agents of domination" rather than "structur[ing] the power dimensions of human interaction so as to ameliorate domination in walks of life" (Shapiro 2006, 5).

Yet another scholarly literature on policy-making and democratic responsiveness has demonstrated how societal mobilization have led to policy change, including the legislative successes of the civil rights movements in the United States (Andrews 2001), rights protections for Afro-descendant populations in Colombia and Brazil (Paschel 2016), and social policy expansion resulting from mobilization by informal-sector workers and partisan competition for their votes (Garay 2017). The present analysis extends these insights to policing, demonstrating the influence of societal mobilization on the distribution of protection and repression. I argue, however, that societal mobilization on policing and security issues (along with patterns of political competition) need not always lead to policy change; instead, it may also favor the maintenance of the status quo, or "nondecisionmaking" (Bachrach & Baratz 1962, 952). Thus, when political leaders seemingly fail to enact police reform in the face of rampant extralegal violence and corruption, as well as weak external accountability, this does not reflect a lack of democratic responsiveness. Instead, mobilization by different societal groups may well indicate to politicians that societal preferences over police reform are fragmented, shifting electoral incentives away from police reform.

Explaining the persistence of authoritarian coercion therefore requires not an understanding of authoritarian legacies but rather an understanding of ordinary democratic processes. As the case studies demonstrate, the practices and structures I've characterized as authoritarian coercion – the exercise of exceptional coercion, serving the interests of political leaders, and weak external accountability – may result from the ordinary processes through which citizens' preferences are translated into policy and bureaucratic behavior. Although these democratic processes may at times result in police reform efforts to promote democratic coercion, the persistence of authoritarian coercion in democracy is a compelling illustration of how "democratic procedures can in any case have perverse consequences" (Shapiro 2006, 7).

Societal Preferences and Criminal Justice Policy: Disentangling Related Approaches

Scholars of criminal justice systems broadly have similarly viewed repression and punitive policies – some of which fall under the rubric of what I call authoritarian coercion – as outcomes of the normal functioning of democracy. Scholars across a range of disciplines have demonstrated how societal mobilization, mass publics, and opinion shape the way states exercise coercive power in response to crime. For this reason, it is worth considering some of these approaches and specifying how my own argument differs, as well as where the observable implications of these related approaches diverge.

Many scholars have written about how democratic processes facilitate the expression of punitive preferences, finding that elected judges become more punitive in their sentencing as they approach reelection (Huber & Gordon 2004) and that democratic countries "where the public has the greatest political influence" have higher incarceration rates than those that are more "hierarchical," such as corporatist structures (Jacobs & Kleban 2003, 746). Miller (2016) largely argues against the notion that mass opinion is inherently punitive, arguing that, in contrast to other democracies such as the United Kingdom and the Netherlands, it is the fragmented, racialized political structures in the United States that make it unresponsive to demands for policies to reduce social inequalities but particularly responsive to demands for greater punishment. While this approach is far more nuanced than many other theories about mass opinion and crime policy, most theories in this literature share the view that mass opinion regarding crime and security is largely uniform and unidirectional. That is, depending on institutional structures, responsiveness to the majority's demand almost certainly leads to more punitive policies; there is little room for changes in mass opinion. While this book concerns itself with police reform rather than criminal justice policy, it is worth raising the distinction between these approaches and the argument presented here. This book advances the argument that mass opinion on security and policing is fragmented and subject to change – from fragmentation to convergence – and, as such, can both favor the continuity of authoritarian coercive institutions and serve as a driver of reform.

Meanwhile, looking specifically at police violence and police reform in the Latin American context, Fuentes (2005) also explains variation in whether governments choose to increase police powers or enact police reform in terms of societal divisions, organized into "pro-order" and "civil rights" coalitions. The author explains variation in outcomes as a function of shifts in power from one coalition to another. In contrast, rather than seeing reform as a product of a shift in the balance of power between different coalitions, the argument presented here – in Fuentes's terms – is that some societal groups not typically part of the "civil rights" coalition, and that even form part of the "pro-order" coalition under the status quo, may temporarily shift their preferences and demands in favor of reform.

Other foundational scholars of policing instead explain police reform (or its absence) in terms of issue salience. Wilson (1978), for instance, wrote decades ago that city governments seldom use their authority over policing because "such matters are not of general interest to the citizenry or to public officials" (228). Goldstein (1977) similarly noted that public concern regarding policing comes in "waves" and that moments of scrutiny and reform have come during "spurts of public interest" following "an exposé of corruption or other wrongdoing" (2). By these accounts, the continuity of authoritarian coercion in democracies is the result of a lack of public interest in or attention to the problem, and the reform processes emerge as a result of the increased salience of the problem. In contrast, I argue that both outcomes are a product of the degree of fragmentation of societal preferences and demands, which reflect continual public interest that is consistently communicated to officials.

Scholars focused on Latin America, meanwhile, have sought to explain variation in the adoption of police reforms in terms of societal attitudes toward the police. Pereira and Ungar (2004), for instance, argue that "there is an inverse relationship between public confidence in the police and the level of police reform," observing few reforms where confidence is high, as in Chile, and a greater number of reforms where confidence is low, as in Argentina (265). While this argument is intuitive, it masks considerable variation within countries and has little explanatory power for understanding within-case variation over time. Argentina, for instance, has dozens of police forces, some of which have been subjected to ambitious reforms – such as the Buenos Aires provincial police – while others, such as the Federal Police, have not. Moreover, even when we look at successful enactment of reforms, public attitudes toward police cannot be seen as the sole cause. By early 1997, a mere 6 percent of citizens expressed trust in the police of Buenos Aires Province following the killing of a journalist by police. According to this argument, we might have expected to see reform occur then; nonetheless, reform did not occur until after midterm elections later that year led to an unexpected shift in the balance of power between the governor's party and the opposition (see Chapter 7). Thus, low public confidence in police is far from sufficient for reform.

It is important to highlight the differences in the predictions of these related theories of societal preferences and politicians' choices regarding security. In the analysis that follows I use process tracing to illustrate how societal preferences over security and policing can reflect fragmentation or convergence and, in turn, shape the decisions of elected leaders. To the extent possible, I will highlight evidence that allows us to distinguish empirically between my argument and the alternative mechanisms described here.

EXPLAINING THE PERSISTENCE OF AUTHORITARIAN COERCION – AND REFORM – IN LATIN AMERICA

In order to test the argument outlined in this chapter, I draw on comparative evidence from periods of continuity and reform across police forces in Buenos Aires Province (Argentina), São Paulo State (Brazil), and Colombia. The choice of two subnational cases within federal countries and one unitary country is intended to achieve congruence between the bureaucracy and the jurisdiction that controls it. Given the research question and the electoral argument at the heart of this book, the appropriate unit of analysis is the "locus of choice" (Arjona 2019), the political-administrative level where politicians make decisions about police reform and where electoral pressures stand to influence such decision-making. The selection of two subnational units and one unitary national unit is not without limitations, as there continue to be important differences that can complicate the comparison. Brazil and Argentina's federal constitutions, for instance, place some important constraints on the content of police reform that is possible at the state and provincial level; in Colombia, meanwhile, its unitary police force faces no such constraint. Despite these limitations, a strength of this analytical approach is that it demonstrates that, irrespective of the administrative level and concomitant constraints, the police's structural power and electoral incentives nevertheless shape politicians' decision-making over police reform in similar ways.

Case selection followed a most-similar and a most-different systems design, based on various structural conditions relevant for reform outcomes (see Table 2.2). Despite structural similarities in federalism, authoritarian past, military strength,[23] and low–medium levels of violence, São Paulo State and Buenos Aires Province differ on outcomes. Colombia, meanwhile, offers a sharp contrast to Buenos Aires Province: it is a unitary country with a long history of being formally democratic and with a national police force and a strong military (Leal Buitrago 1994), as

---

[23] As scholars of Argentina and Brazil have shown, both countries undertook concerted measures to reduce military power following their respective transition to democracy (Acuña & Smulovitz 1991; Diamint 2003; Hunter 1997).

TABLE 2.2 *Case selection: most-similar and most-different designs*

	São Paulo State	Buenos Aires Province	Colombia
Recent dictatorship	Yes	Yes	No
Structure	Federal	Federal	Unitary
Military strength	Weak	Weak	Strong
Violence	Medium	Low	High
Reform	No	Yes	Yes

well as a decades-long armed conflict. Yet both overhauled their police forces in remarkably similar ways during the 1990s.

The selection of these cases allows us to rule out a number of alternative explanations of institutional continuity or reform. While a more systematic discussion for persistence and reform can be found in the respective introductions to Parts I and II of the book, it is worth providing an overview here. Conditions such as previous military dictatorship, strong military, or high levels of violence may complicate reform efforts through authoritarian legacies, additional veto players, or straining state resources and capacity. Yet, Argentina's history of military dictatorship did not prevent bold police reforms from taking place in the 1990s, nor did its federalist structure (Eaton 2008). Meanwhile, neither Colombia's powerful armed forces, nor extraordinary levels violence, nor a weak state battling powerful guerrilla groups and drug cartels precluded the successful passage of comprehensive police reform legislation. This case selection allows us to rule out these static conditions as alternative explanations of continuity and reform.

The analysis presented in this book focuses on the dynamic processes that shape politicians' choices between continuity and reform. Since societal preferences and political opposition strength are subject to rapid change, each case exhibits considerable variation over time. As Table 2.3 shows, the cases presented here highlight variation in independent and dependent variables, in order to test different mechanisms of the argument. Since structural police reform has been absent in São Paulo State, that case study highlights fragmentation and weak political opposition to account for institutional continuity. Where ambitious structural reforms were adopted, the cases focus on how a shift in political opposition strength under preference convergence (Buenos Aires Province) and a change in preferences from fragmentation to convergence in the context

TABLE 2.3 *Overview of cases and variation*

	Societal preferences	Opposition	Outcome	Chapter
São Paulo (1983–1984)	Fragmentation	Robust	No Reform	6
São Paulo (1992)	Fragmentation	Robust	No Reform	6
São Paulo (1997)	Fragmentation to Convergence	Weak	Marginal Reform	6
Buenos Aires (1991–1996)	Fragmentation	Weak	No Reform	4
Buenos Aires (1997–1998)	Convergence	Weak to Robust	Reform	7
Colombia (1990–1992)	Fragmentation	Weak to Robust	No Reform	5
Colombia (1993)	Fragmentation to Convergence	Robust	Reform	7

of a relatively robust opposition (Colombia) changed politicians' calculations in favor of structural reforms. This analysis and case selection underscores that reform becomes likely under the joint occurrence of these factors, helping to reconcile the discrepancy between the literatures of police reform and of institutional change, given the former's tendency to overpredict police reform. Political competition and federalism may serve as obstacles to police reform, but not when societal preferences converge. Societal pressure and mobilization may drive reform but may result in continuity in the absence of convergence and a robust opposition.

Across all cases, I demonstrate how the structural power of the police constrained the policy options available to civilian officials charged with overseeing them, enabling the police forces to succeed in keeping police reform off the agenda and shaping the terms of the debate. The chapters in Part I of the book document the persistence of authoritarian coercion across the three police forces and illustrate how, within this constrained policy space, authoritarian coercion is maintained by the fragmentation of societal preferences, including considerable segments of the population that demand authoritarian coercive practices as the means of achieving protection. Part II of the book shows how, in Buenos Aires Province and Colombia, institutional persistence gave way to comprehensive structural reform after the convergence of societal preferences through scandals and a robust political opposition. The characteristics of each case allow us to demonstrate that neither condition is sufficient to bring about reform on its own. In Buenos Aires Province, a scandal failed to bring about reform until midterm elections produced a change in the strength of the political opposition; in Colombia, a reform proposal failed in the congress, despite a fairly robust opposition, and was revived only after the onset of a scandal. In the case of São Paulo State, meanwhile, I show that alternate paths to reform may nonetheless face barriers due to fragmentation, and, even in moments of convergence, the absence of a robust opposition may preclude reforms altogether.

Methodological Approach

These accounts are based on two-and-a-half years of field research in Argentina, Brazil, and Colombia, during which I conducted 230 interviews and ethnographic observation in community security meetings, police stations, and other settings, as well as archival research. Just as the theoretical framework that informs this project takes both macro- and micro-level perspectives, the mechanics of my research on the ground did as well. At one level, there was the straightforward task of studying a historical process of institutional continuity and reform, seeking out former presidents, governors, mayors, ministers and secretaries of security, police leadership and rank and file, former legislators, and civil society actors, as well as reviewing documents in government, police, NGO, and media archives.

At the same time, my research on the broader political processes that determine whether police reform can be successfully enacted was also informed by a fieldwork strategy that probed internal spatial variation. Due to the challenges of conducting such research at the scale of a national or state/provincial territory, I selected the main metropolitan region in each setting for this part of the field research, which was conducted primarily in São Paulo, Bogotá, and the Greater Buenos Aires region. In Latin America's unequal societies, there is considerable overlap in the spatial distribution of poverty, crime, police violence, and the distribution of police services. I therefore pursued a research strategy based on the selection of communities in different regions of the city/metropolitan area, reflecting differences in socioeconomic and racial composition, as well as experiences with crime and the police. I then conducted ethnographic observation in community meetings and police stations and also interviewed the local police commanders, rank and file police officers, and community leaders. This research strategy aimed to discern the link between macro- and micro-level processes. That is, despite a research question focused on a macro-level political decision regarding a centrally administered agency, the theoretical framework is based on the premise that these political choices are shaped by the day-to-day distribution of protection and repression and police–community relations, which inevitably vary across different communities in three diverse and unequal societies. Because the case of São Paulo represents a "negative case," where comprehensive structural police reform of the sort adopted in Buenos Aires Province and Colombia has not been enacted, the São Paulo chapter in particular draws on ethnographic methods to probe the micro-foundations of preference fragmentation, which I argue acts as an impediment to police reform.

PART I

PERSISTENCE

Introduction: The Renewal of Authoritarian Coercion in Democracy

The chapters in this section probe what drives the institutional persistence of police forces that exercise authoritarian coercion, drawing on empirical evidence from three police forces: the Military Police of São Paulo State (Chapter 3), the Police of Buenos Aires Province (Chapter 4), and the National Police of Colombia (Chapter 5). Notably, while the police forces of Buenos Aires Province and Colombia eventually underwent comprehensive structural reform processes (see Chapter 7), reform was preceded by a prolonged period of "reform deficit" (Weyland 2008), institutional stasis in the face of widespread extrajudicial violence, rampant corruption, and politicized coercion. Considering these cases through a comparative lens thus sheds light on the mechanisms that favor the persistence of authoritarian coercive institutions in otherwise democratic states.

Chapter 3 provides an overview of three decades of continuity among police institutions in São Paulo State, beginning with a successful pressure campaign by police to prevent the inclusion of structural reforms of the Military Police in the constitution drafted during Brazil's transition to democracy, and continuing with an analysis of the endurance of fragmentation of societal preferences through the present day. Chapter 4 examines a decade and a half of institutional stasis of the Police of Buenos Aires Province, beginning with the transition to democracy in 1983 but focusing on the political choice of Governor Eduardo Duhalde to maintain the status quo during the bulk of his two terms as governor, from 1991 through 1997. Chapter 5 similarly examines a period of prolonged institutional decay of the Colombian National Police, beginning in the 1980s with the ramping up of the state's war against drug cartels. As with

Chapter 4 on Buenos Aires Province, Chapter 5 focuses on the administration of a single executive, President César Gaviria, who pushed forward a transformative reform agenda affecting nearly all aspects of the state – but, conspicuously, not the police. In both chapters, careful analysis of the same executive – each of whom explicitly decided to maintain the status quo, only to reverse course and enact police reform in a relatively short period of time – allows us to hold constant a number of conditions in interrogating politicians' choices when deciding whether to reform decidedly authoritarian police forces.

Such comparative analysis allows us to identify important variation in the manifestations of authoritarian coercion and the processes of societal preference formation that sustain them. The cases analyzed in Part I thus help to elucidate different aspects of the book's central argument about how ordinary democratic processes can reproduce authoritarian coercion. At the same time, the selection of these cases provides considerable analytical leverage, demonstrating how similar outcomes of institutional persistence among police forces can emerge even in the context of multiple conditions that have led to or facilitated reform in other policy areas and in the absence of conditions that have served as common obstacles to police reforms.

DRIVERS OF INSTITUTIONAL PERSISTENCE

The police forces studied in Part I are all characterized as authoritarian, in that they routinely exercise exceptional coercion, are subject to negligible external accountability, and primarily serve the interests of political leaders. But even though the three police forces lie at the authoritarian end of the continuum, there is important variation in the exercise of authoritarian coercion, how they leverage their structural power to constrain the policy agenda, and the nature of social structures and contestation that help to sustain authoritarian coercive structures and practices.

The chapters that follow probe this variation, in order to understand the different pathways through which police may emerge and endure as authoritarian enclaves in democracies. In São Paulo, for instance, the most salient manifestation of authoritarian coercion has long been the high rate of extrajudicial killings – both those captured in official statistics and those conducted by police death squads. Analyses of these killings conducted by public officials and scholars over the course of three decades have demonstrated that these killings are often exceptional – that is, not defined or constrained by the law – and are driven instead by characteristics such as race, class, and geography. In Buenos Aires Province, while arbitrary police killings that reinforced societal inequality were also a systematic practice, authoritarian coercion also entailed an expansive illicit network of rent extraction from criminal activity, wherein police were routinely complicit with the very crimes they were charged with preventing. The Colombian National Police, meanwhile, represented a hybrid of these authoritarian coercive practices through the 1980s and early 1990s, which were exacerbated by the country's singularly high rates of drug and guerrilla violence at the time, as well as the resulting institutional crisis. Colombia's police carried out routine social cleansing murders of marginalized groups under the guise of the drug war and also engaged in widespread violence and corruption in connivance with powerful drug cartels, while the state's embattled civilian institutions proved unable to provide external accountability.

The three cases also illustrate how the police's structural power enables them to constrain policy agendas, albeit in different ways. In Buenos Aires Province, politicians across the political spectrum were reportedly involved in the police's illicit rent-extraction system, on which they depended to finance their political parties and electoral campaigns. The Colombian police constrained the policy agenda by leveraging its control over the government's policy priority, the drug war, which allowed them to cultivate a relationship with a powerful backer, the United States. Meanwhile, São Paulo's Military Police conferred the distribution of coercion and repression in accordance with politicians' political interests, strategically withdrawing its service to generate politically embarrassing situations. In each case, and with police forces generally, politicians depended on the police's cooperation in order to achieve a range of political objectives; they proved quite hesitant to alienate their police forces by enacting reform. Police forces thus use their control of coercion in varied ways to induce politicians to pursue accommodation – granting police autonomy in exchange for cooperation. In this way, police forces constrain the policy options available to politicians to address societal demands for security.

In the context of this constrained policy space, the nature of societal preferences and patterns of demand-making are crucial for understanding this book's central argument that such conditions – which on the surface would seem to indicate the failure of democratic responsiveness – are often sustained by ordinary democratic politics. Across all three cases, citizens conveyed fragmentation, wherein attitudes and preferences regarding policing and security are divided among considerable segments of society – typically along existing societal cleavages – such that there may not be a clear majority position. As the chapters that follow demonstrate, political leaders routinely received consistent signals from different societal groups indicating conflicting demands over policing and security, serving as information cues that preferences over police reform were fragmented. In São Paulo, for instance, surveys conducted over several years repeatedly found that large groups of citizens were divided in their views on appropriate levels of police violence. This division was also reflected in the class, race, and geographic distribution of citizen contacts to civilian officials. For instance, interviews with officials from the Police Ombudsman's Office indicated that the vast majority of complaints about police misconduct come from the "three P's" (*pobre, preto e periférico*) – those who are poor, black, and from the city's periphery. In contrast, these officials also indicated they had recently received hundreds of calls from residents of a well-to-do neighborhood praising a recent police action that resulted in the killing of ten alleged robbers.[1] At the same time, as Chapter 3 shows, citizens' views and demands on policing are also fragmented in communities in São Paulo's peripheries, despite – or perhaps as a result of – those areas disproportionately suffering greater levels of crime victimization and police violence. In Buenos Aires Province, meanwhile, surveys showed widespread distrust of police but divided views regarding whether police should have expanded authority to fight crime. Throughout the 1990s, politicians thus had to contend with protests in low-income areas denouncing extrajudicial killings by police, as well as protests in middle-class neighborhoods demanding greater police repression in the face of rising crime and social unrest. In Colombia, surveys conducted in the early 1990s showed that, despite broad distrust of the National Police, low-income individuals were more likely than their middle- and high-income counterparts to express fear and distrust of police, while security officials at the time reported "conflicting visions" among the citizenry about the type of police force they wanted.

These conflicting demands and fragmented preferences of societal groups send a signal to politicians that police reform would not only risk alienating a powerful bureaucracy, whose cooperation politicians need, but may also bring little electoral gain. As citizens convey conflicting demands, they signal to politicians the lack of an electoral counterweight

---

[1] Author interview with anonymous official at Police Ombudsman's Office (Ouvidoria da Polícia), São Paulo, September 15, 2017.

to the structural power of police. The authoritarian coercive practices and structures discussed throughout Part I are thus reinforced by ordinary democratic processes of citizen contestation and politicians' electoral calculations. Thus, even in contexts of police forces that exercise authoritarian patterns of coercion, electoral incentives may favor institutional persistence rather than reform.

POLICE INSTITUTIONS AS A "HARD CASE" FOR REFORM

In addition to understanding variation in pathways to persistence among police institutions, the case studies in Part I underscore the challenges coercive institutions pose for institutional change – and why politicians choose to maintain the status quo when societal preferences over policing are fragmented. The chapters that follow provide similar accounts of institutional persistence across the three cases, where the growing salience of increased crime and violence placed policing and security atop the public agenda but, with rare exceptions, did not lead politicians to undertake police reform to address widespread police violence, corruption, and weak capacity to provide security. The seeming hesitation of politicians to pursue police reform, despite societal demands for improved security and despite rampant police violence and illegality, underscores the extent to which police institutions constitute a "hard case" for reform. What is notable about the specific patterns of institutional continuity and reform among police forces described in this book is not merely the (in)frequency of reform, which can result from many different factors. Instead, as the case studies demonstrate, a set of empirical regularities suggests that police forces may be especially resistant to reform.

In the chapters that follow, I demonstrate that, despite facing a highly salient political issue in which the chief state entity charged with providing security exhibits demonstrable and broadly acknowledged deficiencies, the responses of elected officials largely eschewed the police. Rather than responding to widespread public clamor for improved security by enacting police reforms, Latin American politicians long avoided the police with surgical precision, instead enacting ambitious security policies, establishing stiffer penalties for certain crimes, creating prosecutor's offices, reforming the courts, or banning certain practices such as torture. In the chapters that follow, I demonstrate that, across the three cases analyzed in this book, when politicians did undertake policy changes involving the police, such interventions were typically limited to firing police commanders, or using

emergency powers to expel large numbers of officers en masse for malfeasance, rather than enacting more challenging internal, comprehensive, and
permanent structural reforms. These strategies were particularly common
in Colombia and Buenos Aires Province, where politicians relied on these
responses for many years prior to the eventual enactment of comprehensive
police reforms (discussed in Chapter 7).

A second feature of institutional persistence common across the three
case studies was the way police forces leveraged their structural power to
roundly defeat initial reform attempts or proposals, exerting active opposition to these initiatives. In Buenos Aires Province, police succeeded in
blocking a reform proposal and achieving the removal of a reformist
secretary of security despite rising crime, exceedingly low public trust in
police, and growing scandals of police malfeasance. In Colombia, a timid
reform bill backed by the executive branch died in congressional committee, according to the minister of defense, due to pressure from the
National Police. Similarly, in São Paulo State and throughout Brazil, the
Military Police undertook a concerted campaign to successfully block
several police reform measures proposed during the constitutional convention, even as other institutions were created or transformed during the
country's democratic transition (Chapter 3). Along these lines, the cases
share a third outcome, in which incumbents pursued a range of other
complex and politically challenging reforms in other policy areas and
institutions, even as they avoided reforming the police. The conspicuous
exclusion of police reform from Colombia's expansive "institutional shakeup" – an ambitious reform agenda pushed by President César Gaviria in
the 1990s – provides a compelling illustration of this phenomenon
(Chapter 5).

Comparative analysis of periods of continuity thus adds considerable
theoretical insights to our understanding of institutional change, elucidating the challenges posed by coercive institutions. The three cases lay
out how police leverage their structural power to constrain policy
options, raising the threshold for reform. Police forces successfully
block police reform even as reforms in other policy areas prosper,
resulting in the persistence of authoritarian coercive structures and
practices. The cases also demonstrate, however, that police institutions
represent a "hard case" of reform in part because the fragmentation of
societal preferences shift politicians' electoral incentives away from
reform. The next section lays out how case selection allows us to tease
out the causal role of fragmentation as a driver of the persistence of
authoritarian coercion.

ANALYTICAL LEVERAGE FROM COMPARATIVE ANALYSIS: ADDRESSING ALTERNATIVE EXPLANATIONS

A number of structural conditions likely shape politicians' capacity and willingness to enact police reform, including levels of violence and economic crisis. The selection of cases in this book is therefore intended to enable us to tease out the extent to which shifts in societal preferences and political competition shape politicians' incentives when choosing between continuity and reform. Specifically, Part I of the book focused on institutional persistence draws on a most-similar and most-different systems design, in order to discard a number of alternative explanations for the prolonged periods of continuity of authoritarian coercive institutions, including previous history of dictatorship, strength of the military, high levels of violence, and federalism.

Comparative analysis of the three cases demonstrates that institutional persistence emerges even in the face of conditions that have been conducive to reform in other policy areas and even where common obstacles to police reforms have been absent. The chapters on São Paulo State and Buenos Aires Province, for instance, demonstrate how their respective police forces developed core structures and practices from periods of military dictatorships, seemingly supporting arguments about enduring authoritarian legacies as obstacles to police reform. But the case of Colombia attests to the development of remarkably similar patterns of authoritarian coercion, despite a long history of formal democratic rule.[2] Relatedly, the Colombian case seemingly demonstrates how a strong military can serve as an obstacle to police reform, acting as a veto player to block reform efforts that reduce military influence over police and introduce greater civilian control. Yet police reform to promote democratic coercion also stalled for decades in Buenos Aires and has been elusive in São Paulo, despite the significant decline in military strength after democratic transitions in Argentina and Brazil, respectively (Hunter 1997; Pion-Berlin 1997).

The case studies in Part I also demonstrate that policing practices and structures contrary to the rule of law, such as extrajudicial killings, torture, and widespread corruption, do not necessarily emerge and endure as a result of very high levels of violence or so-called "drug wars."

---

[2] Colombia was briefly ruled by a military dictatorship in the 1950s. In contrast, Argentina experienced six different military coups and periods of military rule during the twentieth century, while Brazil was governed by a military dictatorship for more than two decades.

Scholarly and journalistic accounts of the "war on drugs" in the United States (Forman 2017; Fortner 2015) and the Americas broadly (Krause 2014), as well as of the more recent rise in state-sanctioned killings in the Philippines,[3] attribute the rise of police repression, extrajudicial killings, and other exceptional practices to a societal demand for punitive and repressive policies and a loosening of constraints on police actions in the face of high levels of drug-related violence. Yet, in the three cases studied here, authoritarian coercion became entrenched without meaningful political intervention to enact reform; this outcome emerged in places with low (Buenos Aires Province), medium (São Paulo State), and high (Colombia) levels of drug violence alike.

Finally, the case studies show that the prolonged institutional persistence of police forces occurs in both federal and unitary settings. As discussed in Chapter 2, the institutional change and policing literatures offer conflicting predictions. The former predicts that reform is *more* likely in federal settings due to the availability of more opportunities for innovation and experimentation, while the latter predicts that police reform is *less* likely under federalism, due to competition among politicians at different levels of government. Yet the cases and time periods under examination in Part I provide ample evidence of the challenges of enacting police reform under both federal (Buenos Aires and São Paulo) and unitary (Colombia) settings.

Because of the variation in these structural conditions, and a shared outcome of institutional persistence, case selection grants us considerable analytical leverage, allowing us to discard these static, structural factors as drivers of the remarkable persistence of authoritarian coercion under democratic rule. At the same time, while this analytical account of institutional continuity and change privileges the role of dynamic processes in explaining politicians' choices regarding reform, we must also acknowledge the role of structural factors in shaping broader patterns of policing and citizen demand-making. Indeed, one of the key explanatory variables in this analysis – the degree of fragmentation of societal preferences – is likely rooted in a distinct set of structural factors that shape the formation of preferences and demands being communicated to politicians through democratic channels, as well as political leaders' choices between maintaining the status quo and enacting reform. In all of the cases studied in this book – and, indeed, throughout Latin America – societal demands

---

[3] See, for instance, Vincent Bevins, "Duterte's Drug War Is Horrifically Violent. So Why Do Many Young, Liberal Filipinos Support It?" *Washington Post*, April 28, 2017.

and politicians' policy decisions took place in the context of increasing crime and high inequality, which may well increase fragmentation (Caldeira 2000; Dammert & Malone 2003; Kessler 2009a; Rotker 2002). Each of the cases also experienced distinct conditions that likely shaped societal demands and politicians' choices, including record-high levels of violence in Colombia, widespread social strife and protest in response to neoliberal economic policies in Buenos Aires Province and throughout Argentina, and São Paulo's (and Brazil's) profound racial inequalities and rising prevalence of drug violence. As the chapters that follow make clear, these factors undoubtedly shape how citizens vary in their understanding of security conditions, their experiences with coercive institutions, and the types of demands they make regarding policing and security. They also shape how police exercise their structural power and the concessions they are able to extract from politicians. Thus, while this book's focus is on the dynamic factors that drive politicians' shifting assessments of the electoral costs and benefits of police reform and continuity, the chapters in Part I also underscore how the police's institutional persistence may well be rooted in enduring structural conditions such as patterns of violence and inequality.

But even as we acknowledge the role of these structural factors in shaping policing, the formation of citizens' preferences, and political decision-making, they cannot directly explain the patterns of persistence and change examined in this book. Indeed, as Part II (Chapters 6 and 7) demonstrates, these largely static factors cannot account for the short-term dramatic policy shifts that often characterize police reform processes. In both Colombia and Buenos Aires Province, politicians decided to push for comprehensive structural reforms mere months after choosing to maintain the status quo – while levels of violence, inequality, federalism, and military strength remained unchanged.

In seeking to understand persistence, the chapters that follow undertake careful process-tracing in order to elucidate the underlying mechanisms of the police's institutional persistence. Drawing on extensive interview, ethnographic, and archival evidence, they demonstrate how police constrain policy agendas and why fragmented societal preferences reinforce that status quo of authoritarian coercion. They document concerted police action to control the agenda and block reform efforts, as well as the conflicting demands expressed by citizens through protest, media, and direct contacts. The latter point is of particular importance, as it demonstrates that the challenge of reforming the police is not due to a lack of attention or salience, nor is it the result of uniformly punitive mass preferences, although both are commonly cited in the criminal justice literature as explanations for the lack of reform (see Chapter 2). Instead, the chapters in Part I illustrate that, despite slight variation in some of the pathways, the fragmentation of societal preferences along existing societal cleavages of race, class, and geography is at the core of the police's institutional persistence. The case studies demonstrate that the decision to maintain the status quo is a response by politicians to the fragmentation that emerges from ordinary contestation and demand-making, given a policy space constrained by the police's structural power. The comparative analysis developed in the following chapters thus provides considerable theoretical and substantive contributions to our understanding of a key institution that performs the defining function of the state.

3

The Persistence of "the Police that Kills"

Authoritarian Coercion in São Paulo State

At a women's meeting in a favela in the eastern zone of São Paulo, a resident told us that her nine-year-old son insists on sleeping in her bed every night, out of fear that "the police are going to come into the house and kill everyone. He's afraid because the police recently killed his cousin."[4] The woman's young son was not only dealing with serious trauma due to the loss of a loved one at the hands of the state. He was also demonstrating a tragic awareness of the contours of police violence in his state, which is suffered disproportionately by those who share his characteristics. The conventional wisdom that police violence in São Paulo targets the "three Ps" (*pobre, preto e periférico*) – those who are poor, black, and from the urban periphery – has for decades been borne out by analyses of official statistics (Mariano 2018; Ouvidoria da Polícia do Estado de São Paulo 2000; Sinhoretto, Silvestre & Schlitter 2014). Recent studies, moreover, have shown that children and adolescents constituted one-sixth of victims of police killings in 2017 (Mariano 2018, 23) and that police are the primary source of intentional homicides of children and adolescents in the city of São Paulo.[5] That these stark regularities of police violence have been so clearly understood by a child who is *pobre, preto e periférico* reveals how entrenched these patterns of coercion have become.[6]

---

[4] The meeting, convened by a local NGO, was attended by the author in 2019. Date and location withheld.

[5] The report prepared by the Brazilian Forum for Public Security was reported on in "Polícia é principal responsável por mortes intencionais de crianças e adolescentes em SP," *Ponte Jornalismo*, June 16, 2019, available at https://ponte.org/policia-e-principal-responsavel-por-mortes-intencionais-de-criancas-e-adolescentes-em-sp/.

[6] The phrase used in the title of this chapter, "the police that kills," refers to Barcellos (1992) and the title *Rota 66: A História da Polícia que Mata*.

The remarkable persistence of police violence in São Paulo – with its distribution so clearly stratified by race, class, and geography rather than on the basis of the rule of law – is undoubtedly the most conspicuous manifestation of authoritarian coercion in the state. Indeed, the prevalence of this authoritarian coercion was so conspicuous that it was also palpable in the discourses of police officers I encountered during my fieldwork in São Paulo's *periferias*. For instance, during one of my visits to a community police station[7] in a low-income neighborhood in the northern zone of São Paulo, a low-ranking police agent (*soldado*) and his commanding officer (*tenente*) stopped by at the start of their patrol. As the *soldado* prepared to leave, ready to resume his patrol, the commanding officer called out to him and said, "You'll only get a day off if you kill someone" (*só vai tirar folga se matar alguém*). The *soldado*, visibly startled, said to his commanding officer that he would give me the wrong idea and that I would write in my study that "this is what the police of São Paulo is like." The *tenente*, seemingly unconcerned with how his joke would be interpreted by a civilian and foreign researcher, winked at me and repeated, "You'll only get a day off if you kill someone." Similarly, during a visit to a police station in a different low-income neighborhood in the southern zone of the city, I chatted with the local Military Police commander and the leader of the Community Security Council when the commander announced his impending retirement. When I asked about his post-retirement plans, the commander looked at us, smiled, and said that he might "become a terrorist and collaborate with the cleansing" (*vou virar terrorista e colaborar com a limpeza*) – a reference to the history of "social cleansing" killings carried out by police-linked death squads in the state (Adorno & Cárdia 1998; Barcellos 1992).

Jokes about police violence – police killings, social cleansing, beatings, torture, and violence against people in police custody – were fairly commonplace in my conversations with police officers in São Paulo. While jokes are not necessarily indicative of an individual officer's engagement in these practices, they nevertheless reflect the extraordinary levels of police violence in the state. For instance, in 2017, according to official figures, 940 civilians were killed by police officers – both on and off duty – in the State of São Paulo (Mariano 2018, 10). To put this into comparative

---

[7] Community police stations, or *bases comunitárias de segurança*, are substations of the Military Police located within the jurisdiction of a given *companhia* or police district; the substations are intended to allow greater proximity to the community. Location of the substation and date of visit withheld to preserve anonymity of police officers.

perspective, counts of civilians killed by police in the United States compiled by media sources ranged from 962 (the *Washington Post*) to 1,093 (*The Guardian*) in 2016.[8] São Paulo's police forces thus kill nearly as many civilians as those in all of the United States, whose population is more than seven times larger. The everyday remarks I heard about police violence throughout my fieldwork, from community members and police officers alike, were thus part of a fairly conspicuous discourse that maps onto documented patterns of routine extralegal deadly violence by São Paulo's police.

São Paulo's police forces,[9] particularly the state's Military Police (PM), exemplify the stubborn persistence of distinctly authoritarian modes of coercion, perhaps to a much greater extent than the other police forces analyzed in this book. The São Paulo case is also the most illustrative of how the endurance of these coercive practices – politicized coercion and widespread deadly violence largely unconstrained by the law and external accountability – is sustained through democratic processes rather than in spite of them.

The discussion that follows examines the persistence of authoritarian coercive practices and structures and how these patterns have been reinforced by ordinary democratic politics. I first provide an overview of the role of police under Brazil's last military dictatorship and the absence of police reform from the political agenda during the transition to democracy in the 1980s, highlighting how, even in the context of authoritarian legacies, strictly democratic political logics underlie the persistence of authoritarian coercion in democracies. I show how, in the three decades since the transition to democracy, the state's police have leveraged their control over coercion – through both the selective provision of security in politically beneficial ways and the strategic withdrawal of service – to constrain the policy options available to politicians, who in turn benefit from patterns of accommodation with police. These conditions have raised the threshold for police reform in São Paulo over the last three decades, favoring institutional persistence despite the prevalence of widespread extrajudicial killings, corruption, and other abuses. In the final

---

[8] See the *Washington Post*'s count at www.washingtonpost.com/graphics/national/police-shootings/ and *The Guardian*'s count at www.theguardian.com/us-news/series/counted-us-police-killings.

[9] Article 144 of the Brazilian constitution establishes preventive policing and public order policing as the duties of the Military Police (Sec. 5); and the investigation of crimes as the duty of the Civil Police (Sec. 4). It also establishes the states' Military Police forces as auxiliary forces and reserves of the Army (Sec. 6).

sections of the chapter, I show how the fragmentation of societal preferences over policing and security – rooted in differences in the distribution
of protection and repression along lines of race, class, and geography – has
yielded little electoral incentive for politicians to enact reform. On the
contrary, a large segment of São Paulo's citizens demanding weakened
legal restrictions on the police's use of coercion with little external
accountability have provided a ready constituency favoring the persistence of authoritarian coercion.

A SEAMLESS TRANSITION: AUTHORITARIAN LEGACIES AND THE POLICE'S STRUCTURAL POWER IN DEMOCRACY

Brazil's transition to democracy exemplifies how structures and practices
consolidated during authoritarian rule can come to be sustained by democratic processes. In the discussion that follows I situate contemporary
authoritarian coercive practices and structures within the country's
experience with authoritarian rule, as well as how the police leveraged
their structural power during the transition to shift the incentives of
elected officials away from police reform.

São Paulo's Military Police (*Polícia Militar*, PM) owes much of its
current structure, mission, and practices to a reorganization that occurred
under military rule. Throughout two decades of military rule, beginning
with the military coup in 1964, the state's police forces operated as an
essential component of the regime's intelligence and repressive apparatus
(Hunter 1997, 35). The country's military rulers unified existing police
forces to formally constitute military police institutions in each state
(Decree-Law 317/1967), subordinated these state-level forces to the
armed forces at the federal level (Decree-Law 667/1969), and submitted
these military police forces to the military penal code rather than civilian
courts (constitutional amendment 7/1977). These measures established
the organization's internal hierarchy (which continues unchanged to
this day) and its formal tasks, fighting both ordinary crime at the state
level and political enemies – including armed leftist guerrilla groups – of
the military regime at the federal level. As a result, the police became the
arm of the military regime in the states, serving as "auxiliary forces" and
reserves of the Army, a designation that continues to this day (Brazilian
Constitution, Art. 144, sec. 6).

Along with formal structures, the modalities and purpose of the deployment of state violence saw profound shifts during this period. Once the
armed dissident groups had been decimated, the police's apparatus of

political repression was then oriented to ordinary crime-fighting. The state's fight against the "internal enemy" shifted from the "terrorist" to the "common criminal infiltrated in the popular masses ... using the same techniques and enjoying the same impunity" (Pinheiro 1982, 60–65). This shift effectively represented the transference of National Security Doctrine to crime-fighting, sanctioning the elimination of the internal enemy that threatens the nation and the prevailing social order, with little constraint posed by formal legal rules. As Colonel Luiz Eduardo Pesce de Arruda, who at the time of the transition to democracy in 1983 commanded a unit of the riot police (*pelotão de choque*), put it, "my generation had as its foundation national security [doctrine], strong North American influence, with an enormous preoccupation with the internal enemy, with guerrillas, with national security." As a consequence of this orientation, noted Arruda,

after 21 years of the military regime [the officer] was no longer able to adequately engage with people. Many times he thought his conduct was self-determined, that he wasn't subjected to the law. Another thing that was significant [was] the high rate of lethality. In the 1970s and 1980s, [leaders] from outside the institution ... came to defend the simplistic vision that "a good criminal is a dead criminal," and that it was up to the PM to resolve that problem. The thing became so Dantesque that they rewarded police officers involved in killings of civilians. They rewarded, with cash, in the yards of the police stations for cases of resistance followed by death.[10]

The coercive practices of the state's police forces during the dictatorship reflected the prerogative described by Arruda. During the early 1970s, Civil Police officers formed the "Esquadrão da Morte" (Death Squad), which carried out summary executions of suspected criminals, with the support of the leadership of the Civil Police and even the governor (Caldeira 2000; Pinheiro 1982). Between 1970 and 1975, meanwhile, Military Police officers killed at least 274 individuals in alleged shootouts (Barcellos 1992, 68).[11] This figure, according to journalist Caco Barcellos, "exceeds the number of casualties of a dark period of political repression in the country during the 1960s and 1970s" (Barcellos 1992, 69). According to contemporaneous reports, 215 people died in jails and police stations between 1979 and 1981, and a staggering 432 civilians were

---

[10] Author interview with Colonel Luiz Eduardo Pesce de Arruda, commander of the Metropolitan Region of São Paulo, São Paulo, March 20, 2012. "Resistance followed by death" was the administrative and legal term used at the time to refer to police killings of civilians.
[11] Barcellos finds that the vast majority of these killings – in a police force that at the time had 50,000 officers – were committed by a single unit, the elite tactical unit ROTA (Barcellos 1992, 69).

killed by police in the first nine months of 1982 (Benevides, 1985, 26). These figures prompted the firm declarations by then-governor José Maria Marin, cited at the beginning of Chapter 2, to "go to the final consequences to contain police violence."

Investigations of cases of police killings found a set of recurrent practices – fabrication of evidence, intimidation of witnesses, and false police reports – that called into question the claims that individuals were killed in the course of a shootout with police (Barcellos 1992). In addition to summary executions, the transference of other practices of political repression, such as mass raids and arbitrary detentions, also came to be applied to those suspected of committing crimes, with round-ups and arbitrary detentions of hundreds of thousands of people in Rio de Janeiro and São Paulo alone (Pinheiro 1982, 77). This stands in sharp contrast to the reported 25,000 political prisoners in the country as a whole (Pereira 2005, 21). Moreover, the submission of the Military Police to the military penal code ensured that, with regard to these extraordinary levels of violence, "the risk of punishment was very small" (Mingardi 1992, 68).

Thus, although the military dictatorship in Brazil is seen as far less violent than that of Argentina, it nevertheless established an apparatus of repression based on what Pereira (2005) calls "authoritarian legality," of which both police forces were an integral part. These patterns of violence, exercised with impunity, flourished under the harshest period of military rule (1964–1974) and were consolidated during the extended period of gradual liberalization begun in the mid-1970s (Pinheiro 1982, 61).

Despite these entrenched coercive practices and structures, structural changes intended to install democratic coercion by police were conspicuously lacking in the years after the transition to democracy in Brazil in 1985. According to Brazilian scholars, "the Constitution of 1988 did not achieve structural or functional changes, shifting only the subordination of the Military Police forces from the central government to state governors" (Pinheiro, Izumino & Fernandes 1991, 108). At the state level, earnest attempts to reform the police during the first year of the administration of São Paulo's first democratically elected governor were ultimately thwarted. These efforts will be examined further in Chapter 6.

Early Tensions between Police and Democracy: Police Agency and Structural Power during the Transition

The institutional fate of policing under a new democratic Brazil was heavily contested, with active debate about a series of substantive proposals, and was an early instance of the police's ability to draw on democratic processes to exert strong pressure to thwart those proposals. It is therefore worth exploring in greater detail why the 1988 Constitution did not do more to enact "structural or functional changes" to Brazil's police forces despite the fact that the military police had been engaged in coercive practices and structures under dictatorship that are wholly incompatible with democratic principles.

Indeed, the 1988 Constitution changed relatively little about the police, declaring that the federal government has competence over the "organization" (and other characteristics) of military police forces (Art. 22, XXI), as well as separating the functions of prevention/repression and investigation of crimes between the Military Police and Civil Police, respectively, and subordinating both police forces to state governors (Art. 144). This latter measure – granting the Civil Police constitutional status and subordination of both forces to governors – represents the only meaningful change relative to the pre-transition status quo. Moreover, consistent with the detailed account laid out by Hunter (1997), this shift is perhaps better understood as an effort to challenge and weaken military power than as an effort to reform the country's police forces. Although Stepan (1988) demonstrates that military prerogatives remained strong into the democratic regime, Hunter (1997) convincingly lays out the steps taken by Brazilian politicians to subordinate the armed forces to civilian rule. While the military lobbied fiercely to maintain control over internal security and army control of the states' military police forces, the subordination of the states' military police forces to governors made it "much harder for the military as such to override their decisions and assume direct responsibility for the maintenance of law and order" (Hunter 1997, 52).

Yet, the absence of police reform in the Constitution of 1988 was not because policing was not considered a salient issue, nor was it because the role of police under the dictatorship was not an important problem – or even that the main priority was to weaken the military. The drafters of the Constitution were clearly concerned with authoritarian coercive practices, outlawing torture and inhuman or degrading treatment (Art. 5, III), establishing torture as a crime for which there would be no bail or amnesty (Art. 5, XLIII), and limiting detentions without a judicial order (Art. 136, Sec. 3, III). Yet, despite clear intent to change authoritarian coercive practices, the Constitution did nothing to enact structural change of the entity charged with carrying them out.

The relative silence of the Constitution of 1988 regarding the country's police forces was not for lack of reform proposals; instead, it served as an

early indicator of the tensions police pose for democracy. At the start of
the country's transition to civilian rule, a sociologist noted hearing "with
troubling frequency ... questions about the appropriateness of discussing
such issues: wouldn't messing with police and security be 'dangerous' for
the democratic transition?" (Benevides 1985, 25). Despite these concerns,
a special presidential commission tasked with "develop[ing] fundamental
research and studies ... for the future contribution to the work of the
National Constituent Assembly" (Decree 91.450/1985) considered and
even approved proposals to fundamentally reform policing in the country.
The Provisional Commission of Constitutional Studies (Comissão
Provisória de Estudos Constitucionais) approved a proposal to abolish
the Military Police forces, before ultimately settling on drastically reducing its authority and role.[12] Its proposal called for transferring the
prevention and repression of crimes to the Civil Police, while limiting
the Military Police to the roles of riot police and firefighting.[13] A similar
proposal was introduced in the Constituent Assembly the following year.

   In response to the Provisional Commission's proposal, Military Police
forces around the country mobilized using a range of strategies typical of
social movements in democracies, in order to influence the Commission,
public opinion, and, ultimately, the National Constituent Assembly. The
president of the Provisional Commission, Afonso Arinos, even received
a visit from the commanders of twenty-four Military Police forces in the
country.[14] With the house call yielding few results, PM commanders
mobilized extensively over the next year and a half: organizing national
meetings,[15] writing op-eds,[16] debating Civil Police officials,[17] creating
a group to lobby members of the Constituent Assembly[18] (as did the
Civil Police[19]), and launching an unprecedented campaign in which police
officers hit the streets to collect millions of signatures for a petition calling

---

[12] "Comissão Constitucional volta atrás na extinção das PMs," *Folha de São Paulo*, May 7,
1986; "Conselheiros não querem rever redução de poder das PMs," *Folha de São Paulo*,
July 10, 1986.
[13] Proposal published in "A defesa do Estado e da sociedade civil," *Estado de São Paulo*,
June 5, 1986.
[14] "Contra mudanças, comandos de 24 PM visitam Arinos," *Jornal do Brasil*, June 25,
1986.
[15] "Encontro de PMs critica o anteprojeto," *Folha de São Paulo*, October 4, 1986, 4.
[16] "A Constituinte e as Polícias Militares," *Estado de São Paulo*, December 16, 1986, 38.
[17] "Polícias civis e militares disputam garantia da ordem," *Jornal do Brasil*, April 29, 1987,
9; "A PM continua brigando pelo policiamento preventivo," *Jornal da Tarde*, October 7,
1987, 7.
[18] "PMs tentam pressionar a Constituinte," *Jornal do Brasil*, December 4, 1986, 6.
[19] "Constituição definirá atribuição da polícia," *Jornal do Brasil*, April 12, 1988, 2.

on the Constituent Assembly to maintain the PM's authority over preventive policing.[20] But the Military Police forces also drew on the structural power inherent in their control of the state's coercive authority, publishing a manifesto in various newspapers declaring, "If the proposed text [removing the preventive function] succeeds, there will be nothing left to lose ... More than 350 thousand [Military Police officers] are threatened."[21] Although proposals to transfer preventive policing to the Civil Police[22] and to abolish the Military Police[23] continued to emerge, the definitive text in the 1988 Constitution – which left police institutions intact – serves as a testament to the success of the PM's mobilization efforts and, ultimately, its structural power.

The persistence of what I call authoritarian coercion by São Paulo's police by no means can be attributed solely to the military dictatorship. As many Brazilian scholars have shown, militarization, torture, illegality, etc. have been a constant "from imperial times to this day" (Caldeira 2000, 151; Pinheiro 1994). Yet, the two decades of military rule saw extensive coercive institution-building, and the transition to democracy failed to serve as an opening to dismantle these structures and practices in accordance with democratic principles. When the Constituent Assembly voted to keep policing structures, particularly that of the Military Police, intact, an incredulous Civil Police official declared, "The dictatorship militarized the police and now democracy has consecrated this."[24] We could say the same about the consolidation of authoritarian coercion – including by the Civil Police – under the dictatorship and its persistence under democracy. In the failure to reform its police forces, Brazil's transition to democracy allowed for a remarkable continuity of the repertoire of coercion.

Given the central role of police in a democracy and the persistence of authoritarian coercion, it is evident that the police's seamless transition was a consequential oversight of Brazilian democracy. Indeed, the legacy of the dictatorship on policing continues to be salient decades later in São Paulo, with civil society leaders and police officials alike cognizant of the

---

[20] "PM coleta assinaturas para mudar substitutivo," *Estado de São Paulo*, November 5, 1987, 4; "Sinais da crise de Estado," *Estado de São Paulo*, November 6, 1987, 3; "PM gaúcha vai às ruas contra transferência de poderes à Polícia Civil," *Jornal do Brasil*, November 5, 1987, 3.

[21] "PM paulista não aceita perda de atribuições," *Jornal do Brasil*, September 24, 1987, 5.

[22] "PM quer continuar no patrulhamento ostensivo," *Estado de São Paulo*, September 23, 1987, 4.

[23] "Deputado sugere extinção das PMs," *Estado de São Paulo*, January 10, 1988, 5.

[24] "Polícia Civil perde a função preventiva," *Correio Brasiliense*, November 7, 1987, 5.

challenges posed by the police's role under the dictatorship – even among those who denied that such practices continued under democratic rule. According to a lieutenant colonel with the Military Police, because of this legacy of military rule "we still have a reputation – rather than being seen as a defender of the law, of being a guardian of the State – as a praetorian police."[25] A high-ranking Civil Police official similarly noted that the relationship between police and society since the transition to democracy was "extremely difficult" due to the police's "extra-constitutional" role in political repression: "If there was a student protest, [the police] beat students, if there were labor strikes, they arrested and beat workers, so the relationship was awful."[26] These views were confirmed by the president of the Community Security Council (CONSEG) of a wealthy neighborhood in the western region of the city, who told me, "The whole community, when it sees police, acts with caution. They don't have the courage to get close and talk [to police] ... It's a cultural thing in Brazil, because Brazil had a period of dictatorship ... In the CONSEG, the two police [commanders] are at the table ... for the community to talk to them, to break that view. But many people still don't trust [them]."[27]

SHIFTING PATTERNS OF VIOLENCE AND SOCIETAL DEMANDS

As occurred in many countries in the region, democratization went hand in hand with increased in crime and violence in the State of São Paulo and particularly in the metropolitan region surrounding the capital. In the decades following the state's first democratic elections after military rule in 1982, the steady rise in crime and violence became a top concern on the public agenda, where it has remained a priority to this day. Growing societal concerns over crime and violence, and the urgent demands they generated, created strong pressures for the new democracy, pressures that democratically elected leaders are still struggling to address.

As with other "violent democracies" (Arias & Goldstein 2010), post-transition São Paulo saw an expansion of violence and the emergence of new violent actors that would challenge the state's monopoly of legitimate coercion. As Figure 3.1 demonstrates, homicide rates in the State of São

---

[25] Author interview with anonymous lieutenant colonel of the Military Police of São Paulo, São Paulo, April 29, 2012.
[26] Author interview with anonymous *delegado* (Civil Police official) of the Civil Police of the State of São Paulo, São Paulo, July 10, 2012.
[27] Author interview with anonymous president of a Conselho Comunitário de Segurança (CONSEG, Community Security Council) in the city of São Paulo, June 28, 2010.

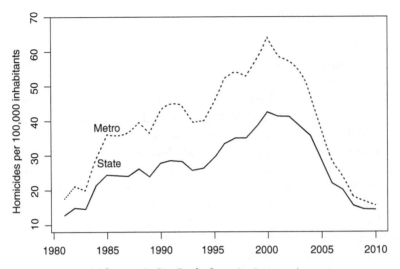

FIGURE 3.1 Homicide rates in São Paulo State (1981–2010)
This figure shows the dramatic variation over time in homicide rates in the State of São Paulo (solid line) and the São Paulo Metropolitan Region (dashed line). Data are from the Ministry of Health's count of "deaths by aggression," rather than homicides reported to the Secretariat for Public Security, in order to allow for a longer time-series. There is commonly a discrepancy between police and health authorities with regard to homicides.
Fundação SEADE (Sistema Estadual de Análise de Dados)

Paulo tripled between 1981 and 2000, from approximately 13 homicides per 100,000 inhabitants to nearly 40. As we might expect, patterns of violence in the state show a great deal of internal variation. In the metro-politan region of Greater São Paulo, for instance, homicide rates rose from 18 per 100,000 inhabitants in 1981 to a peak of 64 in 2000. In the capital itself, meanwhile, homicides reached 67 homicides per 100.000 inhabit-ants by 1999 (Cárdia & Schiffer 2002, 25). This period also saw the growth of violent crime overall, with robberies increasing from a rate of 567 per 100,000 inhabitants in 1988 to a rate of 750 by 1993 (Adorno 2002, 95); and kidnappings rising from a total of 12 cases in 1996 to 63 cases in 2000, with an astonishing 307 cases just one year later (Caldeira 2002, 237). The decades after democratization in the state also saw the rise of the PCC (Primeiro Comando da Capital), a highly structured criminal organization that formed in the prison system in the 1990s and continues to rival the state's monopoly on violence (Feltran 2008; Nunes Dias 2011; Willis 2015).

The salience of crime was felt across all sectors of society. According to a survey conducted in 1999, for instance, 95 percent of respondents in the city of São Paulo believed that violence had increased (Cárdia 2002, 154), and 57 percent believed violence had a very large impact on their city (Cárdia 1999). "Everyone," wrote one Brazilian scholar, "regardless of his/her origins, ethnic characteristics, gender, generation, wealth, and/or race feels threatened and unsafe, be it in terms of property and wealth or in terms of the most precious possession – life" (Adorno 2013, 412). Fear of crime and violence transformed everyday life, with many citizens reporting in surveys that they avoided going out at night (52 percent), avoided certain neighborhoods and streets (39 percent), and changed the route they take to work, school, or home (25 percent) (Cárdia 1999). As Caldeira (2000) has analyzed extensively, increased fear of crime led many citizens to retreat from public spaces toward the "fortified enclaves" of closed luxury condominiums.

Citizens also increasingly came to the conclusion that state institutions under democracy did not offer adequate levels of protection, leading many to favor private solutions. As citizens perceived an ineffective state – with 61 percent of *paulistanos* agreeing that "it is difficult to feel protected by the laws" (Cárdia 1999, 55) – São Paulo saw the growth of private security and private violence. The number of private security agents doubled during the 1990s and grew to outnumber the state's police forces 135,000 to 105,000 (de Mesquita Neto 2011, 71). The rise in crime and violence following democratization was also conducive to the continuity of a long tradition of vigilante or private violence in Brazil, which dates back to the colonial period (Adorno 2013, 418). Lynchings, for instance, endured the transition to democracy, with a documented 272 cases between 1979 and 1988 (Huggins 1991, 25) and considerable public support for so-called *justiceiros* (justice makers) who carried out acts of vigilante violence (Chevigny 1995, 157). A 1999 survey by researchers at the University of São Paulo also found that 52 percent of respondents said they would agree or understand if "someone threatens your neighborhood and someone kills him;" agreement or "understanding" reached 73 percent among those between thirty-five and forty-nine years of age (Cárdia 2002, 178).

Such lynchings are often justified in terms of the failure of the state, and specifically the police, to protect citizens from crime (Sinhoretto 2009), a framing that would become increasingly common under democracy. Following the adoption of the 1988 Constitution, for instance, police and the press – in São Paulo and beyond – pursued a discourse emphasizing purported incompatibilities between the rights guaranteed in the new Constitution regarding detentions and torture and the ability of the police to fight crime.[28] In a case that appeared to confirm these supposed incompatibilities, the press reported on a prominent lynching episode in late 1988, just days after the new Constitution took effect, with the headline: "In Rio, the police obey the Constitution, and a homicide suspect is lynched."[29] According to these reports, a woman in Rio de Janeiro State went to police to report the location of a man who had recently committed a homicide, and she was told (erroneously) by officers that "nothing could be done because the Constitution ... only permits *in flagrante* arrests" – that is, if the person is caught in the act. The woman and her neighbors then confronted the man and lynched him. The incident appeared to call into question the ability of democracy – with its formal constraints on the use of the state's coercive authority – to effectively protect citizens from crime. As I argue in the next section, democracy – which, as laid out in Chapter 1, ought to entail the use of coercion in the interests of citizens, constrained by the rule of law and subject to external accountability – has done little to transform coercive patterns in the state of São Paulo. Instead, democracy has, in many ways, reproduced authoritarian coercion.

VIOLENT DEMOCRACY, AUTHORITARIAN POLICE

In an interview with Colonel Marcelino Fernandes, the internal affairs chief (*Corregedor*) of the Military Police of São Paulo, Col. Fernandes prided himself on disciplining police officers that engage in misconduct: "I don't let anyone get away with a slap on the wrist (*eu não passo mão na cabeça de ninguém*). [There were] 194 [officers] fired last year, I broke the record in the number of arrests, 100 [officers] arrested last year." I asked how he accounted for the conspicuous increase in the number of civilians killed by police since 2013 (see Figure 3.2):

---

[28] "A polícia parando," *Jornal da Tarde*, October 7, 1988, 12; "Prisão ficará impossível, diz Brossard," *Gazeta Mercantil*, February 22, 1988, 29; "Presos em averiguação são soltos conforme determina a Constituição," *Folha de São Paulo*, October 7, 1988, C3; "Os primeiros problemas gerados pela Carta," *Jornal da Tarde*, October 12, 1988, 4; "Ação policial diminui com a Constituição," *Estado de São Paulo*, October 30, 1988, 22.

[29] "No Rio, polícia obedece Constituição e suspeito de homicídio é linchado," *Folha de São Paulo*, October 11, 1988, C3.

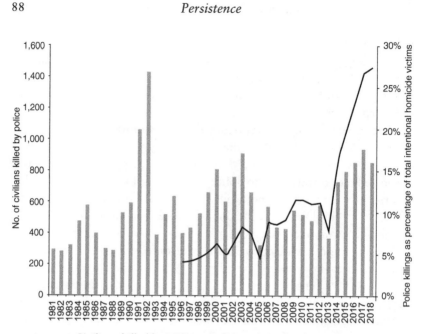

FIGURE 3.2 Civilians killed by Military Police and Civil Police in São Paulo State (1981–2018)

The figure presents the total number of civilians killed by Military Police and Civil Police officers in São Paulo State and such killings as a percentage of all victims of intentional homicides in the state. Sources: 1981–1989: Pinheiro et al. (1991, 97); 1990–2000: Ouvidoria da Polícia do Estado de São Paulo (2000, 79); 2001–2018 police killings and 1996–2018 homicides: Dados Trimestrais (quarterly reports) issued by the Secretariat for Public Security of the State of São Paulo regarding "persons killed in confrontation with police" both on and off duty.

FERNANDES: Police killings increased between 2014 and 2018. It was when there was a change in the law regarding arraignment hearings (*audiência de custódia*) and benefits for criminals to receive furloughs ... It's due to the fact that the majority of people killed in confrontations with the military police – licit or illicit – have a criminal record. So if they had been jailed for their original crime, they wouldn't be on the streets.

YG: Do you mean in statistical terms, as in, it increases the likelihood of coming into contact with police on the streets, or is this the police's reasoning?

FERNANDES: It's both things. Because the police officer is the final degree in society ... the officer is the last recourse. So the police officer, subconsciously, he's going to analyze the following: "The police arrests and the justice system releases, what am I going to do? He's shooting at me, I'm going to kill him . . . The state is not giving me a solution, so I have to find a solution" (*o estado não está dando jeito, eu tenho que dar um jeito*). If the state provided a solution, the police would arrest [the suspect].[30]

Col. Fernandes's assessment of the drivers of the sharp rise in police killings underscores the persistence of authoritarian coercion in the State of São Paulo. According to the top official charged with internal oversight of the Military Police, officers routinely exercise exceptional coercion due to the perceived flaws of the broader justice system in dealing with crime, rather than strictly constraining lethal force against civilians within the scope defined by law, such as self-defense. Indeed, this account is reminiscent of Col. Arruda's characterization, quoted earlier in this chapter, of the officer's perspective under the dictatorship – that his conduct was "not subjected to the law." This rampant deployment of exceptional coercion, meanwhile, has been subjected to little restriction and oversight from civilian officials. Despite the creation of some novel institutions, such as a Police Ombudsman's Office, the exercise of external accountability authority by executive, legislative, and judicial institutions has been uneven at best. A key impediment to robust external accountability has been that, under pressure to respond to the increase in crime rates following democratization and the public's growing demands for improved security, the deployment of coercion is often politicized, responding to the demands of political leaders rather than the needs of citizens or "objective" security conditions.

Exceptional Coercion by São Paulo's Military and Civil Police Forces

The return of democratic rule in São Paulo State was marked not only by dramatic increases in crime and violence It was also defined by high rates of lethal violence at the hands of the state's police forces, particularly the Military Police. As Figure 3.2 (bars) demonstrates, the transition to democratic rule in the state had little impact on the use of lethal violence by police. The number of civilians killed by police rose from 328 following

[30] Author interview with Col. Marcelino Fernandes, São Paulo, March 13, 2019.

the first gubernatorial elections in nearly two decades in 1982 to nearly 600 in 1985. A decline in fatalities at the hands of the state in the second half of his term was followed by dramatic increases under his successors, rising to more than 1,400 police killings in 1992, the year of a deadly massacre at Carandiru prison (see Chapter 6). Although the broad national and international outcry that followed the Carandiru massacre led to a dramatic decrease in police violence, officially recorded police killings under democracy – despite fluctuations – have been comparable or far greater in number to those under the military dictatorship,[31] when police killed with impunity.

Police killings of civilians in São Paulo State have also remained high in comparison to homicide rates, an important discrepancy for assessing the legality of police violence. Homicide rates in the state have fallen by two-thirds since the early 2000s (see Figure 3.1), and other crimes, such as car theft, have fallen "50 percent in a period of ten years," according to the former Military Police commander for the city of São Paulo, Colonel Marcos Chaves.[32] Police killings, meanwhile, have (despite fluctuations) largely increased in the previous decade, even as homicide and other violent crimes have gone down. This discrepancy between patterns of violent crime and patterns of police violence is significant. Noting the disconnect between crime rates and police killings, researchers looking at highly detailed police records from the 1980s also found a discrepancy between the reason most often cited by police for police killings of civilians – robberies, the stated reason in 42 percent of cases – and the actual occurrence of these crimes. The authors found that the regions of the city where most police killings happen – the city's periphery – are not where most robberies take place, the city's center and wealthier areas (Pinheiro et al. 1991, 104–105). Thus, even though the disconnect between crime rates and police killings is not new, it has become even more conspicuous as homicide rates in the state (at approximately 10 per 100,000 inhabitants in 2017) have, according to official figures, reached historic lows and become the lowest of any state in Brazil.[33]

---

[31] It is, of course, impossible to say for certain how many civilians were killed by police during the dictatorship – or even under democratic rule. The comparisons cited here are based on official data shown in Figure 3.2, with the admitted limitations of available data.
[32] Author interview with Col. Marcos Chaves, São Paulo, February 15, 2012.
[33] See "Atlas da Violência," an initiative of the Institute of Applied Economic Research and the Brazilian Forum for Public Security, accessible at www.ipea.gov.br/atlasviolencia/.

But the most striking comparison between homicide rates and police killings is the extent to which, as homicides have declined, police killings have come to constitute an ever-larger source of lethal violence in the State of São Paulo. Figure 3.2 (lines) presents civilians killed by police as a percentage of victims of intentional homicides in the state. As the homicide rate fell to dramatic rates in the late 2000s, police killings reached the equivalent of 10 percent of all homicides; today, the number of civilians killed by police constitute the equivalent of one-fourth of all homicide victims in the state. The state's police forces (particularly the Military Police) have thus become a key source of the very violence they are supposed to prevent.

The staggering figures discussed thus far are only those that are officially reported by the State's Secretariat for Public Security, characterized as "persons killed in confrontation with police." But police violence in São Paulo State is manifest in an additional troubling modality of authoritarian coercion: death squads. In recent years, there have been reports of participation by Military Police officers in *grupos de extermínio* (death squads) who set out to kill suspected criminals, whether for revenge, payment, or some other motive. An investigation by the state's Civil Police, for instance, found that 150 individuals were killed by such PM-involved death squads between 2006 and 2010.[34] In another analysis, São Paulo's State Council for Defense of Human Rights (Conselho de Defesa dos Direitos da Pessoa Humana, CONDEPE), a civil-society led commission that is part of the Secretariat for Justice and Citizenship,

detected, between 2014 and 2016, 139 *chacinas* (multi-victim killings) in the State of São Paulo, mostly in the metropolitan region, with about 230 victims. Basically, all the chacinas we investigated had the same pattern. They were preceded by police stops (*abordagens*) in the territory, and some sort of misunderstanding by the police and some [local] groups. And generally the focus of those police stops was so that the police could find people who were formerly incarcerated or members of a criminal group. Another characteristic was for there to have been a police officer killed in that region, generally while off-duty. And after those episodes you would find a process of retaliation, where three, four, five people would be killed in a single action, on a single night. They were clearly death squads (*grupos de extermínio*), and all with characteristics of police involvement.[35]

---

[34] Tatiana Merlino, "Em cada batalhão da PM tem um grupo de extermínio," *Caros Amigos*, September 2012, 10–13. See also "Grupo de extermínio da PM matou 150 pessoas," *Folha de São Paulo*, March 25, 2011.

[35] Author interview with member of the CONDEPE, São Paulo, September 11, 2017.

Reports of killings by such police-linked death squads have been frequent,[36] and at times have been denounced by Military Police officers[37] and even by a sitting governor.[38] Such participation by police in death squads, often for hire, has been reported by scholars and human rights activists since the start of democratic rule in the state to the present day (Adorno and Cárdia 1998; Alves 2014; Americas Watch 1987; Chevigny 1995).

My interviews with some Military Police officers provide additional evidence that, as these accounts suggest, many civilians are killed by police not in the context of a confrontation but in premeditated fashion. For instance, during a conversation with a retired lieutenant colonel of the Military Police about police hierarchy and authority, he told me that his authority was so unquestioned that if he were to signal something to his subordinates – as he made a gesture of his hand cutting through the air – in relation to a *bandido* (criminal), that person would be taken somewhere and killed. "This has already happened" (*isso já aconteceu*), but, he assured me, "only with *bandidos*."[39] A second retired lieutenant colonel, meanwhile, said that when he resolved to "diminish lethality in my area," he began telling his officers, "you are not the whole system, you don't have to resolve the whole problem. You are a cog in a wheel, you have limits to your actions, you're running the risk of being arrested for abuses. Stay within the limits of the law ... Some bought into it, some didn't, but I ended up being transferred and retiring from the police ... Because I had a different vision of the deployment of [force], I ended up being transferred."[40] These accounts are consistent with journalistic reports of killings by death squads within the Military Police, which "have the approval of high-ranking police officials."[41]

A number of recent analyses have provided systematic evidence that many of these killings by police are indeed taking place outside the scope

---

[36] See, for instance, "PM afasta 25 policiais suspeitos de atuar em grupo de extermínio," *O Estado de São Paulo*, September 25, 2007; also "Grupo de extermínio com PMs já matou 35 na região de Guarulhos," *O Estado de São Paulo*, April 24, 2013.

[37] "Sargento diz que existem grupos de extermínio na Polícia Militar de SP," R7 Notícias, August 4, 2012, available at http://noticias.r7.com/sao-paulo/noticias/sargento-diz-que-existem-grupos-de-exterminio-na-policia-militar-de-sp-20120805.html.

[38] "Serra diz que há grupos de extermínio na PM," *Folha de São Paulo*, February 22, 2008.

[39] Author interview with anonymous lieutenant colonel (ret.) of the Military Police of São Paulo I, São Paulo, June 25, 2012.

[40] Author interview with anonymous lieutenant colonel (ret.) of the Military Police of São Paulo 2, October 16, 2017.

[41] "Exclusivo: Em entrevista, policiais revelam como agem os grupos de extermínio em SP," *Revista Fórum*, July 22, 2013.

of the law. Although, prior to January 2013,[42] such killings had been classified by police as "resistance followed by death" (*resistência seguida de morte*), analyses by scholars, activists, and legal experts have consistently found evidence, such as manipulation of crime scenes and false reports, that what is often reported as confrontations or *resistências* are in fact executions (Americas Watch 1987; Barcellos 1992; Chevigny 1995; Delgado, Dodge & Carvalho 2011; Human Rights Watch 2009). For instance, an unprecedented legal and forensic analysis conducted by the Police Ombudsman's Office of police killings in 2017 determined that, out of 756 civilian victims of "deaths resulting from police intervention" analyzed by the report, only 23 percent of cases were "legitimate defense." Meanwhile, 46 percent of cases were characterized as showing "evidence of excesses in legitimate defense," and 31 percent of cases showed "evidence of excesses in cases where there was no armed confrontation" (Mariano 2018, 16). In another thorough analysis of forensic evidence of 126 police killings that took place between May 12 and May 20, 2006, members of Harvard Law School's International Human Rights Clinic found that 51 cases "presented indicators of having been executions" (Delgado et al. 2011, 73). Thus, the conclusion reached nearly two decades ago by the Police Ombudsman's Office seemingly continues to hold: "the discourse of police authorities that the deaths were inevitable and confirmed to have occurred in cases of 'resistance' or 'shootout,' for example, was not substantiated in many cases investigated by the Ombudsman" (Ouvidoria da Polícia do Estado de São Paulo, 2000, 17).

"Transparency Alone Is Not Enough": The Limits of External Accountability

Despite clear and consistent evidence that the deployment of coercion routinely contravenes the rule of law, efforts by state actors to subject police forces to external accountability have been uneven and unsystematic. Authoritarian coercion by the police forces of São Paulo State has been deepened by the actions of elected officials in the executive and legislative branches, as well as the judiciary, who have seldom used their authority to systematically investigate the use of force by the police or to sanction officers in cases of abuse.

---

[42] In January 2013, the state's Secretariat of Public Security issued Resolution SSP-05 (7-1-13), which directed police to instead classify such killings as "deaths following police intervention" (*morte decorrente de intervenção policial*).

São Paulo State has created a number of entities that seek to strengthen the ability of civilian institutions to hold police accountable, primarily through greater transparency. But while these institutions have provided broad and unprecedented access to information about police abuses, in doing so they have ultimately laid bare the glaring inaction by other state entities to sanction those abuses. As the first police ombudsman put it in a report summarizing his five-year tenure, "transparency alone is not enough" (Ouvidoria da Polícia do Estado de São Paulo 2000, 4).

The unevenness of external accountability mechanisms is especially stark within the executive branch, despite the fact that the state's police forces are formally under its jurisdiction. The Secretariat for Public Security, for instance, has formal oversight authority over the police and has a number of divisions that facilitate police accountability – including the Office of Analysis and Planning (Coordenadoria de Análise e Planejamento, CAP) and the Police Ombudsman's Office (Ouvidoria da Polícia). The CAP compiles, analyzes, and publicizes data on crimes and police activity in the state, including the number of civilians killed by police. The Police Ombudsman's Office, meanwhile, receives complaints about police abuses from citizens[43] and channels those complaints to the police's internal affairs divisions (whose chief, Colonel Marcelino Fernandes, was quoted at the beginning of this section) and the civilian justice system. But while these entities provide broad and unprecedented access to essential *official* data about, for instance, police killings and abuses that are largely unavailable in most other states and countries, this transparency has not translated into accountability.

Consider the limitations of the Police Ombudsman's Office, which ought to work to facilitate internal and external police accountability by forwarding and accompanying citizen complaints to the police's internal affairs entity and the civilian justice system. In practice, the effectiveness of the agency in promoting accountability within the police or in the courts has been uneven. For instance, according to a study by Brazilian scholars, of 734 killings investigated by the Ouvidoria da Polícia between 2009 and 2011, a mere 1.6 percent of officers involved were charged with a crime (Sinhoretto et al. 2014, 27). Moreover, across the general spectrum of complaints of police abuse received by the Ouvidoria da Polícia – which ranges from poor service and discrimination to torture and homicide – the

---

[43] The Ouvidoria also receives complaints from police officers who wish to denounce abuses by their superiors.

TABLE 3.1 *Results of complaints received by the Office of the Police Ombudsman (1998–2013)*

Police type	Officers denounced	Officers punished
Civil Police (all)	13,468	989 (7%)
Military Police (all ranks)	25,244	5,355 (21%)
Superior ranks (PM)	2,409	30 (1%)
Intermediate ranks (PM)	5,942	352 (6%)
Low ranks (PM)	16,893	4,973 (29%)

Office of the Police Ombudsman of São Paulo (Ouvidoria das Polícias) 2013 Annual Report

record of accountability has been largely mixed. According to data published by the Police Ombudsman's Office, presented in Table 3.1, relatively few officers who are denounced receive any type of punishment within the police's internal disciplinary systems. Among the Civil Police, a mere 7 percent of the police officers against whom citizens have filed complaints between 1998 and 2013 have been punished. Among the Military Police, 21 percent of officers received some sort of punishment. However, there is great disparity across ranks, with only 1 percent and 6 percent of high- and mid-ranking officers, respectively, receiving some sort of sanction. The ability of the Police Ombudsman's Office to serve as a check on the police and scrutinize its use of coercion has thus been highly limited by the inaction of entities with authority to sanction police abuses.

In addition to the Police Ombudsman's Office and the CAP, the limitations of executive branch officials to constrain the use of extralegal coercion by police are exemplified by the Special Commission for the Reduction of Lethality, an entity created by the Secretariat for Public Security in 2000 to monitor and analyze cases of lethal police violence and provide recommendations to reduce such instances.[44] Despite its intentions, interviews with two civil society representatives who participated in the commission indicate the challenges of meaningfully monitoring and reducing police violence. One civil society member of the commission said, "The lethality commission, in which I've participated for years, it's very difficult for anything to come out of it, very difficult. It's very difficult to work with the police … You have to be very cautious because they're very sensitive to

[44] Secretariat for Public Security, Resolution 526, December 26, 2000.

criticism, they're very closed off. Anything is interpreted as criticism, as suspicious."[45] Another civil society member of the commission similarly pointed to tensions with the police, and the lack of prioritization by the government: "The commission in reality hasn't worked in a long time, because it's not a priority, it's not a policy priority, not for the government nor for the police. In the commission there's a constant tension – we seek out information, we seek out data, the police doesn't provide it, they refuse – so it's very difficult to work. It's a very tense process. So we've achieved very little."[46] The commission thus faced considerable challenges in achieving its intended objective and has been inactive since 2011 (Pekny, Bento & Morin 2017, 56)

A key impediment to the ability of the Police Ombudsman's Office – and other executive branch agencies that promote transparency such as the CAP – to promote external accountability of the state's police forces is the nature of the relationship between the executive branch and the police, which is largely defined by accommodation and deference. For instance, when asked about the police's relationship to the governor and the secretary of security, the former commander of the Military Police, Col. Álvaro Camilo, reported a high degree of autonomy from the primary civilian officials charged with overseeing the police:

[Regarding] the relationship with the secretary and the governor, I never had any problem. I had a lot of freedom to command. There was no interference from the secretary nor from the governor in my command, and that's very important for the commander ... For instance, the secretary could've said, "Place this colonel in the transit police, or put this one and not this one, understand?" In my administration that didn't happen.[47]

The deference extended to police by executive officials has also been common among state legislators. Although legislators have a number of tools at their disposal to conduct robust oversight of the police (or any executive bureaucracy), the formal avenues of police oversight within the legislature have rarely focused on the prevalence of authoritarian coercion. For instance, a review of meeting minutes of the legislature's Committee on Public Security and Penitentiary Affairs during the 2015–2019 legislative session – a period in which police killings rose sharply and came to constitute the equivalent of

---

[45] Author interview with anonymous civil society security expert 1. Date and location withheld to preserve anonymity of interviewee in light of criticisms expressed.
[46] Author interview with anonymous civil society security expert 2. Date and location withheld to preserve anonymity of interviewee in light of criticisms expressed.
[47] Author interview with Col. Álvaro Camilo, São Paulo, May 28, 2012.

more than 20 percent of all homicides in the state – shows that only five out of thirty-five meetings of the committee mentioned police killings.[48] In four of the meetings, legislators approved requests for an invitation to the secretary for public security or the commander of the Military Police to respond to questions about specific episodes of police killings.[49] The secretary for public security attended two committee meetings during the legislative session to address questions about his administration but only received and addressed questions about police killings on one of those occasions, on November 24, 2015.[50]

Meanwhile, another potential legislative instrument to advance police oversight, information requests, were also rarely used to investigate extralegal coercion by the state's police forces. As summarized in Table 3.2, only 18 percent of information requests about policing issued by legislators and legislative committees during a ten-year period (2009–2019) sought greater information on potential extralegal coercion by the police, and only 3 percent of these – a total of eight requests in a ten-year period – inquired about police killings.[51] Although these information requests and the meetings of the public security committee are far from the only avenue through which the legislature could exercise police oversight, this snapshot of two routine legislative instruments suggests reluctance by the legislature as a whole to exercise oversight of the state's police forces during a period of growing extralegal police violence and lethality.

An additional indicator of the reluctance of the state's legislature to use its authority to serve as a mechanism of external accountability has been the actions by prominent legislators to oppose even basic constraints on police authority and practices. Chevigny (1995) documented several cases of elected officials in the state of São Paulo that failed to denounce exceedingly high rates of police violence during the first decade of

---

[48] The author consulted the meeting minutes and, where available, meeting transcripts of the Committee on Public Security and Penitentiary Affairs during the 2015–2019 legislative period and coded the items included in the meeting minutes or discussed in the transcripts.

[49] The fifth meeting featured testimony by then-ombudsman Júlio César Fernandes Neves, who was compelled to appear before the committee to explain remarks criticizing a police killing.

[50] Notably, in an August 11, 2015 meeting, the Committee on Public Security and Penitentiary Affairs rejected a request to invite the secretary to "explain allegations regarding the embezzlement of 21.5 million reais of the Military Police of the State, due to a fraud scheme in contract bids by the General Command of the force, between 2005 and 2011."

[51] For the sake of comparison, three information requests during this period dealt with the treatment of animals.

TABLE 3.2 *Policing information requests by São Paulo State Legislative Assembly (2009–2019)*

Issue	Percentage
Police services/facilities	40%
Personnel	14%
Crime/violence	11%
Operations	8%
Police repression of protest	6%
Other police violence	5%
Police malfeasance	4%
Other	4%
Police killings	3%
Police conditions	3%
Police authority	3%
Total requests	277

Legislative Assembly of the State of São Paulo, "Pesquisa de Proposições." Review of all *"requerimentos de informação"* (information requests) issued by legislators to the Secretariat for Public Security specifically about the Military Police or Civil Police between 2009 and 2019

democratic rule; indeed, they consistently celebrated it as evidence of success in fighting crime. More recently, the cadre of politicians defending these coercive practices has increasingly come to include former police officials, constituting the so-called "bullet caucus" (*bancada da bala*) in the state's Legislative Assembly. The Military Police officers-turned-legislators include Colonel Camilo, the former commander general of the Military Police cited earlier, and Colonel Paulo Telhada, who has admitted to personally killing thirty-six civilians as a police officer, a fact he cited widely during his campaigns for the São Paulo City Council and later for the state Legislative Assembly.[52]

Led by Camilo and another former (civil) police officer, *Delegado* Antonio Olim, the Assembly's Commission on Public Security and Penitentiary Affairs has, in recent years, failed to serve as an effective

[52] "Ex-policiais da Rota eleitos em SP somam 77 mortes," *Estado de São Paulo*, October 8, 2012.

source of oversight – though such oversight has long been far from robust. For instance, in 2016, proposed legislation introduced by Colonel Camilo sought to change the selection process for the police ombudsman (*ouvidor*), such that it would undermine the entity's institutional independence.[53] That same year, the Commission on Public Security ended its legislative work for the year, not by analyzing the rise in police killings for the fourth year in a row and the highest rates of fatalities at the hands of police in more than a decade but rather by compelling the ombudsman to attend a hearing to address his recent public critiques of specific police killings.[54] In a heated exchange with then-ombudsman Julio César Fernandes Neves, Col. Camilo chastised the ombudsman for his public criticism of the police: "I would like to ask you, sir, where it's written [in the ombudsman's formal duties] to go to the location of the occurrence and criticize the police's actions, without having knowledge of the facts? ... That mode of criticizing the police of São Paulo will turn the population against the police."[55] During a subsequent interview, Fernandes Neves expressed surprise at Col. Camilo's sharp criticism of the Police Ombudsman's Office as a legislator, relative to his previous orientation as Military Police commander:

I was surprised when he began verbally attacking me ... When he became a legislator he started to criticize me. I have a hunch that he's done this to use the work of the Ombudsman's Office to get media attention to appeal to his electorate, which is police officers. Everything that the Ombudsman's Office did he spoke up to criticize it. [But] when he was the commander of the police, he was part of the Commission on Lethality, and he was very concerned about it.[56]

The state's criminal justice system – including the Ministério Público (Prosecutor's Office) and the civilian courts – have also failed to fulfill their role in holding police officers accountable in specific cases of extra-legal killings. Recall the analysis of police killings in 2017 by the Police Ombudsman's Office, which showed that there was no armed confrontation to justify the shooting in as many as 31 percent of cases and that an additional 46 percent of cases showed evidence of "excesses." While this analysis is only for a single year, it suggests that police killings in São Paulo require legal scrutiny and that a significant proportion of these killings are

---

[53] Projeto de Lei Complementar 21 de 2016.
[54] "Ouvidor das polícias peita bancada da bala na Assembleia de SP," *Folha de São Paulo*, December 16, 2016.
[55] Transcript of the meeting of the Committee on Public Safety and Penitentiary Affairs, December 14, 2016, available at www.al.sp.gov.br/spl/2018/02/Transcricao/10002016 33_1000151194_Transcricao.pdf.
[56] Author interview with Julio César Fernandes Neves, São Paulo, September 12, 2017.

likely unjustified under the law. Yet, interviews with legal professionals within state entities who deal with cases of police killings suggest reluctance within the Prosecutor's Office and civilian courts to investigate, charge, and try officers. One prosecutor (*promotor*) with São Paulo State's Ministerio Público told me, "Some prosecutors will hold the officer responsible and gather evidence ... Others will archive the investigation, saying it was legitimate defense ... This is not my opinion, it's a question of numbers. If you put in one column the cases of police lethality and in the other column you put convictions for police lethality, you'll have your answer."[57] Similarly, a public defender said the Public Defender's Office of São Paulo State began taking on the role of prosecutorial assistant (*assistente da acusação*) in cases of police killings "to pressure the Prosecutor's Office. Because it's an institution that accommodates a lot in these prosecutions."[58] These officials' assessments have been borne out by scholarly analysis. In his investigations of police killings where the victim was not involved in a violent confrontation with police – that is, where there was strong evidence that the victim's rights had been violated by the state – Brinks (2008) finds that the rate of conviction in these cases during the 1990s in São Paulo was a mere 6 percent (57). As the author observes, "precisely in those places where the police use lethal force most indiscriminately," São Paulo and Bahia, "the justice system punishes police homicides least often" (Brinks 2008, 11).

Even in high-profile, extraordinary acts of police violence, the courts' record of holding officers accountable has been no better than in cases of "ordinary" extralegal killings by police. Judicial outcomes in response to the deadliest police massacres in the state since the transition to democracy are illustrative. Decades after the Military Police's violent actions to quell a prison riot in 1992 resulted in the deaths of 111 inmates (see Chapter 6), as noted by the *Globo* network, "only one of the accused police officers is in prison. For a different crime."[59] Meanwhile, the actions of the state's police forces during a week of extraordinary violence between the police and the PCC in May 2006, in which hundreds of civilians and dozens of police officials lost their lives, have received little official scrutiny by the courts.

---

[57] Author interview with anonymous prosecutor, Ministério Público do Estado de São Paulo. Date and location withheld.

[58] Author interview with anonymous public defender, Defensoria Pública do Estado de São Paulo. Date and location withheld.

[59] "Massacre do Carandiru faz 24 anos com júris de policiais anulados," *Globo/G1 São Paulo*, October 2, 2016, available at http://g1.globo.com/sao-paulo/noticia/2016/10/massacre-do-carandiru-faz-24-anos-com-juris-de-policiais-anulados.html.

During what has come to be known as the "Crimes of May," planned prison rebellions and attacks on security officials coordinated by the PCC led to police-imposed curfews and indiscriminate violence concentrated in the mostly poor and mostly black communities in the periphery of São Paulo and the city of Santos (Nogueira 2007). Approximately 500 civilians were killed in just over one week; as noted already, approximately 120 have been formally attributed to the police – with nearly half showing clear evidence of being summary executions (Delgado et al. 2011, 73) – and the remainder to masked gunmen belonging to death squads. A decade and a half after these events, two military police officers only have been convicted, though not jailed.[60] The investigation of these extraordinary acts of violence by state-level officials has been so deficient that Brazil's attorney general (*procurador-geral*) – heeding the request of the Mothers of May (*Mães de Maio*),[61] mothers of victims killed during the Crimes of May – called upon the country's top court to "federalize" (transfer the investigation of the cases to federal jurisdiction) some of the homicides committed during this period: "We have verified that highly serious failures and omissions have permeated the entire investigatory process, which has not taken into consideration the fundamental role of the Military Police during the episode, and much less the context of retaliation on the part of public security agencies."[62]

The relative timidity of the civilian justice system to bring to trial and convict police officers in extrajudicial killings is notable because, in contrast to other modes of police malfeasance, homicides by Military Police officers of civilians in Brazil are handled by the civilian courts rather than by the military justice system (Federal Law 9.299/1996). An early analysis conducted in the late 1990s by a prosecutors' group found that, in the years after the transfer in jurisdiction, the civilian justice system was twice as likely to convict officers accused of homicides than was the military justice system prior to the transfer (48 percent vs. 23 percent).[63] Far fewer

---

[60] Artur Rodrigues, Rogério Pagnan, and Avener Prado, "As feridas de maio, sem respostas," *Folha de São Paulo*, April 20, 2016, available at http://arte.folha.uol.com.br/cotidiano/2016/04/20/as-feridas-de-maio/.

[61] The letter written by the Mothers of May to then-president Dilma Rousseff can be accessed here: www.global.org.br/blog/maes-de-maio-entregam-carta-a-presindente-dilma-rousseff/.

[62] The press release announcing the formal request can be accessed at www.mpf.mp.br/pgr/noticias-pgr/pgr-pede-federalizacao-de-caso-relacionado-aos-crimes-de-maio-1.

[63] Analysis conducted by the Centro de Apoio Operacional das Promotorias de Justiça Criminais. Reported in "Justiça comum condena o dobro da Militar," *Folha de São Paulo*, January 10, 1999, available at www1.folha.uol.com.br/fsp/cotidian/ff10019901.htm.

cases of police killings, however, make it to the trial phase in the civilian courts. The aforementioned analysis found that, while the military justice system tried 205 cases of such killings prior to the legal change in 1995, the civilian courts tried only 64 police killings in 1998, despite the fact that police killing rates remained fairly stable during this period.

As the preceding discussion has shown, São Paulo's police forces conform to our definition of authoritarian coercion in that their exercise of the state's monopoly of legitimate use of physical force has been largely arbitrary, for the most part unconstrained by the rule of law or external accountability.

Coercion in the Interest of Political Leaders

The police of São Paulo State, particularly the Military Police, have thus engaged in widespread extralegal coercion for decades, while interventions by civilian officials to provide mechanisms of external accountability have been weak or ineffective. A key reason for this has been the deference and accommodation that has defined the relationship between the police and the political leaders that ostensibly oversee them. Police routinely exercise coercion in the interest of political leaders, which the police then leverage to maintain autonomy and thwart external accountability mechanisms.

In my interviews with police officers and commanders, they often described how the intervention of political leaders shaped the distribution of police resources (see Chapter 8) as well as the distribution of protection and repression. One of the starkest examples of such intervention occurs in the context of protests, according to a Military Police captain[64] working in a São Paulo district where many protests take place. Depending on the visibility and support of the group participating in the protest, the PM captain told me, police commanders often receive messages from the mayor or the governor about how the police ought to act. He said, for instance, in reference to the city's gay pride parade, if the police were to go in beating participants, "it's over for São Paulo, it's over for Brazil" (*acaba São Paulo, acaba o Brasil*), because the whole world would be watching. In other occasions, according to the captain, politicians might recommend more force, particularly as, when dealing with a group that isn't popular, people might actually want the police to have a heavier hand. The

---

[64] Author interview with anonymous captain of the Military Police of São Paulo, São Paulo, April 29, 2012.

distribution of protection and repression in the context of these protests was thus not determined by the nature of the demonstration itself or security conditions but rather by the interests and demands of the governor.

Considered alongside the discussion regarding the lack of police accountability to executive branch officials, this account suggests the prevalence of the type of accommodation described in Chapter 2, wherein politicians grant police autonomy in exchange for cooperation in achieving political ends. Indeed, Col. Camilo, the former commander of the Military Police, cited earlier in this chapter declaring that "there was no interference from the secretary nor from the governor in [his] command," nonetheless described the pressure to respond politically to the governor:

I always felt pressure, from the beginning. The governor always makes demands (*cobra*), "see what you can do." [So] I always reacted first because we would follow the news and what was happening and the crime reports, so that, when the governor came to talk, we would've already addressed many of the problems he would talk about. He would talk about Morumbi [a wealthy neighborhood], and I would say, "We already made this many arrests," or this and that. I always worked to face these pressures head on.

In theory, this type of responsiveness to elected officials is what might be expected and desirable in a democratic context. Pressure from citizens leads their elected representatives to call upon police to shift resources and operations in accordance with citizen demands. Yet, as the accounts presented here suggest, this relationship is one of accommodation between police and politicians rather than responsiveness. Politicians do not engage in such intervention as a routine matter in ensuring good performance and equitable distribution of resources, nor in holding police accountable for abuses and extralegal violence, but rather in response to complaints and demands from well-positioned sectors of society, such as the residents of Morumbi. In this context, the provision of security functions less like a public good, non-excludable and non-rival, and more like a resource that can be distributed in accordance with the interests of political leaders, a condition in line with what I've defined as authoritarian coercion.

A retired lieutenant colonel who commanded a battalion in the São Paulo metropolitan region also provided an account of another manifestation of the politicization of the police's coercive authority. Although he was careful to clarify that he had always had a good relationship with the governor himself, he said that within the police there was a clear intent to exercise coercion to serve the governor's political interests:

In my area there were two mayors who were from an opposition party [rather than the governor's party]. I didn't care about that – I just needed to engage with them because they are the principals in the solution to public security in the region. I know that there were people that didn't like it. Because I was having a lot of contact with municipal administrations and political parties that opposed the chief executive ... within the police I heard this criticism. And before I knew it, I had been transferred. One day I received a call saying I was being transferred the next day.[65]

In addition to the problem posed from the perspective of democratic coercion, such accommodation with police also poses a great risk to politicians if police officers decide to withdraw their cooperation. Such risks became readily apparent to the former mayor of São Paulo, Fernando Haddad, who sought to cultivate a mutually beneficial exchange with the Military Police through what came to be known as Operação Delegada (OD, Operation Delegated). Operação Delegada was an agreement between the Military Police and the municipal government of the city of São Paulo (which exercises no formal control over the state police forces), through which the city hires Military Police officers who are officially on their day off to patrol, in uniform, commercial areas of the city. In 2013, Military Police officers created a substantial political problem for the mayor after he failed to pay wages for OD in a timely manner. In retaliation, officers were deliberately lax in their patrols during a high-profile large cultural event, leading to a spike in crimes, including two murders. Mayor Haddad then had to deal with headlines declaring record levels of violence at the Virada Cultural festival.[66]

The police's control over coercion – a service politicians wish to distribute in electorally advantageous ways – and the credible threat of its withdrawal thus allow the police to extract concessions from politicians in the form of autonomy. In the context of a police force that routinely deploys that coercion in extralegal fashion, as in the case of São Paulo's police forces, this accommodation with police and the concomitant autonomy allows the police to evade external accountability and raises the threshold for reform. As the following section demonstrates, however, societal preferences over policing in São Paulo are profoundly fragmented,

---

[65] Author interview with anonymous lieutenant colonel (ret.) of the Military Police of São Paulo 2, date and location withheld.

[66] Wanderley Preite Sobrinho e Ricardo Galhardo, "Prefeitura de São Paulo tenta despolitizar violência na Virada Cultural," IG São Paulo, May 20, 2013, http://ultimosegundo.ig.com.br/brasil/sp/2013-05-20/prefeitura-de-sao-paulo-tenta-despolitizar-violencia-na-virada-cultural.html; "Virada Cultural de 2013 acaba com dois mortos, seis esfaqueados, e três baleados," *Folha de São Paulo*, May 19, 2013.

such that politicians receive conflicting demands and face little electoral cost for the persistence of authoritarian coercive practices and, consequently, little electoral counterweight to the structural power of police.

PREFERENCE FRAGMENTATION AND THE CONSTITUENCY FOR AUTHORITARIAN COERCION

A common Brazilian expression I heard often during my fieldwork in São Paulo is the belief that "a good criminal is a dead criminal" (*bandido bom é bandido morto*). As such, there is perhaps no better indicator of the fragmented preferences over policing and security in Brazil than the divided opinion on this oft-repeated phrase. According to a 2015 survey, 50 percent of Brazilians expressed agreement with the phrase, while 45 percent expressed disagreement (Fórum Brasileiro de Segurança Pública, 2015, 7). This common logic undoubtedly informed the response of residents attending a meeting of the Community Security Council (CONSEG) in a low-income district in the northern zone of São Paulo, when the local police commander told them of recent alleged shootouts with "*marginais*" (criminals). On two occasions, when the Military Police captain spoke about an alleged shootout in which "the *bandido* was unfortunately killed," many of the residents around the room approved – with phrases such as "Not unfortunately, fortunately!" and "*Graças a deus!*" (thank god!) – and applauded.[67]

These accounts suggest a sizable constituency for extralegal police violence pointing to one of the main drivers of the persistence of authoritarian coercion in democracy. Despite the egregious patterns of exceptional coercive practices, politicians in São Paulo likely see little incentive to enact reforms to address them and little electoral cost for failing to do so.

Instead, politicians' incentives to enact reform or maintain the status quo of authoritarian coercion are shaped by patterns of fragmented societal contestation and demand-making around policing and security that result from the vastly divergent experiences of different societal groups with the state's coercive apparatus. Differences in the distribution of protection and repression often reproduce social cleavages and inequalities; in the case of São Paulo, this manifests along the lines of race, class,

---

[67] A meeting of the local Community Security Council (CONSEG, Conselho Comunitário de Segurança) attended by the author in a low-income neighborhood in the northern zone of São Paulo in 2012.

and geography. As I discuss in this section, this stratification of protection and repression lead to an enduring fragmentation of societal preferences over policing, indicating to politicians that they can make appeals to a sizable constituency that favors authoritarian coercion, while continuing to reap the benefits of accommodating the police.

"The State Has Abandoned Us": Unequal Protection in São Paulo

Understanding societal demand-making over policing requires us to consider variation in citizens' everyday experiences with police, shaped by palpable disparities in the distribution of protection. Beginning soon after the transition to democracy, researchers documented how police interactions with citizens in São Paulo's *periferias* – the mostly poor, mostly black districts in the far ends of the city – came to be largely defined by the absence of protection: weak preventive policing, a reluctance to respond to citizens' calls for help (Americas Watch 1987), and an overreliance on heavily armed, repressive actions by "elite" forces such as the ROTA (Pinheiro et al. 1991, 102). The police, this last set of authors observes, kill more in regions where they patrol less.

The unevenness in the distribution of protection is illustrated well by a comparison between two areas of the city where I conducted interviews and ethnographic work. The first community is a low-income community in the northern zone of the city, located within a *subprefeitura* (administrative district) with a population that is half black (*preta e parda*) and where the median household income in 2010 was R$2,500 (Secretaria Municipal de Promoção da Igualdade Racial 2015).[68] During a visit to the main police station, I asked the acting commander of the *companhia* (precinct) about the challenges of policing this particular district. The lieutenant directed my gaze away from the DVD of *Twilight: Breaking Dawn* on his desk (which he told me he had just been watching) and pointed to the two large windows behind him, revealing a view of the district's expansive territory with several hills dotted with favelas. I spent several months in 2012 visiting the main police station, a community police station (*base comunitária de segurança*) in the district, and the local Community Security Council (Conselho Comunitário de Segurança, CONSEG).

Across these settings in this low-income community, the lack of access to resources to offer effective police protection was a recurring concern.

---

[68] For the sake of comparison, the city's population was about 37 percent black in the 2010 census.

For instance, after leaving the CONSEG meeting one night, the PM captain who regularly commands the district complained that, despite greater need, his district received fewer resources from the Military Police's central command. "I received two motorcycles," said the captain, "Do you know how many Perdizes received? Twenty-six."[69] The captain's frustration with the lack of resources and the inability to offer adequate protection was echoed by his subordinates in the community police station. During one of my visits, two *soldados* told me that the *base* had been operating without a police car (*viatura*) for a month.[70] Prior to that, they said, they informed their superiors that the car was run-down and would soon stop functioning altogether; they were told to keep using it, and eventually it did break down completely. The officers at the *base* put in a request for another vehicle, but they did not seem hopeful that they would receive it any time soon. They said that because they are in "a low-income area" (*uma área carente*), they are not as much of a priority, whereas if they were in a wealthier area they'd have more resources. I asked them how they respond to crimes (*ocorrências*) without a patrol car. "We don't respond," one of the officers said, "we have no way of doing so" (*Não atendemos … não tem como*). I asked what happens if someone from the community comes in asking for help. They said that, unless they can go on foot, there's not much they can do except put out a call over the radio (which defeats the purpose of the *base* in the first place).[71] The two *soldados* told me that earlier that day they received a call about a stolen car that had been found, but, since they had no patrol car, they had to ride there with the tow truck and that, on the way back, "we had to ask the victim to give us a ride" (*tivemos que pegar carona com a vítima*). Later that afternoon, the two commented to one another that they had done the right thing by riding back with the victim's husband because, if they had waited for a patrol car (*viatura*) to come, they would probably still be there waiting.

The situation facing this low-income community in the city's periphery stands in sharp contrast to another community in the city's center, where

---

[69] Perdizes is a wealthy district of the city that is one-quarter the size of the district commanded by the captain.

[70] One of the officers insisted that the lack of a patrol car in the *base* was something I should know and write about in my book, telling me that it is part of my work to know such things.

[71] Indeed, later that afternoon, two men came to the *base* to report that a man was threatening others with a broken glass bottle nearby. The two officers went to investigate the situation on foot and returned fifteen to twenty minutes later.

more-advantaged residents mobilized effectively for more police resources. This district is located in a *subprefeitura* where the population is less than one-quarter black and the median household income in 2010 was R$8,000; the Battalion (*batalhão*) itself is located in the district's wealthiest neighborhood, which the commander called the "Beverly Hills command." Unlike the commander of the low-income district, the lieutenant colonel who commands the Battalion corresponding to this district was nearly on the verge of complaining of having *too many* resources. "I have too many *bases* ... I probably have three or four per *companhia* (precinct) ... But that's too many, they tie up too much of my staff." When I asked the commander why he had so many *bases*, he replied this was "because, precisely, there was political mobilization." As a result, officers working in this district are unlikely to face the resource constraints faced by those in the low-income community. According to the lieutenant colonel, "I've been in the Military Police for twenty-nine years, and I've lived through periods of misery ... [But] today we have many resources, I would even say resources that are very close to the ideal, considering the situation of the country."[72]

While this may seem an atypical statement from a police official – and indeed, the lieutenant colonel, who served me hibiscus tea, played calming music, and lit incense during our interview, is an atypical police official – the lieutenant colonel's assessment of the resources at the disposal of the Military Police concurred with what I heard from the institution's highest-ranking officials. Col. Marcos Chaves, the municipal commander, for instance, recounted with pride the investments made in the Military Police in recent years, such as placing computers in all 12,000 patrol cars in the state (presumably those that are operational) and acquiring twenty-three helicopters. According to Col. Chaves, "today there is not a citizen in São Paulo who is more than ten minutes from a helicopter, an air vessel (*aeronave*), from a rescue [vehicle], from assistance in any situation." The lack of resources faced by the low-income district in the city's northern periphery is thus likely to be a distributive question rather than a result of broader resource constraints within the institution.

Despite the relative availability of resources conveyed by high-level Military Police commanders, the unevenness of protection – and the resources presumably needed to provide it – was a salient concern in other low-income communities. In another low-income community in

---

[72] Author interview with anonymous lieutenant colonel of the Military Police of São Paulo, São Paulo, April 29, 2012.

the southern zone of the city, a PM captain who at the time commanded the district expressed his frustration about the lack of support from central police leadership and political leaders in rather telling terms: "the state has abandoned us."[73] This selective presence and "abandonment" of the state leaves police officers in these communities to substitute for other state institutions, offering recreational spaces, providing food baskets to needy families, and even serving as de facto ambulances for women in labor (González 2017, 506). Communities made up of the three Ps – *pobre, preto e periférico* (poor, black, and from the periphery) – thus lie at a nexus of vulnerabilities, in which they depend far more on police services than fellow citizens that are more well-off, but they are less likely to receive adequate protection.

At the same time, this segment of society is also disproportionately likely to bear the brunt of police repression, particularly that which falls outside the scope of the law, as well as less likely to see police held accountable. One of the clearest manifestations of these contradictions I observed during my fieldwork was while accompanying the two officers cited at the beginning of this chapter who joked about killing someone in order to get a day off. As they drove around, we saw a group of four black youth, who appeared to be in their late teens, hanging out near their car in a wooded area. The officers, who are white, stopped the patrol car, and one asked the other, "Are they smoking weed?" (*'tão fumando maconha?*), even though only one person in the group was smoking a cigarette. The two officers then approached the group and yelled this question at the teenagers repeatedly, addressing only the young men. The officers searched the young men's bags and pockets and roughly patted them down, including the groin area. The young men kept their heads lowered, acting very deferential to the officers. The officers returned to the patrol car and yelled at the group to leave the area. The officers followed the car for a few minutes, during which I asked whether the young people had, in fact, been smoking marijuana; one of the officers replied that they had not. A few minutes later, we drove by an area with small clusters of humble and precarious homes. As the patrol car passed by, two little boys looked at the officers, smiled, and gave them the thumbs-up sign.

The juxtaposition of an *abordagem* (stop and search) that appeared to fall outside the scope of the legal standard of "justified suspicion" (*fundada suspeita*) and instead matched the familiar pattern of racialized police practices with the positive reception by young children in a low-income community with scant state presence was a fitting representation of the relationship between the police and the mostly poor, mostly black citizens living in communities on the city's periphery. It is just one manifestation of broader disparities in the distribution of protection and repression, which produce vastly different experiences with, and relationships to, the state's police forces across race, class, and geography.

Unequal Repression: São Paulo's "Two Police Forces"

Upon taking over as commander of the "elite" tactical unit ROTA, Lt. Col. Ricardo Augusto Nascimento de Mello Araújo sparked much debate in São Paulo, declaring in a news interview that police officers had to treat citizens differently while conducting stops in the city's urban peripheries and in wealthy areas of the city, such as the Jardins neighborhood.[74] Luís Adorno, the journalist who interviewed the ROTA commander and reported his controversial remarks, told me that the fervor over the commander's comments was not because they were novel or untrue but rather because "he said what you are not supposed to say. Everyone knows it, but you're not supposed to talk about it, because it will be seen as latent prejudice, discrimination of people, revealing castes."[75]

Despite the controversy over the commander's remarks, they reflect the stratified policing strategies described by interviewees, from the police and civil society alike. One official, who commanded a Military Police battalion in the metropolitan region of São Paulo, described the demands he heard from the citizenry as follows:

The society felt abandoned because crime rates were high. But they also complained a lot about police actions. That the police were too brutish with the residents of the periphery. That was a recurring account, and it's been proven to be that way: that we have two police forces, a police force in the periphery that is more violent and arbitrary, and the police in the well-off areas (*áreas nobres*), which is more cordial and civic-minded. And we even had a discourse from officers that accepted these two police forces in one.[76]

---

[74] Luís Adorno. "Abordagem no Jardins tem de ser diferente da periferia, diz novo comandante da Rota," *UOL Notícias*, August 24, 2017.

[75] Author interview with Luís Adorno, São Paulo, September 14, 2017.

[76] Author interview with anonymous lieutenant colonel (ret.) of the Military Police of São Paulo 2, date and location withheld.

There is ample evidence that the ROTA commander and the retired lieutenant colonel indeed reflect broader patterns of stratified, and in particular racialized, policing practices. As a young black police officer told me during a visit to a police station, "if you see a white guy and a black guy walking, the white guy could be carrying stolen merchandise, but you stop the black guy."[77] The conventional wisdom expressed by the *soldado* that "you stop the black guy" was formalized by a unit of the state's Military Police in the city of Campinas, where a local commander issued a Service Order (*Ordem de Serviço*) to his subordinates mandating that, when conducting police stops in the well-to-do area of Taquaral, they should "focus stops and searches of pedestrians and vehicles with suspicious disposition (*attitude suspeita*), particularly mixed-race and black individuals (*de cor parda e negra*)."[78] The prevalence of racial discrimination in police stops has evidently been sufficient to be of concern to recent police leadership. The former commander of the Military Police of São Paulo State, Colonel Álvaro Camilo, told me in an interview of his concern with reducing racial prejudice, emphasizing to his officers that "you don't have to disrespect, you don't have to be racist. Because sometimes the officer comes and says [a racial slur]. The officer should call the person 'citizen.'"[79]

The "racial filter" (Barros 2008) identified by these police officials was reflected in citizens' experiences with police. Data from a rare survey conducted in the city of São Paulo in the 1990s specifically about attitudes toward police found, for instance, that those who identified as black (46 percent) were more likely than those who did not (34 percent) to say they had been stopped and searched by police. Black respondents were also more likely to say they had been "verbally offended" by police (25 percent vs. 17 percent) and more likely to report being subjected to "physical aggression" by police (12 percent vs. 6 percent).[80]

---

[77] Date of visit and location of police station withheld to preserve anonymity of the PM *soldado*.

[78] Ordem de Serviço No. 80 BPMI-822/20/12, dated September 21, 2012. Reported in "Ordem da PM determina revista em pessoas 'da cor parda e negra' em bairro nobre de Campinas (SP)," *Notícias UOL*, January 23, 2013, available at http://noticias.uol.com.br /cotidiano/ultimas-noticias/2013/01/23/ordem-da-pm-determina-revista-em-pessoas-da-cor-parda-e-negra-em-bairro-nobre-de-campinas-sp.htm.

[79] Author interview with Coronel Álvaro Camilo, former commander of the Military Police of São Paulo State, São Paulo, May 28, 2012.

[80] "A imagem da polícia," survey of São Paulo residents conducted by the Datafolha Institute on April 2, 1997. Dataset accessed via the CESOP database maintained by the University of Campinas (Unicamp), DAT/SP97.ABR-00805.

Conversations with black and low-income civil society activists from all corners of São Paulo's peripheries similarly revealed what I call "stratified citizenship," wherein policing strategies are determined by markers of inequality such as race, class, and geography, thereby promoting divergent access to rights and relationships to state institutions (González 2017). A human rights lawyer who works with victims of police violence in the eastern zone of São Paulo, for instance, said:

> When police come to a favela, it's a no man's land. No resident is going to come up to a police officer and say, "You can't enter, you don't have a warrant" ... There are constant police abuses in the region. When a person is stopped, they are seen by police as criminals, just for being poor. [They experience] humiliation, torture, aggressions ... They are treated like criminals just for living in the *periferia*. The police stop will be violent – he will be treated like a criminal.[81]

Another human rights activist in the far eastern zone of São Paulo similarly described "the audacity of the officer when he raids a home ... the violence of the police officer when he arrives. And you know that the officer is also black, that he is also poor, that he was also raised in the community. But this is the effect of the state itself [on him]."[82]

A young black activist and artist from the northern zone of São Paulo, meanwhile, candidly summed up the consequences of these modes of policing: "The police are supposed to provide people with security, but here in the community you see a police car and you feel afraid, because he can come out with his gun drawn and put a bullet in you."[83] The activist's frank analysis has indeed been confirmed for decades by public officials and scholars alike, in studies showing that young black men disproportionately suffer higher rates of homicides committed by police. According to the Police Ombudsman's Office, 57 percent of victims of police killings were identified as black (*negro*) during the 1990s, despite the fact that only about a quarter of the state's population identified as black at the time (Ouvidoria da Polícia do Estado de São Paulo 2000, 20). A decade later, another study found that black *paulistas* continue to be killed at the hands of police at much higher rates than other groups. Looking at cases of police killings denounced before the Police Ombudsman's Office between 2009 and 2011, Sinhoretto, Silvestre, and Schlitter (2014) find that 61 percent of those killed by police were black and that black *paulistas* were

---

[81] Author interview with anonymous human rights lawyer, São Paulo, September 25, 2017.
[82] Author interview with activist with Associação Amparar, São Paulo, September 4, 2017.
[83] Author interview with activist and artist from northern zone of São Paulo, March 21, 2019.

three times as likely to be killed by police than their white counterparts (26). Scholars have also found considerable disparities in police violence by geography, which, in São Paulo, overlaps heavily with race and class. Brinks (2008), for instance, in his analysis of a sample of police killings during the 1990s, finds that 64 percent of victims lived in favelas, whereas only about 10 percent of the population of São Paulo lived in favelas at the time (51).

A more recent study by the Police Ombudsman's Office demonstrates not only the continuation of these patterns but also that the stratification of state violence extends to extralegal coercive practices. On the one hand, the analysis found that the victims of lethal police violence continue to come from the "three Ps": 65 percent of victims of police killings in 2017 were black (Mariano 2018, 24), and 76 percent of victims had only completed primary education (Mariano 2018, 27) – by contrast, less than 1 percent had more than a high school education. On the other, the study also found that black victims comprised 60 percent of cases where the ombudsman's analysis showed there had been no armed confrontation, and 69 percent of cases where there was evidence of excessive force (Mariano 2018, 26).

The preceding discussion helps to elucidate one factor that underlies the persistence of the distinctively authoritarian modes of coercion by São Paulo's police forces. Although these practices are routine and widespread, they are concentrated within a single segment of the population, that which typically also possesses the least political power. Those sectors of society that are more well-off – whether in wealthier areas of the city or those within communities that are low-income overall – are exposed directly to extralegal and unaccountable coercive action to a much lesser degree. As I suggest in the next section, these divergent experiences, reflecting patterns of social inequality, shape the nature of contestation and types of demands that politicians perceive as divided preferences and conflicting demands, with considerable sectors of society supporting the types of practices characterized here as authoritarian.

Divergent Experiences, Divergent Demands

After decades of democratic rule defined by authoritarian coercion that is nevertheless experienced disproportionately by citizens depending on their race, class, and residential location, societal contestation and demand-making on policing and security issues have come to reflect considerable fragmentation, in both predictable and counterintuitive ways. Societal preferences over policing – as expressed through surveys, direct contacts, protests, or other means – indeed reflect fragmentation that often aligns with usual cleavages of race, class, and geography. But, an additional consequence of the uneven distribution of protection and repression that has characterized São Paulo for decades has been an additional layer of fragmentation even within the broad segment of the population most likely to suffer repression and least likely to receive protection.

To get a sense of this multilayered fragmentation, consider the following accounts of Community Security Councils (CONSEGs) in vastly different regions of the city of São Paulo. In an interview with the lieutenant colonel cited above, he was explicit in characterizing the fragmented preferences he encounters from the citizenry – including demands for the police to use extrajudicial force – in the context of the monthly meetings of the CONSEGs in a wealthy district close to the city center. According to the lieutenant colonel,

We have 90 percent of people that are very liberal but that never go to these meetings. When you have these meetings, the ones who attend are the 10 percent. And so, there are 2 percent there that want to kill homosexuals, they don't want *nordestinos* (people from the mostly poor, mostly black northeastern region of Brazil) and don't accept Bolivians in the country, and then the other 2 percent that defend these groups . . . So it's common for us to attend a meeting and come across someone that's very pro-repression, the guys that say, "I don't understand! You're police officers and you don't kill the thief!" But I'm not here to kill the thief, and you still have people that don't understand our role . . . We're here in a very rich area of the city, a very cultured region where you'd think you wouldn't hear this, but you do hear this.[84]

A similar set of demands emerged in a CONSEG in a spatially and socially distant district in the eastern zone of São Paulo. According to the human rights lawyer who works in the region,

[The CONSEG] could be an important space for people to really speak out about what's happening in the neighborhood, but it's a space that has been undermined. The majority of participants are business owners who support police, so there's a discourse that seeks to undermine human rights . . . They criticize us saying we are there to support criminals, that human rights are rights for criminals (*direitos humanos é direitos dos manos*), so we haven't seen much progress [in the CONSEG]. It's a space that, if it worked [as intended], I think it would be a space for constructing something, better alternatives, [to] ask how we could

---

[84] Author interview with anonymous lieutenant colonel of the Military Police of São Paulo, São Paulo, April 29, 2012.

dialogue with police about some of these cases, or ask why the police has to be so violent here. These are the answers we're looking for.[85]

These two snapshots illustrate the multiple layers of fragmentation inherent in societal demand-making over policing. On the one hand, we observe privileged sectors of society expressing "pro-repression" views, as the police commander put it, conveying demands that police exert repression against other social groups with less privilege. On the other hand, we see similar divisions emerge in a context that, within the broader stratification of Brazilian and São Paulo society, is overall considered disadvantaged. Within each context, politicians and public officials receive signals of fragmented preferences and conflicting demands, with a robust constituency expressing support for authoritarian coercion.

Fragmentation has long defined societal contestation over policing in São Paulo. While Chapter 6 will explore in greater detail how enduring fragmentation has shaped politicians' incentives against police reform during key decision points, it is worth providing an overview of societal attitudes and, consequently what politicians might infer about societal preferences for reform. Public opinion surveys conducted in São Paulo in the decades since the transition to democratic rule have revealed similar divisions in attitudes toward the police and what the police ought to do. For instance, a 1990 survey showed considerable fragmentation in citizens' evaluation of the police: 26 percent of respondents evaluated the police as good or very good; an additional 30 percent of respondents view the institution as average, while 41 percent think the institution is bad or very bad.[86]

These differences in opinion also manifest as what some scholars call a "paradox" (Caldeira 2002), in which citizens hold what appear to be seemingly incompatible views about the police. For instance, a 1995 survey[87] by the firm Datafolha that asked specifically about the "image of the police" showed that a large proportion of citizens believed that the police were very or somewhat effective in fighting crime: 70 percent. The same survey also revealed that societal actors believe that the police are engaged in fairly extensive malfeasance. When asked about the extent to

---

[85] Author interview with anonymous human rights lawyer, São Paulo, September 25, 2017.
[86] Findings from a 1990 survey by the firm Datafolha. Respondents were asked "In general do you think [the police] is Very Good, Good, Regular, Bad, or Very Bad?" Accessed via de Consórcio de Informações Sociais database maintained by the University of São Paulo.
[87] "A imagem da polícia" survey conducted by the survey firm Datafolha on December 19, 1995. Dataset accessed via the CESOP database maintained by the University of Campinas (Unicamp). DAT/SP-RJ95.DEZ-00532.

which the police use torture when interrogating suspects, 65 percent of respondents said they believe the police always or sometimes use torture. Regarding the existence of death squads within the police, 75 percent of respondents said they believe such death squads continued to exist. Finally, 88 percent of respondents believed that the police are involved with organized crime. Yet, this same survey showed, as will be discussed in more detail in Chapter 6, respondents were divided on the extent to which they trusted (46 percent) or feared (52 percent) the police, and their views of police violence, with only 44 percent considering the Military Police to be too violent – despite the fact, it bears repeating, that large majorities believed police engaged in torture and participated in death squads. Thus, citizens' attitudes toward police do not appear to result from a lack of knowledge about police misconduct, including the reliance on authoritarian coercive practices.

The recurring survey question regarding the appropriateness of police violence is a fruitful point from which to assess broader preferences toward police. Not only has this question shown a consistent pattern of fragmentation, but it also refers to a consistent pattern of authoritarian coercion that has long defined the state's police. The Datafolha Survey Institute has asked the same question about police violence (specifically by the Military Police) over the course of two decades. Figure 3.3 shows the distribution of respondents' opinions for several surveys conducted between 1995 and 2013 that included this question. With the exception of the survey conducted in 1997, when attitudes converged in response to a high-profile incident of police violence (see Chapter 6), public opinion toward police violence has been fairly fragmented across those who believe the Military Police is too violent and those that believe the level of violence utilized by the PM is either appropriate or *not enough*. The first time the survey was conducted, in 1995, 44 percent of respondents said the Military Police was more violent than it should be, 34 percent believed that the police were "violent to the right extent," and 19 percent believed that the police was less violent than it should be. Save for the two iterations of the survey conducted just days after high-profile episodes of police violence – following the "Favela Naval" incident in 1997 and the violent police response to mass protests in June 2013 – there has been only slight variation between those who believe the police are too violent and those who believe levels of violence have been appropriate, while the constituency calling for a more violent police has remained fairly consistent for nearly two decades, at about one-fifth of respondents. These proportions have stayed roughly similar over time, varying little in the

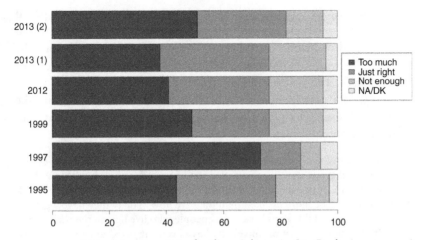

FIGURE 3.3 Citizens' assessment of police violence in São Paulo (1995–2013) Surveys by Datafolha Survey Institute. Respondents were asked "Would you say that the Military Police is more violent than it should be, violent to the right extent, or less violent than it should be?" Responses presented in the chart as "too much," "just right," and "not enough." See report "Protestos sobre aumento nas tarifa dos transportes II PO813688," issued June 18, 2013, on the Datafolha website: http://datafolha.folha.uol.com.br/opiniaopublica/2013/06/1297619-cresce-apoio -a-protestos-contra-a-tarifa-de-onibus-entre-paulistanos.shtml

face of the dramatic decline in the number of homicides in the city (and state) of São Paulo (Figure 3.1) and fluctuations in levels of lethal police violence (Figure 3.2).

What inferences should elected leaders and police officials draw from such surveys about the public's preferences regarding levels of police violence? A key observation is that policing – and police violence – are consistently subject to contestation. Across the citizenry as a whole, there has been an enduring fragmentation that, as Brazil's and São Paulo's politicians know all too well, has ensured the persistence of a sizable segment of the population that favors a highly violent police and can serve as a reliable electoral constituency for those advocating for greater police discretion in fighting crime (Ahnen 2007).

But a second key inference from the survey data is that this contestation, and enduring fragmentation, has also emerged within the sectors of society that are most vulnerable to extralegal coercive practices by the state's police. The Brazilian human rights lawyer from the eastern zone of São Paulo emphasized "a bit of a division in the periphery." He highlighted a distinction between those who live in "favelas" and those who live in the *"asfalto"* (more well-to-do areas, literally asphalt or paved roads) in their relationships with the police, even when both are located in the same low-income periphery. "The more vulnerable sector," he observes, "is within the favelas [of the periphery] where you have a lot of violence ... The police come at any hour, kick down the door of any *barraco* (precarious home), and do whatever they want ... even take someone's life ... The police in the favelas are seen as the enemy." In contrast, he notes,

those that live in the *asfalto* are a bit safer. Someone who lives in a house, even if it's in the periphery, if they live in a paved road, the police abide by the law. They will only enter those houses with a warrant ... So in the streets of the *asfalto* I think the police used to be more disliked than they are now. Today they have a greater level of acceptance. I think it's because ... people who live here in the peripheries, as they're heading to work or university, have been subjected to robberies ... so that's why this group from the *asfalto* sees the police as a solution ... So in the periphery we have people, even people I know, that say, "Criminals have to be killed. They have to be killed– it's him or you."

THE NESTED STRATIFICATION OF POLICING AND THE ENDURING FRAGMENTATION OF SOCIETAL PREFERENCES

The São Paulo case, in contrast to the other two police forces examined in this book, by and large represents a negative case for structural reforms to promote democratic coercion. Despite extensive authoritarian coercive practices – from extrajudicial killings to death squads – and perpetrating an increasing proportion of all homicides in the state, São Paulo's police forces, particularly its Military Police, have largely avoided the instances of profound scrutiny and comprehensive reform of its structures and practices that befell the Colombian police and the police of Buenos Aires Province. A key driver of this institutional persistence has been an enduring fragmentation of societal preferences, which has prevented the emergence of an electoral counterweight to the structural power of a colossal police force.

In many ways, this persistent fragmentation has developed as a result of the "two police forces" strategy that has left São Paulo's peripheries subjected to unequal protection and repression, producing nested processes of stratification. Police respond to demands for security from privileged sectors of society by disproportionately concentrating repression on the "three Ps." At the same time, by underproviding protection for this same sector, policing generates additional processes of stratification within disadvantaged sectors that demand a state response, even if that response is repressive (and authoritarian) in nature. The activist and artist from the northern zone illustrated well the consequences of this nested stratification for demand formation:

There is strong support for the death penalty, for the expansion of gun ownership, in the *periferia* itself. Why is that understandable? . . . Here [the resident] perceives everyday violence. You would not perceive it in a condominium. It's a territorial question. If you were to ask "how many people here have been mugged?" in Moema [a wealthy neighborhood], probably no one. But here, out of fifteen people, fifteen will tell you they've experienced it, because it's much more present in their everyday life, in their imaginary. That's the problem of the periphery; that's what fear does."

The preceding discussion should not be taken to mean that all democratically elected leaders in São Paulo have stood idly by as the state's police forces have exercised blatantly authoritarian coercive practices. Nevertheless, for politicians and police leaders, the main takeaway from the demands and calls they receive on a daily basis from different groups of citizens is that the fragmented preferences of the citizenry create little incentive to undertake institutional reform in an effort to change authoritarian coercive practices. The fragmentation of preferences and the conflicting demands conveyed to politicians make the electoral gains of reform uncertain at best and, considering the structural power of police, politically disadvantageous. Most political leaders have instead sought to shape citizens' preferences in favor of greater police authority and violence: from Governor Luiz Antônio Fleury, who openly advocated for more police killings (Chapter 6), to Governor Geraldo Alckmin, who repeatedly celebrated and defended police killings,[88] and Governor Joao Dória, who began his tenure declaring that, under his administration, "criminals won't go to the police station or prison, they'll end up in the cemetery."[89] Such discourses likely reinforce support for authoritarian coercion among large segments of the citizenry, while suggesting to others

---

[88] "Polícia e Alckmin elogiam ação que matou 10 no Morumbi: 'inteligência' e 'eficiência de Deus,'" *UOL*, September 4, 2017, available at https://noticias.uol.com.br/cotidiano/ulti mas-noticias/2017/09/04/policia-e-alckmin-elogiam-acao-que-matou-10-no-morumbi-i nteligencia-e-eficiencia-de-deus.htm.

[89] "Dória diz que agora em SP 'bandido não vai para a delegacia, nem para a prisão, vai para o cemitério,'" *Revista Fórum*, January 15, 2019, video available at https://revistaforum .com.br/politica/video-doria-diz-que-agora-em-sp-bandido-nao-vai-para-a-delegacia-nem- para-a-prisao-vai-para-o-cemiterio/.

who are neutral or even those who are its primary targets that their government will offer few other policy alternatives to protect them from crime. In this context, the persistence of fragmented preferences over police reform, and the enduring constituency for authoritarian coercion, may not only shape but also be shaped by politicians' incentives.

Even in the case of principled politicians who have sought to enact reforms to reduce police violence, the fragmentation of societal preferences has proven to be an important obstacle (Chapter 6). In accounting for persistence – and in many ways the intensification – of authoritarian coercive practices in the three decades since the transition toward democratic rule, it is important to look to the large segments of the citizenry that demand such authoritarian coercion, even among the sectors of society that are most likely to be its victims. Thus, the absence of comprehensive structural reforms of the sort observed in Buenos Aires Province (Chapter 7) and Colombia (Chapter 7) in the three decades since the transition toward democratic rule in São Paulo is, at least partly, an exercise of democratic responsiveness to (some) citizens' demands.

4

The Endurance of the "Damned Police" of Buenos Aires Province

On May 8, 1987, not long after Argentina's much-lauded transition to democracy in the aftermath of one of the region's most brutal dictatorships, the Police of Buenos Aires Province carried out the first high-profile "*gatillo fácil*" (trigger-happy) killing under democracy in the city of Ingeniero Budge. The case of Ingeniero Budge is illustrative of the persistence of authoritarian coercion under democratic rule, calling into question the capacity of democratic institutions to rein in rampant extralegal police violence against disadvantaged citizens. Pedro Ramírez, a 23-year-old warehouse worker and resident of Ingeniero Budge, plainly laid out the contradictions inherent in the persistence of arbitrary coercion and contestation over policing in the context of both growing inequality and democratization:

We know we are a surplus population. That young people today don't have jobs. We even know that, to more privileged sectors, we are marginal. We've heard of this so-called democracy, but we still live in dictatorship. Because they [the police] come here, they take people away, they come into businesses, they come into homes, raids at 5 in the afternoon, they hit you ... they take your money. What kind of Argentines are we? We are all equal, we all know how to think, we all see reality, [but] what happens is we don't know what to say or do not dare to speak out. But today we are daring [to speak out] together."[1]

The Ingeniero Budge case represents an important juncture, "coming to be known in history as the first case of '*gatillo fácil*' since the return to

---

[1] Quoted in Laura Gingold, "La muerte viaja en patrullero," *CEDES*, Buenos Aires, May 1991. Retrieved August 2017 from the archives of CELS (Center for Legal and Social Studies) in Buenos Aires.

democracy."[2] From that point on, some civil society actors began questioning a recurring set of authoritarian coercive practices by the provincial police. One human rights lawyer with CORREPI (Coordinadora Contra la Represión Policial e Institucional, Coordinator against Police and Institutional Repression), an anti-police-violence NGO, situates the origins of the group as being

> May 8, 1987, when the Budge massacre took place. From then on, a small group of *compañeros* ... began problematizing headlines [like] 'Young Delinquent with Extensive Criminal Record Defeated by the Forces of Order' ... The [alleged] confrontation fell apart when we found the bullet hole in the back of the neck or in the back, when the gun that was attributed to the victim turned out to be what the police themselves call *'perro,'* a malfunctioning firearm that was 'planted' to fabricate the scene of the [armed] confrontation, bodies that were [manipulated] prior to forensic exams ... We began to realize we were not witnessing a series of curious coincidences but rather a systematic practice.[3]

This transitional moment at once illustrated modes of authoritarian coercion inherited from a prior period of dictatorship and an authoritarian coercive practice that would become the modus operandi of police violence in democracy – "trigger-happy" killings. Like their counterparts in São Paulo State, the Police of Buenos Aires Province, or Policía Bonaerense, served as an instrumental part of the apparatus of political repression installed by the military regime in the 1970s and 1980s and survived their country's transition to democracy in 1983 with their institutions, structures, and practices largely intact. Even as democracy took hold in Argentina – at least at the national level, per Gibson (2013) – the country's police forces, particularly that of Buenos Aires Province, have maintained coercive practices that are distinctly authoritarian, as the case of Ingeniero Budge suggests. The *Bonaerense*'s use of coercion has faced little constraint from the rule of law, with seamless continuity of the same tactics common under dictatorship, including torture, disappearance, and extrajudicial executions framed as armed confrontations. The provincial police force continued these practices well into the democratic period with little oversight by democratic institutions in the executive branch, the legislature, and the courts.

Instead, as I demonstrate in this chapter, these authoritarian coercive practices were often reinforced by democratic processes. As in the case of São Paulo, I argue the roots of the stubborn persistence of authoritarian

---

[2] "A 30 años de la masacre de Budge," *Página/12*, May 8, 2017.
[3] Author interview with María del Carmen Verdú, CORREPI, Buenos Aires, October 11, 2011.

coercion lie in the Buenos Aires police's successful leverage of its structural power to constrain the policy options available to politicians and raise the threshold for police reform. In the discussion that follows, I show how the fragmentation of societal preferences over policing and security – rooted in differences in citizens' experiences with police along lines of race, class, and geography – has yielded little electoral incentive for politicians to enact reform to promote democratic coercion.

These conditions favored institutional persistence despite the prevalence of widespread extrajudicial killings, corruption, and other abuses characterized here as authoritarian coercion. As I demonstrate in Chapter 7, the convergence of societal preferences over policing in the context of a scandal, and an increase in the strength of the political opposition, led a governor who for years had consistently pursued accommodation with police to shift his strategy in favor of an ambitious structural reform – only the second such reform of the provincial police in a century (Barreneche 2007, 226). It is this joint occurrence of the convergence of societal preferences and the emergence of a robust political opposition that distinguishes the case of Buenos Aires Province from that of São Paulo State – which saw the contemporaneous emergence of an egregious police violence scandal but weak political competition (see Chapter 6) – and can help us to account for these divergent reform outcomes despite structural commonalities.

As a case that exhibits both prolonged persistence of authoritarian coercion under democratic rule and ambitious structural police reform a decade and a half after the transition period, the case of the Police of Buenos Aires Province illustrates the role of ordinary democratic politics as a driver of both continuity and change among police forces, even in countries with a strong authoritarian legacy. The sections that follow begin by tracing the origins of many of the *Bonaerense*'s authoritarian coercive practices to Argentina's last military dictatorship, illustrating how the transition to democracy neglected to address these practices through structural reform. I then discuss the increase in rates of crime and violence that accompanied the transition to democracy and the effect on citizens' security preferences and demands. Despite this rising violence and growing citizen demands for security, I show that the response of the provincial government was to maintain the status quo, enabling the persistence of authoritarian coercion.

As I demonstrate, politicians chose to maintain the status quo because they perceived the fragmentation of societal preferences, rendering the electoral gains from police reform uncertain at best. In this post-transition period, growing inequality and social unrest generated a demand for repression from middle-class sectors. The inference for politicians was that the more powerful sectors of society favored increasing rather than constraining police power, providing little incentive for reform. As a result, police successfully leveraged their structural power to constrain the policy options available to politicians, who opted to engage the provincial police in accommodation. The result was stalled reform and the persistence of authoritarian coercion years after the start of democratization.

THE PROVINCIAL POLICE'S INCOMPLETE TRANSITION TO DEMOCRACY

During an interview with a retired *comisario* (commander) of the Police of Buenos Aires Province in a noisy café, he leaned over and whispered to me what his commander whispered to him at the start of the dramatic reform of the police force in 1998: "We have to stop collecting [fees]" (*tenemos que dejar de recaudar*).[4] *Recaudación*, an elaborate system of rent extraction carried out by the Police of Buenos Aires Province, epitomizes the notion of authoritarian coercion and the challenges to eradicating such coercive practices under democratic rule. In a practice that was consolidated under dictatorship and has flourished under democracy, the provincial police has routinely exercised its coercive power to collect "fees" from licit and illicit economic activity in order to fund its own operations (Dewey 2012). Because some of the revenue generated through this system of "collection" has reportedly been utilized to finance politicians' electoral campaigns and political parties (Eaton 2008, 19), many civilian officials not only failed to hold the police accountable for these coercive practices but were also complicit in it, with their electoral success contingent on it.

The persistence of *recaudación* and other authoritarian coercive practices long after the end of the dictatorship calls into question why police were not subjected to reforms to change police structures and introduce greater oversight during the transition period. Despite their role as an integral part of the state's coercive apparatus during Argentina's most brutal episode of military dictatorship, transition-era reform efforts largely sidestepped the country's police forces and instead focused almost exclusively on the military. Even in the face of extensive police involvement in grave human rights violations during the dictatorship – including

---

[4] Author interview with anonymous *comisario* (ret.) of the Police of Buenos Aires Province 1, date and location withheld to preserve anonymity of the officer.

torture, killings, and enforced disappearances – a decade and a half would pass before the institution would face the societal and political scrutiny that would bring about comprehensive reform.

A Legacy of Authoritarian Coercion

The exercise of arbitrary coercion in the interest of political leaders without external accountability has long characterized the *Bonaerense*. The incorporation of police forces into an authoritarian coercive apparatus can be traced back to the first of several military coups in Argentina over the course of the twentieth century – the 1930 overthrow of the democratically elected President Hipólito Yrigoyen. Police forces and the military engaged in broad-based surveillance and repression of political groups opposed to the military regime, a practice that became "bureaucratized and routinized" during this period (Kalmanowiecki 2000, 42). This incorporation of police into the state's repressive apparatus at the service of the national government became consolidated over the following decades. Whether democratic or military regimes, leaders would rely on the country's police forces as a tool to gain and maintain power through surveillance and repression (Saín 2015, chapter 1; Ungar 2002, 258). During this period, the police of Buenos Aires Province not only saw a reorientation of its purpose and practices but also underwent a formal reorganization of its institutional structure, mirroring military hierarchies (Barreneche 2007, 226). This militarization of police structures and doctrine shaped the development of the Buenos Aires Province police in fundamental ways, refocusing it away from traditional police roles of fighting crime and orienting it toward the routine practice of "extralegal action against putative enemies of the regime" (Kalmanowiecki 2000, 49).

   With the onset of the country's most brutal military regime from 1976 to 1983, the country's police forces "became an integral part of the terrorist state" (Kalmanowiecki 2000, 49). With the formal subordination of the country's police forces to the Army, the Police of Buenos Aires Province came under the control of the First Army Corps (I Cuerpo del Ejército), commanded by Colonel Ramón Camps. The *Bonaerense* "constituted the institutional basis of the repressive apparatus mounted in the provincial context" (Saín 2015, 70), with nearly two-thirds of the regime's 148 clandestine detention centers in Buenos Aires Province operating inside functioning police stations (Saín 2015, 72–73). Everyday policing tasks thus coincided with the clandestine and extralegal repressive strategies that characterized this period: the kidnapping, torture, and subsequent enforced disappearance of individuals suspected of being involved with guerrilla groups, communism, or simply leftist ideologies. Most were killed through methods intended to conceal the role of the state (Pereira 2005). Initially, many of the disappeared were kidnapped and their bodies would reappear days later on the streets, with the military and police reporting that they had died in a shootout with security forces (CONADEP 1984). Subsequently, the preferred strategy became to dispose of the bodies altogether so that they would not be visible, either in unmarked graves or by dropping them from airplanes in the Río de la Plata (Verbitsky 1995).

These repressive practices in the service of the military regime were carried out jointly by police and military officers in *"grupos de tarea"* (task forces), a modality that, according to Saín (2015), "spread systematically following the establishment of democracy in 1983," serving as the "principal institutional legacy of the dictatorship in the Province of Buenos Aires" (82–83). An early precursor of the subsequent networks of *recaudación*, the "task forces" self-financed their activities through the "illegal appropriation of funds through the direct or indirect 'regulation' of illicit activities undertaken by a diverse set of criminal organizations or groups" (Saín 2015, 82). The police's intelligence apparatus, moreover, was central to the operation of the *grupos de tarea*, "provid[ing] a good part of the information used towards political persecution in the military genocide that began in 1976."[5] Even police units that were not directly involved in the kidnappings and murders were systematically complicit in the broader repressive apparatus. As described in *Nunca Más* (*Never Again*), the report of the National Commission on Disappeared Persons, local police stations would be alerted of activity of a "task force" in a given area, and, if they received a call from that area of a home invasion or kidnapping, they would instruct their officers not to respond, constituting a "liberated zone" (*zona liberada*) for the operation of the "task force" (CONADEP 1984).

Thus, although the military, particularly the army, was the architect and main executor of the regime's repression, the police's territorial reach, infrastructure, and strategies – the illegal use of force, including torture and executions, intelligence, and "liberated zones" – became integral to

---

[5] Author interview with Luis Lugones, chief of the civilian intervention of the Police of Buenos Aires Province begun in 1997, La Plata, September 14, 2011.

the implementation of the military regime's authoritarian coercive practices. Nevertheless, at the moment of the transition to democracy following the most brutal military dictatorship in Argentine history, the country's police forces were largely left intact.

How the Democratic Transition Excluded Police

COMISARIO A: Beginning that year [1984], they attacked the military institutions, paramilitary institutions, and they left out the police institutions, which had military training. So the military structure, the military hierarchy, the military training, remained. It was a transition ...

COMISARIO B: [But] we didn't participate [in the transition]. If we spoke up we were done (*volábamos*). We couldn't even think ...

COMISARIO C: I was trained separately from them.

A: Thank God.

C: Yes, I entered [the police academy] before them, and it was under a militarized regime because I entered before 1983, so they can't really speak to that ...

A: I bet the CONADEP was looking for you! [*Laughs.*]

C: ... but I can speak to that because I entered [the police academy] in 1979 ...

A AND B: Oooh! You were right there with [Army Colonel] Camps!

C: ... when there was a military government. I was seventeen years old when I entered the police academy.

YG: Did you see any continuity between the training in '79 and after the transition?

C: I went through all kinds of things. Combat inside the police academy with subversive groups, inside the police academy with subversive groups! [*To other comisarios*] You must have heard of this ...

A: No, we're from a different generation.[6]

While having coffee with three active-duty *comisarios* (commanders) of the Police of Buenos Aires Province – two that entered the police force

---

[6] Author conversation with three active-duty *comisarios* in Buenos Aires Province. Names, locations, and date of meeting withheld to preserve anonymity of the *comisarios*. At this point in the conversation, *Comisario* A asked me to stop the audio recording, at which point he explained to us how specifically police cadets engaged in "combat within the police academy with subversive groups" during the military dictatorship.

shortly after the transition to democracy, and a third who entered in 1979, still during the military dictatorship – I asked them about their experience during the transition to democracy. As our conversation suggests, the police officers themselves perceived the rupture marked by the moment of the transition to democracy, but they were also well aware of the limited reach of the transition within the police force itself.

The presidency of Raúl Alfonsín marked a transformative period that broke the cycle that saw democratically elected governments toppled by military coups six times between 1930 and 1976. Among the drivers of the shift in institutional dynamics that put Argentina on an unprecedented path to decades of uninterrupted democratic rule were undoubtedly the measures taken by President Alfonsín to subordinate the military to the state's civilian authorities (Acuña & Smulovitz 1991; Diamint 1999, 2003). Yet for all of the extensive changes to military structures, rules, and practices, which were as significant as they were risky, the country's federal and provincial police institutions were left largely untouched, despite the fact that they were highly integrated into the military apparatus and no less implicated in the repression that took place under military rule. In this section I contrast the numerous measures taken to reform the military with the dearth of comparable initiatives to democratize the police, despite recognition for the need for police reform in the years after the transition to democracy.

President Alfonsín took important measures to hold the military accountable for human rights abuses committed under the dictatorship, including overturning the "self-amnesty" law enacted in the last months of the military regime (Law 23.040), reforming the Military Code in order to allow for civilian prosecution of those accused of human rights violations (Law 23.049), establishing an independent commission to investigate disappearances (Decree 187/1983), and ordering the trial of the commanders of the military juntas (Decree 158/1983). The president and the congress also took steps to formally separate defense and internal security (National Defense Law, Law 23.554/1988), and reduce the size of the military and military expenditures (Hunter 2006). These initial measures during the Alfonsín administration were intended to reduce the influence of the military in national politics and helped ensure that "in the long term, the military actor would be without capacity to question, and therefore subordinate to, the constitutional authorities" (Acuña & Smulovitz 1991, 2). After decades of adherence to national security doctrine (Pion-Berlin 1988), in which the armed forces took on a direct role in governing and sought to eliminate perceived *internal* threats to political stability and economic development, these reforms were an important step toward bringing the state's coercive institutions in line with the new democratic order.

Throughout this contested but largely successful military reform process, however, the country's police institutions were left formally intact. Eduardo Estévez, a defense and security advisor to legislators from the Radical Party in the Congress (Unión Cívica Radical, UCR) who was involved in debates over how to establish civilian control over the armed forces following the transition to democracy, explained in an interview why reforming the police was not prioritized:

> At the time, public security was not as visible a phenomenon from the perspective of citizen preoccupation with the issue, or from the [possibility of] conflict of the police institutions with a democratic government. [In contrast,] there was a big, significant fear regarding the possibility of a military coup ... which was reinforced by the uprisings by the *carapintada* sectors [in the army]. Although there were security problems, it was not seen as a primordial necessity ... There were other problems, [such as] the military issue, [and] the economic situation that was quickly deteriorating.[7]

Yet, despite this broader set of concerns, there is ample evidence that early democratically elected leaders recognized that the new democratic order required institutional change in policing. In the early years following the return to democratic rule, torture was made a felony, and federal laws were amended, to limit police authority to extract confessions and conduct unlawful detentions and to recognize other rights of the accused (Chevigny 1995, 188). But while these legal and policy changes indicate that the president and legislators recognized grave problems in the practices of their police institutions, they stopped far short of addressing the structural conditions at the root of the continuity of authoritarian coercive practices such as torture and unlawful detentions. At the provincial level, Radical Governor Alejandro Armendáriz (1983–1987) and his Peronist successor Antonio Cafiero (1987–1991) evidently also recognized the challenges posed by a police force that had been so deeply embedded in the military dictatorship's repressive regime. Armendáriz sought to address this recent legacy by removing police commanders and shifting mid-ranking officers to different parts of the provincial territory (Saín 2015, 90). Cafiero, meanwhile, appointed a reformist secretary of

---

[7] Author interview with Eduardo Estévez, June 5, 2013. Estévez was also the director of the Institute for Security and Crime Policy created under the auspices of the Ministry of Security during the reform in 1998.

government (then charged with overseeing the police), Luis Brunati, who zealously investigated police misconduct and fired hundreds of officers.

Neither governor pursued structural police reform, in large part due to police resistance, as I discuss later in this chapter. But their efforts demonstrate that there was indeed a debate about what would later come to be called the "police question" (González 2007) in the early years of democratization, in the province and nationally (Peregrino Fernández 1983). Political leaders showed at least some concern over the deep roots of the police's authoritarian coercive practices, seemingly aware that the transition to democracy would not automatically cause a rupture with the path it had been on over the course of the previous half-century. But neither these early governors nor their successor Eduardo Duhalde, until the very end of his term, sought to undertake the challenge of structural police reform, despite the fact that even the legislation governing all aspects of the provincial police (Decree-Law 9.551/1980) was enacted during the dictatorship. As former minister of security Carlos León Arslanian noted, the structures and practices acquired under military rule "permeated the institution deeply and the onset of democracy did not take care of this problem."[8]

RISING VIOLENCE, SHIFTING DEMANDS

Scholars have noted that one of the key challenges facing police forces in countries transitioning from dictatorship to democracy is the inadequacy of the tools of political repression for crime fighting (Tanner 2000). The failure to reform the provincial police in accordance with a new democratic order in the years following the transition to democracy had significant repercussions in the context of rising crime and violence, as well as mounting social tensions and unrest in the face of the dramatic economic crisis afflicting Argentina starting in the late 1980s. The pronounced increases in unemployment, poverty, and inequality during this period, and the resulting social protests, placed the police at the center of acute societal demands for security and repression of marginalized citizens. The *Bonaerense*, however, proved largely incapable of addressing these increasingly complex challenges.

As in the case of São Paulo State, democratization was accompanied by an increase in crime rates in Buenos Aires Province. Although homicide

---

[8] "La policía se cambia desde adentro, y toma por lo menos una década," *Página/12*, March 4, 2007.

rates in the province did not see dramatic increases during the 1990s, varying between 7 and 11 per 100,000 inhabitants, overall crime rates doubled, and both violent crime and property crime rates tripled between 1991 and 1999.[9] During this time, crime also became a more complex phenomenon, with the development of different, and more violent, forms. Though these changes became more pronounced after 2000, the 1990s saw the growth of drug trafficking for an internal market, illegal arms trafficking and sales, car theft and dismantling (which saw the highest increase and became one of the most profitable crimes), and organized crime, as well as kidnappings and carjackings (Saín 2004, 6).

In the face of these worsening security conditions, however, the *Bonaerense* had reached a dire state. According to Carlos Beraldi, a former secretary of security, by the time he served in the late 1990s the provincial police had undergone

a process of deterioration that practically began with the transition to democracy ... [This deterioration] was characterized by deficient execution of even the most basic tasks, such as patrolling, relations with the community ... an inability to solve high-impact crimes ... [deficiencies] in training. There were police officers who had not received training in shooting in twenty years ... It was really a situation of an institution that had collapsed.[10]

The dual challenges posed by rising crime and violence and the institutional deterioration described by Beraldi were broadly palpable among the province's citizens, who were vocal in their expressions of dissatisfaction with how the government was handling crime and public security and in their demands for improved security. Surveys conducted in the 1990s in the province's most populous area, the *conurbano*,[11] found that 55–60 percent of respondents evaluated the government's handling of public security and crime as "bad." These same surveys also showed that 76 percent of respondents found the Greater Buenos Aires area (*conurbano*) to be unsafe, 72 percent expressed fear in simply walking around on the streets, and 96 percent agreed that crime had increased considerably over the previous year.[12] As a former opposition provincial

---

[9] See "Informe Anual de Estadísticas Policiales. Año 2002," Sistema Nacional de Información Criminal, Ministerio de Justicia, Seguridad, y Derechos Humanos. Retrieved from www.jus.gob.ar/media/1124692/SnicARGENTINA2002.pdf.

[10] Author interview with Carlos Beraldi, Buenos Aires, October 7, 2011.

[11] The *conurbano* comprises twenty-four municipalities in Buenos Aires Province that surround the city of Buenos Aires, which is not part of the province.

[12] Surveys conducted between 1991 and 1996 by the survey firm Estudio Graciela Romer y Asociados. It included a probabilistic sample of residents from the city of Buenos Aires

legislator wrote in the 1990s, "the demand for security coming from the population of the province has grown to the point of emerging as one of the central demands of society toward their political representatives" (Sigal, Binder & Annichiarico 1998, 28).

This societal demand for security emerged not only as a result of rising crime; it was also shaped in important ways by the profound economic crisis of the late 1980s and 1990s and the widespread social unrest it engendered. Argentine scholars have written extensively about these contemporaneous phenomena, starting with the fallout from hyperinflation in 1989 as a turning point: "In this period there was an important increase in crime at the national level and there came to be, in the public sphere, a close association between the social question and the criminal question" (Kessler 2009a, 77). In the face of rising unemployment[13] and poverty,[14] social discontent caused by these conditions came to be expressed in increasingly contentious forms, from hundreds of instances of lootings in 1989 (Cerruti 2011) to hundreds of protests annually throughout the 1990s, including the increased use of roadblocks (Schuster et al. 2006).

These changes in the nature of protest repertoires in response to economic upheaval, austerity, and the decline of the Argentine welfare state shifted citizens' understanding of rising crime and violence and their concomitant demands for policing and security. These demands manifested as the criminalization and repression of protest (CELS 2003), on the one hand, and, on the other, the criminalization and repression of marginalized social sectors seen as the source of both rising crime and rising protest – what Kessler (2009a) calls "strong causal attribution between the social crisis and crime" (77).

---

(300) and the *conurbano* (405). Results reported here are only from the latter sample. The survey was accessed via the Latin American Databank housed at the Roper Center Public Opinion Archives at the University of Connecticut.

[13] Unemployment rose from 4.6 percent in 1984 to 7.7 percent in 1989 and to 15 percent by 2000. Data from CEPALSTAT database, UN Economic Commission on Latin America and the Caribbean. Retrieved from http://estadisticas.cepal.org.

[14] According to household surveys conducted by Argentina's statistical agency, INDEC, more than half the residents of Greater Buenos Aires (the national capital of the city of Buenos Aires, as well as the surrounding twenty-four municipalities of the Province of Buenos Aires) came to live under the poverty line in the face of hyperinflation (56 percent in 1989 and 50 percent in 1990), falling to 20 percent by 1994, before rising again to 33 percent by the end of the decade. Data from Encuesta Permanente de Hogares, INDEC. Retrieved from www.indec.gob.ar.

Demands over policing in the face of rising violence thus became inextricably linked to the social transformations brought about by the economic crisis. But such demands were themselves transformed in the face of the *Bonaerense*'s institutional decay. As Cerruti (2011) writes, "the 'neighbors' demand 'greater police protection' and, in its absence, take protection into their own hands" (12). Perceiving the police to be incompetent in protecting them from crime and their elected representatives unwilling to improve security, many citizens opted for private security (Eaton 2008, 6) and private violence (Chevigny 1995, 186). According to one news report from 1993, there were 800 private security companies in Argentina, of which 350 were in the Province of Buenos Aires alone, with a total of 40,000 official guards (and as many as 30,000 unofficial guards).[15] But citizens "taking the law into their own hands" also became an increasingly common phenomenon throughout the 1990s, with one prominent newspaper going so far as to declare "a virtual war of all against all."[16]

Security conditions thus posed a number of significant challenges for Argentina's nascent democracy. As crime increased in Buenos Aires Province, the police became the center of urgent societal demands for security, a growing pressure that was exacerbated by the country's massive economic crisis. But the *Bonaerense* proved incapable of responding to the shifting patterns of crime and violence, demonstrating to the citizenry that it could not count on its police force to provide the security necessary to engage in the everyday activities that are constitutive of democratic citizenship. Instead, residents of Buenos Aires Province responded to what they saw as police absence and incompetence by "taking the law into their own hands," relying on modes of private violence that not only contravene the rule of law but also contest the state's very monopoly of legitimate coercion. As I discuss in the next section, the state's response to these challenges was the consolidation of authoritarian coercion in democracy, an expansion of the very coercive practices and structures citizens had endured under the dictatorship, while democratic institutions and leaders showed little capacity and little will to enact structural reforms to promote democratic coercion. As I demonstrate in subsequent sections, the fragmented nature of societal demands over policing helped convince politicians that undertaking such reforms would not be electorally advantageous.

---

[15] "Un ejército privado," *Clarín*, June 27, 1993.
[16] "Una virtual guerra de todos contra todos," *Clarín*, March 13, 1993, 31.

THE PERSISTENCE OF AUTHORITARIAN COERCION
IN DEMOCRACY

The state's response to citizens' demands for the security that is essential to any democracy was not to develop the police's capacity to protect citizens from crime. Instead, the *Bonaerense* built a perverse capacity to perform not what Taylor (2011) calls its "routine" role of providing security but rather an expansive system of "exceptional" coercion, by which it regulated criminal activity through means that fall outside the scope of the law. Despite resulting in widespread violence and predation against the population, democratically elected leaders in the province sought to accommodate the police, granting it extensive autonomy in exchange for cooperation with their political objectives. Although this ability to constrain the policy options available to politicians is character-istic of all police forces by virtue of their control of coercion, the *Bonaerense*'s structural power enabled them to consolidate a sprawling system of authoritarian coercion. The provincial police not only engaged in widespread arbitrary deployment of coercion, from the predatory system of *"recaudación"* to extrajudicial killings and torture; it also did so in the interest of political leaders and largely unconstrained by mech-anisms of external accountability. Despite the great strides toward dem-ocratization by Argentine leaders during this period, the provincial police remained an authoritarian enclave.

Arbitrary Deployment of Coercion – the Age of *"Gatillo Fácil"*

One key manifestation of authoritarian coercion in Buenos Aires Province since the transition to democracy has been the persistence of high levels of extralegal violence against civilians. Coercive practices typical under the dictatorship – such as torture, executions made to appear as shootouts, and even disappearances[17] – remained common during the 1980s and 1990s. In a joint report on the subject, the US human rights NGO Human Rights Watch and the Argentine human rights organization CELS reported that, between 1985 and 1989, the Buenos Aires provincial police killed 705 civilians in the municipalities of Greater Buenos Aires (Americas Watch & CELS 1991, 12). Between 1990 and 2000, meanwhile, approximately 1,200

---

[17] For instance, among twenty cases of police violence reviewed by the provincial Supreme Court in 1993, three involved enforced disappearance, though the victim's body was subsequently found in one of the cases. See "La Suprema Corte bonaerense investiga a la Policía por 20 muertes y desapariciones," *Clarín*, October 25, 1993, 40.

civilians were killed at the hands of the provincial police in the *conurbano* (Brinks 2008, 45). Torture, "the distinctive horror of life under the military dictatorship" (Americas Watch & CELS 1991, 19), also continued well into the democratic period. Although there are no systematic counts of instances of torture – neither official data that are publicly available nor media-based counts by civil society organizations – one count of proceedings initiated by criminal court judges found nearly 1,800 cases for *"apremios ilegales,"* the legal charge under which instances of torture were often categorized, in just 1989 and 1990 (Americas Watch & CELS 1991, 19).

The nature of lethal coercion exercised by the provincial police is indicative of the extent to which it routinely contravened the rule of law. Table 4.1 reports data on police killings during the 1980s and 1990s obtained from a database of such killings maintained by CELS, culled from daily news reports. The data presented correspond to the decade-and-a-half period between the transition to democracy in 1983 and the enactment of ambitious structural reforms in 1998. Though these data are not without their limitations,[18] they provide an estimate of 1,600 civilians killed by police in Buenos Aires Province during this "pre-reform" period, approximately 100 people each year.

Aside from the elevated numbers of civilians killed by police officers, some characteristics of these killings presented in Table 4.1 suggest their exceptional nature, indicative of authoritarian coercion. First, the available data indicate that the number of police killings each year is equivalent to a significant proportion of total homicides in the province. In 1984, for instance, there were a total of 678 homicides in the province and 160 civilians killed by police – the equivalent of nearly one-quarter of homicides (Americas Watch & CELS 1991, 13). Although this proportion fell considerably by the 1990s, the *Bonaerense* was nevertheless responsible for the equivalent of 10 percent of homicides during this period. Second, an additional feature of the violence that many human rights groups point to in questioning the extent to which the police's use of deadly violence conforms to the requirements of the law is the discrepancy between the number of civilians killed and the number of officers killed, the majority of them while off duty (Americas Watch & CELS 1991; CELS 1997; Chevigny 1995). The difference between

---

[18] Publicly available official data in Buenos Aires Province about the number of civilians killed by the police are very difficult to come by. For this reason, CELS and another NGO, CORREPI, construct their own databases from news reports and reports by family members of victims. For a critique of newspapers as data sources, see Ortiz et al. (2005).

TABLE 4.1 *Pre-reform police killings and fatalities in Buenos Aires Province* (conurbano)

Year	Civilians killed	Police killings as % of homicides**	Police officers killed	Percentage killed off-duty
1984	160			
1985*	78			
1986	148			
1987	102			
1988	92			
1989	72			
1990	48			
1991	108	10%		
1992	102	7%		
1993	123	11%	23	43%
1994	94	9%	9	78%
1995	123	12%	28	79%
1996	115	10%	45	53%
1997	123	9%	39	64%
1998	114	10%	43	
Total	1602			

Data for 1984–1990 are from Americas Watch and CELS (1991). Data for 1991–1998 are from CELS annual reports *Informe sobre la situación de los derechos humanos en Argentina* (CELS 1994, 1997, 1998).
* The number of civilians killed for 1985 refers only to the second semester of that year.
** Annual data on homicides retrieved from "Informe Anual de Estadísticas Policiales. Año 2002," Sistema Nacional de Información Criminal, Ministerio de Justicia, Seguridad, y Derechos Humanos.

civilians and police officers killed in what the police claim as shootouts "indicates a modus operandi on the part of state agencies that privileges the elimination of the suspect, rather than other peaceful means of deterrence" (CELS 1997, 17).[19]

---

[19] The provincial police's organic law at the time required police officers, including off-duty and retired officers, to carry their firearms at all times and to intervene if they observe a crime being committed (Decree-Law 9550/1980, Art. 14). However, the proportion of police killings committed by off-duty officers in Buenos Aires Province is much higher than in the city of Buenos Aires, where the same obligation applies. In Buenos Aires Province, 39 percent of civilians killed were shot by off-duty officers in 1997; in the city of Buenos Aires, meanwhile, only 10 percent of civilians were killed by officers who were off duty (CELS 1997, 8).

Additional characteristics are indicative of the arbitrary nature of cases of fatal police violence in Buenos Aires Province. While we do not have systematic information about all police killings (since these figures come from newspaper reports), there is ample evidence that police officers routinely deploy exceptional coercive practices after many of these killings, suggesting that the police officers involved did not have legal justification for the use of lethal force. In a study of dozens of cases of police violence in Argentina, Human Rights Watch and CELS provided an analysis of "patterns of police conduct intended to impede or confuse the investigation of killings": the construction of a false version of events that incriminates the victim, including through the placement of a firearm after the victim has been killed and framing the victims for crimes they did not commit; hiding, fabrication, or destruction of evidence; and threats and retaliation against witnesses (Human Rights Watch & CELS 1998, 56). Similarly, in his study of 260 criminal trials involving police killings in Buenos Aires City and the surrounding municipalities of Greater Buenos Aires between 1990 and 2000, Brinks (2008) finds widespread evidence of this extralegal conduct by police. The provincial police in particular "threaten witnesses and lawyers, plant guns, rearrange the scene of the crime to simulate a shootout, and similarly corrupt the record in 73% of the cases in which one of their colleagues is a defendant" (Brinks 2008, 123). The fact that 13 percent of the killings studied by Brinks were deaths resulting from torture also indicates extralegal use of force. These analyses demonstrate that police officers routinely use a common set of extralegal coercive practices to conceal the facts surrounding killings, providing strong evidence that the killings themselves fell outside the scope of the rule of law.

Long before the enactment of comprehensive structural reforms, there was widespread awareness in Buenos Aires Province that the *Bonaerense* routinely used extralegal violence against the citizenry. As noted in the introduction to this chapter, Argentine civil society actors coined the term *"gatillo fácil"* (trigger-happy) to describe what would come to be a familiar modality of police violence, epitomized in what came to be known as "the massacre of Ingeniero Budge." In that case, three police officers shot thirty-nine rounds at three young men who were drinking beers at a bar on a street corner; the officers were searching for them because they had been involved in an altercation at a different bar.[20] What followed was a familiar pattern of extralegal police practices to conceal an

---

[20] "Llegó la hora de la verdad para los policías acusados," *Clarín*, June 24, 1994.

extrajudicial execution: the fatal shooting of three unarmed victims sub-sequently characterized as a confrontation,[21] the "planting" of guns next to the victims' bodies,[22] the concealment of evidence,[23] and threats against witnesses.[24] The "massacre of Ingeniero Budge" may be known as the "first case of '*gatillo fácil*' since the return to democracy,"[25] but it would be far from the last in Buenos Aires Province. From Roberto Ramón Roldán – a father rushing his three-year-old daughter to the emergency room fatally shot by police when he did not stop his car[26] – to Cristian Campos – a sixteen-year-old who was out buying diapers when he was shot and burned alive by police as retaliation for an earlier disagreement[27] – the routine deployment of extralegal coercion by the provincial police was widely reported and acknowledged even by state officials with the authority to hold the police externally accountable. As one such provincial official, a Radical Party legislator who requested a Supreme Court review of twenty cases of police killings and disappear-ances in 1993, put it, "it's alarming the frequency with which part of the police force engages in practices we thought we had overcome."[28]

Arbitrary Deployment of Coercion – "*Recaudación*"

The most far-reaching manifestation of the authoritarian nature of pro-vincial police's coercive practices was the system of rent extraction described above as "collection" or *recaudación*. The *Bonaerense* utilized its coercive authority to extract these rents from both licit and illicit enterprises. As a policing expert with the NGO CELS described it, the police of Buenos Aires Province maintain "an iron-clad territorial control, with important linkages to the networks of illegality in the province,

---

[21] "Un testigo clave vio cómo los policías mataban a los 3 jóvenes desarmados," *Clarín*, June 16, 1994.
[22] "Un testigo vio cuando colocaban las armas al lado de los cadáveres," *Clarín*, June 15, 1994.
[23] "Reclaman entre 20 y 18 años de cárcel para los 3 policías acusados," *Clarín*, June 22, 1994.
[24] "Denuncian amenazas dos mujeres que participaron en el juicio de los policías," *Clarín*, June 28, 1994.
[25] "A 30 años de la masacre de Budge," *Página/12*, May 8, 2017.
[26] "Un policía mató a un hombre que iba a internar urgente a su hija," *Clarín*, February 23, 1996.
[27] "El chico asesinado por los policías aun vivía cuando lo quemaron," *Clarín*, March 12, 1996.
[28] "La Suprema Corte bonaerense investiga la Policía por 20 muertes y desapariciones," *Clarín*, October 25, 1993.

[entailing] the control of legal and illegal businesses."²⁹ In the case of the former, the police demand periodic payments from legal businesses in exchange for protection³⁰ but also in order to avoid being subjected to future police operations, inspections, and other inconveniences.³¹ Police involvement in illicit businesses, meanwhile, is more complex and varied. It ranges from collecting a monthly fee from establishments engaged in prostitution, illegal gambling, etc., (the sort of practices on which *recaudación* had traditionally been based) in order to be allowed to operate without the intervention of state officials; to the protection and collaboration with car-theft rings,³² drug-trafficking groups, and other types of organized crime; and murder-for-hire, as in the killing of photo-journalist José Luis Cabezas (described in Chapter 7). Luis Lugones, a provincial legislator subsequently appointed to lead the civilian inter-vention of the *Bonaerense* in December 1997, explained in an interview how the system works:

> Some police commanders managed structures linked to a certain crime, for example, car theft or drug trafficking. There were police units dedicated to each issue and the commanders made them autonomous [relative to the rest of the police force] and they turned [these units] into their own hunting reserve, their own fiefdom. The same thing happened with territorial jurisdictions correspond-ing to the structural divisions of the police, the Regional Units.³³

Recaudación, an extralegal system of predation against the population, was also interlinked with extralegal violence, as the provincial police's vast involvement in crime ultimately led to more crime and violence rather

---

²⁹ Author interview with Marcela Perelman, security policy and institutional violence coordinator, CELS, Buenos Aires, August 26, 2011.

³⁰ See, for instance, "¡Peligro!, policía protege la zona," *Página/12*, September 22, 1995; "Una vaquita atada: Comerciantes platenses cuentan como pagan la 'protección,'" *Página/12*, September 23, 1995.

³¹ See, for instance, a news report on the practice: "Bailanta con cámara oculta," *Página/12*, August 2, 2000.

³² This particular mode of police–crime linkage was so well known it was even reported on in the *New York Times*: "Thieves would steal a car and sell it with fake registration papers to an unsuspecting buyer, [a prosecutor] said. The police would then seize the car, threaten the new owner with jail unless he paid hefty bribes, and give the car back to the thieves. The cycle would be repeated sometimes three or four times before the car would be turned over to a chop shop and dismantled. The sums raised through such schemes are huge: as much as $30,000 a month in profits and bribes from the richest of the province's 300 police stations, according to prosecutors and former police officials." See Larry Rohter, "Police Corruption Plagues Argentine and President," *New York Times*, August 4, 2004.

³³ Author interview with Luis Lugones, La Plata, September 14, 2011.

than less. Arslanian, the minister of security who led two waves of profound structural reforms, noted in an interview that police sometimes "would fabricate some serious crime, take action by killing [the perpetrators], but that crime had been fabricated by [the police], sending in unsuspecting people, *perejiles*,[34] as they say, to carry it out."[35] Another former high-ranking provincial security official, Marcelo Saín, similarly wrote about the linkage between extralegal violence and the system of extralegal rent extraction: "Torture, extrajudicial executions, enforced disappearances . . . these illegal practices permitted the seamless reproduction of the system of illegal self-financing resulting from the sophisticated network of illegal collection of dirty funds" (Saín 2015, 121).

The highly lucrative[36] nature of the system of *recaudación* has undoubtedly contributed to its endurance over time and across regime types, from the "task forces" that operated during the last military dictatorship, which "had to finance themselves independently of the public coffers" (Saín 2002, 64), to the contemporary system of self-finance to compensate for an insufficient budget (Dewey 2012). But the durability of this entrenched system of arbitrary coercion is also due to its ability to adapt to the exigencies of democratic politics. As I will discuss, *recaudación* has also served as a highly valuable corollary to the provincial police's coercive authority that, like coercion generally, police deploy strategically in the interest of political leaders – and that it can also credibly threaten to withdraw.

Coercion in the Interest of Political Leaders

Understanding why the provincial police continued to engage in coercive "practices we thought we had overcome," as the legislator cited earlier put it, becomes easier once we consider how those authoritarian coercive practices are deployed selectively in the interest of political leaders. Although many politicians engage in mutually beneficial exchanges with police, accommodation in Buenos Aires Province entailed the use of extralegal coercive practices – from surveillance and repression of political

---

[34] In Argentine slang, *perejil* (parsley) refers to something so abundant as to have very little value.

[35] Author interview with Carlos León Arslanian, Buenos Aires, September 12, 2011.

[36] According to a 2010 investigative report by the magazine *Noticias*, these activities in total gross up to $300 million pesos (about US$75 million) between the more than 300 police stations in the province. See "Pruebas y confesiones de la corrupción policial," *Noticias*, April 30, 2010.

opponents to sharing the profits of the system of *recaudación* – for the benefit of politicians.

Following a long tradition of authoritarian leaders utilizing the police's coercive and surveillance structures against political opponents (Kalmanowiecki 2000), journalists documented how the *Bonaerense* spied on political opponents of Governor Eduardo Duhalde during the mid-1990s,[37] including Ramón "Palito" Ortega, who, like Duhalde, was vying to be the Peronist candidate in the upcoming presidential elections. Duhalde also utilized the police selectively to repress protests by political opponents (Saín 2006). Perhaps it was due to such cooperation that Duhalde said he viewed police chief Pedro Klodczyk as a "true guarantee" and prohibited his secretary of security from removing Klodczyk in 1994, despite an acknowledged "crisis" facing the *Bonaerense*.[38]

But without a doubt the most significant manifestation of the exercise of coercion to serve the interests of political leaders has been the role of politicians and political parties in the vast network of *recaudación*. Although, for obvious reasons, the phenomenon has not been subject to much empirical investigation,[39] many observers claim that "politicians offer protection to police officers in exchange for a cut of the funds that the police raise through a variety of protection rackets" (Eaton 2008, 19). These funds from illicit activities are then reportedly funneled to political parties and electoral campaigns of particular mayors. As one former chief of the *Bonaerense* put it, "for every corrupt police officer there is a corrupt politician."[40]

While it is difficult to obtain systematic evidence of the contours and structures of the police-political networks of *recaudación*, interviews with security officials in the province provide a sense of the types of linkages it entailed and the expectation of protection that formed part of the exchange relationship. One key element of the police–politician network was the role of mayors, particularly those of the *conurbano*, the municipalities surrounding the city of Buenos Aires that were then home to one-quarter of the national population (and electorate) and larger than many provinces. Tellingly, although Duhalde said he viewed the police chief as

---

[37] "Secretos compartidos," *Página/12*, May 10, 1998.
[38] "Piotti aceptó el timón de la seguridad bonaerense," *Página/12*, February 18, 1994; "Piotti promete remover la cúpula de la policía," *Página/12*, February 19, 1994.
[39] Nevertheless, accounts of these relationships have existed for at least three decades; see Americas Watch and CELS (1991, 8).
[40] "Plata sucia: La masacre de Ramallo y el financiamiento de la política," *Página/12*, September 26, 1999.

a "true guarantee" while serving as governor, the two first formed a relationship while Duhalde was the mayor of the municipality of Lomas de Zamora in 1987.[41] Although mayors did not have any formal powers over policing under the Argentine Constitution at the time, they nevertheless formed close ties to their local police chiefs, a relationship that provincial security officials often linked to the system of *recaudación*. Marcelo Saín, a scholar, politician, and former vice minister of security in the province, describes the relationship as follows:

The *Bonaerense* police is a part of [mayors'] governance structure at the local level: the *comisarios*, the financing of politics, the intelligence tasks, the pressure on political opponents. It's a great political tool. The police plays [the game] with the Peronist party and the local mayors ... Almost all of the local mayors participated in this consortium."[42]

For many observers, the clearest evidence that police deploy coercion in the interest of politicians – and the debt the latter owe the former – is the massive intervention of mayors (and legislators) to prevent the removal of their local commanders during the anti-corruption purges carried out by secretaries and ministers of security since the 1980s.[43] One example was Luis Patti, a former police commander subsequently convicted[44] for torture and homicide committed during the dictatorship who at the time was the mayor of the municipality of Escobar. According to Eduardo de Lázzari,[45] who was brought in as secretary of security to battle corruption within the *Bonaerense*:

I had a problem with Patti, the famous Patti – who was the mayor of Escobar at the time – because I removed a police commander that he had in his zone. At first he started off well: 'This commander is really good,' etc., until finally when I emphatically said 'no,' I remember it clearly, he said, 'From this moment on, you have an enemy.' And he hung up.

According to Secretary de Lázzari, the fervent protection Patti and other mayors granted to their local police chiefs was not due to programmatic reasons:

---

[41] "Decidieron el recambio del jefe de la Policía Bonaerense," *Clarín*, March 20, 1996.
[42] Author interview with Marcelo Saín, Buenos Aires, October 17, 2011.
[43] See, for instance, the experience of Luis Brunati, charged with overseeing security in the late 1980s: "La historia de un precursor," *Página/12*, April 11, 2004. Another former official who was involved in implementing the purges during the civil intervention of the police that began in late 1997 recalled that in just one day he received seventy-four calls from mayors (and judges) to lobby for their local police chief. "Plata sucia: La masacre de Ramallo y el financiamiento de la política, " *Página/12*, September 26, 1999.
[44] "Condenaron a Luis Patti a prisión perpetua," *La Nación*, April 15, 2011.
[45] Author interview with Eduardo de Lázzari, La Plata, October 19, 2011.

The mayors create alliances with certain chiefs of their respective police district. So if I tried to touch a police officer that was shielded by some mayor, that mayor would come to me in a fury, with the demand that I not remove this chief to put in that other chief ... It is extremely clear that there was a political motive in relation to the police in [the mayor's] zone. It's not casual, it's not free; it's not because they like the [commander's] face. It's because ultimately they form a series of relations between the local mayor and the local police for mutual benefit.

Some mayors deny that their intervention on behalf of police is done in support of or due to complicity with extralegal coercive practices. I interviewed a former Peronist mayor of one of the municipalities of the *conurbano* who held office at the time of the reform in the 1990s. He was emphatic that he never accepted any money from police and that the claim of alleged connivance between police and mayors is an "erroneous supposition." Instead, he attributed his own opposition to the widespread removal of police officials to the "confusion" it generates within the institution, since "it was never clear to me why the ones who are kicked out are kicked out and why the ones that stay, stay ... I'm not saying that they were good or that they have to stay. But if these [officers] go for this reason, why is that other one staying despite having done the same thing?"[46]

A provincial legislator from the opposition made a similar distinction about the relationship of mayors to the system of *recaudación*. In an interview, Graciela Podestá, who served as president of the Security Committee in the provincial Chamber of Deputies in the late 1990s, underscored how the police's control over coercion makes it both a valuable political instrument and a potent threat:

The police had a certain power over the mayor because it controls everything, gambling, prostitution, etc., and so the honest mayors didn't get involved because they knew it was a very delicate space and they were fearful. There were other mayors that, without them, prostitution, gambling, chop shops, etc. would've never been able to exist ... Some mayors celebrated what we were doing, that we were questioning all of this, and they encouraged us and gave us tools to keep doing this work. And there were other mayors that, by deduction, we might say, by action or inaction were part of criminal acts ... They were either afraid of it or they were part of it.[47]

Though it has been denounced by security officials and directly referenced by scholars (Dewey 2012; Eaton 2008), to date there have been no

---

[46] Author interview with anonymous mayor, location and date withheld.
[47] Author interview with Graciela Podestá, Vicente López, Buenos Aires Province, November 2, 2011.

systematic, far-reaching official investigations exposing the use of illicit police funds to finance politicians or political parties. But even if the police's "contribution" to the exchange relationship remains opaque, what they receive in return from politicians is clear: protection and autonomy. Civilian security officials over a decade-long period denounced obstruction efforts from municipal and provincial politicians, shielding police from external accountability and perpetuating extralegal coercion, bolstering the claims of those who assert that these arbitrary coercive practices serve their political interests and are functional to their electoral goals.

Weakness of External Accountability

As the previous section suggests, the provincial police force successfully leveraged its political relationships to thwart external accountability. Former minister of security Arslanian described how this accommodation of police by politicians all but guaranteed there would be no external interference:

The police responded fundamentally to the political power ... There was a pact between the police and the political authorities. The pact consisted of self-governance (*autogobierno*) by the police; it was a completely 'corporativized' institution. It was like a closed nutshell that had a stem of sorts that was the police chief. The political authorities would refer or link to the police through that chief, who they might occasionally replace if there were things that were not satisfactory or didn't function well. But what they could not do – because they were not in a position to and did not have the political will to do – was break open that nutshell and see what was inside: what had to be disposed of and what had to be reorganized inside of that nutshell."

Arslanian's metaphor of not breaking open the nutshell aptly characterizes the stark limitations of external accountability in Buenos Aires Province. The *Bonaerense* thus exemplifies what I argued in Chapter 1, that a police force's control over coercion endows it with a great deal of structural power that it can leverage to defend its interests and preserve its autonomy. Although a number of civilian officials occasionally sounded the alarm about the extent of police involvement in extralegal violence or corruption, there were few formal mechanisms of external accountability, whether within the executive branch, the legislature, or the judiciary.

The constrained sphere of action of the primary entity charged with external oversight of the provincial police in the pre-reform period, the Secretariat of Public Security, is illustrative of the weakness of external accountability mechanisms. In interviews, Duhalde's first two secretaries of security – Eduardo Pettigiani (1992–1994) and Alberto Piotti (1994–1996) – indicated that their central task was far from ensuring that the provincial police adhered to the limits of the law, sanctioning conduct that fell outside the scope of the law, or having much of a role in setting security policy at all. When he began his tenure as the province's first secretary of security under Governor Eduardo Duhalde in January 1992, Eduardo Pettigiani recalls that his predecessor's office "had been virtually deactivated, it had been directed de facto by officers from the police force."[48] Although Pettigiani insisted that policing and security were a major priority for Governor Duhalde, as evidenced by the creation of the Secretariat of Security and an increase in financial, human, and material resources (Saín 2015, 101), this prioritization did not extend to civilian oversight of the police. Pettigiani observed that, by the end of his tenure, "in practice, the management [of the institution], as well as the achievements obtained, were the product of the execution of a plan designed and implemented by the [police] itself."

Pettigiani's successor, Alberto Piotti, took over as secretary of security during what he characterized as a "crisis facing the police force in recent months."[49] In an interview, however, he described his only mandate from Governor Duhalde as "to take charge (*hacete cargo*), don't bring me any problems, take responsibility (*poné la cara*)." Piotti came to the Secretariat with plans to "remove the police's command structure," but he admitted that he had been prohibited by Governor Duhalde from removing the police chief, Pedro Klodczyk.[50] Of his term as secretary, Piotti spoke of the impossibility of resolving problems or even thinking about meaningful change while he was ostensibly in charge of overseeing the *Bonaerense*:

From that euphoria when you come in thinking, 'I'm going to solve something, I'm going to improve something,' ... you go on to frustration, *desazón*, and then you realize that what you're doing, every single day, is patching holes on a tire that every day becomes more deformed, and you become conscious of the fact that you cannot resolve these things ... [You come in] thinking that you're going to be Messi in Barcelona, and you end up being some no-name in the Deportivo Flandria.[51]

---

[48] Author interview with Eduardo Pettigiani, who at the time was serving as the Chief Justice of the provincial Supreme Court. Interview conducted in writing; responses were received on December 5, 2011.

[49] "Piotti promete remover la cúpula de la policía," *Página/12*, February 19, 1994.

[50] "Piotti promete remover la cúpula de la policía," *Página/12*, February 19, 1994.

[51] Author interview with Alberto Piotti, Buenos Aires, November 2, 2011. Lionel Messi is considered the best soccer player in the world and plays for the Futbol Club Barcelona.

Even Piotti's successor, Eduardo de Lázzari (1996–1997), despite undertaking arguably the most far-reaching, if ad hoc, intervention by civilian officials to roll back the authoritarian coercive practices by the *Bonaerense* in the pre-reform period, described his time in this post as "a sensation of trying to disarm a bomb that is about to explode and then you discover that there is another bomb."

These reflections by three consecutive secretaries of security from the pre-reform period underscore the extent to which the focus of the entity they led was not to provide meaningful oversight of a police force that was both ineffective in addressing citizens' increasingly urgent demands for security and engaged in widespread violence and predation against them. Instead, the top civilian entity in the province charged with the governance of security under the Duhalde administration was focused on problem management, to paraphrase Duhalde's explicit charge to Piotti. Consider, for instance, Pettigiani's response to a growing concern about police violence throughout 1993, with journalists and civil society actors reacting with alarm to five recent killings of teens at the hands of the provincial police, referring to the killings as *gatillo fácil*.[52] Pettigiani was forced to respond in an op-ed in Argentina's main newspaper, *Clarín*, addressing societal concern after the recent killings, which the newspaper called "inexplicable." Although "it has become commonplace to speak of the 'trigger-happy police,'" he wrote, "the police response has been proportional to the aggression. There are many isolated arbitrary acts among its members, considering that the Police of Buenos Aires Province has 45,000 officers in active duty. Elevating these exceptional cases to the level of a norm would be incurring upon a fallacy, confusing public opinion."[53] Thus, despite ample evidence that a large proportion of police killings were taking place well outside the bounds of the law, the civilian official directly responsible for overseeing the police, and the elected officials to which he reported, did not intervene to reduce the provincial police's unquestionably authoritarian coercive practices. Instead, he sought to reduce criticism of the provincial police.[54]

Deportivo Flandria is a soccer club in the interior of Buenos Aires Province that plays in the low-level C Division of the Argentine football league.

[52] "¿Por qué esta locura criminal?," *Clarín*, August 8, 1993, 36.

[53] Eduardo Pettigiani, "Esta policía no es de gatillo fácil," *Clarín*, August 12, 1993.

[54] In an indication of the extent to which the Secretariat of Security was focused on managing the public relations problem, one of the men who served as secretary of security under Duhalde told me in an interview, "During my first few days [as secretary], a journalist came to interview me. He said, 'I represent a group of journalists; you

Two instances in which secretaries of security attempted to use the main instrument of external accountability exercised by the executive branch – purges – are illustrative of the obstacles impeding the ability of that entity to serve as an instance of external accountability in the pre-reform period. In 1987, Luis Brunati, then minister of government,[55] attempted to root out corruption among the *Bonaerense* police by firing dozens of high-ranking police officials and hundreds of rank-and-file officers suspected of involvement in the system of *recaudación* and investigating corrupt activity in police stations. Brunati's efforts were met with staunch police resistance throughout 1988. Police leaders published a document criticizing his policies; rank-and-file officers "reduced patrols and left banks and public buildings with practically nonexistent security during several days"; and more than 1,000 police officers marched to the provincial government building, chanting "the police, united, will never be defeated" (Saín 2015, 93–95). In an interview decades later, however, Brunati cited political pressure, not police resistance, as the reason for his removal. Brunati recalled being summoned to a meeting with the governor and nearly all Peronist legislators, during which he was told that his policies "generated a lot of tensions, generated a lot of noise. Supporting such policies had become too costly."[56]

Nearly a decade later, Eduardo de Lázzari was brought on as secretary of security to carry out a similar "cleansing of the police personnel," to similar results.[57] In 1996, amid a series of police scandals that prompted the resignation of police chief Klodczyk[58] – Governor Duhalde's "true guarantee" – the governor brought de Lázzari on board to once again root out corruption in the *"maldita policía"* (the damned police), as a recent news exposé had labeled the *Bonaerense*.[59] De Lázzari said that "the philosophy of this effort was first and foremost to establish a civilian authority above the police force," but the outcome of his effort attests to

---

know how these things work.' It turns out that he said, 'This group of journalists tries to publicize the good work of each [secretary] in the press. There has to be a contribution each month.' He hands me a piece of paper: 'This guy 5,000 pesos, this other guy 3,500 pesos,' etc ... There were well-known names." The name of the interviewee, as well as date and location of the interview, withheld due to the nature of the allegations made by the interviewee.

55 Prior to the administration of Duhalde, the provincial police was under the jurisdiction of the minister of government.

56 "La historia de un precursor," *Página/12*, April 11, 2004.

57 Author interview with Eduardo de Lázzari, La Plata, October 19, 2011.

58 "Decidieron el recambio del jefe de la Policía Bonaerense," *Clarín*, March 20, 1996.

59 Carlos Dutil and Ricardo Ragendorfer, "Maldita Policía," *Noticias*, August 1996.

the obstacles to doing so. He began by drafting legislation declaring a state of emergency in the police force (Law 11.880/1996), enabling the rapid firing or forced retirement of large numbers of officers. Per de Lázzari, he fired more than 1,000 rank-and-file officers; "filed criminal complaints for illicit enrichment against high-ranking police commanders, in a case that incriminated fifty commanders"; "executed search warrants in police stations where we had reports of bribery"; and audited the system of contracts and purchases, "where we found many things that weren't right."

Like Brunati, de Lázzari described considerable resistance from police: "This resistance resulted in threats, attacks against my former residence, in the sense of bullet holes ... I was spied upon. They set up shop in the building across the street and captured all of my conversations. These were police officers." De Lázzari said police "circulated pamphlets saying I wanted to destroy the police, that I was a Marxist," and complained to state legislators. De Lázzari also shared an anecdote to illustrate the contempt in which he was held by the police due to his efforts: "During a celebration for [a police official], they had a doll sitting at one end of the table, and it had my face on it. One by one the officers would pass by the doll and urinate on it." De Lázzari also recalled clashing with the new police chief, Adolfo Vitelli. In a scene quite similar to that described by Brunati, news reports claimed that when de Lázzari went to communicate his displeasure with Vitelli to Duhalde, "Duhalde received him with Vitelli at his side. The one who left his post was de Lázzari."[60] De Lázzari told me in our interview that he left of his own accord and that he felt he had the governor's support throughout his tenure. What is undeniable, though, is that de Lázzari, like Brunati, served in this position for less than a year and was replaced by Carlos Brown, a Peronist operative.

The fate of Brunati and de Lázzari attest to the obstacles to external accountability, even by the very entity explicitly charged with civilian oversight of the police. In both cases, the police exerted their structural power by withdrawing their services and leveraging political relationships to thwart the efforts of civilian officials charged with overseeing them – and ultimately have them removed. Elected officials accommodated the police, reinforcing what de Lázzari described as the police's view of periodic efforts to root out corruption: "They [the police] will always be here; the [civilian] officials come and go."

---

[60] Horacio Verbitsky, "Bonaerenses," *Página/12*, August 18, 2002.

Even these purges, the main instrument of external accountability exercised by the executive branch throughout the 1990s, underscore the extent to which civilian officials saw their policy options as constrained. Although de Lázzari and Brunati tout the number of ostensibly corrupt officers they fired during their terms, the use of ad hoc and legally dubious purges fell far short given the magnitude of the *Bonaerense*'s vast extra-legal practices and structures. Such periodic purges resulted in the expulsion of 3,805 police officers suspected of corruption and criminal activity between 1992 and 1996 – approximately 8 percent of the police force.[61] Not only did these firings not disrupt the underlying systems of *recaudación* and other extralegal structures, they also, as journalists noted at the time, created "thousands of unemployed people, whose only experience is limited to the use of firearms."[62]

Even as the executive branch showed remarkable reluctance to provide systematic oversight of the police force, the legislative branch was no more effective an instrument of external accountability. Although individual legislators were active and vocal in their expressions of concern about the state of policing and security in the province, there was little systematic effort by the provincial legislature to use its authority to conduct external oversight of the *Bonaerense*.

Consider, for instance, the nature of legislative debate around policing in the years prior to the enactment of reform but following widespread awareness about rampant extralegal violence and corruption by the provincial police.[63] Table 4.2 provides a summary of all legislative actions[64] on the issue of policing in the provincial Senate for the years 1995 and

---

[61] This figure is also less than the 6,000 officers that joined the force during Duhalde's first term (1991–1995). See Governor Eduardo Duhalde's speech to the provincial legislature inaugurating his second term, December 11, 1995. *Diario de Sesiones*, Senado de Buenos Aires, Período 123, Reunión 29.

[62] "Al borde del sistema," *Clarín*, April 20, 1997.

[63] Recall, for instance, that Secretary of Security Alberto Piotti admitted that the provincial police was facing a crisis upon beginning his tenure in 1994.

[64] I coded legislative actions (including announcements, declarations, bills, and requests for information submitted to the legislative branch) regarding the provincial police during two legislative periods – the 123rd (beginning March 1, 1995, and ending February 1996) and the 124th (beginning March 1, 1996, and ending February 1997), during which the Senate met eighty-two times. Data are from the *Diario de Sesiones*, the Senate's legislative record of proceedings. There are limitations to this analysis: it does not include the provincial Chamber of Deputies, nor does it offer a comprehensive accounting of all legislative actions that may have occurred in specific committees, such as the Security Committee or the Human Rights Committee. However, it does serve as an indicator of legislative priorities during this period.

TABLE 4.2 *Legislative action on policing in Buenos Aires Province Senate*
(1995–1996)

Legislative actions on issues specific to policing[a]	181
Information requests submitted to executive branch regarding policing[b]	45
Information requests regarding specific cases of police violence/ misconduct[b]	18
Information requests for statistical data regarding police violence[b]	1 (1 rejected)
References to police operations/services[b]	23
Notifications designating buildings to be converted into police stations or creation of new police stations[b]	12

Senado de Buenos Aires, *Diario de Sesiones*, 123rd (1995–1996)–124th (1996–1997) periods
a Includes all legislative actions (announcements, bills, information requests) relating to policing, count includes legislative actions repeated across multiple sessions
b Count includes only unique instances

1996, including announcements, declarations, bills introduced,[65] and requests for information submitted to the legislative branch. As can be seen from Table 4.2, there were 181 legislative actions regarding policing in the Senate during this period. Regarding what we might consider the legislature's oversight function, the Senate submitted only forty-five distinct information requests about police to the executive branch over the course of eighty-two meetings, of which only eighteen were requests about specific cases of police violence or misconduct and only one was a request for aggregate official data on police violence (an additional request proposed by a senator was voted down by the full Senate). In the context of the dire security conditions facing the province, the urgency of societal demands for improved security and turn toward vigilantism, and the widespread extralegal coercive practices by the provincial police, these legislative actions are conspicuously insufficient.

Rather than exercising its legislative authority to conduct external oversight of the police in light of the province's dire policing and security problems, the official position of the legislative branch was one of deference to the governor, the secretary of security, and the police chief.

---

[65] Legislative bills introduced in the Senate will be discussed in the final section of this chapter.

Graciela Podestá, who at the time was a member of the provincial Chamber of Deputies with the opposition FREPASO party and served as the president of the Security Committee in that chamber, recalled the surprise of other legislators at the information requests issued by her committee, with one Peronist legislator telling her, "'We've never had these types of information requests.' They didn't question what the executive did in security matters. From both chambers, they just didn't have that habit."[66]

This deferential position relative to the executive was reinforced by the majority Peronist Party – the governor's co-partisans – to temper criticisms of the police and block autonomous legislative reform efforts. For instance, after the provincial police engaged in dramatic repression of university student protesters in the provincial capital in February 1996, the head of the majority Peronist legislative caucus in the senate, José María Díaz Bancalari, rejected a request for information to the executive branch about the organization and execution of the police operation at the student protest, saying that the executive branch had already taken action to punish the lower-ranking officers responsible and that the most egregious violence at the protest hadn't been provoked by the police.[67] Senator Díaz Bancalari also said the Peronist caucus would vote against a declaration requesting that police chief Pedro Klodczyk clarify remarks in the press where he appeared to justify police corruption due to low salaries, unless the opposition senator who proposed the request "changed the text so that it doesn't have such an assertive character."[68]

In the midst of the deferential position enforced by the majority party, opposition senators repeatedly urged their colleagues to assert their legislative authority to address the province's grave security and policing problem. Amid a heated debate about the February 1996 repression, Senator Eduardo Sigal of the opposition party FREPASO urged "a needed reflection by the Legislative Branch to determine whether this is simply an isolated, casual act, or whether there are foundational problems that require legislative action."[69] In another instance, Peronist senator

---

[66] Author interview with Graciela Podestá, Vicente López, Buenos Aires Province, November 2, 2011.

[67] *Diario de Sesiones*, Senado de la Provincia de Buenos Aires, Periodo 124, 2nd Reunión, March 7, 1996, 58–59.

[68] *Diario de Sesiones*, Senado de la Provincia de Buenos Aires, Periodo 123, 20th Reunión, October 12, 1995, 1401.

[69] *Diario de Sesiones*, Senado de la Provincia de Buenos Aires, Periodo 124, 2nd Reunión, March 7, 1996, 61.

Horacio Román urged his colleagues to pass legislation submitted by the executive branch declaring the provincial police to be in a state of emergency in order to "give a more effective weapon to the Secretary of Security to reorganize the police force." Senator Ricardo Alberto Tojo of the opposition Radical Party responded by pointedly telling his colleagues:

> It's time for this Legislature to put on its big-boy pants . . . We are being asked to give [the executive branch] a weapon, as though it were the exclusive jurisdiction of the executive branch to resolve security problems, as though we're painted on here (*cartón pintado*), as though the Legislature has nothing to do with it, as though we didn't have in our hands the instruments needed to resolve things . . . It would be preferable if we got to work immediately on the Organic Law of the Police, redesigning the police force if needed."[70]

It would be another year and a half before the provincial legislature heeded Senator Tojo's call, undertaking comprehensive structural police reform in 1998 (see Chapter 7). In the interim, the legislative branch continued its institutional deference to the executive, delegating its authority to conduct external oversight of the provincial police.

The third branch of the provincial government, the judiciary, was similarly limited in the use of its authority to hold police accountable for misconduct and extralegal violence during the pre-reform period. According to the human rights organization CELS, judicial oversight of police in Buenos Aires Province was "almost nonexistent," as judges routinely failed to investigate unlawful detentions, torture, killings, and cover-ups by police (CELS 1998, 35). The instances in which the judicial branch acted to hold police accountable for rampant extrajudicial violence actually serve to demonstrate the deficiencies in judicial accountability for police violence and the extent to which these deficiencies may have been intentional. In October 1993, the provincial Supreme Court took the unprecedented decision to conduct an audit of judicial proceedings in twenty cases of police killings and disappearances dating back to 1991, in which judicial investigations were unduly delayed. The Court ordered its inspector general (*procurador general*) to instruct judges and prosecutors in the cases to speed up the investigation, as well as to accompany the proceedings.[71] Nearly two years later, the Supreme Court's inspector

---

[70] *Diario de Sesiones*, Senado de la Provincia de Buenos Aires, Periodo 124, 33rd Reunión, November 7, 1996, 3223.
[71] "La Suprema Corte bonaerense investiga a la Policía por 20 muertes y desapariciones," *Clarín*, October 25, 1993, 40.

general – future Secretary of Security Eduardo de Lázzari – had to intervene once again in response to undue judicial delays in investigations of police violence. De Lázzari removed a judge that, by "strange coincidence," was presiding over two prominent cases of police violence, the enforced disappearances of Andrés Núñez and Miguel Bru. The judge, Amílcar Vara, was denounced by a police officer who accused him of blocking the investigation of the cases.[72] As these examples illustrate, the judicial branch had to take extraordinary measures to hold itself accountable, acting to address the deficiencies in exercising judicial authority to hold police accountable for extralegal violence.

Societal Preference Fragmentation and the Absence of an Electoral Counterweight to the *Bonaerense*

The preceding discussion suggests a grave failure of democratic institutions. Elected leaders and appointed officials charged with enforcing the rule of law were seemingly unresponsive to urgent societal demands for improved security and incapable of holding police accountable in order to protect the citizenry from egregious extralegal violence and predation. As the discussion that follows suggests, however, these conditions did not reflect a failure of democratic responsiveness; they were the result of ordinary democratic politics.

In the context of rising crime and growing social unrest amid economic upheaval, there was considerable societal contestation over policing and security, with important implications for politicians' electoral incentives. Societal concern and mobilization about *gatillo fácil* police killings went hand in hand with increased vigilantism due to the perception that the state was negligent in its duty to protect citizens from rising crime. As citizens from predominantly low-income communities marched against police violence (Verdú 2009), others held *marchas del silencio* (silent marches) denouncing impunity for crimes and demanding more policing to address the insecurity brought by the economic crisis (Cerruti 2011), while still others celebrated *justicieros* or "urban vindicators" (Fernandez Roich 2017) who took the law into their own hands.

These stark societal divisions presented politicians with conflicting demands over policing and security. This fragmentation of preferences means that politicians likely saw little electoral gain in reforming the police, even in the context of extensive and entrenched authoritarian

[72] "El amigo de los policías," *Página/12*, September 8, 1995.

coercive practices. Police effectively constrained politicians' policy choices through the threat of withdrawing their cooperation – and the lucrative system of *recaudación* – raising the threshold for reform. Observing fragmented preferences and conflicting demands for the citizenry, political leaders faced little electoral counterweight to the police's structural power.

Unequal Distribution of Protection and Repression and the Mobilization against *Gatillo Fácil*

Societal divisions in demands and preferences over policing corresponded with disparities in the distribution of protection and repression. As the range of extralegal coercive practices undertaken by the *Bonaerense* came to align starkly with social cleavages of class and geography, one set of demands faced by the province's political leaders emerged in the form of ongoing mobilization by the affected social sectors, who sought greater restrictions on the provincial police and called for an end to *gatillo fácil*.

In the context of the economic crisis and concomitant increases in unemployment, poverty, and inequality, disparities in the distribution of protection and repression in Buenos Aires Province correlated with characteristics such as class and geography. As in the case of São Paulo, low-income citizens of Buenos Aires Province were both subjected to the under-provision of protection and disproportionately victimized by extralegal violence at the hands of police. One survey of residents of Greater Buenos Aires, for instance, showed that 40 percent of low-income residents reported having been a crime victim, a much higher proportion than middle-class (28 percent) and upper-class residents (12 percent) (Fraga 1998).

This same segment of the population also bore the brunt of police repression. For instance, as a lawyer for victims of police violence, María del Carmen Verdú, noted in an interview, two-thirds of the victims of *gatillo fácil* (trigger-happy) killings in the database maintained by CORREPI, her NGO, are male, young, and poor.[73] Indeed, in his analysis of court cases involving police killings, Brinks (2008) calculated the likelihood of being the victim of deadly police violence and found that, in Greater Buenos Aires, someone living in a *villa* (shantytown) was six times more likely to experience police violence than someone who does not (Brinks 2008, 53). For the *conurbano*, he found that 72 percent of

---

[73] Author interview with María del Carmen Verdú, Buenos Aires, October 11, 2011.

victims were lower class or working class and 15 percent of victims lived in a shantytown, compared to 3 percent for the general population of the *conurbano*. Meanwhile, 60 percent of victims of police killings had only completed primary education, and 33 percent were unemployed (Brinks 2008, 114).

This class-based differentiation extends to the societal and state responses to these instances of police violence, despite the fact that the cases analyzed by Brinks were cases in which the victims were not armed and not engaged in a confrontation with police. Nevertheless, Brinks (2008) finds important differences in the rates of conviction of police officers depending on the class background of the victim: for lower- and working-class victims, the police officer was convicted 25 percent of the time; for those who were not from these social groups (a much smaller number overall, to be sure), the conviction rate was 44 percent (Brinks 2008, 69). For Verdú, the human rights lawyer, the perceived social class of the victim is a determining factor of how state and societal actors respond: "Look at the *desaparecidos* (disappeared) of La Plata. Why do we all remember Miguel Bru and not Andrés Núñez? The case of Andrés was even more clear [than Bru's]. But Andrés Núñez was a construction worker. He wasn't a journalism student [like Miguel Bru]."[74]

In the face of these patterns of state violence, the pre-reform period was characterized by robust mobilization by affected communities and their allies in the human rights movement (Pita 2010), constituting what Fuentes (2005) calls the "pro-civil-rights" coalition. The massacre of Ingeniero Budge in 1987, referenced at the start of this chapter, not only consolidated the modus operandi of police violence in democracy – "trigger-happy" police killings – but also marked one of the first instances of mobilization by low-income and working-class communities against these modes of police violence. As memorialized in the files of the Intelligence Division of the Police of Buenos Aires Province,[75] residents of Ingeniero Budge began mobilizing immediately after the killings, forming the Committee of Friends and Neighbors (Comisión de Amigos y Vecinos,

---

[74] Both Andrés Núñez and Miguel Bru were detained and subsequently disappeared by the members of the Police of Buenos Aires Province: Núñez in 1990 and Bru in 1993.

[75] The Intelligence Division of the Police of Buenos Aires Province (DIPPBA), created in 1956 and dissolved in 1998 as part of the structural reform, routinely collected records on political and social organizations in the province, including thousands of files produced on a number of groups organizing against police violence. The files of the DIPPBA are housed in the archives of the Provincial Commission for Memory, parts of which can be accessed electronically at www.comisionporlamemoria.org/archivo/la-dippba/.

CAV). Just days after the killings, the CAV called the residents of Ingeniero Budge to action: "Neighbors, you as parents and youth – who are the primary target, who are killed daily – have the obligation to come and demand immediate justice and clarification of the facts . . . [and] imprisonment of those responsible. No more killings of Argentine youth!"[76]

For months and even years after the killings (or disappearances) of Maximiliano Albanese, Andrés Núñez, Sergio Durán, Rubén "Cachi" Romero, Miguel Bru, and countless others,[77] the mostly low-income communities to which the victims of police violence belonged, supported by human rights organizations,[78] organized meetings and *"marchas del silencio"* (silent marches) in their communities, and protests in front of police headquarters and the Casa de Gobierno (provincial government building) in the provincial capital of La Plata, and even in Plaza de Mayo in the national capital, the city of Buenos Aires, decrying "impunity" and calling for an end to *"gatillo fácil."*[79] Rosa Schonfeld Bru, the mother of Miguel Bru, a journalism student detained and disappeared by the *Bonaerense* in 1993, recalls their mobilization during this time:

We demanded justice. People related to other cases would also come, because the police had also killed their children. And when another mother was demanding [justice] we went and accompanied her. It was constant, today for me, tomorrow for you . . . One of the places [we protested] was the Casa de Gobierno; a few times we marched by the police headquarters, where they would put out *tanquetas* (armored vehicles). It was pure indignation; we were the victims and they were protecting themselves from us."[80]

The mobilization of families and communities was commonplace enough that, in some instances, those who would subsequently become victims of

[76] Flyer of the Comisión de Amigos y Vecinos, May 1987. Retrieved from the files of the Intelligence Division of the Police of Buenos Aires Province (DIPPBA), Provincial Commission for Memory, Legajo 26185, Tomo I.
[77] Flyers announcing protests demanding justice for these and other victims, compiled by the DIPPBA and maintained today by the Provincial Commission for Memory, can be accessed online at www.comisionporlamemoria.org/investigacion/project/inteligencia-y -violencia-institucional/.
[78] Some of the human rights organizations, such as CORREPI (Coordinator Against Police and Institutional Repression) and COFAVI (Commission of Families of Innocent Victims of Police Violence), were formed specifically in response to police violence after the democratic transition in 1983; other organizations, such as Mothers of Plaza de Mayo, the Permanent Association for Human Rights, and others, were formed during the military dictatorship.
[79] See, for instance, "Marcha de repudio al gatillo fácil," *Página/12*, July 29, 1995.
"Los policías de la provincia son animales cebados con sangre." *Página/12*, August 3, 1995.
[80] Author interview with Rosa Schonfeld Bru, La Plata, August 23, 2017.

police violence had previously participated in marches for earlier victims. They joined their fellow citizens in denouncing police violence, never explicitly imagining that they would fall victim to it themselves. Rosa Bru, for instance, recalled:

Miguel used to go to the marches of the Albanese young man,[81] and he used to come home and tell me about the parents of this young man who had been killed by police, and I used to read about Lalo [the father of the victim] in the newspapers ... [I thought] we were low-income people (*humildes*) – we weren't political activists. What could happen to us? ... The dictatorship, when they used to kidnap people, had ended.

Nicanor Bogado, whose son Marcelo was killed by provincial police in 2004, similarly recalled his own earlier participation in protests against police violence in the 1990s:

A few times I went to the marches for [Walter] Bulacio, and here in Morón I went twice [to protests] for the case of Sergio Durán, because the regional unit of Morón brutalized him completely. Remember the bakery where we went? I remember one of the times I went, we did a partial roadblock around there. It was symbolic, it wasn't a complete block, [but] a lot of people mobilized ... But I never, ever thought then that we would go through what we ended up going through.[82]

Low-income and working-class communities mobilized throughout the pre-reform period to protest pervasive authoritarian coercive practices, conveying a clear demand to political leaders in favor of greater constraints on police use of force and stronger accountability mechanisms.

The Rise of Vigilantism and the Constituency for Authoritarian Coercion

During this period, however, politicians also faced strong demands calling for exactly the opposite of what low-income and working-class communities were asking for. As Argentine scholars and policy experts have observed, "the demand for security is linked to the levels of social unrest in society" (Sigal, Binder & Annichiarico 1998, 42), such that "increasing unemployment, urban migration, and the presence of large, socially marginalized urban populations feed the demand for more violent action on the part of the police" (Brinks 2008, 120).

---

[81] Maximiliano Albanese was shot by a provincial police officer while waiting in line to enter a student party in La Plata in 1990, at the age of seventeen.

[82] Author interview with Nicanor Bogado, Morón, Buenos Aires Province, August 31, 2017.

The rise in crime of the post-transition period, compounded by the pressures of the economic crisis, generated two interrelated sets of demands that ultimately favored *"mano dura"* or "iron fist" policies, an expansion of police authority to fight rising crime and violence. One manifestation of these demands was the phenomenon of the *"justicieros,"* the defense of vigilantism in the face of police ineffectiveness and state neglect. In one such instance, bereaved residents mourning the killing of three teens in the municipality of González Catán held their own *"marchas del silencio"* and warned, "There better not be impunity like the last time. Because we will not be organizing protests here: I assure you that from here on out the men of the neighborhood are arming themselves, because we cannot trust the police."[83] News reports throughout the 1990s declared, "There are increasingly more *'justicieros'*" (justice makers),[84] alleged crime victims who killed the alleged perpetrators of the crime, in most instances a robbery.[85] In other cases, these acts of vigilantism were collective responses to heinous acts of violence, such as the residents of the neighborhood of Villa Martelli in the municipality of San Martín, who faced off against fifty police officers in an attempt to lynch a young man suspected of raping and murdering a nine-year-old girl.[86] In line with this turn to vigilantism in response to rising violence and dissatisfaction with the response of state institutions, a survey conducted in the late 1990s found that 56 percent agreed with "taking the law into one's own hands in extreme cases" (*justicia por mano propia en casos extremos*) (Fraga 1998, 55). As Fernández Roich (2017) has written about these "urban vindicators," "the widespread perception that they are doing the right thing by fighting back ... is one of the conditions of production of the so-called 'iron-fist' discourse, the kind of discourse that justifies killing in response to minimum threat" (3).

[83] "Por la inseguridad, dicen los vecinos se arman para hacer justicia por su cuenta," *Clarín*, March 26, 1993.
[84] Front page, *Clarín*, November 4, 1994.
[85] The newspaper *Clarín* provided details on twenty-eight of the forty cases of "justicieros" it says took place in 1994; in all twenty-eight cases the alleged perpetrator of a robbery was killed by the alleged victim. See "Larga lista de sangre," *Clarín*, November 4, 1994, 47; "40 casos en el '94," *Clarín*, January 25, 1995, 36. There were also countless reports of individual instances of vigilantism, for example, "Un nuevo justiciero: Mató a dos ladrones y quedó libre," *Página/12*, September 20, 1995; "La ley del revólver," *Página/12*, January 24, 1995; "El joven asumiría la responsabilidad de ser el que disparó contra el ladrón," *Clarín*, January 25, 1995.
[86] In an indication of the police's deficiencies, the dozens of officers on the scene reportedly sought to prevent this act of vigilante violence by shooting their guns into the air. See "Detuvieron 4 hermanos por el descuartizamiento de una nena," *Clarín*, March 2, 1995.

The elevation of the "*justicieros*" went hand in hand with support for harsher legal and even extralegal treatment of criminal suspects. Scholars and activists alike cite broad support for police violence in the post-transition period (Americas Watch & CELS 1991, 7) and the belief that "all forms of control and regulation of police activity would severely limit its performance and efficacy" (Saín 2002, 62). The existence of support for police violence among some sectors of society is perhaps best illustrated by the question of torture, which, unlike police killings, is not justified under any circumstance under the Argentine legal framework. According to a 1991 poll in Greater Buenos Aires, just over half of respondents opposed the use of torture, while 38 percent approved of its use in at least certain cases (Chevigny 1995, 195).

A clear illustration of the support for torture among certain sectors of society in the province is the case of Luis Patti.[87] Patti was a local police commander accused of participating in torture, disappearances, and killings during the military dictatorship. While serving as police chief of the municipality of Pilar, he was indicted by a judge in 1990 on charges of using torture against two robbery suspects. After he was charged, thousands of residents from Pilar held a demonstration on his behalf in September 1990 arguing that crime had dropped since he became the local police chief (Americas Watch & CELS 1991, 22). Moreover, no less than President Carlos Menem, the governor of Buenos Aires Province Antonio Cafiero, and then-candidate for governor Eduardo Duhalde,[88] as well as prominent Argentine journalists, came to Patti's defense and heavily criticized the judge who had ordered his arrest.[89] According to human rights advocates, this outpouring of mainstream support for the use of torture served as evidence that "society appears to be divided, when not in direct confrontation, between those that are directly harmed [by institutional violence] ... and [those] who defend institutional violence as a form of obtaining that ever valued individual security" (Abregú 1993, 71).

---

[87] Recall Eduardo de Lázzari's reference above to "the famous Patti," then the mayor of the municipality of Escobar.

[88] "Duhalde propone como modelo a comisario Patti," *Clarín*, August 6, 1991.

[89] The judge was eventually forced to resign, Patti went back to being chief of the Pilar station, and Menem appointed Patti to serve in a federal commission to investigate a prominent killing of a young woman in Catamarca. Patti was subsequently elected mayor of the municipality of Escobar, as well as a federal legislator (though he was eventually stripped of legal immunity, tried, and sent to prison) (Abregú 1993, 73).

Fragmented Preferences, Conflicting Demands

Democratically elected leaders in Buenos Aires Province thus faced societal contestation and demand-making in favor of both reform and maintaining the status quo of extralegal coercive practices. Patterns of societal mobilization during this pre-reform period suggest fragmentation, such that attitudes and preferences regarding police and security are divided among considerable segments of society, along existing class and geographic cleavages, often with no clear majority position.

Survey data from the 1990s attest to this fragmentation. Table 4.3 presents data from surveys of residents of the *conurbano*[90] asking respondents their opinion of the provincial police in the years 1991–1993.[91] As the table shows, survey respondents were divided in their assessments of the police, with about one-quarter of respondents viewing the police as "good" or "very good," one-third to one-quarter of respondents viewing the police as "bad," and the largest proportion of respondents, approximately 40 percent, holding a neutral view of the provincial police. There was greater consensus when, starting in 1994, the question wording was changed to instead ask about trust.[92] As Table 4.4 shows, there was much

TABLE 4.3 *Opinion of the police of Buenos Aires Province (1991–1993)*

	Good/very good	Average/neutral	Bad
1991	22%	43%	33%
1992	27%	42%	30%
1993	25%	43%	25%

Surveys conducted in the municipalities of Greater Buenos Aires by the firm Estudio Graciela Romer y Asociados. Survey data accessed via the Latin American Databank housed at the Roper Center Public Opinion Archives at the University of Connecticut.

[90] The *conurbano bonaerense* refers to the twenty-four municipalities of Buenos Aires Province surrounding the city of Buenos Aires.
[91] The survey asked, regarding a range of institutions, "what opinion does [institution] merit, considering their contributions to the well-being of the country?"
[92] "Thinking about the way in which the following institutions or social groups are functioning today in Argentina, how much trust do you have in them? Do you think [institution] is very trustworthy, trustworthy, untrustworthy, or very untrustworthy?" Table 4.4 combines very trustworthy/trustworthy and untrustworthy/very untrustworthy.

TABLE 4.4 *Trust in the police of Buenos Aires Province*
(1994–1997)

Year	(Very) trustworthy	(Very) untrustworthy
1994	22%	75%
1995	29%	70%
1996 (March)	16%	79%
1996 (May)	10%	89%
1997 (March)	6%	92%

Surveys conducted in the municipalities of Greater Buenos Aires by the firm Estudio Graciela Romer y Asociados. Survey data accessed via the Latin American Databank housed at the Roper Center Public Opinion Archives at the University of Connecticut.

greater consensus in levels of trust toward the provincial police, which never reached 30 percent and fell to single digits by the late 1990s. But other survey data from this period nevertheless reflects fragmentation over policing and security policy, even if citizens largely agreed that the police were untrustworthy. A survey conducted in the late 1990s by the organization Centro de Estudios Unión para la Nueva Mayoría revealed important divisions: 45 percent agreed with "increasing police authority to combat crime," while 44 percent disagreed that "there should be restrictions on individual rights for greater security," and 53 percent agreed that "more police officers on the streets will help solve the crime problem" (Fraga 1998, 59–63). Thus, even with a police force that was almost universally distrusted, citizens were divided regarding what police ought to do or how much authority it should be granted.[93]

Available survey data from this period also suggest that some of the fragmentation in preferences and demands regarding policing aligned with existing social cleavages. Figure 4.1 breaks down responses from the survey presented in Table 4.3 by level of education for 1993 – the year that the provincial Supreme Court sounded the alarm about the *Bonaerense* and that mainstream media outlets framed police violence as "*gatillo fácil*" (trigger-happy). If we use level of education as a proxy for socioeconomic status, we observe that those with higher levels of education were more likely to be neutral toward police (57 percent) than those with the lowest level of

[93] By contrast, there was much more convergence regarding other criminal justice policies: 84 percent of survey respondents agreed with longer sentences for crimes, and 71 percent agreed with trying sixteen-year-olds as adults (Fraga 1998, 53).

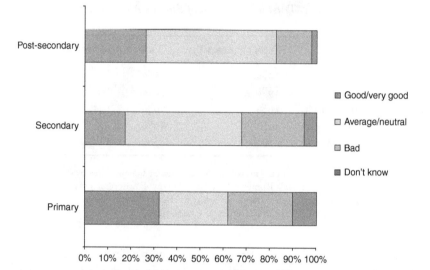

FIGURE 4.1 Opinion of the police of Buenos Aires Province by education level (1993)
Surveys conducted in the municipalities of Greater Buenos Aires by the firm Estudio Graciela Romer y Asociados. Survey data accessed via the Latin American Databank housed at the Roper Center Public Opinion Archives at the University of Connecticut

education (30 percent), who were more likely to say the police were "bad" (28 percent vs. 15 percent). It should be noted, however, that even those from lower socioeconomic strata held fragmented views toward police, likely due to the complicated relationship between police and lower-income communities, who are more likely to be victimized by crime but lack access to the resources that wealthier citizens can invest in private security measures, leading the former to depend much more on police for protection.[94]

Taken together, the preceding discussion of societal mobilization and attitudes expressed in public opinion surveys suggests considerable fragmentation of societal preferences and demands. This fragmentation of preferences and demands between outrage at police violence and support for that violence was familiar to security officials in the province. Arslanian, the province's first minister of security and leader of the reform that would begin in 1998, recalled the fragmentation of societal demands on the issue of security leading up to the reform:

[94] A similar argument was made by security experts at the time. See Rosendo Fraga, "La seguridad de los pobres," *La Nación*, May 28, 1996.

It was a very erratic demand, frankly erratic, because of what I'm about to tell you. In the collective imaginary there has always been the idea of the criminal law as a talisman and, fundamentally, the idea that the efficacy of the fight against crime depended on the degree of authority and freedom [of action] that the government granted the police so that it could [perform this task] ... But on the other side, there was this social demand that was evident: you cannot have such a corrupt, punitive, and terrible police, in which there were daily occurrences of youths, adolescents, disappearing or being killed by the repression; they were shot in the back, executions of various types, under democracy. [It was] a legacy of police excesses under dictatorship. So from this other perspective there was a strong social demand for change.

ORDINARY DEMOCRATIC POLITICS AND THE PERSISTENCE OF AUTHORITARIAN COERCION

In the face of these "erratic" demands, provincial leaders in the province likely concluded that there would be little electoral benefit in pursuing police reform. The provincial police exerted their structural power to constrain the policy agenda, pressuring politicians to preserve police autonomy and raising the threshold for reform. The result was stalled reform, enabling the persistence of the *Bonaerense*'s authoritarian coercive practices, including extrajudicial killings, disappearances, torture, and an expansive system of extralegal rent extraction.

Reform stalled, even though numerous reform proposals were considered in the executive and legislative branches. Some two-dozen bills introduced in the provincial Senate in 1995 and 1996 directly pertained to the provincial police, many of which sought to reform police structures and practices. These reform proposals sought to curb arbitrary detentions by police,[95] create a judicial police to improve investigations,[96] decentralize the police force,[97] create an internal affairs division,[98] establish a psychological aptitude exam for police officers,[99] institute a code of

---

[95] *Diario de Sesiones*, Senado de la Provincia de Buenos Aires, Periodo 124, 6th Reunión, April 11, 1996.

[96] *Diario de Sesiones*, Senado de la Provincia de Buenos Aires, Periodo 124, 8th Reunión, April 25, 1996.

[97] *Diario de Sesiones*, Senado de la Provincia de Buenos Aires, Periodo 124, 13th Reunión, June 6, 1996.

[98] *Diario de Sesiones*, Senado de la Provincia de Buenos Aires, Periodo 124, 21st Reunión, August 14, 1996.

[99] *Diario de Sesiones*, Senado de la Provincia de Buenos Aires, Periodo 124, 3rd Reunión, March 14, 1996.

conduct for police officers,[100] and change internal disciplinary practices,[101] among others. However, the only legislation about policing that was approved during this period, according to the Senate's *Diario de Sesiones*, was a law instituting an award for "police merit" to be granted on the Day of the Bonaerense Police (Law 11.699/1996) and the law declaring the provincial police to be in a state of emergency (Law 11.880/1996). As Saín (2015) has noted, moreover, even Governor Duhalde touted – but never delivered – a "profound reform" of the provincial police in 1996, which included many of the same plans considered in the legislature, such as the creation of an internal affairs agency, decentralization of the police, and civilian oversight (Saín 2015, 131).

Reform stalled, despite the remarkable salience of policing and security throughout Duhalde's administration. This chapter has provided ample evidence that policing and security issues were central to the policy agenda during this period, as affected communities marched in the streets for years (with some demanding more aggressive police and others an end to police violence), prominent news outlets repeatedly featured the rise of both "*gatillo fácil*" police killings and vigilantism, and the top security official in the province openly referred to a "crisis" in the provincial police.

Reform stalled because of ordinary democratic politics. Although many of the *Bonaerense*'s egregious extralegal coercive practices can be traced back to the last military dictatorship, the persistence of authoritarian coercive institutions was a function of everyday contestation among the citizenry and how it shaped the electoral incentives of the province's political leaders. Rather than being the result of authoritarian legacies, the *Bonaerense*'s authoritarian coercive practices endured because politicians concluded that reform would be electorally disadvantageous. In Chapter 7, I show how shifts in societal preferences from fragmentation to convergence, and the emergence of a robust political opposition, led politicians in Buenos Aires Province to change their electoral calculations, shifting their strategy from accommodation of police to pursuing audacious structural reforms to promote democratic coercion. But, for a decade and a half following the return of democratic rule, democratic processes served to reinforce authoritarian coercive practices – from torture to extrajudicial

---

[100] *Diario de Sesiones*, Senado de la Provincia de Buenos Aires, Periodo 124, 4th Reunión, March 21, 1996.
[101] *Diario de Sesiones*, Senado de la Provincia de Buenos Aires, Periodo 124, 34th Reunión, November 7, 1996.

killings – because of how fragmented societal demands shaped the incentives of democratically elected leaders to hold police externally accountable. In the words of the judges who issued the first verdict in Buenos Aires Province convicting a police officer in a case of torture followed by death in 1994:

These types of occurrences happen due to shared responsibility. On the part of society, which in some cases demands that police authorities solve crimes without concern for the means employed to achieve it. On the part of police authorities that do not punish subordinates when they are denounced for these practices. And on the part of the judicial authorities, who do not adequately investigate these types of crimes.[102]

---

[102] The victim, Ramón Buchón, died in the hospital in March 1993 after being tortured by police, wrongfully arrested, and tortured in a police station. "Perpetua a policías que torturaron y mataron," *Página/12*, May 14, 1994.

5

Policing in Hard Times

Drug War, Institutional Decay, and the Persistence of Authoritarian Coercion in Colombia

A major from the Colombian National Police, who had survived two terrorist attacks and a kidnapping at the hands of the Medellín Cartel and the guerrilla forces, described his early years on the police force as follows: "In the era of Pablo Escobar, the simple fact that you were a police officer made you a target for them. And during that time we didn't know who could kill us; it could be Pablo Escobar's men or it could be our own colleagues in the police [due to infiltration]. Even the Army was infiltrated back then."[1] Colombian police officers of a certain age bear the scars of policing at the nexus of a multiplicity of wars. As the major's experience attests, Colombia's war against drug cartels and armed conflict positioned the police as the target and perpetrator of extraordinary levels of violence.

The Colombian case differs along a number of significant dimensions from the other two cases analyzed here. It is a unitary country with a national police force without a long history of authoritarian rule.[2] Moreover, Colombia's experiences with political and drug violence, and their resulting impact on state institutions, have been singular in the region. By the early 1990s, Colombia had been engaged in a decades-long war against guerrilla organizations and a more recent but devastating battle with drug cartels. These conflicts fundamentally eroded the

---

[1] Author interview with anonymous major of the Colombian National Police I, Bogotá, August 12, 2012.

[2] Although Colombia did not experience decades-long authoritarian rule as in many other Latin American countries, it was briefly governed by military dictatorship in the 1950s, during which the country's police underwent significant structural changes.

legitimacy of the Colombian state and laid bare the precariousness of its institutions. Colombia has thus grappled in recent decades with broader challenges of governance and order that distinguish it from the other cases considered in this book.

Despite these important differences, however, the Colombian National Police confronted a number of challenges similar to those faced by the police forces of Buenos Aires Province and São Paulo State. As in these other settings, urban security conditions around Colombia had also deteriorated, reaching historically high rates of homicide and other violent crime by the early 1990s. Meanwhile, the National Police proved to be unprepared not only to respond to the challenges posed by armed criminal and guerrilla organizations but also to perform basic security functions such as preventing and investigating crimes. Most importantly, the National Police routinely exercised authoritarian coercion, with rampant extrajudicial killings, torture, corruption, and other exceptional actions falling outside the scope of the law, with negligible external accountability.

The Colombian case underscores that the institutional persistence of authoritarian coercion in democracies cannot be reduced to enduring authoritarian legacies. Instead, the case illustrates how such authoritarian coercive practices are bolstered by ordinary democratic politics, as contestation over policing and security among the citizenry shape politicians' incentives away from reform. The discussion that follows lays out why politicians may have viewed police reform as electorally disadvantageous, despite the National Police's profound institutional decay and widespread authoritarian coercive practices. Although overall trust in the National Police was relatively low, societal preferences nevertheless reflected considerable fragmentation, often along class lines. As this chapter demonstrates, even as Colombia's political leaders responded to widespread societal discontent and institutional deterioration with broad reforms in other policy areas, patterns of societal contestation and conflicting demands regarding the distribution of protection and repression meant there was little electoral incentive to reform the National Police. In the face of fragmented societal preferences over policing, politicians likely concluded there would be little electoral benefit in enacting police reform, choosing instead to accommodate the police and maintain the status quo. In the discussion that follows, I show how, in spite of the National Police's prolonged and profound institutional crisis, ordinary democratic politics failed for many years to bring about an electoral counterweight to the police's structural power, helping to sustain systematic authoritarian coercive practices and structures.

The Colombian case also underscores – to a greater degree than the other cases studied in this book – the extent to which police in particular constitute a "hard case" for reform. Even as a grave crisis of legitimacy created the impetus for profound and far-reaching institutional reforms across all areas of the Colombian state, the National Police remained largely untouched. The National Police's puzzling continuity in the face of the president's "institutional shake-up" demonstrates how police leverage their structural power to constrain the policy options available to elected leaders, effectively raising the threshold for police reform. Indeed, the Colombian National Police is illustrative of the ways in which police exchange cooperation in one dimension for autonomy in another dimension. As I argue in this chapter, the police's cooperation with the objectives of the drug war, the government's policy priority and the focus of the country's relationship with the United States, raised the threshold for politicians to enact reforms to hold the National Police accountable for its authoritarian coercive practices. For more than a decade, however, societal preferences and demands over policing reflected important divisions. Without such an electoral counterweight to the police's structural power, politicians had few incentives to enact police reform and risk antagonizing a key bureaucracy.

The chapter is organized as follows. I first provide an overview of the effects of the drug war on the Colombian police, detailing the extensive institutional deterioration it experienced throughout the 1980s and early 1990s. I then describe the profound consequences of this institutional decay for the police's capacity to perform its basic functions and how these conditions facilitated a range of authoritarian coercive practices. The chapter then dives into the distinctive puzzle of the institutional continuity of the Colombian police, providing a discussion of a transformative period of institutional reforms across all areas of the Colombian state, while police reform stalled. The final section accounts for the police's continuity by discussing how the National Police leveraged its structural power – specifically its control over the drug war – to constrain policy options and block reforms, as well as how the fragmentation of societal preferences likely led politicians to conclude there would be little electoral gain in enacting police reform. These conditions persisted for many years, until the convergence of societal preferences in the form of a scandal and a newly strengthened political opposition changed the president's incentives in favor of reform in 1993. This shift is examined further in Chapter 7.

"OUR BODIES WERE NOT IMPENETRABLE": INSTITUTIONAL CONSEQUENCES OF THE DRUG WAR

In describing the strain caused by the fight against drug trafficking waged primarily by the National Police throughout the 1980s and 1990s, retired Brigadier General Guillermo León Diettes (former commander of the police in Cali and Bogotá and sub-director of the National Police) referred to the physical threat facing police officers, who were frequent targets of bombings and other forms of violence. "Unfortunately," Diettes told me in an interview, "our bodies were not impenetrable" (*nuestros cuerpos no fueron impermeables*).[3] But his statement could easily be applied to the impact of the drug war on the institutional body as a whole, which faced not only extensive infiltration and corruption by drug cartels but also a growing tendency toward authoritarian coercive practices against the citizenry. This confluence of threats was at the heart of the institutional decay experienced by the Colombian police in the years and decades preceding the reform enacted in 1993 (see Chapter 7). Former national security and defense advisor Camilo Granada described the dual impact of the drug war on the police: "The National Police became the eye, the center, of the great battle against drug trafficking in Colombia, for better and for worse. There were major heroes and major corrupt [officers]. There were many police officers that were murdered, and many police officers that were murderers."[4]

The National Police's central role in the war against drug cartels, as well as its more minor role in the armed conflict, had a similar institutional impact as the Buenos Aires and São Paulo police forces' incorporation into the repressive apparatus of their respective country's military dictatorship. Though Colombian experts agree that the low level of institutional development of the National Police preceded the crisis that reached its peak in the 1980s (Camacho 1993; Llorente 1997; Llorente 2005; Pardo Rueda 1996), much of the institutional decay can be traced back to the drug war. First, the adverse consequences of the pressures of fighting guerrilla and drug-trafficking groups placed an irreparable strain on material, financial, and human resources, which took its toll in the form of diminished operational capacity, corruption, and rampant extralegal violence. Second, the National Police's militarization shaped police education, structures, and strategies in such a way that undermined the

[3] Author interview with Brigadier General Guillermo León Diettes, Bogotá, July 16, 2013.
[4] Author interview with Camilo Granada, Bogotá, July 17, 2013.

police's traditional role and relationship to society, contributing to the use of extralegal violence by police. Finally, in addition to the strains caused by the armed conflict, urban crime and violence increased to historic levels throughout the 1980s, while the police repeatedly proved incapable of adequately providing security in the country's cities.

The National Police as a Primary Target of Violence

The drug war had a transformative impact on the distribution of protection and repression. One of the key determinants of this distribution was the extraordinary violence targeting police officers during this period. The vulnerability of the National Police to frequent deadly attacks diminished the police's already deficient capacity to provide protection and, as discussed later in this chapter, was used to justify the deployment of coercion in urban communities well outside the scope of the law.

The drug cartels' violent campaign against the National Police was systematic and lucrative. Pablo Escobar, leader of the infamous Medellín Cartel, offered a reward of between 1 million and 1.5 million pesos for every police officer killed.[5] General Miguel Antonio Gómez Padilla, the director general of the National Police at the time, recalled during an interview the toll of the drug war: "It cost us the lives of many officers. [Drug cartels] offered money for the heads of police officers according to their ranks. For yours truly, [the bounty] was 5 million US dollars ... The police were the first line in confronting this type of crime ... In Medellín, they killed one of our police officers every day."[6] Drug cartels also targeted local police substations known as CAIs (*Centro de Atención Inmediata*, or Immediate Attention Centers) for attacks, often leading to the deaths of several officers at a time.[7] Nearly 3,000 police officers were killed in the line of duty between 1982 and 1992 in Colombia (Goldsmith 2000, 172).

The lethal violence against the National Police was not restricted to drug cartels. Although the fight against the guerrilla was primarily the responsibility of the Army, the National Police was a frequent target of violence from guerrilla groups. In fact, former defense minister Rafael Pardo noted in an interview that the number of police casualties from

[5] "Pablo Escobar, autor de los crímenes de policías," *El Heraldo*, November 7, 1992.
[6] Author interview with General (ret.) Miguel Antonio Gómez Padilla, October 12, 2013. According to the minister of defense at the time, in 1990, 420 members of the National Police were killed in Medellín alone (Pardo Rueda, 1996, 344).
[7] See, for example, "Plan para evitar atentados a los Centros de Atención Inmediata," *El Tiempo*, January 5, 1991.

attacks by guerrilla groups far exceeded the number of army casualties.[8] The guerrilla forces FARC (Revolutionary Armed Forces of Colombia) and the ELN (National Liberation Army) regularly targeted isolated police stations in rural areas,[9] leading the police to respond by diminishing the number of rural police stations[10] and increasing the number of agents in each station as a self-defense measure. The result, however, was "a larger police force, without a sufficient command structure, more costly budget wise, less well equipped per person, with less territorial coverage, and offering in general, less security" (Pardo Rueda, 1996, 339). Indeed, as a result of the onslaught of attacks against police stations, less security is precisely what many citizens felt, leading residents in a number of small towns in the Antioquia department to formally petition the Constitutional Court to move or remove their police station, with the claim that its presence violated the residents' right to life.[11]

The Institutional Deterioration of the National Police

In addition to its staggering human toll, the drug war also accelerated the National Police's institutional unraveling. The incessant demands of the fight against drug cartels led to a chaotic growth strategy, which, in turn, eroded recruitment and training standards, rendered internal oversight all but impossible, and enabled widespread corruption and extralegal violence. The Colombian National Police increased from about 46,000 uniformed agents, noncommissioned officers, and commissioned officers in 1982 to approximately 76,000 in 1992 (Pardo Rueda, 1996, 341). This increase, however, was disproportionately among the lowest ranks. In 1992, there were only about 4,000 noncommissioned officers and 2,700 commissioned officers to command the remaining 70,000 noncommissioned officers. As military and police scholar Francisco Leal Buitrago put it, that is "a very small head for a very big body" (Leal Buitrago 1994, 199).

---

[8] According to Pardo, this led to tension between the police and the army. The police would accuse the army of not providing them protection and support, while the army would accuse the police of giving in to the guerrilla groups and inadequately defending themselves. Author interview with Rafael Pardo Rueda, Bogotá, October 16, 2012.

[9] "Asesinados 26 policías ayer," *El Tiempo*, November 8, 1992.

[10] According to Llorente (2005), "from the 1980s into the early 1990s, the force withdrew from almost 30 rural stations" (190).

[11] "Los policías no son hombre de 2a categoría," *El Espectador*, April 17, 1993, 10A; "Freno a 'trasteo' de cuarteles," *El País*, March 12, 1993, 8B.

The disproportionate growth of the "body" came at the expense of adequate training, resources, and, most crucially, oversight. As the president's former security and defense advisor Camilo Granada noted, "the police grew in order to try to respond to security needs, but it had grown without a plan to reinforce the institution." As an example, in order to recruit so many new officials in such a short period of time, the training period was cut from twelve to eight and finally to six months (Presidencia de la República 1994, 132). This is particularly alarming considering that the training and the "quality" of police recruits was already tenuous at best. A major of the Colombian National Police joked in an interview about the low educational standards, even for officers (noncommissioned officers had even lower requirements): "Previously, it was enough to have a high school degree. 'Great, you're in.' Actually, if you had a professional degree they would say to you, 'No, your profile is too high to be a police officer. Rejected. You're overqualified.' I'm talking about twenty years ago. Before, in order to be a *patrullero*, a street agent, you didn't even need a high school diploma. 'What have you got? First year of secondary school? Perfect, you're the one we need.'"[12] Officers interviewed in the newspaper *El Tiempo*[13] in 1993 outlined the challenge before them. "The government orders us to increase the size of the force by five thousand men, so we have to open the doors to recruit them," said one officer. Meanwhile, another noted that "if the control over the selection process were strictly complied with, the institution would not be able to meet its [recruitment] needs. Of those five thousand men required, one thousand would enter at most."[14] The growth among the lowest ranks was not accompanied by a corresponding increase in the number of commanding officers (including both officers and noncommissioned officers), leaving these poorly trained agents without adequate supervision and oversight.[15]

This weakening of recruitment standards, training, and internal oversight structures was seen by many officials and observers as a key source of the reliance on exceptional coercion by the National Police, manifesting as

---

[12] Author interview with anonymous major of the Colombian National Police II, Bogotá, November 26, 2012.

[13] "La deformación de la policía," *El Tiempo*, March 21, 1993.

[14] It goes without saying that another consequence of this massive recruitment of poorly trained agents was the exacerbation of already low salaries and precarious conditions of most police officers (Restrepo Riaza et al. 1994a, 66).

[15] Llorente (1997), for instance, compares the ratio of commanding officers to rank and file agents in Japan, Canada, Australia, Great Britain, and the United States, where it ranges from 1:1.3 to 1:5, to the Colombian National Police, which in 1993 had a ratio of 1:7.8 (17).

widespread corruption, violence, and the deterioration of institutional integrity (Pardo Rueda 1996, 339). Indeed, police involvement with drug cartels and drug trafficking was rampant throughout the 1980s and early 1990s. As will be discussed in greater detail, mass expulsions from the police for corruption, violence, and drug trafficking were frequent and involved officers of all ranks, in all parts of the country. Police involvement with crime was so widespread that, between August 1992 and March 1993, the *Consejo de Estado* (Colombia's highest administrative court) held the state legally, and financially, responsible for crimes committed by the police in eighty-six separate verdicts out of a total of 211 (Leal Buitrago 1994, 204).

Militarization and the Implications for External Oversight

An additional challenge exacerbated by the drug war, and by Colombia's decades-long armed conflict, was the police's far-reaching militarization and the prevalence of National Security Doctrine, which served to insulate the National Police from external, civilian oversight, despite the profound institutional deficiencies described in the previous section. The armed conflict and the resulting militarization of police posed a similar challenge to that of military dictatorships in Argentina and Brazil, consolidating organizational structures and practices incompatible with democratic rule.

Despite the Constitution's designation of the National Police as a civilian institution, it is also subordinated to the Ministry of Defense, which until 1991 had an Army general as its top official. Moreover, the National Police is considered the fourth entity of the *Fuerza Pública* (Public Force), along with the three branches of the military. The Colombian National Police became constituted as a national force – it had previously been a collection of municipal and departmental organizations – in the 1950s, when the National Police's internal command structure, system of discipline, education, and other characteristics came to mirror those of the Army (Decree 883/1954, Law 193/1959).[16] By the time it was constituted as a unitary institution, it had already been under military control for several years, thereby shaping in fundamental ways its development as a national entity. The various police forces throughout the country were brought under the Ministry of War (the predecessor of the

---

[16] Policía Nacional de Colombia, "Estructuras Orgánicas de la Policía Nacional 1890–2010: Una historia por conocer," acquired in the Archives of the Colombian National Police, August 2013.

Ministry of Defense) and subordinated to the General Command of the Armed Forces in 1953 (Decree 1814/1953). The National Police had thus been extensively militarized by the 1950s, a pattern that intensified as a result of the armed conflict.

For Colombian scholars, the tension between a civilian police mission and a highly militarized structure and orientation complicates the possibility for democratic coercion (Camacho 1993; Restrepo Riaza et al. 1994b). An external consultative police reform commission (see Chapter 7) composed of academics, political leaders, and societal representatives was especially concerned with the potential contradiction inherent between the National Police's proximity to the armed forces and its constitutionally defined civilian status (Presidencia de la República 1994, 121). For the experts in the reform commission, the ongoing armed conflict in the country distorted the police's mission, such that its principal task became protecting the political order itself, rather than the citizen (Camacho 1993, 3). The prioritization of defending the state from internal enemies is at the core of the National Security Doctrine framework, an ideology that had fallen into disuse elsewhere in South America as countries emerged from military dictatorships but remained solidly in place in Colombia as a result of its internal conflict (Leal Buitrago 1994).

While the high rates of deadly attacks posed an existential threat to countless police officers, the National Police's profound militarization provided a structural framework for justifying extralegal violence against citizens while delegitimizing civilian oversight. As one police officer put it, "the agent creates mechanisms of defense to avoid being killed on the street."[17] In the case of Medellín in the late 1980s and early 1990s – the epicenter of the drug war – local scholars described a situation of constant clash and confrontation between police and citizens as a result of the war on drug trafficking in the city: "Due to the permanent sensation of danger in its work, [the police] not only isolates itself from the part of the population it perceives as dangerous, but also from citizens in general. In this sense, for the police in the city of Medellín, any citizen [is] a potential enemy of the police" (Restrepo Riaza et al. 1994a, 41). Police officers themselves perceived the tension between the police's traditional role in a democracy and the militarization adopted in the context of an ongoing war. Three police officers interviewed shortly after participating in an internal reform commission in 1993 (see Chapter 7) acknowledged both the incompatibility of these models and their resignation to it,

---

[17] "La deformación de la policía," *El Tiempo*, March 31, 1993.

given the ongoing conflict: "the Police hasn't prepared itself for war just because; it has done so because the country is at war. People ask themselves why the neighborhood officer no longer exists. The cause is the decomposition of society and the neglect of the state."[18]

The militarized policing strategies adopted in response to the guerrilla forces and drug cartels, and the persistence of National Security Doctrine ideology, thus undermined the central mission of a police force in democracy: to prevent and investigate crimes in the service of the citizenry. As I discuss in the following sections, this militarization had important implications for the police's deployment of coercion against citizens, facilitating rampant abuses and undercutting the willingness of civilian institutions to conduct meaningful oversight.

THE PROLIFERATION OF URBAN VIOLENCE AND AN ILL-EQUIPPED POLICE

The National Police faced additional challenges that did not stem from the drug war or armed conflict but were instead common across many police forces throughout the region. As occurred in Argentina and Brazil, Colombia saw an increase of crime and violence across its urban centers throughout the 1980s and 1990s, as well as a similarly deficient response by its police force, which proved incapable of fulfilling citizens' growing demands for security. In the face of rising fear and frustration with a seemingly unresponsive state, many citizens similarly came to favor the privatization of violence, leading to the emergence of rampant "social cleansing" murders in Colombia's cities. Alongside the challenges of the drug war and the armed conflict, the National Police thus also had to contend with eroding societal trust and the growing criticism of high-ranking civilian officials, who repeatedly sounded the alarm about the police's profound institutional decay.

During the 1980s, violent crime in Colombia rose dramatically. Homicide rates skyrocketed from about 32 per 100,000 inhabitants in 1980 to 86 in 1992; to provide a sense of the alarming rate of increase, the rates then rose to 106 in 1993 and 127 in 1994 (Franco Agudelo 1997, 95). Meanwhile, kidnappings went from being virtually nonexistent prior to 1980 to numbering more than 1,500 cases by 1990; bank robberies quadrupled – from about 200 to approximately 800 – between 1988 and 1992 (Pardo Rueda 1996, 327). According to Camilo Granada, the

---

[18] "Las salidas son esperanzadoras," *El Tiempo*, May 15, 1993, 12A.

president's national security and defense advisor at the time, citizens' demands also intensified as a result of – in addition to the high murder rates – the increase in crimes such as street robberies, which are "a more quotidian aggression, much less dramatic; but it is one that causes more alarm." Granada also described the impact of "narcoterrorism" – attacks by drug cartels in urban centers that became more prevalent in the early 1990s – on the collective psyche of the citizenry, which experienced what he called the "banalization of violence":

> In the darkest hours of terrorism, people couldn't go out in the street, couldn't go to the movies, couldn't go to the mall, due to fear of bombs . . . Bombs of that sort were everywhere; anyone, doing anything, could become a victim. You no longer had to be involved in politics or be the neighbor of a minister or be a police officer to run that risk. Going out into the street was synonymous with risk.[19]

Citizens thus grew increasingly dissatisfied with the police's performance in addressing such crimes, resulting in the deterioration of police–society relations and the rise of vigilantism and "social cleansing" murders. Political and societal leaders at the time acknowledged frayed relations with great urgency, as in a public hearing in Medellín in late 1992, where officials observed a "tacit confrontation between the citizenry (*ciudadanía de bien*) and the Police. Let's not kid ourselves. When one sees a police officer or patrol car approaching, that action does not generate [a sense of] protection, it does not generate [a sense of] security."[20] Human rights organizations at the time argued that the combination of growing fear, distrust of police, and the perception of state inaction in the face of rampant crime served as a key driver of "'social cleansing' killings and their widespread acceptance in many communities" (Human Rights Watch 1994).

By the early 1990s, the National Police found itself with insufficient training, capacity, and resources to meet the demands of deteriorating urban security conditions, an internal armed conflict, and the combatting of drug cartels. Deficiencies in training, capacity, and resources were extensive. For instance, in the mid-1990s, Colombia had 26 police officers per 10,000 inhabitants; in contrast, Peru, a neighboring country similarly engaged in an internal armed conflict during the same period, had 35 police officers per 10,000 inhabitants (Llorente 1997, 24). Goldsmith (2000) makes a similar comparison, noting that, during the period of

---

[19] Author interview with Camilo Granada, Bogotá, July 17, 2013.
[20] "Policía: a ganar credibilidad," *El Mundo*, November 21, 1992, 9A.

sectarian conflict in Northern Ireland, there was one police officer for every 125 inhabitants, whereas in Colombia the ratio was just over one police officer for every 500 inhabitants (172). Scholars and security experts also emphasized the lack of specialized skills for crime prevention and urban security (Camacho 1993, 6), and the low salaries and precarious conditions of most police officers (Restrepo Riaza et al. 1994a, 66). Indeed, the minister of defense described the security institutions he oversaw as follows: "The precariousness was considerable; suitable and well-trained personnel were insufficient in all of the agencies, their training scant and their means of transport and communication was very deficient" (Pardo Rueda 1996, 212).

Such deficiencies were quite apparent in Medellín the center of the state's battle against drug cartels, where police proved to be equally inept at protecting citizens, leading many to reject the police altogether. María Victoria Llorente, security expert and former advisor to the Ministry of Defense, recalled in an interview the "strong questioning [of the police] to the point where the governor of Antioquia and the mayor of Medellín would ask the national government to remove the police because they were clearly considered part of the problem."[21]

But perhaps the most poignant symbol of the National Police's limited resources and capacity is the very program that was meant to salvage the police's relationship with society and improve urban security: the Immediate Attention Centers (*Centro de Atención Inmediata*, CAI). The CAIs are based on the Japanese *koban*, local neighborhood police stations that are intended to increase police presence in communities and allow for a faster response to crime. Begun in 1987, the CAIs grew at a rapid pace in Bogotá and throughout the country;[22] by 1994 there were 300 around the country, about half of them in Bogotá.[23] The CAIs, however, presented two sets of problems for the National Police: they were frequent targets of attacks by cartels, and they required a larger number of officers than the National Police was able to provide. The CAI was another highly visible example of the National Police's "growth without planning" (Pardo Rueda 1996, 340) and thus became another contributor to the police's decline in the public's opinion. Indeed, in 1994, General Octavio Vargas

---

[21] Author interview with María Victoria Llorente, Bogotá, September 19, 2012.
[22] Pardo Rueda (1996) attributes the rapid growth of the CAIs to the fact that they were "easy, cheap, and quick to set up," which also made them a favorite currency used in municipal political campaigns (340).
[23] "CAIs cambian o se acaban," *El Tiempo*, October 1, 1994.

Silva, then director of the National Police, acknowledged that "the dis-
credit (*desprestigio*) they cause is greater than the service they deliver."[24]
Citizen complaints about the CAIs were abundant around this time, as
indicated by this reader's letter to the newspaper *El Tiempo*: "The two
times I was robbed it was near a CAI, and both times I found that inside
there was only one officer who, upon being informed [of the crime], can't
do anything beyond calling a phone number that is always busy."[25]

The CAIs also exemplified how the drug war undermined ordinary
security provision, leaving the police with diminished resources and capacity to provide urban security. The former commander of Bogotá's
Metropolitan Police, Brigadier General Guillermo León Diettes,
explained in an interview how this occurred:

When the CAIs were created ... the idea was that in each CAI there would be
a second lieutenant (the commander of the CAI), two or three sergeants, and
twenty agents. That's how it was born; it was a very good idea. But what
happened? When drug trafficking began to be a big problem ... where did they
go first? The Bogotá Metropolitan Police had and still has the largest number of
police officers. And [police commanders] would say, "There's a problem in
Medellín, twenty police officers were killed, same thing in Cali." And they
would say, "We have to take out 100 police officers from Bogotá"; where did
they get them from? "We can take 10 police officers from 10 CAIs, and there we
have the 100 officers." So what happened to the CAIs? Previously, the philosophy
had been, we would hear of a case in the neighborhood and two police officers
would go on a motorcycle ... It's in the name [Immediate Attention Center],
immediate reaction ... So [a neighborhood resident] would call and say,
"There's a robbery," and two police officers would race over. But then
a moment came where, after losing so many police officers, what remained in
the CAI? One or two officers. So now [the resident] would call and say, "There's
a robbery." The officer takes down the address and says "Yes, right away." He
hangs up the phone and what does he do? He calls the central police station,
whereas before they would send [an officer on] a motorcycle. The "immediate
reaction" part was lost.[26]

But the police's low capacity to provide security in the country's urban
centers did not stem solely from the strains of the drug war. An additional
challenge to the National Police's capacity was its low level of specialization, as reflected in its organizational structure. One of the earliest areas of
specialization for the National Police was the creation of a judicial police
in the 1960s, but this function and division was not permanent until the

[24] "CAIs cambian o se acaban," *El Tiempo*, October 1, 1994.
[25] "La comunidad comienza a reaccionar," *El Tiempo*, September 25, 1991.
[26] Author interview with Brigadier General Diettes, Bogotá, July 16, 2013.

1991 Constitution. Even this institutionalized unit was highly deficient, however. A survey of judges in the Antioquia department asked them to evaluate the police's capacity and performance in its judicial police role. More than three-quarters, or 76.5 percent, of respondents said the National Police does not perform its functions or does so insufficiently (Restrepo Riaza et al. 1994b, 59). The National Police's deficiencies in this arena did not stop at a lack of capacity or specialization, as officials routinely condemned police malfeasance. In one instance, the country's attorney general denounced the lack of cooperation by police and military in anti-narcotics operations in the department of Caquetá and hinted at "deceptive maneuvers" to frustrate the regional prosecutor's investigation.[27] In a sign of the evaluation of the National Police's judicial police capacities, a reform proposal submitted by the country's chief prosecutor, inspector general, and other legal entities in 1993 advocated for removing the investigatory function from the National Police altogether.[28]

In the 1980s, the National Police also created anti-narcotics, kidnapping, and extortion units, increasing its level of specialization. Though the anti-narcotics unit was considered an "island of excellence,"[29] however, agents and officers were routinely transferred across units, for instance from rural policing to anti-narcotics, in order to meet the challenges of fighting the guerrilla forces and the drug cartels. The reality of public security in Colombia therefore limited the degree to which these were specialized units in practice. Another shortcoming of the police's organizational and functional structure was the lack of a specialized intelligence unit that was distinct from criminal investigation. Security scholar Álvaro Camacho (1993) and other members of the Consultative Commission also expressed particular concern about the lack of specialization in fighting regular crime, recommending the creation of separate units for urban and rural policing, given the vast differences in security challenges facing each.

In the face of worsening security conditions due to the drug war and the armed conflict, as well as growing citizen demands for improved security, the National Police's institutional decay resulted in a greatly diminished capacity to perform its basic functions. The many deficiencies of the National Police did not go unnoticed by government officials, as many public officials and political leaders sounded the alarm about the broad

[27] "Policía y Ejército no apoyaron a la Fiscalía," *El Tiempo*, October 8, 1992.
[28] "Piden 'desmilitarizar' a la Policía Nacional," *El Espectador*, April 20, 1993.
[29] Author interview with Rafael Pardo Rueda, Bogotá, October 16, 2012.

structural problems facing the police. Gustavo de Greiff, the attorney general at the time, rebuked the police for its conspicuous inability to protect its own members from violence. Following the brutal killing of a police captain in Medellín, de Greiff denounced the "inefficiency and incredulity of the police. This is worth saying, on behalf of all Colombians, because it's incredible that in the city with the largest police force, it's possible to assassinate one of its members in this way."[30] In another instance, Horacio Serpa, a prominent Liberal politician, lambasted the "irresponsible, negligent, arbitrary, and even delinquent [officers] in the National Police that have caused the institution to lose legitimacy and credibility."[31] But the most consistent rebuke of the National Police came from the Consejo de Estado, Colombia's highest administrative court, which, as noted, repeatedly issued verdicts holding the state financially responsible for the crimes of the National Police. In one such verdict in a case where police commanders levied only a sixty-day suspension against officers who tortured and burned alive two young men suspected of a theft, the Consejo de Estado declared unequivocally, "Something is failing in the recruitment, oversight, and administration of the Public Force."[32]

THE PERSISTENCE OF AUTHORITARIAN COERCION

As in the other cases studied in this book, Colombia's National Police responded to rising crime and violence and to citizens' demands for protection not by building capacity but by engaging in widespread authoritarian coercive practices. Echoing the linkage drawn in the preceding sections between the extraordinary violence the Colombian state confronted in the form of the armed conflict and the drug war, and the authoritarian coercive practices wielded in response by its security institutions, Colombia's inspector general (*procurador general*) lamented in 1992 that the "most uncivilized and least democratic practices are used to guarantee the existence of the state" (Amnesty International 1994b, 37).[33] The inspector general's remarks were notable not only because they

---

[30] "La Policía no cuida ni a sus miembros: Fiscal General de la Nación," *El Nuevo Siglo*, December 22, 1992, 12A.

[31] "Denuncia Serpa Uribe: 'En la policía hay negligencia y corrupción,'" *El Colombiano*, December 28, 1992, 2A.

[32] "Critican proceso de selección de policías," *El Nuevo Siglo*, November 5, 1993.

[33] Page numbers cited for this report correspond to the PDF version available online at www.amnesty.org/download/Documents/180000/amr230011994en.pdf, accessed October 21, 2018.

situate rampant state violence in the context of the threats posed by the guerrillas and drug cartels, but also because they underscore the incompatibility of the state's ongoing coercive practices and structures with democracy. This section discusses how security provision at the nexus of the Colombian state's multiple wars, the police's extensive militarization alongside the prevalence of National Security Doctrine, and the lethal violence targeting the police resulted in distinctly authoritarian modes of coercion. As I detail in the next section, these conditions perpetuated the routine deployment of coercion well outside the scope of the law and in the service of political and private interests, while impeding external accountability of the National Police by civilian state entities.

Arbitrary Deployment of Coercion

Throughout the 1980s and early 1990s, as the Colombian state intensified its war against drug cartels, the National Police engaged in widespread exceptional violence against the citizenry – not based on the dictates of the law but in the form of extrajudicial executions, enforced disappearances, torture, and other forms of abuses. Citizens from around the country interviewed by the Consultative Commission to Reform the Police (see Chapter 7) told commission members that the national police "ignores the rights of the citizens," "acts with unnecessary violence," and engages in "abuse and systematic trampling [of rights]" (Presidencia de la República 1994, 142). Official data support these claims. The National Police was the state entity most frequently accused of violating human rights in reports issued by the Inspector General's Office (Procuraduría) during the early 1990s detailing data from citizen complaints received by their office. In the most comprehensive of these reports, corresponding to complaints received between January 1990 and April 1991, the National Police was implicated in 259 homicides, 14 massacres, the enforced disappearance of 89 victims, the torture of 319 people, the causing of physical injuries to 743 people, and the arbitrary detention of 625 people.[34] All told, the National Police was responsible for 55 percent of human rights violations reported to the Inspector General's Office.[35]

---

[34] "Informe sobre Derechos Humanos 1990–1991," Procuraduría General de la Nación, report accessed at the archives of the Centro de Investigación y Educación Popular (CINEP) in August 2018.

[35] Subsequent reports named police as responsible for 58 percent of rights violations in 1992 and 44 percent of violations in 1993. See "III Informe sobre Derechos Humanos 1993–1994," Procuraduría General de la Nación, 14.

One modality of the National Police's use of arbitrary coercion is worth detailing further, as it presents perhaps the starkest illustration of exceptional coercion: the police's rampant involvement in so-called social cleansing killings. An exhaustive journalistic investigation of the phenomenon demonstrated that, starting in 1981, "reports of the involvement of police and DAS agents in these types of events became increasingly frequent" (Rojas 1996, 19). According to Llorente (2005), "police gangs formed in several cities to carry out armed robberies and 'social cleansing,' that is, the selective killing of criminals, prostitutes, beggars, and the mentally ill" (191). Human rights organizations documented cases of police participation in such death squads throughout the country. A 1994 report by Amnesty International cited alarming figures from the Intercongregational Commission for Justice and Peace, which recorded instances of such killings: 1,900 "social cleansing murders" occurred between 1988 and 1992 in Colombia's primary cities, including 500 in 1992; 229 were in the city of Cali alone (Amnesty International 1994b, 3). Police officers in the city of Pereira were implicated in the killing of sixty indigent persons in the month of July 1991, and the municipal ombudsman in the city of Popayán found dozens of police killings of "people the security forces consider to be 'disposable'" throughout the early 1990s (Amnesty International 1994b, 3). In perhaps one of the most prominent cases of such killings in Colombia, three police officers were implicated in an egregious example of social cleansing and organ trafficking, in which dozens of indigent people in the city of Barranquilla were killed by private security agents and sold to a local medical school in 1992.[36]

The police's involvement in what were widely recognized as "social cleansing" killings underscores the exceptional nature of the police's deployment of coercion. In the context of the extraordinary levels of violence targeting the Colombian police during this period, police officers conducted hundreds of killings each year, targeting not the actors responsible for these attacks but instead the most vulnerable segments of the population, where no justification of self-defense or legality could plausibly be made.

Colombian police officers were also implicated in countless high-profile killings that similarly had little to do with curbing rising crime and

---

[36] Comisión Interamericana de Derechos Humanos, 1993, "Segundo Informe sobre la Situación de los Derechos Humanos en Colombia," OEA/Ser.L/V/II.84 Doc. 39 rev. October 14, 1993, www.cidh.org/countryrep/Colombia93sp/cap.7a.htm, accessed October 14, 2018.

violence, instead reflecting considerable malfeasance. In early 1992, police were implicated in the killing of Tsuyoshi Mokuda, the vice president of Colombia's branch of the Japanese car company Mazda.[37] Police were also charged with the killing of Luis Mora Gonzalez, a former regional prosecutor, in Sincelejo, in what was allegedly a murder for hire ordered by a local rancher.[38] Moreover, many police killings in low-income communities were often thinly veiled acts of revenge following killings of police officers. In one instance, masked and heavily armed police officers responded to the fatal shooting of two police officers in Medellín by raiding a poor neighborhood and killing nine children (Amnesty International 1994b, 4). In addition to rampant extrajudicial lethal violence, police were also routinely implicated in enforced disappearances, such that "over 1,500 people are believed to have been 'disappeared' after detention by the security forces between 1978 and 1992" (Amnesty International 1994b, 2). Human rights organizations also reported testimonies of torture of children at the hands of police, including "beatings, rape, electrical shocks, near-drownings in filthy water, and near-suffocation" (Human Rights Watch 1994).

So frequent was the National Police's use of coercion outside the bounds of the law that, as stated previously Colombia's highest administrative court, the Consejo de Estado, routinely ordered the state to compensate the families of victims of the police's crimes. In one case involving the torture and murder of a bus driver, the court chastised the police, apparently considering it necessary to remind the police of the importance of adherence to the law in carrying out its functions: "The state can use with all rigor – within the limits imposed by the principle of proportionality – all means to impede a person from engaging in illegal conduct. But it does not have the power to take the life of or torture a human being."[39]

Coercion in the Service of Political and Private Interests

Since its consolidation as a national police force and subordination to the Ministry of War (subsequently Defense) in the 1950s, Colombia's National Police has largely avoided extensive politicized coercion in the form that occurred in the case of the Buenos Aires police (Chapter 4). As

---

[37] See "Policías Mataron a un japonés," *El Tiempo*, February 16, 1992; "A Consejo de Guerra policías que asesinaron a industrial," *El Tiempo*, February 18, 1992.

[38] "A juicio dos policías," *El Tiempo*, September 1, 1990.

[39] "Llaman la atención a la Policía," *El Colombiano*, December 5, 1992, 7C.

experts such as Camacho (1994) have observed, however, the National Police has pursued "a new form of privatization, consisting of its subordination to private local power groups that substitute state presence and action" (29). Indeed, Leal Buitrago (1994) similarly argues that some members of the National Police have effectively privatized the police's function, placing it at the service of large landowners, business owners, industrialists, and even organized crime groups dominant in different regions, often committing human rights violations to protect the interests of their patrons (204).

Thus, rather than being strictly a response to the country's war against drug cartels, much of the National Police's extrajudicial violence was the result of the deployment of coercion toward political and private ends. Moncada (2016) notes that, in cities like Cali, police "had a history of participating in varied forms of extrajudicial violence, including social cleansings, at the behest of local political and economic leaders as part of maintaining the exclusionary political order" (101). Human rights organizations came to similar conclusions, observing that "most killings of 'undesirables' in the cities appear to be carried out by police agents, often from the F-2 intelligence branch, many of whom are contracted by local [business owners] seeking to protect their economic interests" (Amnesty International 1994b, 5). Even when city governments tried to adopt local security reforms that promoted democratic coercion, the business sector often provided funding directly to the police, undermining the ability of local government to exercise oversight and accountability over police, as mandated by the 1991 Constitution (Art. 315). As Moncada (2016) documents, business leaders used their financial support and influence "to increase the repressive capacity of local security forces" in support of their own interests (102), to such an extent that "support from the private sector had clearly enabled the police to assume greater autonomy vis-à-vis local government" (104). The financial support of local business thus not only helped to promote the police's deployment of arbitrary coercion in support of its interests but also helped to undermine external accountability.

Weakness of External Accountability

By the time that reform was eventually enacted in 1993, the inadequacy of the police's internal oversight mechanisms was evident. Many citizens interviewed by the Consultative Commission that year said that the "police are as feared as the wrongdoer" and reported police involvement in crimes such as robbery and assault, as well as complicity with mafias and *sicariato* (the business of hired killings). Some also said that, when they reported these crimes to superiors, their complaints "fell on deaf ears," and others said they feared retaliation (Presidencia de la República 1994, 141).

Yet external oversight mechanisms routinely did not fare much better. Formally, the National Police is subject to oversight by a number of entities within the executive branch, as well as the judicial and legislative branches. Despite the routine and widespread arbitrary uses of coercion by the Colombian police, however, the extent to which these entities act to hold police accountable has been uneven at best.

Within the executive branch, the Inspector General's Office has been a key entity charged with external oversight of the National Police, receiving and investigating citizen complaints of human rights abuses. Yet, human rights organizations routinely observed that officers implicated in egregious rights violations, including political killings and disappearances, were "seldom punished" (Amnesty International 1994b, 36). An analysis of "social cleansing" killings committed by police, meanwhile, found that adequate investigation by the Inspector General's Office of police involvement in "social cleansing" cases was repeatedly "thwarted by the decision of the Personnel Division of the National Police, which on various occasions transferred the accused to diverse areas of the country, delaying the [investigative] process repeatedly" (Rojas 1996, 75). Perhaps as a result of the strategies used by the National Police to interfere with the inspector general's investigations, few cases of human rights violations reported in 1990 and 1991 resulted in a final determination, and even fewer resulted in sanctions against the accused officers (see Table 5.1). In a subsequent report, the Inspector General's Office complained that "the difficulties entailed for the Inspector General's Office in cases involving the National Police and the Armed Forces have resulted in excessive delays in disciplinary determinations."[40] As a result, according to Colombian scholars, "oversight entities such as the *Procuraduría* (Inspector General's Office) and the *Fiscalía* (Attorney General's Office) have not been willing to control and sanction criminal acts by members [of the police] in a systematic manner" (Ruiz Vasquez, Illera Correal & Manrique 2006, 194).

In addition to the National Police's efforts to thwart investigation by the inspector general, the executive branch, particularly the Ministry of Defense,

---

[40] "Informe sobre Derechos Humanos 1993–1994," Procuraduría General de la Nación, 17.

TABLE 5.1 *Inspector general's final determination in human rights violations by National Police (1990–1991)*

Type	No. of cases	Absolved	Sanctioned
Homicide	259	9	23
Massacre	14	0	2
Disappearance	89	5	5
Torture	319	5	12
Physical injuries	743	40	148

"Informe sobre Derechos Humanos 1990–1991." Procuraduría General de la Nación.

to which the National Police is subordinated, often served as an obstacle to external accountability by other state entities. For instance, when the Consejo de Estado held the state financially responsible for some of the National Police's most egregious crimes, the Ministry of Defense often refused to accept the court's judgments. In one verdict in which an indigent person was killed by police in the Antioquia department in 1986, the Ministry of Defense refused to issue the payment ordered by the Consejo de Estado, arguing that the victim "was neither useful nor productive, either to society or to his family, but who was a vagrant whose presence nobody in the town of Liborina wanted" (Amnesty International 1994b, 6).

An additional obstacle to the ability of the judiciary to serve as an instance of external accountability was the constitutional provision subjecting the National Police to the military justice system (Art. 221). As a result, few cases of police killings went to civilian courts, which often ended up dropping the charges against police officers. In one instance, a civilian court dropped charges against three high-ranking police officials implicated in the kidnapping and killing of a university student in Bogotá (Amnesty International 1994b, 40). Civilian officials in the early 1990s decried the subordination of the police to the military legal system, citing the obstacle posed to civilian oversight (Presidencia de la República 1994, 172).[41] In its 1993 human rights report, the Inspector General's Office was unequivocal in its critique of the challenges posed by the military justice system for external accountability:

[41] See also "Piden 'desmilitarizar' a la Policía Nacional," *El Espectador*, April 20, 1993, 8A; "Civiles y no generales deben mandar en Policía Nacional," *El Tiempo*, April 20, 1993, 1A.

Certainly the military justice [system] has demonstrated little effectiveness in the judgment and conviction of violators of human rights among the ranks of the state's security and defense entities ... In not a few cases, the verdicts of the military justice system are in open contradiction with the determinations of the Inspector General's Office, in which case the disciplinary sanctions [issued by the inspector general] lose a great deal of their deterrent effect."[42]

The legislative branch similarly exercised little systematic oversight of the National Police, perhaps in part because the decades-long state of exception enabled the president to enact measures relating to defense and security through executive orders. In late 1992, as Congress debated a bill to regulate the declaration of state of exception in accordance with the Constitution, there were "calls by members of Congress for the suspension of some fundamental human rights during the government's offensive against organized crime and guerrilla groups" (Amnesty International 1994b, 38). In the face of this effort to cede to police and the military greater exceptional coercive authority, the inspector general wrote to congressional leaders with an urgent call to preserve democratic coercion:

In the face of these constitutional principles, it is terrifying that, given the crisis faced by the country, there are those that think the solution is achieved when oversight authorities, especially the Inspector General of the Nation, turn their backs on their legal and constitutional obligations and tolerate repressive mechanisms that have no place in our legal order.[43]

Indeed, with the exception of a bill introduced by Conservative Senator Fabio Valencia Cossio in early 1992, and a subsequent bill introduced by the administration to undercut it (see Chapter 7),[44] there were few other efforts by the legislative branch to rein in the National Police.

Rather than the actions of the entities formally charged with oversight of the National Police, the most consistent instrument of external accountability was the use of mass purges of police officers by the Minister of Defense, with the intention of expelling police officers suspected of malfeasance (Decree 2010/1992). Rafael Pardo, former minister of defense, said in an interview that thousands of officers, as much of 10 percent of the force, were expelled through such purges. However, the use of purges as the main mode of external accountability suffers from a number of

---

[42] Procuraduría General de la Nación, "Informe sobre Derechos Humanos 1993–1994," p. 17.
[43] "SOS de Procurador a Senado y Cámara," *El Tiempo*, October 31, 1992.
[44] "Debate sobre la Policía," *El Nuevo Siglo*, November 4, 1992, 12A.

deficiencies. First, human rights organizations found that "the 'purge' has seldom been extended to those implicated in political crimes" (Amnesty International 1994b, 43). Second, the ad hoc application and legal dubiousness of such purges through a "discretional authority to retire [officials] without explanation"[45] undermined their effectiveness as instruments of accountability. Pardo explained the purges were "controversial" and that "it's possible that there were arbitrary actions, but in essence it gave the citizenry a sense that the police could be purged."

But the primary problem with purges as a response is that they simultaneously represent an acknowledgment by the state of the widespread systematic extralegal violence and corruption by the National Police *and* an unwillingness to use formal institutional oversight mechanisms to exercise effective external accountability. State officials undoubtedly recognized the extent of the problem. Mass expulsions of police officers for suspected corruption and violence were frequent and far-reaching, particularly under Defense Minister Pardo,[46] but such purges were the extent of external accountability faced by police. For instance, the case of the killing of sixty indigent people in the city of Pereira in 1991 resulted only in the expulsion of thirteen police officers (Amnesty International 1994b, 3).

Despite an abundance of evidence of the widespread authoritarian coercive practices and corruption by the National Police, and acknowledgment of the magnitude of the problem by state officials, there was little effort to undertake systematic civilian oversight, whether through the executive, the legislature, or the judiciary. Instead, the National Police was given considerable autonomy to run its own affairs and evade reforms.

THE COLOMBIAN STATE'S CRISIS OF LEGITIMACY AND TRANSFORMATION (EXCEPT THE POLICE)

In order to understand the institutional deterioration of the National Police and the remarkable autonomy it nonetheless enjoyed during this

---

[45] Author interview with former minister of defense Rafael Pardo Rueda. According to former minister Pardo, this authority was used to carry out purges because of the difficulty of sustaining allegations of corruption and illicit enrichment.

[46] "Expulsan a 29 hombres de la policía," *El Tiempo*, August 13, 1992; "Expulsan a 55 policías," *El Tiempo*, September 19 1990; "En Cali destituyen a catorce policías," *El Tiempo*, September 7, 1990; "Director del DIJIN acusa a coronel R," *El Tiempo*, August 12, 1990; "El policía escondido," *El Tiempo*, April 4, 1992.

period, it is essential to situate the police's challenges within the grave crisis of legitimacy afflicting the Colombian state as a whole. It is also essential to ask why the National Police was exempted from the broad agenda of institutional transformation adopted in response to that crisis. Just as policing constituted a key oversight of democratic transitions in Argentina and Brazil, the National Police remained absent throughout a transformative period of institutional reforms that reached every sector of the Colombian state – except the police.

The extent of Colombia's social, political, and institutional upheaval resulting from the proliferation of violent actors – guerrilla forces, drug cartels, paramilitary groups – is difficult to overstate. The resulting institutional crisis – which Paschel (2010) has characterized as "domestic political disequilibrium" – was perhaps best represented by the existential threat facing the Colombian state and its representatives, as well as the precariousness of the security apparatus purportedly charged with protecting them from violence. By January 1990, about 1,000 officials and political leaders in Bogotá alone had official escorts from one of the state's security forces (Pardo Rueda, 1996, 212). Nevertheless, violence against high-level leaders, and in general, was rampant: four presidential candidates were killed leading up to the 1990 elections, including Liberal Party candidate Luis Carlos Galán, considered the front-runner. Former Liberal Party senator José Blackburn, who still keeps in his office a large framed photo of himself and Galán, recalled that period as "the worst possible political climate. I challenge anyone complaining [about the current climate] to put up with what we lived through in that era." He described a climate of fear in which presidential candidates were being assassinated; he recalled planning for meetings with Galán in which participants were afraid to talk about plans and meeting places by phone and instead had to pass along this information on "little pieces of paper ... and we would hold meetings in the most unheard of places" due to security concerns.[47] César Gaviria, who would go on to win the 1990 election as Galán's successor within the Liberal Party, also described it as a "very complex period. The truth was that in that election there was a climate of fear and apathy, of disenchantment and crisis."[48]

Perhaps the clearest manifestation of this crisis and the impotence of the Colombian state in combating the multiple armed actors challenging its monopoly of legitimate violence was the near-permanence of a state of

---

[47] Author interview with former senator José Blackburn, Bogotá, July 15, 2013.
[48] Author interview with former president César Gaviria, Bogotá, July 11, 2013.

exception declared throughout the 1970s and 1980s.[49] Over the course of this period, the state of exception became the norm: the executive effectively ruled by decree, and many fundamental rights were suspended. Former president Gaviria said in an interview that one of his aims in an effort to get the state back to a normal state of operation, was "taking the country out of the idea that problems are resolved through decree, which is what happened for decades. All the problems were resolved by decreeing a state of exception or a state of economic emergency ... [Under my administration] that disappeared. Now the state is obligated to emit legislation as it should, through the Congress." The country's high rates of violence thus interfered with the normal functioning of democracy in important ways.

Colombia's democratic regime faced an additional distortion resulting from the extensive violence experienced throughout the 20th century, the elimination of ordinary partisan competition. Starting in 1946, the Liberal and Conservative parties entered into a power-sharing pact known as the Frente Nacional (National Front). The National Front established what Leal Buitrago (1995) called a "bipartisan monopoly," in which the two parties not only alternated in the presidency but also shared power through the inclusion of both parties in government posts. As one might expect, however, such a pact – in which "politics were absorbed by bipartisanism, [and] which co-opted most spaces in an incipient civil society" – also created incentives for those in power to close off entry to other political expressions (Leal Buitrago 1995, 23). As a result, by 1978, the National Front had become "immobilized," the political class had lost its credibility, and the political system as a whole was seen as lacking in legitimacy (Pardo Rueda 1996, 246).

Colombian scholars have documented the effects of a "permanent state of war" on governance and state–society relations (Comisión de Estudios sobre la Violencia 1987; Uribe de Hincapié 1995), as well as society's "general pessimism due to the impotence of the state to contain the multiple drivers of violence" (Torres Forero 2007, 31). In this context, former defense minister Rafael Pardo Rueda offered an unequivocally grim diagnosis of the crisis facing the Colombian state as a whole:

In 1989 and early 1990, the stability of the political system was in real and imminent danger of collapsing ... [The] accelerated delegitimization of the

---

[49] The 1991 Constitution reined in the president's ability to declare a state of siege (Art. 213) by limiting its duration to ninety days and the number of times it could be extended to two periods.

establishment, which demonstrated itself to be incapable of resolving the problems of the governed, presented a devastating panorama. (Pardo Rueda 1996, 211)

From Crisis of Legitimacy to "Institutional Shake-Up"

In line with much scholarship on crisis and institutional change,[50] what emerged from this "devastating panorama" was a vast transformation of the political system, forged through a political consensus to address widespread societal discontent and alienation from the state. As former president César Gaviria, who took office in 1990, told me, "all that violence delegitimized the political system ... and that is why there was so much desire and will to transform it."

After winning the 1990 presidential elections, Gaviria sought to implement a series of reforms to address the crisis of legitimacy that had permeated the Colombian state for years. His agenda, which he called the *revolcón institucional* or "institutional shake-up," intended to strengthen the Colombian state and reestablish its credibility. In the first six months of his administration, Gaviria pushed forth a Law of Public Services, privatized the concessions of ports, created a pensions fund and a new health systems law, deepened the decentralization of education as well as fiscal decentralization, made the Central Bank autonomous, and pushed reforms to the criminal justice system, including highly controversial policies for prosecuting drug trafficking organizations.

According to Gaviria, his "institutional shake-up" was bold not only in content but also in strategy. In order to push through these initiatives at the start of his administration, "we used a methodology that is a bit different from what is done in the United States and in Latin America, which was to promote all of these reforms at the same time, rather than one by one ... We took them all to the Congress and promoted them simultaneously ... I think that facilitated the economic reforms, which in turn facilitated the political ones."[51] Gaviria thus pushed through a number of highly controversial policies in a short period of time, including central bank independence, which, according to the former president, "was quite costly politically."

Undoubtedly among the most politically risky policies of Gaviria's "institutional shake-up," however, were two policies relating to the

---

[50] See, for instance, Carpenter and Sin's (2007) overview and critique of crisis-based arguments.

[51] Author interview with César Gaviria, Bogotá, July 11, 2013.

drug war. The first of these was the policy known as *justicia sin rostro* or "faceless justice" (Decree 2790/1990), under which the identities of judges, investigators, and witnesses were to be concealed in criminal proceedings. In response to the grave threat facing judges presiding over cases relating to drug trafficking,[52] they were literally made "faceless," covering their faces in the presence of the accused and omitting their names and signatures from official records.[53] In our interview, President Gaviria referred to the "faceless justice" policy as "a secret justice system emanating from a state of exception ... an extreme institutional situation." A similarly extraordinary measure was the policy of "submitting to justice" (*sometimiento a la justicia*, Decree 303/1991), an important shift in the state's approach to prosecuting high-level drug traffickers under the Colombian justice system rather than extraditing them to the United States.[54] These policies intended to reestablish the Colombian state's ability to enforce its own laws, but they were also a "shake-up" in the conduct of the drug war, particularly in the potential challenge posed to the United States by the shift in extradition policy.

Even more remarkable than the changes Gaviria was able to implement, however, was the fact that he was able to do so with broad political support, including an approval rating above 70 percent.[55] Having come into office in the wake of complete delegitimization of the political system, the collapse of the National Front pact, and a highly weakened state apparatus, Gaviria could have easily faced the continuation of the "devastating panorama" described by his defense minister. Instead, Gaviria recalled a broad political consensus in favor of reforms:

My administration always managed to maintain a very broad coalition in support of its initiatives in the Congress because there was a reformist spirit, of which my administration was not the owner. Everyone felt part of that reformist spirit. It's

---

[52] Some thirty-two judges overseeing drug-trafficking cases were killed between 1984 and 1990. In contrast, two were killed between 1991 and 1996. See "Arrancan jueces sin rostro," *El Tiempo*, January 13, 1991; and "A prueba de balas," *Semana*, January 1, 1996.

[53] Identities were anonymized using fingerprints, unique numeric identifiers, and even pseudonyms.

[54] The 1991 Constitution would subsequently prohibit the extradition of Colombians (Art. 35). Prior to that, a number of drug traffickers, most notably Pablo Escobar, had formed a group called Los Extraditables (The Extraditables) dedicated to committing assassinations and other violent acts in opposition to the Colombian government's extradition policy. They declared their preference for a "grave in Colombia to a jail in the United States." See "Extraditables: Fin del terror," *El Tiempo*, July 4, 1991.

[55] "Calificación: Apenas Regular," *El Tiempo*, August 7, 1992.

not that it was exclusively the administration; the whole country found itself in a reformist climate, and that meant we didn't have a monopoly on that.[56]

The "reformist spirit" resulting from widespread societal discontent did indeed lead to a set of institutional reforms as transformative as Gaviria's "institutional shake-up": the 1991 Constitution. The Constitutional Assembly itself is an example of the broad demand for reform that emerged throughout Colombian society. Although constitutional reforms had been debated throughout the 1980s, the country's political leaders took little action to move the reform process forward. In response to the inaction of political leaders, broad despair over the violence consuming the country, and disillusionment about the capacity of the current political system to address the country's problems, widespread societal mobilization led by student groups emerged in 1989 and 1990.[57] In one of the early marches held in 1989, the student groups declared both their "support for our democratic institutions in their fight against all those forces that seek to destabilize them, be it drug trafficking, guerillas, paramilitary groups, and others" and their demand for a plebiscite "of the people to reform those institutions that impede the resolution of the current crisis" (Torres Forero 2007, 31).

With tens of thousands of students marching in the streets and a plebiscite in which 89 percent of voters voted in favor of a Constitutional Assembly in May 1990 (Quintero Ramírez 2002, 133), newly elected president César Gaviria had indeed received a mandate from voters demanding an "institutional shake-up." Shortly after taking office, Gaviria issued an executive order establishing the terms of the Constitutional Assembly and the election of its members. The Constitutional Assembly similarly represented an instance of widespread societal mobilization, with considerable participation by societal organizations. The Constitution that ultimately emerged from this process indeed reflected this broad societal participation and political consensus to overhaul the Colombian state, with the creation of a host of new institutions, including a new Constitutional Court and a new Prosecutor's Office (Fiscalía), novel participatory mechanisms (Mayka 2019), and broad rights and protections for ethnic and racial minorities (Paschel 2016). Gaviria described in our interview the robust political consensus that drove the constitutional reform process:

---

[56] Author interview with César Gaviria, Bogotá, July 11, 2013. .
[57] As Quintero Ramírez (2002) notes, the key catalyst of the mobilization was the assassination of Liberal Party presidential candidate Luis Carlos Galán in August 1989.

The constitutional convention, the way it functioned, was done with ... enormous political will. The votes were not questioned, the rules were respected, there was a tripartite presidency ... One needed a great deal of political will to move that forward, and we had it ... [due to] the deep crisis we faced as a result of the violence that had been generated throughout the electoral process.

Stalled Police Reform amid an "Institutional Shake-Up"

But the broad-based political will described by Gaviria seemingly did not extend to the National Police, which escaped the ongoing overhaul of the Colombian state despite being engulfed by the same profound institutional crisis. The police's continuity in the face of an "institutional shake-up" did not escape notice by political leaders at the time. Indeed, during a congressional hearing in 1993, one dissident Liberal Party senator asked why the president's many executive orders to restructure and modernize state institutions neglected the police, "an entity so essential for the security of the citizenry, [and] the prevention and repression of crime."[58] Exactly one year before the scandal that would lead to long-overdue reform (Chapter 7), Colombia's Inspector General Carlos Gustavo Arrieta sounded the alarm about the urgent need to "purify" (*depurar*) the National Police and enact "very severe internal oversight mechanisms," as he announced an investigation into the police force's role in the massacre of twenty indigenous people in the Cauca department.[59]

In the next section I explain the lack of structural reform of the National Police during this period by demonstrating how the police leveraged their structural power to constrain the policy agenda and how the fragmentation of societal preferences indicated to politicians that reforming the police would not be electorally advantageous. Before proceeding to this account, however, it is important to address a number of alternative explanations for the absence of police reform. In this section I discard two related alternative explanations: that politicians did not prioritize police reform due to a policy agenda that was already too crowded; and that policing and security were not salient during this period. These explanations cannot account for the absence of police reform since a number of institutional changes brought about by

[58] "La Policía debe ser totalmente reestructurada," *El Nuevo Siglo*, March 19, 1993.
[59] "Procuraduría urge necesidad de depurar la Policía," *El Nuevo Siglo*, February 29, 1992; "Pide aligerar proceso de depuración," *El Mundo*, February 29, 1992.

Gaviria's crowded policy agenda – particularly the 1991 Constitution – mandated structural police reforms in order to be implemented. Moreover, Gaviria's agenda demonstrates recognition of the police's profound crisis and the salience of security issues, but his response was limited to marginal reforms.[60]

How the 1991 Constitution Mandated Police Reforms

A possible explanation for the lack of police reform during this period is that, with no shortage of pressing matters to address, the policy agenda during the early 1990s was simply too crowded to enact police reform. Yet, a crowded policy agenda was characteristic of the Gaviria administration and, indeed, was part of his strategy to enact his "institutional shake-up," as discussed. Moreover, the omission of the National Police from these extensive reforms remains curious because many of the institutional changes brought about by Gaviria's "shake-up" and the 1991 Constitution themselves mandated structural and operational police reforms in order to be implemented in practice. For instance, the new Constitution established that governors and mayors would be the "first authority" on police matters in their respective jurisdictions and compelled the National Police to comply and cooperate with their orders (Art. 315). It also gave the National Police the role of judicial police, placing it under the jurisdiction of the judicial system and Prosecutor's Office (Fiscalía), newly created by the 1991 Constitution (Arts. 249, 250). These institutional changes had important implications for the police, formally introducing new functions and new chains of command, and therefore required structural reforms in order for these measures to be implemented in practice. As former defense minister Pardo noted in an interview, the "double dependence" of the police on the judicial branch (only with respect to its role as judicial police) and to mayors and governors, in addition to the Ministry of Defense and the national government, introduced new layers of complexity and "generated resistance within the police and so we would have to establish it by law later on in the reform."[61] The administration was therefore aware of the potential tensions generated by the new Constitution and the need for those tensions to be addressed through legislation.

---

[60] In Chapter 7 I address a third alternative explanation – that police reform would have been enacted eventually anyway, in light of the National Police's institutional crisis – by examining a failed police reform effort in 1992.

[61] Author interview with Rafael Pardo Rueda, Bogotá, October 16, 2012.

The Constitution also established the National Police as a "permanent armed body that is civil in nature" (Art. 218), which, as part of the *Fuerza Pública* along with the armed forces, would subject the police to the military legal code. This distinction between a civil entity subject to the military legal code and subordinated to the Ministry of Defense required further statutory clarification. Moreover, the 1991 Constitution also required that members of the police and military receive "education in the foundations of democracy and human rights" (Art. 222), which at the very least implied changes to the educational curriculum of the police academy.

One might say that, given the short time elapsed between the new Constitution (1991) and the police reform that was subsequently enacted (1993), the Constitution was actually the catalyst for reform, simply with a slight delay. But the legislative sessions that followed the drafting of the new Constitution were heavily focused on laws intended to put into effect new institutions and policies introduced by the Constitution. A new tax law, a new law for citizen participation, and important changes to the structure and operations of the Congress itself were among the laws passed within that first year (Ungar Bleier 1995). It is unlikely, then, that the 1991 Constitution served as the catalyst for police reform two years later, as other constitutionally mandated laws were passed in the year that followed, while a 1992 reform bill stalled (see Chapter 7). It is also unlikely that police reform was excluded from the broader "institutional shake-up" because the policy agenda was too crowded, since enacting legislation mandated by the Constitution was clearly a priority for the Congress and the Gaviria administration.

Policing and Security as Policy Priorities, through Marginal Reforms

One might also reason that, with so many other important changes to be enacted in other policy areas, security issues may not have been salient among the citizenry and, therefore, not a priority for the Gaviria administration. But ample evidence suggests this was not the case. In the face of historically high levels of crime and violence and a police force that had shown itself to be ineffective in addressing the problem, President Gaviria and the police's leadership attempted a number of interventions that demonstrated the public salience and the government's acknowledgment of the policing and security crisis. These measures, however, were largely limited to marginal reforms – policies involving changes to external entities alone.

The "institutional shake-up" involved efforts by the national government to reinstate civilian control over defense and security policy. Among these was the appointment of the first civilian minister of defense in four decades and the first since the start of the armed conflict. But Gaviria's actions to expand civilian intervention in security policy went much further. Maria Victoria Llorente, an advisor in the Ministry of Defense at the time, recalled that Gaviria's was the first administration to focus on designing public policies in the area of security.[62] Gaviria created the Office of Presidential Advisor for Security and National Defense in 1990, drawing for the first time a distinction between the two, and reinserting civilians in policymaking in these issue areas for the first time in decades. The security and defense advisor's office developed a National Strategy against Violence as its first policy to reduce rising crime and violence, representing, according to the presidential advisor at the time,

a reclaiming of a civilian public policy on security. Both parts [of that] are very important, both the civilian and the public parts ... [It was civilian because] during nearly fifty years, military and police issues had been completely delegated to the armed forces. In 1990, a process began to reclaim for the government's civilian officials [dominance] over these issues ... [It was public] because it was open, it was publicized. Printed copies [of the policy] were distributed in newspapers all over the country; there was a great deal of publicity around the policy. There were forums with the so-called "violentologists," experts in security and violence in Colombia; the policy was debated publicly a lot. And it became a state policy that was converted into a series of budget policies, judicial reforms, [and] legal reforms. But it was also what we call a presidential directive, which involved and gave the presidential advisor [for security and defense] the authority to coordinate, promote, and nearly control the compliance with this policy by other executive and state agencies.[63]

The National Strategy against Violence demonstrates the importance of security on Gaviria's policy agenda. It also demonstrates that Gaviria was willing to challenge long-running conventions and power structures to assert civilian control over security policy. This raises the question, however, of why this bold strategy did not include needed changes to internal police structures and practices.

Indeed, even measures that involved the police directly were nevertheless largely marginal. In 1991, for instance, the Congress enacted a law allowing young men to perform mandatory military service in the police as an alternative to the branches of the armed forces. The measure was intended to improve relations with the citizenry and, as Defense Minister Pardo put it, " to stir up the institution from the inside a bit."[64] The Gaviria

---

[62] Author interview with Maria Victoria Llorente, Bogotá, September 19, 2012.
[63] Author interview with Camilo Granada, former presidential advisor for security and national defense.
[64] Author interview with Rafael Pardo Rueda, Bogotá, October 16, 2012.

administration also sought to introduce "greater public scrutiny" through a hotline that allowed citizens to report police corruption and misconduct (Pardo Rueda 1996, 343). Moreover, the administration also took on a concerted effort to improve the living and working conditions of police officers through salary increases[65] and investment in infrastructure.[66]Like the National Strategy against Violence, however, these measures left internal police structures and practices intact.

The fact that Gaviria's "institutional shake-up" did not entail police reform is suggestive of the specific challenges of reforming the police. By the time César Gaviria took office, the National Police had already undergone significant institutional deterioration due to the strains of the drug war, and Colombia already had one of the highest homicide rates in the world. Despite the abundance of politically costly reforms – including those that challenged the United States and economically powerful interests – and a range of constitutional, judicial, legal, and security-sector reforms that mandated changes to the National Police's structure, there was not a concerted effort to reform the police. This was not, however, due to a lack of alternatives: police reform proposals had been floating around for years,[67] and at least two police reform bills were introduced in the Congress in late 1992 (Pardo Rueda 1996, 342), though they ultimately floundered. In the section that follows I demonstrate how the National Police leveraged its control of the drug war to constrain politicians' policy options and how fragmented societal preferences shifted politicians' incentives away from reforming the police, even as they enacted other sweeping institutional changes.

STRUCTURAL POWER AND FRAGMENTED PREFERENCES: WHY THE NATIONAL POLICE ESCAPED REFORM

Despite many years of institutional decay and systematic authoritarian coercive practices, the National Police remained largely untouched by the

---

[65] Decree 335/1992 increased salaries for police officers at all levels. It should be noted, however, that there had been a general salary increase for all public employees through Decree 334/1992.

[66] Speech by Defense Minister Rafael Pardo Rueda, March 23, 1993 (Presidencia de la República 1994, 19).

[67] For example, Jose Maria Rico, "Presupuestos para una reforma de la policía," Bogotá, January–March, 1985; Asociación Nacional de Oficiales en Retiro Policía Nacional, "Propuesta de reforma constitucional al título de la Fuerza Pública," *Gaceta Constitucional*, No. 34, Bogotá, April 2, 1991, 27–28.

"reformist spirit" driving institutional transformations in other parts of the Colombian state. In this section I explain the National Police's remarkable continuity in the face of sweeping change across the Colombian state by demonstrating how the National Police constrained the policy options available to politicians and how, in this constrained policy space, fragmented societal preferences over the distribution of protection and repression indicated to political leaders that police reform would bring little electoral benefit. Without an electoral counterweight to the structural power of the police, Colombian leaders chose to maintain the status quo, engaging in accommodation with the National Police and granting it broad autonomy in order to ensure cooperation with the drug war.

How the Colombian Police Leveraged its Structural Power to Block Reform

In Chapter 2, I distinguished between the police's routine or formal tasks and their exceptional (often extralegal) tasks,[68] noting that police forces may exchange cooperation in one dimension for autonomy in the other. As I demonstrated in Chapter 4, the police of Buenos Aires Province cooperated with politicians in maintaining a lucrative network of illegal rent extraction, which allowed them to operate with considerable autonomy from civilian authorities in performing their formal role of preventing and investigating crimes. The Colombian National Police engaged in a different sort of exchange, wherein they cooperated on a routine task, conducting the drug war in accordance with government priorities, in exchange for considerable autonomy in carrying out exceptional tasks, including widespread corruption and extrajudicial violence. The National Police was thus able to maintain broad discretion and deference from political leaders, thwarting reform in the face of extensive institutional deficiencies.

While police forces are generally endowed with structural power due to their control over coercion, the National Police exercised considerable structural power specifically due to their central role in the drug war. Former defense minister Pardo noted that police's Anti-narcotics Division functioned as "an island of excellence. The Anti-narcotics Division had high standards, a great deal of confidence from the government and the citizenry; not so for the rest of the police."[69] By performing this formal task with competence, the National Police was able to extract concessions

---

[68] See Taylor (2011).
[69] Author interview with Rafael Pardo Rueda, Bogotá, October 16, 2012. .

and greater autonomy from the executive. Llorente, who served as an advisor in the Ministry of Defense during the early 1990s, discussed in an interview how the National Police succeeded in constraining the policy options available to the executive due to its control over drug trafficking: "What's at stake for a national government in trying to move an institution like the police, which is so critical in the fight against drug trafficking and the citizens' image of the government's [handling] of security conditions? The police has huge power over the executive."[70] This power stemming from control over the drug war likely exacerbated what security officials and other security experts called the National Police's "self-sufficiency"[71] and autonomy, which not only led civilian officials to leave security issues in the hands of the police[72] but also enabled the police to "[act] as an independent entity and its members [to] attempt to maintain to the extreme its autonomy of decision" (Ruiz Vasquez, Illera Correal & Manrique 2006, 193).

In addition to the police's dominance on matters relating to drug trafficking and overall competence in this task, we must also consider the role of the United States.[73] During the first half of the 1990s, the Colombian National Police received hundreds of millions of dollars "for equipment, such as helicopters and fixed-wing aircraft, weapons and ammunition, logistical support, and training," a figure that would increase to $2.6 billion by the end of the decade with the introduction of Plan Colombia.[74] By 1992, "with the decided economic support from the United States, the air fleet of the anti-narcotics division of the Colombian police became the most powerful in Latin America."[75] Armando Borrero,

---

[70] Author interview with María Victoria Llorente, Bogotá, September 19, 2012.

[71] Author interview with Rafael Pardo.

[72] According to former presidential advisor for defense and security Armando Borrero, "civilian officials became accustomed, because we had so many public order problems, to evading the problem ... If there was an issue with public order or insecurity, [they would say,] 'Go talk to the [police] commander.'" Author interview with Armando Borrero, Bogotá, September 10, 2012.

[73] The United States government kept close tabs on the National Police. For instance, a State Department cable from December 1993 observed in great detail the appointment of a new director of the National Police, General Octavio Vargas Silva, rumored in the cable to have ties to the Cali Cartel, and the fact that outgoing director General Miguel Antonio Gómez Padilla's "resignation was not anticipated and his remarks at the change of command suggested some bitterness." US State Department Cable, "New National Police Chief Appointed," document number 1993BOGOTA19286.

[74] Government Accountability Office, "Drug Control: Narcotics Threat From Colombia Continues to Grow," June 1999, www.gao.gov/archive/1999/ns99136.pdf.

[75] "Policía aumenta su capacidad aérea," *El Tiempo*, August 7, 1992, 12A.

who served as a security and defense advisor to Gaviria's successor Ernesto Samper, recalled that during this period "the police began to be subsidized by the United States. The United States began to distance itself from the Colombian military, to the point that, when I was advisor in the 1990s, the problem of the internal armed conflict did not exist for the embassy. One could not talk about that there – it was only drug trafficking."[76] The National Police's ties to the United States, and the resources it brought in for a cash-strapped agency, were undoubtedly another factor that increased the agency's leverage to preserve its autonomy and thwart reform.

While the rest of the Colombian state apparatus was undergoing an "institutional shake-up," the National Police was able to exert its structural power to enact institutional changes it found favorable and to block others that would limit its autonomy. During the 1991 Constitutional Assembly, for instance, National Police officials in uniform were highly conspicuous during the process. According to a Colombian scholar and policing expert who was an observer during the constituent assembly, police officials "went directly and lobbied the seventy Constitutional Assembly members that drafted the 1991 Constitution ... They held lunches, they met with *constituyentes* (members of the Constitutional Assembly), negotiated, [and that's] reflected in the Constitution."[77] Indeed, as Conservative Senator Fabio Valencia Cossio observed, "The truth is that during the Constitutional Assembly, despite the fact that a diverse set of proposals were presented regarding the police, the final form adopted by the Assembly, definitively and without much debate, was introduced by the police itself."[78] Accordingly, the 1991 Constitution was the first in Colombia's history to grant the National Police constitutional status, reflecting the efforts of police officials to protect their institutional prerogatives. Meanwhile, as will be discussed further in Chapter 7, legislative proposals to enact structural police reform in late 1992 failed due to police pressure.

Despite the National Police's reliance on widespread authoritarian coercive practices, the relationship of civilian and elected leaders to the police was largely one of deference and accommodation rather than external oversight. The overarching political discourse from the executive branch sought to minimize the extent of the problem. As one scholar

---

[76] Author interview with Armando Borrero.
[77] Author interview with Juan Carlos Ruíz Vásquez, Bogotá, October 18, 2012.
[78] "Controversia por la Reforma de la Policía," *El Tiempo*, April 19, 1993, 6A.

noted, "the national government, however, appeared to have deaf ears and seemed satisfied with the no longer credible explanation that the evils affected only a few police officials, and that the rotten apples did not damage the rest of the distinguished institution" (Camacho 1993, 27). Indeed, just two years before confidence in the police crashed and reform became all but inevitable, but well after the National Police was widely seen as an inefficient and corrupt agency, President Gaviria called the police "a source of pride for the country."[79]

Fragmented Preferences and a Societal Demand for Authoritarian Coercion

The National Police was thus able to leverage the agency's structural power to raise the threshold for reform, making such reform more costly. As I demonstrate in this section, however, civilian leaders in Colombia also faced little electoral incentive to reform the police to promote democratic coercion, due to the fragmentation of societal preferences and demands over policing and security. This fragmentation between those who wanted to expand the authority of the police (and the military) and those who wanted to constrain it was characterized in compelling terms by the country's inspector general, who declared in a letter to Congress in late 1992:

> The Inspector General's Office is concerned about the troubling polarization that the country suffers today ... between those that consider bypassing the rule of law an indispensable requirement for advancing in the fight against the subversion and [organized] crime, and those of us who consider that [the rule of law] is the supreme condition that sustains our coexistence.[80]

As in the other cases examined in this book, one of the drivers of these fragmented preferences was that the distribution of protection and repression in Colombia reflected existing societal inequalities along class, race, and geography. While information about the characteristics of the victims of state violence is not widely available for this time period, a report issued by the Colombian Inspector General's Office in the early 1990s detailing human rights complaints received by that office suggests that human rights violations committed by police and military officers disproportionately affected low-income citizens. Although the occupation of many of

---

[79] "La policía es un orgullo del país, dice Gaviria," *El Tiempo*, November 6, 1991.
[80] "SOS de Procurador a Senado a Cámara," *El Tiempo*, October 31, 1992.

TABLE 5.2 *Human rights complaints against police and military, by victim's occupation*

	Homicide	Massacre	Enforced disappearance	Torture	Physical injuries
Unknown	50%	12%	27%	27%	48%
Rural/peasants	14%	36%	27%	34%	10%
Workers	14%	22%	21%	14%	25%
Professionals	2%	0%	3%	1%	2%
Military and security forces	3%	4%	6%	2%	4%
Public employees	3%	7%	2%	0%	2%
Union and other activists	4%	1%	2%	4%	1%
Homemakers	1%	0%	1%	0%	2%
Students	3%	2%	4%	2%	2%
Prisoners	0%	1%	0%	9%	1%
Indigenous	2%	2%	1%	3%	1%
Minors	0%	1%	2%	0%	0%
Criminal suspects	1%	3%	0%	1%	0%
Guerrillas	1%	6%	0%	1%	0%
Others	1%	1%	2%	1%	1%
Total	559	589	617	664	939

Procuraduría General de la Nación, Informe Derechos Humanos 1990–1991, 30
Note: The report did not disaggregate victim occupation by police and military.

the victims reporting human rights violations remains unknown, where the occupation was reported the majority of victims were either peasants (*campesinos*) residing in rural areas or workers from largely urban areas (see Table 5.2).[81] Across a range of reports of human rights violations – from homicides and massacres to torture – these forms of extrajudicial violence disproportionately targeted low-income people.

This stratification of extrajudicial violence (in this case by police and military) along class lines was also reflected in societal opinions and demands regarding security and policing – divisions that were exacerbated by the extraordinary levels of violence afflicting Colombia at the time.

---

[81] The category "workers" includes informal-sector workers, self-employed workers, and skilled workers.

Among the most stark manifestations of this fragmentation were the conflicting demands conveyed to officials around the practice of social cleansing, which, as described already, targeted the most vulnerable sectors of society, was rampant in Colombian cities throughout the 1990s, and frequently involved police officers. Human rights organizations routinely denounced the promotion of social cleansing and vigilantism by business owners and other middle-class citizens. A report by Human Rights Watch (1994) included an account from a municipal ombudsman who had "received a visit of about ten local merchants, state employees, and lawyers who threatened to 'take justice into their own hands' if nothing was done about crime" and included a flyer posted in a low-income area of Bogotá by "industrialists, businessmen, civic groups" calling for the "extermination" of "delinquents." A police official interviewed in 1993 observed that demands for social cleansing "come from the same people that see that the police doesn't change and so they decide to pay the police to carry out the cleansing. But where does the pressure come from? From people with means (*gente pudiente*), from people who are disgusted by the *ñero* (indigent)."[82]

While these are an extreme manifestation of the demands of middle- and upper-class citizens that cannot be said to be widespread or systematic, additional evidence suggests that these sectors nevertheless favored an expansion of police authority and discretion, rather than placing constraints. For instance, an editorial in the *El Mundo* newspaper, a liberal newspaper founded by business groups, defended the measures being taken by police to address concerns about corruption and misconduct and rejected "extreme positions": "The Police can and should restructure, critique, and purify itself. And in fact, it is doing so."[83] Along these lines, while speaking at a gathering of small-business owners denouncing growing insecurity, a Liberal politician complained of "permissive justice, where procedures are slow and cumbersome, where the laws that made justice expedient have disappeared."[84]

At the same time, government officials received frequent petitions and protests from citizens from low-income neighborhoods in cities throughout Colombia complaining that the distribution of protection subjected them to police repression and favored more well-to-do citizens. Such complaints were common in the populous and largely low-income

---

[82] "La justicia se confiesa," *El Espectador*, October 3, 1993, 6A.
[83] "Policía: ¡a dignificarla!," *El Mundo*, February 25, 1992, 3A.
[84] "Volver a la justicia de antes: Carlos Lemos," *El Tiempo*, February 21, 1992, 9A.

Bogotá district of Engativá,[85] where residents mobilized to demand a police station.[86] They could also be heard in low-income areas of Barranquilla, where that city's mayor complained that "unfortunately, the police in Barranquilla only protect the rich," citing the location of police stations (CAI) and the placement of officers near banks, industrial centers, and other entities that could afford private security, to the detriment of other areas of the community seen as lacking police protection.[87]

Moreover, residents of some of the most impoverished areas of Colombia's major cities routinely denounced police repression to their public officials. In the community of La Iguaná, Medellín – characterized by anthropologist Peter Wade as a "settlement on the lowest rungs of Medellin society" (Wade 1995, 201) – 550 residents signed a petition to the mayor denouncing unlawful detentions, warrantless searches, and other abuses, declaring: "It would seem, Mr. Mayor, that we, the residents of La Iguaná who are poor, hard-working, honest, and defenders of our rights, have to endure all the weight of the insecurity lived in this city, which permanently blames us for the various [criminal] acts that occur in this city."[88] Officials in Bogotá's low-income district of Ciudad Bolívar received similar complaints, reporting in 1992 that "the communities complain of an increasing wave of police violence that goes from mistreatment to homicides and disappearances."[89] Residents of Ciudad Bolívar had protested and sent petitions to the mayor and other local officials for years, denouncing police participation in "social cleansing" killings – including a massacre of twelve youths – and the lack of investigation into hundreds of suspected "social cleansing" killings of youth (Forero Hidalgo & Molano Camargo 2015, 130).[90] Such protests over police violence were not limited to urban centers. Hundreds of residents in a rural indigenous community in the department of La Guajira protested the killing of one of their residents by a police officer, including by burning a police car and blocking roads.[91]

[85] https://bibliotecadigital.ccb.org.co/bitstream/handle/11520/2883/6227_perfil_economico_engativa.pdf.
[86] "Estación de Policía para Engativá," *El Espectador*, June 19, 1993, 6D.
[87] "Vigilancia de la Policía no tiene distingos de clase," *El Heraldo*, June 15, 1993.
[88] "Denuncian atropellos policiales," *El Mundo*, June 11, 1992, 6A.
[89] "La policía pide pruebas al personero," *El Tiempo*, August 14, 1992, 1D.
[90] See also "Ciudad Bolívar: Cara ...," *El Tiempo*, September 20, 1992.
[91] "Vuelve la calma a Mingueo La Guajira," *El Tiempo*, April 12, 1993; "Disturbios en Mingueo," *El Tiempo*, April 11, 1993; "Vuelve la paz a Mingueo," *El Heraldo*, May 1, 1993.

In this context, political leaders likely perceived that societal preferences over police reform were fragmented, divided among considerable
segments of society, along existing class cleavages. This fragmentation
was also reflected in survey data. Although survey data about attitudes
toward police disaggregated by class, race, or geography are hard to come
by for the 1980s and early 1990s, one survey conducted in late 1992 in the
city of Medellín demonstrated considerable variation in how people of
different socioeconomic strata[92] perceive the National Police (Restrepo
Riaza et al. 1994b). When asked about the frequency with which the
National Police acts within the bounds of the law, for instance, the
differences across socioeconomic groups was stark. Of those at the very
lowest socioeconomic stratum, 73 percent responded that police never or
almost never act within the bounds of the law. Among those in the low to
medium-high strata, there appears to be little variation: between 50 percent and 55 percent of these respondents believe that police do not act
within the bounds of the law. However, among those at the highest
stratum, 27 percent believe that the police never or almost never act
lawfully (Restrepo Riaza et al. 1994b, 56). Moreover, citizens at the
lowest socioeconomic category were also far less likely to say that the
police inspire protection and respect than those in the middle and high
categories, and they were more likely to say that they feel distrust and fear
toward the National Police (53). News reports of that same survey
emphasized the divergences in opinion: "The highest negative perception
of the police is among youth between 15 and 24 years old from the lowest
strata ... The most positive image of police is held by people from high
social strata, above 40 years of age."[93]

The variation in attitudes of these different societal groups reflected
differences, particularly along class and geography, in the distribution of
protection and repression. As the authors of the study noted, interactions
between police and those in the lowest socioeconomic strata are "marked
by confrontation," while the "highest strata, on the other hand, have
a relation of service with the agent; that is, their image of the police is
different since it is not conditioned by confrontation" (Restrepo Riaza
et al. 1994b). Furthermore, the study provided evidence that citizens are

[92] Colombia uses a methodology of categorizing socioeconomic status in which people are
classified into one of six groups, called *estratos*, depending in part on the physical
characteristics of their homes and surroundings. As such, the classification belongs to
the home and not to the individual or household. The categories used in the survey were:
low-low, low, medium-low, medium-medium, medium-high, and high.
[93] "La imagen deteriorada," *El Mundo*, May 4, 1993, 8.

aware of these discrepancies. The survey also asked respondents whether they perceived that police officers conduct themselves in the same way in all neighborhoods. Large majorities in all strata held the perception that police conduct differs according to the neighborhood (80 percent for the lowest stratum, 64 percent for the highest stratum). When asked *why* they believed the police behave differently in different neighborhoods, majorities of most socioeconomic groups said they believed this was due to discrimination: 66.7 percent of those in the lowest and 57 percent of those in the highest stratum (55). Citizens, at least in the city of Medellín, thus appeared to form differentiated relationships with the police depending on their socioeconomic status.

Thus, although the National Police engaged in widespread extralegal violence and corruption, the information cues politicians received through public opinion surveys, media reports, organizational advocacy, and citizen contacts indicated divergent opinions among different social groups regarding trust in police, evaluation of police performance, and views of police discretion and authority. These information cues would indicate to politicians that there was considerable fragmentation in societal preferences over police reform. In this context, politicians likely concluded that police reform would be electorally disadvantageous.

As in the case of Buenos Aires Province, the fragmentation of preferences also reflected contradictory views regarding trust in police and the desire to grant police greater discretion and authority in response to high levels of violence. As was also the case in Buenos Aires, citizens from across society were aware of the deficiencies of the National Police. It is instructive to compare the rates of confidence in the police with those of confidence in the Army. In the early 1980s, levels of trust in the two institutions did not differ greatly. Over the course of the decade, however, the two began to diverge. The poll numbers in Table 5.3 map the deterioration of the National Police over time and provide an institutional "counterfactual" of sorts, the Army. Societal trust in the National Police declined steadily, while the Army went on to achieve very high levels of trust.[94] Colombian citizens, then, were well aware of the many deficiencies that plagued the National Police throughout the 1980s and early

---

[94] Note that some surveys ask about the Army specifically, while others ask about the armed forces. In 1983 and 1992, respondents were asked specifically about the Army; surveys from 1989 and 1993 asked about the armed forces. For comparison, note that in 1992 trust in the armed forces was 49 percent while the Army enjoyed a higher level of trust, at 76 percent.

TABLE 5.3 *Levels of trust in the Colombian
National Police and military*

Year	Trust in police	Trust in army/military
1983	18.1^a/37^b	22^a/40^b
1989	30–39^c	40–49^c
1992	23	76
1993	20	NA

Note: (a) 18–25 years of age; (b) above 25 years of age; (c) Data
provided in ranges only.
For 1983, see Lemoine (1986); for 1989 and 1992, see Lemoine
(1993); for 1993, see Lemoine (1997).

1990s, and their levels of trust varied accordingly. In a survey conducted
in 1992, only about 23 percent of respondents expressed trust in the
police, while one year later this trust had declined to 20 percent of
respondents.

Despite low levels of trust in the National Police, Colombian society –
after decades of wars with guerrilla groups and drug cartels – was nevertheless divided in its attitudes and preferences, with some societal sectors
supporting greater police discretion and authority to fight crime and
violence. María Victoria Llorente, the former advisor to the Ministry of
Defense, described the "conflicting visions" found in society: some held
"very romantic visions of the corner policeman, the friendly policeman,
and [others said,] 'Well, in a society co-opted by drug trafficking, I don't
want the friendly policeman.'"[95]

CONCLUSION: ORDINARY DEMOCRATIC POLITICS
AND AUTHORITARIAN COERCION

From many perspectives, the Gaviria administration (1990–1994) was an
era in which Colombia returned to ordinary democratic politics after the
distortions produced by widespread political violence, the power-sharing
National Front pact, and a near-permanent state of exception. But while
ordinary democratic politics was manifest early on in Gaviria's administration – through the broad social mobilization leading to the 1991
Constitutional Assembly and the emergence of political competition – it

---

[95] Author interview with María Victoria Llorente, Bogotá, September 19, 2012.

did not initially result in reforms to promote democratic coercion. Instead, societal contestation on the issue of security and policing revealed that, while these issues were highly salient across Colombian society, continued fragmentation of preferences made police reform electorally disadvantageous despite widespread police corruption and extrajudicial violence. Facing conflicting demands from the citizenry, and thus little electoral pressure for reform, politicians pursued mutually beneficial patterns of accommodation with the National Police, which largely succeeded in blocking reforms.

The Colombian case illustrates well how ordinary democratic contestation – patterns of political competition and societal preferences and demand-making – can both sustain authoritarian coercion (when preferences are fragmented) and enable reform processes to foster democratic coercion (under preference convergence and robust political competition). While the first three years of Gaviria's administration saw the persistence of authoritarian coercion under the fragmentation of societal preferences, the final year of his administration saw the enactment of comprehensive and ambitious reform legislation in 1993, a process I discuss in detail in Chapter 7. The challenge for would-be police reformers in Colombia and beyond, however, is that societal and political pressures for police reform rarely materialize. The dichotomous outcomes, and the challenges posed by fragmentation, were summed up well by the reflections of Colombia's inspector general on the 1993 reform process:

In 1993, the National Police was subjected to constant scrutiny by the media and the community after the verification of grave events such as the murder of a minor in a police station in Bogotá ... We must highlight the effectiveness of the pressure exerted by public opinion and the media, which achieved considerable results and should be [sustained] permanently and effectively. Unfortunately, Colombian civil society is extremely erratic in its opinion when it comes to condemning human rights violations.[96]

---

[96] Procuraduría General de la Nación, *Informe sobre Derechos Humanos 1993–1994*, 15.

PART II

REFORM

Introduction: Pathways to Democratic Coercion

Alberto Piotti, the former secretary of security of Buenos Aires Province, emphasized in an interview the dilemma posed by security, a policy area he viewed as producing few political benefits even when things go well. As Piotti put it, "inaugurating a jail is not the same as inaugurating a hospital." For this reason, Piotti described his mandate from the governor as "plugging holes, not searching for fundamental solutions." While Piotti is especially pessimistic about his time as security secretary (see Chapter 4), his remarks are illustrative of the broader hesitation of political leaders to undertake police reform, resulting in the high degree of institutional persistence documented in the preceding chapters. When faced with police forces implicated in politicized coercion and a range of conduct that systematically contravenes the rule of law with negligible external accountability, political leaders across the three cases, like Piotti, routinely sought to "plug holes" rather than "search for fundamental solutions." Over the course of three decades, successive leaders in São Paulo State, and more broadly at the federal level in Brazil, contemplated similar reform strategies – including demilitarization, unification of the two police forces, and strengthening civilian oversight – but have consistently avoided structural reform of a highly violent and unaccountable police (Chapter 3). In Buenos Aires Province, meanwhile, the provincial police successfully blocked reform and civilian intervention throughout the 1980s and 1990s, despite repeated diagnoses of a police force in crisis and out of control (Chapter 4). Colombia's President Gaviria took on an ambitious "institutional shake-up" that somehow excluded the embattled National Police, which had faced profound institutional decay for a decade (Chapter 5). The result was the persistence of authoritarian coercion, during a period in which each country undertook a concerted effort to build democratic institutions.

The chapters in Part II examine the relatively rare moments when political leaders in each of these settings decided to enact reform to promote democratic coercion after prolonged periods of continuity of authoritarian coercive practices and structures. Each chapter uses process tracing to tease out the causal mechanisms underlying police reform, leveraging shifts in preference fragmentation and political opposition strength to explain short-term changes in politicians' choices regarding police reform. Chapter 6 focuses on São Paulo, examining a series of "close calls" in which police reform seemed likely but politicians ultimately decided to maintain the status quo. Close analysis of these specific events provides considerable insight into why São Paulo's police forces have endured for more than three decades without meaningful structural reforms. In contrast, Chapter 7 examines the decision of executives in Buenos Aires Province and Colombia to enact comprehensive structural reforms affecting every aspect of policing – from recruitment and training to organizational structure and external oversight – months after explicitly choosing to maintain the status quo.

The relatively short time period under analysis in each case provides considerable analytical leverage, allowing us to hold constant a range of alternative explanations, static conditions that have been offered by scholars as explanations for institutional continuity and change. Accordingly, the chapters demonstrate how short-term changes in politicians' electoral incentives lead them to make radically different decisions when choosing between continuity and reform. When they observe a scandal – indicating the convergence of societal preferences over police reform – and face a robust political opposition, politicians are more likely to choose reform. When one or both of these conditions are absent, however, politicians are more likely to maintain the status quo. The cases examined in each chapter demonstrate how these two conditions – the convergence of societal preferences and a robust political opposition – jointly constitute an electoral threat for politicians, shifting their incentives in favor of reform. This means that the choice to maintain the continuity of authoritarian coercion and to enact reform to promote democratic coercion both result from ordinary democratic politics: citizens conveying preferences to politicians through everyday forms of contestation and politicians responding to electoral incentives.

The chapters are organized as narratives that pay special attention to temporally bounded sequences of events that result in politicians' decision to either enact police reform or maintain the status quo. As Falleti and Mahoney (2015) argue, the temporal ordering of a series of events can tell us a great deal about the relationship among them and their consequences. Accordingly, a systematic comparison of sequences – a "temporally ordered set of events taking place in a given context" (Falleti & Mahoney 2015, 213) – can provide important insights about the causal mechanisms underlying a range of historical and political outcomes. By analyzing sequences around reform attempts and high-profile episodes of police malfeasance, we can advance our understanding of the causes of politicians' decision to undertake reform not long after choosing to maintain the status quo.

This sequential approach enables comparison within and across cases in order to elucidate causal mechanisms. Using process tracing, the chapters compare policy choices before and after a given set of events over a short period of time, demonstrating how the convergence of societal preferences and a robust political opposition change politicians' incentives, making reform more likely. But the chapters also allow for comparisons across cases, with two similar cases (São Paulo and Buenos Aires) producing different outcomes, as well as the emergence of highly similar reform processes in two structurally different cases (Buenos Aires and Colombia). The discussion that follows provides a brief overview of how these within- and cross-case comparisons enable us to tease out the drivers of reform and rule out alternative explanations.

THE PATH TO REFORM: CAUSAL SEQUENCES AND THE DRIVERS OF POLICE REFORM

Although the argument developed throughout this book is not a sequential one per se, implicit within the theoretical framework is a sequence of events that it predicts ought to lead to reform: a high-profile act of police malfeasance brings about the convergence of societal preferences, which leads to a change in politicians' incentives if they face robust opposition, ultimately deciding to enact police reform (see Figure II.A). The chapters that follow draw on this causal sequence, laying out how the absence of one of the three events results in the maintenance of the status quo rather than reform.

In the case of São Paulo, the absence of comprehensive structural reforms over more than three decades poses a challenge for the book's

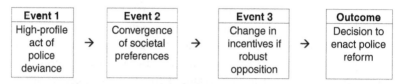

Event 1		Event 2		Event 3		Outcome
High-profile act of police deviance	→	Convergence of societal preferences	→	Change in incentives if robust opposition	→	Decision to enact police reform

FIGURE II.A Causal sequence implicit in the book's theoretical framework

theoretical framework, since the lack of reform can plausibly be caused by a range of factors. The sequential approach, however, is helpful for analyzing temporally bounded events that can elucidate why structural reform has remained off the table in São Paulo since the start of Brazil's transition to democracy in the 1980s. Chapter 6 therefore focuses on three specific sequences since the 1980s that I refer to as "close calls," instances when reform seemed imminent but ultimately fell short. Two instances were selected due to being repeatedly identified in interviews as especially salient cases of egregious police violence that led to calls for reform; the third instance, meanwhile, was an ultimately failed effort by a sitting governor to enact police reform to promote democratic coercion. Chapter 6 presents a comparative sequential analysis of these sets of events to demonstrate how the state's Military Police exerted pressure to limit policy options and how fragmented preferences and the absence of political competition led political leaders to conclude that structural police reforms would not be electorally advantageous.

Each of the cases examined in Chapter 6 demonstrates how deviation from the causal sequence outlined in Figure II.A results in the maintenance of the status quo rather than reform. The chapter begins by considering the first half of Governor Franco Montoro's term in the mid-1980s. As the first democratically elected governor of São Paulo State after two decades of military dictatorship, Montoro vowed to "return to the rule of law" and had an ambitious reform agenda to build a "new police" by tackling rampant violence and corruption. Montoro's reformist agenda emerged not as a result of a high-profile instance of police malfeasance but rather as part of a principled desire to promote democratic coercion. But the absence of the first event in the causal sequence also led to deviation from subsequent events. As the case study shows, Montoro's initial steps to reform police took place in the context of considerable police resistance and preference fragmentation, leading Montoro to conclude that reform would not be electorally advantageous, such that he chose instead to maintain the status quo. The second sequence analyzed in the chapter – concerning a massacre of more than

100 prisoners by the Military Police in 1992 – begins with a high-profile act of police violence. This egregious act, however, did not result in the convergence of societal preferences, such that the governor's incentives did not shift in favor of reform. Notably, this infamous act of police violence took place in the context of a robust political opposition – a rare occurrence in São Paulo State – demonstrating that competition alone is insufficient to create incentives to enact police reform. Chapter 6 goes on to examine a high-profile instance of police violence that did lead to the convergence of societal preferences, with widespread condemnation of the police, including from sectors that are typically supportive or neutral toward police. However, this scandal did not result in police reform, I argue, due to the absence of a robust political opposition. Without an opposition that could pose an electoral threat to the governor and his party, the incumbent had little incentive to enact difficult police reforms, opting instead for symbolic responses and bolstering an existing marginal reform.

Considering the specific cases as sequences of events that fail to bring about comprehensive structural reforms thus helps to elucidate the police's remarkable continuity in São Paulo State presented in broad strokes in Chapter 3. This comparative sequential analysis demonstrates how long-term institutional persistence has been driven by the absence of an electoral counterweight to the structural power of the police due to enduring fragmentation of societal preferences and weak political competition in the state.

Because the cases of Buenos Aires Province and Colombia did eventually result in ambitious structural police reforms, Chapter 7 presents a detailed sequential analysis of the events that brought about reform in each instance, leveraging changes over time in societal preferences and the strength of the political opposition. As with São Paulo, each of these two cases demonstrates how the absence of one or more events in the sequence outlined in Figure II.A fails to produce the outcome of reform. In the case of Buenos Aires Province, the sequence begins as predicted in Figure II.A, with a high-profile police killing of a photojournalist, followed by widespread mobilization and repudiation of police by a broad range of societal sectors. Notably, however, although societal mobilization was sustained for several months, the chapter demonstrates that the governor had little intention to enact reform prior to midterm elections that led to the emergence of a robust political opposition in the province (and nationally). It was only after the newly strengthened political opposition – along with the sustained convergence of preferences following the killing of the journalist – constituted an electoral counterweight to the structural power of police that the governor ultimately decided to enact reform. The sequence of events in Buenos Aires Province is summarized in Figure II.B.

The Colombian case study similarly begins with a set of events that deviate significantly from the sequence presented in Figure II.A. Over the course of 1991 and 1992, Colombia saw the beginnings of true political competition for the first time in decades. In this context, a police reform bill was introduced in the Congress, but it was ultimately shelved due to pressure from the National Police. As in the case of São Paulo's Governor Montoro, this initial reform attempt occurred in the absence of a high-profile instance of police malfeasance and in the context of fragmented societal preferences. In contrast to São Paulo, however, a different sequence of events subsequently brought about reform. Months after the initial bill was shelved in the Congress, a high-profile act of police violence generated widespread repudiation. Following the brutal rape and murder of a young girl in a police station, a broad swath of Colombian society called for reform, and the president's political opponents in the Congress vowed to hold executive officials accountable. In this context, with the presidential campaign under way, the president's incentives – which six months prior led him to shelve his own administration's legislative proposal – shifted in favor of reform. The sequence of events in Colombia is summarized in Figure II.C.

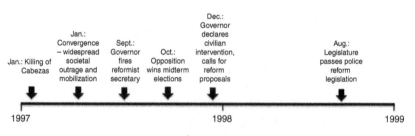

FIGURE II.B Sequence of events in Buenos Aires Province

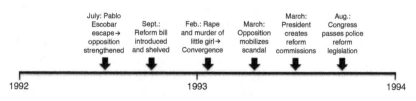

FIGURE II.C Sequence of events in the Colombian case

The sequential analyses presented in the following chapters elucidate the factors that shape politicians' incentives when choosing between continuity and reform, demonstrating how those incentives change in response to short-term shifts in societal preferences and political competition. The accounts of Buenos Aires Province and Colombia complement one another well, demonstrating that neither of these conditions is likely to bring about reform on its own. In each case, we observe an explicit decision by the executive to maintain the status quo when faced with the convergence of societal preferences (in the case of Buenos Aires Province) or a robust political opposition on its own (as in Colombia). After both conditions were present, however, the two executives chose to enact comprehensive structural reforms just months after opting for the status quo. By analyzing politicians' choices before and after the joint occurrence of these conditions, we obtain a greater understanding of the mechanisms underlying institutional persistence and change among police forces.

BRINGING THE CASES TOGETHER: CROSS-CASE COMPARISONS AND INSIGHTS ABOUT INSTITUTIONAL CHANGE

In addition to rich within-case analysis, the chapters also enable fruitful comparisons across the cases that provide considerable insight about the drivers of institutional change. Considering the cases together elucidates the causal mechanisms of reform to promote democratic coercion and helps call into question the extent to which a number of explanatory factors cited by other scholars as drivers of reform are applicable to the case of police.

Considering the three cases together, for instance, demonstrates that, despite the remarkable institutional persistence of police, institutional change can occur in the form of "dramatic and discontinuous" (Weyland 2008) decisions by politicians to enact comprehensive reforms. This path to reform contrasts with many prominent theories of institutional change, which predict gradual, endogenous change (Mahoney & Thelen 2009; North 1990). Such frameworks may well describe the institutional development of São Paulo's police forces, which have faced negligible external intervention by civilian officials and may have, at best, been subject to gradual, endogenous change. In contrast to such theories, however, the cases of the Colombian National Police and the Police of Buenos Aires Province show how exogenous shifts in political conditions led to abrupt decisions by executives to dramatically overhaul formal security and policing institutions after many years of continuity, immediately following the onset of a scandal and an electoral defeat, respectively.

Such joint analysis also suggests that whether or not police reform takes place may have little to do with a range of structural and historical conditions that have also been cited in the literature. As noted in Chapter 2, for instance, federalism has been said to be both conducive to (Falleti 2010) and an obstacle to (Eaton 2008) reform. Other scholars have attributed the persistence of what I call authoritarian coercion in democracy to the legacies of military dictatorships (Pereira & Ungar 2004). Another area of scholarship on the corrosive effects of violence on state institutions in Latin America (Arias & Goldstein 2010; Davis & Pereira 2003) suggests that undertaking challenging police reforms may be especially difficult in the context of high levels of drug-related violence and powerful non-state armed groups.

Yet, considering the cases together indicates that these conditions do little to explain variation in the cases of police reform and institutional persistence studied here. São Paulo State and Buenos Aires Province, both subnational units within federal countries with long histories of military dictatorships, diverge on outcomes despite these structural similarities. While São Paulo State's police have enjoyed remarkable continuity, these conditions did not prevent the enactment of ambitious and extensive police reforms in Buenos Aires Province. This institutional persistence of São Paulo's police may well be attributed to the higher rates of drug violence in the state and in Brazil more broadly, particularly in light of the rise of the PCC (Primeiro Comando da Capital, First Capital Command), an armed criminal organization that poses a growing challenge to the state's monopoly of violence (Willis 2015). Yet, Colombia eventually enacted ambitious reforms of not only the police but also the state apparatus as a whole, during a period when it had the world's highest rates of violence and as state forces contended with powerful drug trafficking organizations.

At the same time, while the analysis that follows emphasizes the social and political drivers of institutional continuity and reform, it also adds nuance to political explanations of police reform. The following chapters, and Chapter 7 in particular, help tease out the proposed causal mechanism, illustrating that the threshold for public pressure and electoral threat to shift politicians' incentives in favor of reform may well be higher than what much of the literature suggests. For instance, many police reform scholars argue that the enactment of police reform is a matter of "political will" (Neild 2001; Stanley 1995), with a variant of this argument suggesting that concerted citizen pressure (Sabet 2012) and "pro-reform societal mobilization" (Moncada 2009, 433) can be important drivers of reform.

These political explanations, however, fail to take into account how the structural power of police constrains the policy options available to politicians, even when they face strong public pressure or hold a principled stance on reform. The São Paulo case in particular demonstrates that political will and public pressure may well be insufficient to bring about reform. It would be difficult to find greater political will than that of Governor André Franco Montoro, who came to office in the 1980s with a commitment to "return to the rule of law" and worked with advisors even before taking office to develop a plan to reform the police. Years later, the Favela Naval scandal led to widespread public condemnation and pressure on Governor Mário Covas – both in the state and nationally – to reform the police. Both politicians, however, ultimately failed to enact structural reforms, instead accommodating the police after facing resistance.

Considering the case of São Paulo alongside that of Buenos Aires Province, however, provides a more nuanced understanding of the political conditions that constitute an electoral counterweight to the police's structural power and that can therefore shift politicians' incentives in favor of reform. For most of 1997, the governor of Buenos Aires Province faced widespread mobilization and media reports denouncing the killing of photojournalist José Luis Cabezas and declaring the provincial police to be in crisis. As Chapter 7 demonstrates, the governor showed little interest in police reform – and even backtracked on timid anti-corruption efforts by firing a reformist secretary of security – prior to his political party's defeat in midterm elections. Just one month after those elections, however, the governor began an ambitious reform process. The governors of São Paulo and Buenos Aires faced contemporaneous police violence scandals in 1997; the latter alone enacted comprehensive structural reforms, but only after he faced a robust political opposition.

Collectively, then, the case studies presented in the following chapters add important nuance to existing theories of institutional change in general and police reform in particular. The chapters in the previous section illustrate the drivers of institutional persistence, demonstrating how the police leverage their structural power to constrain the policy agenda and how the fragmentation of societal preferences makes police reform electorally disadvantageous. As a result, politicians choose to maintain the status quo, favoring the continuity of authoritarian coercion. The chapters that follow develop the theoretical framework further, elucidating the causal mechanisms underlying rare moments when politicians choose to undertake police reforms that promote democratic coercion. Each of the case studies features sequential analysis that teases out how the convergence of societal preferences in the form of a scandal and the emergence of a robust political opposition fail to bring about reform when they occur individually – but also how they shift politicians' incentives when they occur jointly. Taken together, the case studies demonstrate that politicians' choices between maintaining the status quo of authoritarian coercion or undertaking reform to promote democratic coercion result not from static structural conditions such as federalism or patterns of violence. Instead, such decision-making is a dynamic process shaped by the everyday forms of societal contestation and mobilization and the shifts in political competition that constitute ordinary democratic politics.

6

"New Police," Same as the Old Police

Barriers to Reform in São Paulo State

"The poorer they are, the less Brazilians trust the police." Colonel Airton Alves, then the operational coordinator of the Military Police of São Paulo, began the meeting of the working group to reform the police's procedure for street stops (*abordagens*) by reading aloud from recent news stories about low trust in police among the poor and about the 2 percent "hit rate"[1] among the millions of street stops conducted by the Military Police in 2011. Col. Alves, a black man, expressed great frustration to the dozen or so officers, academics, and civil society representatives around the room:[2]

When we read this news that the *periferia* (periphery), the lowest classes, feel degraded and attacked, [I ask] where are we from? Where are the majority of our troops from? Who is causing this problem of racism in the street stops? Who is it that usually has a problem with the black person? When there is a problem with a black person, 99 percent of the time, the team [of officers] includes a black officer. The black person is treated worse by the black officer than the others. This is one of the things we're seeing [in this study]. Two percent, man? We're doing this for quantity, we are not doing this for quality. We are not being professionals. Certainly not. What authorizes me to say this? Thirty-three years as a police officer."

For Col. Alves, the unjust treatment received by citizens who are poor, black, and from the periphery – the "three Ps" – by street-level officers that, in many instances, share these characteristics, and the repercussions for the image of the Military Police, were important motivation for

---

[1] "Hit rate" refers to the proportion of stops that yield a finding that the person who was stopped illegally possessed drugs, weapons, or other contraband – outcomes related to the purported purpose of the stops.

[2] Meeting of the "Abordagem Consciente" working group at the headquarters of the Military Police of São Paulo, May 17, 2012. The author was in attendance.

undertaking the effort to reform the agency's procedure for street stops. The police leadership created the Abordagem Consciente (AC, Sensible Stops) program under the administration of Colonel Álvaro Camilo, the Commander of the Military Police of São Paulo between 2009 and 2012, in order to reduce "aggressive" and "arbitrary" conduct by police officers during stops. According to Col. Camilo, the program sought to "change the relationship to society. We conduct a lot of stops, [so] if the police officer is more polite and educated during stops, you change the view that the population has of the police."[3] The program consisted of a working group composed of police officers of diverse ranks and civil society experts charged with researching and evaluating current procedures, proposing reforms, and conducting trainings with officers. The AC program began under Col. Camilo and continued under his successor, Colonel Roberval Ferreira França, who invested considerable institutional resources into developing the program. I participated in meetings of the working group in May and June of 2012, shortly before the program was interrupted. In June 2012 and the months thereafter, a spike in violence between police officers and the criminal organization known as the PCC (Primeiro Comando da Capital, First Capital Command) – and particularly an increase in the number of police officers killed on and off duty – led to concern among the leadership about how the program would be perceived by both the public and the rank and file.

The interruption of the Abordagem Consciente program reflects the tensions and contestation inherent in police reform and reveals some of the obstacles that explain the absence of structural police reforms in São Paulo State. Would-be reformers, even those within the police, must contend with the need to ensure that a large, armed workforce that controls a fundamental function of the state – the use of coercion – continues to provide that service, which it can credibly threaten to withdraw. As I argue in Chapter 1, this credible threat of withdrawing its service endows the police with considerable structural power to constrain the policy options to political leaders. Moreover, the fragmentation of societal preferences over policing and security means that a sizable constituency will support maintaining a status quo in which police exercise coercion unconstrained by the rule of law and external accountability. Under these circumstances, reformers will be hard pressed to mobilize a majority in favor of reforming the police, while leaders who prefer to

---

[3] Author interview with Colonel Álvaro Batista Camilo, former commander of the Military Police of São Paulo, São Paulo, May 28, 2012.

maintain the status quo will perceive little electoral benefit in enacting police reform and will continue to accommodate a powerful police force.

In Chapter 3, I illustrated the structural power of São Paulo's police and how it has raised the threshold for police reform, such that, in the absence of an electoral threat, politicians are unlikely to risk antagonizing the police by enacting reforms. I also demonstrated that, particularly in the São Paulo case, enduring preference fragmentation and conflicting demands from the citizenry has provided a strong constituency that favors authoritarian coercive practices and made structural police reforms to promote democratic coercion electorally disadvantageous.

In the discussion that follows, I use process tracing to demonstrate how ordinary democratic politics may result in the persistence of authoritarian coercion. In the introduction to Part II of the book, I restated the book's theoretical framework as a causal sequence (Falleti & Mahoney 2015) of police reform: (1) a high-profile event that leads to, (2) a convergence of preferences, and (3) a shift of politicians' incentives if they face a robust opposition, (4) leading them to enact reform. This sequential approach enables us to analyze short-term shifts in the societal contestation and politicians' incentives and decision-making that constitute everyday democratic politics. This sequential analysis is particularly important in the case of São Paulo, which has yet to undergo comprehensive structural reform in more than three decades of democratic rule. While the absence of structural reform over such an extended period can be caused by multiple factors, sequential analysis of temporally bounded events can elucidate how the fragmentation of societal preferences and weak political competition can shift politicians' incentives away from police reform. I therefore focus on three temporally bounded events that emerged in my interviews as highly significant moments of scrutiny of the state's police forces but which did not result in reform. These "close calls," summarized in Table 6.1, feature some, but not all, elements of the sequence, ultimately resulting in the persistence of authoritarian coercive practices and structures.

Through sequential analysis of the first two cases, I probe how the fragmentation of societal preferences toward policing can serve as an impediment to police reform, providing little incentive for self-interested politicians to enact reform – as in the case of Carandiru – and leading even reform-oriented politicians to reverse course, as occurred during the state's democratic transition. I also demonstrate how, in instances of convergence of societal preferences, the overall absence of a robust

TABLE 6.1 *Overview of cases according to causal sequence*

	High-profile event	Preference convergence	Shift in politicians' incentives	Structural reform
Transition to democracy (1983–1984)	No	No	No	Attempted, marginal
Carandiru (1992)	Yes	No	No	No
Favela Naval (1997)	Yes	Yes	No	Marginal

political opposition in the state has reduced the incentive for structural reforms, as occurred following the Favela Naval case.

Although this analysis focuses on individual cases across two decades, these brief "snapshots" can shed considerable light on two enduring obstacles to reform of São Paulo's "police that kills": the persistent fragmentation of societal preferences, even in the context of egregious instances of police violence; and weak political competition. Indeed, it is the relative absence of a robust political opposition that led São Paulo to deviate from the proposed causal sequence in 1997, in contrast to Buenos Aires Province, a case that shares a range of structural characteristics. As we observed in Chapters 3–5, all three cases examined in this book saw the persistence of authoritarian coercive structures and practices for long periods of time, with little intervention by elected leaders. Across these three cases, leaders faced fragmented preferences and conflicting demands regarding policing and security, reducing the electoral incentive to enact structural police reforms. In Buenos Aires Province and Colombia, however, a moment of convergence of societal preferences, in the form of a scandal, occurred in the context of a robust political opposition, posing an electoral threat to the incumbent that raised the costs of not reforming the police. In Buenos Aires and Colombia, these two conditions led to comprehensive efforts to overhaul deeply entrenched authoritarian coercive structures and practices (Chapter 7). In São Paulo, meanwhile, the dominance of a single political party – first the Partido do Movimento Democrático Brasileiro (PMDB, Party of the Brazilian Democratic Movement) and then its spin-off party, the Partido da Social Democracia Brasileira (PSDB, Brazilian Social Democracy Party) – has meant that, even in moments when societal preferences over policing have

converged, there has not been a strong opposition party that could leverage the institutional and political resources to mobilize the broadly shared
discontent and criticism of police as a profitable avenue for threatening
the incumbent's electoral success. As a result, police reform in São Paulo
has been limited to short-term, ad hoc responses in moments of scandal, as
well as marginal reforms enacted by leaders tied to pro-democracy and
human rights social movements, while attempts at structural reforms were
actively thwarted.

FROM THE "RETURN OF THE RULE OF LAW" TO THE CONSOLIDATION OF THE "OLD POLICE" (1983–1984)

Franco Montoro began his term as the first democratically elected governor of São Paulo after nearly two decades of military rule in 1983.
Montoro was, by all accounts, a committed democrat and principled
politician. Luiz Carlos Bresser Pereira, a prominent Brazilian economist
and national public official who served as Montoro's secretary of government, recalled Montoro's approach during an interview: "He was a very
democratic governor. He had a very strong belief in democracy and the
participation of the people in democracy; it was something deeply
ingrained in him."[4]

Montoro also sought to promote what is defined in this book as
democratic coercion: coercive practices deployed for the purpose of protecting citizens from crime, with their input; constrained by the rule of
law; and subject to external accountability. According to Brazilian
scholars, "Montoro was the first governor in the republican history of
São Paulo who sought to put limits to the illegal violence of the state"
(Pinheiro 1992, xvii) and who pursued a set of reform proposals based on
the belief that "the police should shift to serving the population, not the
government or regime" (Mingardi 1992, 83).

A "New Police" for Democratic São Paulo

Even prior to the democratic opening that allowed for popularly elected
governors in the states in 1982, Montoro and his party, the PMDB, had
assembled various party experts and police officials to develop an extensive proposal to reform both police forces with the objective of ushering in

---

[4] Author interview with Luiz Carlos Bresser Pereira, São Paulo, June 19, 2012.

a "new police" (Mingardi 1992, 77–79). The proposal included changes to recruitment and training for the civil police, eliminating a key component of the military regime's intelligence apparatus, DOPS (Departamento de Ordem Política e Social, Department of Political and Social Order), greater independence for an internal oversight body (*corregedoria*), establishing objective criteria for promotion, and building technical capacity to prevent and solve crimes. Many of these measures were enacted at the start of Montoro's term in 1983 (Decree 20.872/1983). Most reforms dealt with the Civil Police, because the continuation of military rule at the federal level entailed the ongoing subordination of the Military Police to the Army. As one security official who was a civil police officer at the time put it, Montoro "didn't have much force to change the Military Police. Back then it was still the military regime, so the commander of the Military Police had to be approved by the Army's General Inspectorate of the Military Police."[5] Montoro did, however, attempt to enact changes to the ROTA (Rondo Ostensiva Tobia de Aguiar, Tobias de Aguiar Ostensive Patrol) – an "elite" unit within the PM responsible for most killings of civilians (Barcellos 1992) – and remove it from policing the city's periphery (Caldeira 2000, p. 171). Montoro also appointed a secretary of security and a Civil Police chief committed to fighting corruption and promoting human rights, and he also dismissed more than 1,800 Military Police officers between 1983 and 1986 (Chevigny 1995, p. 153).

With few exceptions, however, Montoro's early efforts to reform the Military and Civil Police, even in these preliminary ways, failed unequivocally. By the end of Montoro's first year in office, the reformist secretary of security and under-secretary, the head of the Civil Police, and the head of the internal oversight agency had all been replaced by other officials with ties to the previous regime. Montoro's own press secretary admitted in 1983 that the replacement of a reformist Civil Police chief had been due to "excessive rigor in the fight against corruption and police violence" (Mingardi 1992, p. 115). Michel Temer – the future president of Brazil, who would go on to pursue greater accommodation with the police rather than reform – became Montoro's "third secretary [of security] in nine months ... [and] was very well received by the police forces."[6] As I demonstrate in the next section, Montoro's ambitious reforms came undone in a short period of time due to highly effective police resistance

---

[5] Author interview with security official who requested to remain anonymous, São Paulo, June 6, 2012.
[6] Author interview with Michel Temer, Brasília, September 24, 2012.

and the fragmentation of societal preferences, which continued to reflect a demand for police violence.

The Police's Structural Power and Resistance to Reform

In many ways, Montoro's efforts to reform the state's police forces appear to contradict the causal sequence proposed in Figure II.A, since he pro-actively sought to enact police reform in the absence of a high-profile instance of police malfeasance and without the convergence of societal preferences. Yet the absence of these conditions, I argue, is precisely what led to the failure of his reform effort, since there was no electoral counter-weight to the structural power of the police.

Governor Montoro faced extensive obstacles to reform, particularly in a complicated political context that the police forces were able to leverage to exert effective resistance to Montoro's proposals. Not only was Montoro charged with stewarding the state's first democratic government in two decades, but he also faced considerable social unrest in the context of "the biggest economic crisis experienced by Brazil in the last half-century, a crisis that has projected in a particularly adverse form in our state."[7] To understand the significance of police cooperation (or lack thereof), it is worth discussing the police's adherence to Montoro's instructions in a crisis that emerged at the very start of his administration. During a demonstration against unemployment and social strife brought about by the economic crisis at the time, a large crowd marched to the Palácio dos Bandeirantes, the governor's mansion, and threatened to break down its gates. Montoro and his cabinet were aware of the risks involved in using repression to quell the unrest. Montoro's communications secretary at the time recalled the challenge facing Montoro: "One fatal victim in the confrontation could put an end to the democracy that had barely begun" (Câmara dos Deputados 2009, 21). Montoro would later write in his memoirs that the military regime had ordered a mobilization of the army in response to this event: "The president was very concerned with the events in São Paulo and was closely following the situation, fearing it would contaminate the rest of the country" (Montoro 2000, 174). Montoro, instead of ordering repression, told the Military Police to stand down, and he went to talk to the protesters directly to listen to their demands. One of the Military Police officers who commanded the

---

[7] Democratic Government of the State of São Paulo, Budget Proposal 1984, 3, accessed in the library of the Secretariat of Planning of the State of São Paulo in September 2012.

governor's security team at the time recalled the precariousness of that moment in an interview:

People invaded the [governor's] palace, broke down the gates and invaded ... We perceived the governor's apprehension, and he perceived that the police defended him the same way we defended the previous government ... [When] we swear the oath it is to defend the authority to which we are subordinated ... and he was that authority – it didn't matter if he was right, center, left.[8]

The stakes of the police's cooperation with Montoro could not have been higher. As another police commander put it, "if the PM had not stood firm, the State of São Paulo would've had to ask for federal intervention; and if there had been federal intervention in São Paulo, the whole process of redemocratization would've been undermined."[9]

The police's adherence to the governor's order and commitment to defending him demonstrates that the police were initially willing to cooperate, an inclination that would turn to resistance as a result of Montoro's attempts to enact police reforms. Police exercised resistance by withdrawing their service in the context of the social unrest unfolding as a result of the economic crisis. Over the course of several months, protests in a commercial area of the city turned to rioting and looting, as the Military Police failed to follow the orders of the secretary of public security to intervene in the protests (Galdeano Cruz 2009, 32). According to the secretary of public security at the time and other high-ranking officials interviewed by Mingardi (1992), the PM's withdrawal of service was intended to "give the public the impression that the new system did not work" (115). Crucially, the secretary also accused the police of deliberately trying to stoke disorder with the objective of provoking federal intervention (Mingardi 1992, 101), understanding this as posing an existential threat to Montoro's administration and democracy itself.

The Civil Police also rebelled against Montoro's reforms. Civil Police officials issued an open letter denouncing the policies of the governor. The open letter, approved by the general assembly of the Civil Police's *delegados*, told citizens of São Paulo that "believing in promises, we chose the wrong governor, the wrong party, the PMDB ... They, the criminals (*bandidos*) are protected by the so-called human rights, something that the [Montoro] government believes that you, honest and working citizen,

---

[8] Author interview with anonymous retired colonel of the Military Police of the State of São Paulo, São Paulo, May 23, 2012.

[9] Author interview with Colonel Luiz Eduardo Pesce de Arruda, commander of the Metropolitan Region of São Paulo, São Paulo, March 20, 2012.

do not deserve" (Mingardi 1992, 195). They expressly backed an opposition candidate for mayor of the city, Jânio Quadros, rather than the candidate from the governor's party, Fernando Henrique Cardoso (Storino dos Santos 2008, 86). Police stations, according to one observer, became "pro-Jânio fronts" (Galdeano Cruz 2009, 33).

Citizens' Fragmented Preferences as an Obstacle to Reform

Police resistance, as suggested by the state official cited in the previous subsection, was intended to turn public opinion against Montoro's reform efforts, in order to shift the governor's incentives against his own policy. Despite winning a majority of votes with his reformist agenda to "Return to the Rule of Law" (Galdeano Cruz 2009, 30) a year earlier, the police's actions indeed contributed to fragmentation in citizens' views of Montoro's reformist measures, reflecting the "third face" of power (Lukes 1974). Given rising crime[10] and social unrest due to economic crisis, Montoro's attempts to change the police led to a clear shift in popular preferences in a relatively short period of time. The 1982 elections saw considerable popular mobilization in defense of human rights because the middle class had been subject to police repression during the dictatorship. However, as Caldeira (2000) notes, "popular support for the defense of human rights disappeared when the victims of abuse were no longer either middle-class or political prisoners" (157). Meanwhile, in the face of police resistance, powerful sectors of society – primarily the business sector, concerned with looting and rioting – threatened to call upon the Army to intervene (Mingardi 1992, 115).

Montoro's efforts to reduce police violence by removing the ROTA unit from patrols also generated societal opposition. Montoro's officials described daily visits from citizens demanding the ROTA return to the streets of the city's periphery to combat crime: "That is what people ask for here in my office daily. They come in groups asking for ROTA, knowing that it is going to kill" (Caldeira 2000, p. 171). Bresser Pereira, Montoro's secretary of government, explained these demands in terms of the tension between Montoro's democratic approach and the notions many citizens held about police and security, including citizens from the periphery:

[10] Mingardi (1992) argues that the previous military-selected government manipulated crime data "with the objective of hiding from the public the real extent of crime in the State," with the implication that the increase in crime under democratic rule was in many ways a function of this prior manipulation (104).

We were coming from twenty years of a military period, and the idea of security [as a civil right] was not an idea to which we were sympathetic ... The history of [the police], that they were repressive, that they killed, all of that could be true, and it was true. But the concrete fact is that for them the police was the meaning of security. I remember a meeting where a community leader from a low-income neighborhood ... [said] he was worried about the safety of his kids when they came home at night, and the only guarantee he had was the police.[11]

At the same time, less-prominent residents of the city's periphery conveyed different demands. Black activist groups such as the Unified Black Movement – founded in response to a black man's torture and death at the hands of police in 1978 – denounced continued violence in the city's *periferias*, where ROTA "killed many black people, [accusing them] of being involved in crime, [but] it was just for being black, for being in a certain place ... The genocidal project that existed under the military dictatorship continued into democracy."[12] In response to black social movements protesting the racism that was "becoming increasingly explicit in acts of police violence,"[13] Montoro created a Council for the Participation and Development of the Black Community in 1984, but he did not renew his police reform efforts. In the face of fragmentation and conflicting demands, Montoro pursued a "segmented" (Luna 2014) strategy.

Although some Brazilian scholars homogenize society as being singularly in favor of a violent police, it is more accurate to say that, rather than creating a uniform opposition to police reforms, the governor's attempts to reform the police deepened fragmentation of preferences. Mingardi (1992), for instance, claims that a lack of societal organization and mobilization in favor of reforms – before and after the 1982 elections – doomed the reforms to failure, since there was no bottom-up pressure to sustain it. Caldeira (2000), too, says Montoro's reform efforts "have been opposed by the population, who prefer violent, extralegal, and private methods of dealing with criminality to the recognition and respect of rights" (138). But the discussion in this subsection and available survey data from this period suggest fragmentation rather than uniform opposition. For instance, a survey conducted in 1983, the first year of Montoro's

---

[11] Author interview with Luiz Carlos Bresser Pereira, São Paulo, June 19, 2012.
[12] Author interview with Milton Barbosa, founder, Movimento Negro Unificado, São Paulo, September 5, 2017.
[13] "Conselho de Participação e Desenvolvimento da Comunidade Negra: 26 anos de História," Governo do Estado de São Paulo, 2010, 11.

administration, asked citizens to evaluate the governor's security policy: 41 percent did so positively while 39 percent did so negatively (Caldeira 2000, 170–171). In the face of fragmented preferences and conflicting demands, few others in Montoro's administration supported his efforts to reform the police, and legislators were also unsupportive because "to try to control police discretion was to displease voters" (Pinheiro 1992, xix).

The Reversal of Reform

The fate of Montoro's reform efforts suggest the perils of "jumping" to the end of the sequence, adopting reforms in the absence of a high-profile act of police violence that can catalyze the convergence of societal preferences. As a result of the opposition to his reforms from a fragmented citizenry, police resistance, and strategic behavior by politicians, Montoro reluctantly accepted accommodation as a strategy, granting the police greater autonomy and rolling back his earlier proposals. His security secretary, Michel Temer, took a noticeably different approach than his predecessors. Temer described in an interview what he was called on to do – manage the police forces without ruffling feathers:

[The governor] said, 'listen, you are going to be the secretary of security.' And I said, 'But, Governor, I don't have the slightest idea about that.' [And the governor said,] 'No, I need someone who can unify the military and civil police.' Because a big problem back then was that there was a huge division between the two police forces ... And that was it. I was able to really unify the two police forces. I achieved a good rapport with them ... I preached a lot about democracy, but democracy without radicalism, without any of that which would touch the police."[14]

Indeed, a former security official agreed about the shift in policy that Temer initiated. Temer, according to this official, "only accommodated [the police] ... He didn't mess with anything. For better or for worse, he accommodated, and that's the phase when the reform started to regress."[15]

With Temer as secretary of security, the Montoro administration implemented a number of important changes. Temer, for example, created Community Security Councils (Conselhos Comunitários de Segurança, CONSEGs), through which residents and police commanders could

---

[14] Author interview with Michel Temer, Brasília, September 24, 2012.
[15] Author interview with anonymous security official who requested that he not be identified when speaking about the then-vice president, São Paulo, June 6, 2012.

discuss local community problems (Decree 23.455/1985), as well as a specialized police station (Delegacia da Defesa da Mulher, Police Station for the Defense of Women) to serve women who had been victims of physical and sexual violence (Decree 23.769/1985). While these reforms allowed the police to improve service to citizens, particularly regarding the distribution of police resources, they did little to improve accountability (González 2016), reproduced demands for what I characterize as authoritarian policing (Galdeano Cruz 2009), and largely excluded the voices of poor, black *paulistas* that are the main targets of police violence (Alves 2014).

The marginal reforms that Montoro succeeded in enacting were ultimately compromise measures intended to address societal pressure and discontent (González 2019a). Reforms such as the CONSEGs thus did not "touch" the internal structures and practices of the police and were unquestionably marginal to the extensive structural problems facing the institution. Attempts to enact structural reforms, meanwhile, failed. What followed was accommodation – greater police autonomy in exchange for their cooperation in security provision – and more modest marginal reforms. After Montoro's administration, his successors would go on to adopt "tough on crime" approaches to security, giving the police wide latitude to use killings and torture as means of crime control (Chevigny 1995).

Three decades since the start of the first democratically elected government, few of São Paulo's elected leaders, whether the governor or members of the legislature, have championed efforts to intervene in the internal structures of the police that failed at the start of the first democratically elected government. Bresser Pereira, Montoro's secretary of security, summarized the lesson of Montoro's reform attempts that future governors appeared to heed:

> Given the failures of the secretaries of security that had been previously named, Montoro appealed to Temer and it was really a success. He administered security well, gave it another [approach]. Because the democrats, they were a little soft, and you need to have a certain firmness with security.[16]

CARANDIRU: A HORRIFIC MASSACRE AND A MISSED OPPORTUNITY FOR REFORM (1992)

In contrast to Montoro's failed reform efforts, the scrutiny faced by the Military Police under his successor, Governor Luiz Antônio Fleury,

---

[16] Author interview with Luiz Carlos Bresser Pereira, São Paulo, June 19, 2012.

followed a high-profile case of police violence, in which Military Police officers killed 111 inmates in what had been Latin America's largest prison. This high-profile event, however, did not lead to the convergence of societal preferences. The enduring preference fragmentation, in turn, likely led politicians to infer there would be little electoral benefit to enacting reforms, despite occurring in the context of a rare moment of robust political competition in São Paulo State. The fragmented societal reaction to the distinctively horrific nature of the Carandiru massacre epitomizes both the stubborn persistence of authoritarian coercive practices under democratic rule in São Paulo and how such modes of coercion are sustained by democratic processes of citizen contestation and demand-making. The case underscores the particular challenge posed by the fragmentation of societal preferences for addressing authoritarian coercion through structural police reforms.

Governor Fleury, a former Military Police official who served as secretary of security from 1987 until he was elected governor in 1990, did not share Montoro's commitment to reforming the state's police forces in order to rein in their authoritarian coercive practices and structures. In fact, he came to office by explicitly calling for a violent police as a means of fighting crime, ushering in unprecedented levels of police violence. As Figure 3.2 shows, police homicides increased by 81 percent from 1988 to 1989, and similarly between 1990 and 1991, when police killed a staggering 1,066 civilians. In 1992, police killings of civilians reached a record, with 1,492 victims. As secretary of security during the late 1980s, Fleury accounted for the astonishing increase in police violence as evidence that the police were being more "active" in the fight against crime and were responding to societal demands for improved protection (Holston & Caldeira 1998, 272). Following along these lines, Governor Fleury's secretary of security famously declared in 1991 that such killings were justified by the levels of crime: "The police has to respond with force, and it is not expected to give a rosebud to the riff-raff" (*não dá para dar botão de rosa para marginal*) (Americas Watch 1993). Less than a decade after the state's transition to democracy, Fleury openly made authoritarian coercive practices his official security policy.

A High-Profile Act of Authoritarian Coercion

In a period of astonishingly high rates of police killings, a single police operation caused national and international outrage. In October 1992, the Military Police intervened after a riot broke out in the Casa de

Detenção, or Carandiru prison, then the largest prison in Latin America. The ROTA and other elite units entered the prison to quash the riot, with some officers reportedly shouting "Here is *choque* (riot police), death has arrived."[17] In an interview, a colonel with the Military Police, despite not being present during the massacre, nonetheless provided the police's perspective of the operation:

Carandiru was a tragedy from the beginning of the operation: they didn't have adequate maps [of the prison], there was political interference in the decision to invade [the Casa de Detenção], the officers were terrified [because] there was the threat that the inmates had syringes filled with blood contaminated with HIV, and in 1992 nobody knew if there was a cure for AIDS. The officers were terrified due to the risk of AIDS ... The [riot] occurred during late morning, and at 4pm they gave the order to invade the Casa de Detenção, [but] it was not an opportune time to invade ... There were no external hostages in the rebellion, there was no need to invade at that moment, but they complied with the order and proceeded [to invade]. The first to enter was Colonel Ubiratan Guimarães, who had been injured ... When he was injured, an officer carried him out crying, 'They killed the commander! They killed the commander!' That's when they lost control, [and the situation] degenerated."[18]

Perhaps as the result of the lack of preparation and operational justification, the scene inside the prison was highly chaotic, and police malfeasance in the case was made apparent immediately. Police initially claimed to have acted in self-defense in the face of inmates armed with weapons and, according to the above account, AIDS.[19] Nevertheless, news reports in the days following the massacres – accompanied by gruesome images of bloodied corpses and bodies piled one on top of the other – provided detailed accounts of heavily armed police shooting unarmed men, attacking them with police dogs, and forcing inmates to carry the corpses of other inmates.[20] According to the accounts of the inmates, the Military Police brutally slaughtered the 111 prisoners after the vast majority had already gone into their cells and surrendered (Varella 1999). Despite claims of self-defense, not a single police officer was killed in the operation.

The extraordinary violence at the hands of the state inside the prison walls was exacerbated by the sensitivity of the political context. The

---

[17] "O horror, o horror," *Veja*, October 14, 1992, 20.
[18] Author interview with Colonel Luiz Eduardo Pesce de Arruda, commander of the Metropolitan Region of São Paulo, São Paulo, March 20, 2012.
[19] Caldeira (2000) also discusses this police account about darts with "HIV-contaminated blood" (176).
[20] See, for example, "Massacre deixa 111 presos mortos," *Estado de São Paulo*, October 4, 1992.

massacre took place the day before municipal elections in which the governor's co-partisan was running for mayor of the capital, leading to assertions of "political interference," as the colonel put it, in the order to invade.[21]

Enduring Fragmentation of Societal Preferences

Unlike most instances of police killings – which had already reached record highs in the preceding years – the massacre received wide coverage in the media, generating strongly critical editorials from news outlets ranging from São Paulo's largest newspapers (*Folha de São Paulo* and *O Estado de São Paulo*) to the conservative magazine *Veja* and the tabloid *Notícias Populares*.[22] A range of public officials, human rights organizations, intellectuals, and ordinary citizens condemned the actions of the police (Caldeira 2000, 176). In contrast to most instances of police violence, the event also came to be widely known by citizens – in a survey conducted in the days after the massacre, 98 percent of respondents reported having heard about it.[23]

Yet the reaction to the horrific violence in the Casa de Detenção did not represent a convergence of societal preferences as occurred in the case of Favela Naval (see next section), providing little electoral incentive for incumbent and opposition politicians to include police reform in their response to the massacre. The poll conducted days after the massacre showed that a slim majority of respondents (53 percent) said the police acted wrongly during the massacre, but about 30 percent of respondents believed the police acted correctly. Respondents, moreover, were divided in who was to blame for the deaths, with 39 percent blaming the police and 36 percent blaming the prisoners for the massacre to which they fell victim. Other polls taken in the days following the massacre, meanwhile, showed as many as one-third to 44 percent of respondents approved of the way police handled the situation, and media reports showed "the public in general ... split between supporters and critics of police action" (Caldeira

---

[21] "Cadáveres sob a urna," *Veja*, October 14, 1992.
[22] *Notícias Populares* dedicated its front page to the massacre on twelve consecutive days, detailing the brutality of the police. One editorial in *Notícias Populares* was titled simply "Vergonha!" (Shame!). A long report on the violence by the conservative magazine *Veja* was titled "The horror, the horror" (*O horror, o horror*).
[23] The survey of 1,079 São Paulo residents was conducted on October 6, 1992, by the Datafolha Institute. Dataset accessed via the CESOP database maintained by the University of Campinas (Unicamp), DAT/SP92.OUT-00314.

2000, 176–177). Moreover, supporters of the police were also vocal in the media and on the streets. One week after the massacre, as many as 500 people held a demonstration in front of the ROTA battalion to protest the removal of commanders involved in the massacre.[24]

An important implication of these divergent reactions to the massacre is that it indicates to politicians that societal preferences over police reform are similarly fragmented and that enacting police reform would, as a result, be electorally disadvantageous. Accordingly, in response to the massacre, Governor Fleury initially defended the police's actions and claimed that the majority of society approved of it (Caldeira 2000, 177). However, he was eventually forced to reverse his policy of tolerating, and even encouraging, police violence (Chevigny 1995, 160). After the first few days of concealing and then defending what occurred at Casa de Detenção, Fleury fired the police commanders who oversaw the massacre. He also fired the secretary of security, "who, in addition to being his advisor, is [also] his friend"[25] but whose permanence in the position "became unsustainable in light of the international repercussion of the massacre."[26]

Fleury called upon a familiar face to handle the situation. Michel Temer, who had been called upon to solve a crisis in public security in the state by Governor Montoro in the 1980s, said he "returned to security in 1992, after that episode of the 111 [killings] at Carandiru. I was called to be secretary once again, after I had been serving as a federal legislator."[27] Temer took on a very different discourse from that of Fleury's previous secretary of security and actively discouraged police violence. He reinvested in community participation through the CONSEGs, held meetings with a range of civil society representatives, and took officers involved in violence against citizens off the streets, placing them in administrative roles.[28] Under Temer's watch, police killings plummeted to 377 the year after the massacre. While Temer's success in reducing the astronomically high rates of police killings in the state should not be

---

[24] See "Banho de sangue no Carandiru deixa 111 mortos," *Folha de São Paulo*, January 15, 2014, available online at http://f5.folha.uol.com.br/saiunonp/2014/01/1393908-banho-de-sangue-no-carandiru-deixa-111-mortos.shtml.

[25] "Cadáveres sob a urna," *Veja*, October 14, 1992.

[26] "'Trauma do Carandiru é fruto do sistema autoritário,' diz Michel Temer." *IG São Paulo*, April 7, 2013, available at http://ultimosegundo.ig.com.br/brasil/sp/2013-04-07/trauma-do-carandiru-e-fruto-do-sistema-autoritario-diz-michel-temer.html.

[27] Author interview with Michel Temer.

[28] Mário Simas Filho and Josie Jeronimo, "O papel de Temer," *Isto É*, July 24, 2015, available at http://istoe.com.br/429011_O+PAPEL+DE+TEMER/.

underestimated, it is notable that the Carandiru massacre, perhaps the most egregious single act of police violence in democratic Latin America at the time, did not lead to reform of the police.

Politicians' Anti-reform Incentives amid a Strong Political Opposition

Because societal preferences remained fragmented following the Carandiru massacre, the interpretation of political leaders was likely that reforming the police was not an electorally advantageous response, despite the national and international repercussions of the event.[29] That politicians would see little electoral incentive to reform the police force after the Carandiru massacre is especially significant because it occurred during a moment of partisan shift, one of the few periods of robust political competition since the transition to democracy in the state (see Table 6.2). During the late 1980s, the political party that had served as the main opposition to the military regime and governed the state since the transition to democracy, the PMDB (Partido do Movimento Democrático Brasileiro, Party of the Brazilian Democratic Movement), saw an important rift that led to the creation of a new political party led by many of its founders and most prominent members (including Governor Montoro, future governor Mário Covas, future president Fernando Henrique Cardoso, among others). The new political party, the Partido da Social Democracia Brasileira or PSDB, divided the PMDB's electoral support, leading to a first-round loss for the PMDB candidate in the 1990 gubernatorial elections, Luiz Antônio Fleury. Although Fleury would eventually prevail in the subsequent runoff elections, his margin of victory was the party's smallest since the transition, with Fleury defeating his opponent, Paulo Maluf, by only 3 percentage points. During the 1990 elections, the governor's party would also decrease its vote share in legislative elections to 23 percent, from 44 percent during the previous statewide elections in 1986 (see Table 6.3).

The Carandiru massacre took place in this context, hours before the polls opened for municipal elections, in which the governor's party once again faced off against Maluf for the mayoralty of the capital city of São Paulo. Fleury was likely concerned about the potential consequences of the massacre on the elections that would begin just hours later. Media reports at the time accused Fleury of attempting to cover up the massacre

[29] See the Amnesty International report from 1993, "'Death has arrived': Prison Massacre at the Casa de Detenção, São Paulo," AMR 19/008/1993.

TABLE 6.2 *Results of gubernatorial elections in São Paulo State*
(1982–1994)

Year	Candidate	Party	Percentage
1982	Andre Franco Montoro	PMDB	44.92
	Reynaldo De Barros	PDS	23.53
	Janio Quadros	PTB	12.48
	Luiz Inacio Lula Da Silva	PT	9.87
1986	Orestes Quercia	PMDB	36.1
	Antonio Ermirio De Moraes	PTB	23.78
	Paulo Salim Maluf	PDS	17.27
	Eduardo Matarazzo Suplicy	PT	9.76
1990 – first round	Paulo Salim Maluf	PDS	34.28
	Luiz Antonio Fleury Filho	PMDB	22.2
	Mario Covas Junior	PSDB	11.97
	Others		10.35
1990 – second round	**Luiz Antonio Fleury Filho**	PMDB	43.81
	Paulo Salim Maluf	PDS	40.82
1994 – first round	**Mario Covas Junior**	PSDB	35.71
	Francisco Rossi	PDT	16.94
	Jose Dirceu	PT	11.32
	Others (including PMDB)		12.24
1994 – second round	**Mario Covas Junior**	PSDB	48.8
	Francisco Rossi	PDT	38.15

SEADE (State System for Data Analysis), *Informações Eleitorais*

on the day of the elections in order to help his party's candidate for mayor.[30] Maluf won the first round of the mayoral election on October 3, 1992, and would go on to win the runoff the following month as well. Thus, taking into consideration a number of the indicators of political opposition strength, the governor's party was facing an especially robust challenge at the time of the massacre, having won his own election by a close margin, having lost half of his party's representation in the legislature, and looking ahead to an upcoming municipal election where his co-partisan was competing against his former opponent.

---

[30] "111 Killed When Police Storm Brazilian Prison during Inmate Riot," *New York Times*, October 4, 1992; "Cadáveres sob a urna," *Veja*, October 14, 1992.

TABLE 6.3 *Results of legislative elections in São Paulo State (1982–1994)*

Political party	1982	1986	1990	1994
PC do B			1%	2%
PDC			1%	
PDS	26%	13%	13%	10%
PDT		4%	4%	3%
PFL		11%	10%	5%
PL		1%	2%	5%
PMDB	50%	44%	23%	24%
PRN			2%	
PRONA				1%
PRP				2%
PSB			1%	1%
PSD				2%
PSDB			11%	18%
PST			2%	
PT	11%	12%	17%	17%
PTB	13%	15%	13%	7%
PV				1%

SEADE (State System for Data Analysis), *Informações Eleitorais*

At the time of the massacre, Governor Fleury thus found himself facing the strongest challenge his political party had faced in the preceding decade, from Maluf and his party, the PDS (*Partido Democrático Social*, Democratic Social Party). Even as the PDS had also seen a decline in its share of the popular vote in the legislative elections between 1982 and 1990 (see Table 6.3), the performance of Maluf in the 1990 gubernatorial elections and the 1992 mayoral elections likely presented Governor Fleury and the PMDB with a "daunting threat of replacement" (Grzymala-Busse 2007).

The book's theoretical framework would predict that, had there been preference convergence in response to the Carandiru massacre, its concurrence with this new political challenger might have made police reform more likely. One important limitation to this counterfactual is that Maluf and his party, the right-wing PDS (Power & Zucco 2009, 222), may have been particularly reluctant to seize upon such an unprecedented act of police violence and make the case that police malfeasance represented a broader institutional problem as a means of attacking the incumbent governor and party. Right-wing politicians and political parties may well be more supportive of police discretion and more likely to support the use of lethal force as an instrument of crime control (Ahnen 2007).

But, while it is far from certain that the convergence of societal preferences in favor of reform would have led Governor Fleury to push for reforms due to facing a right-wing party, the evidence presented thus far shows that he was responsive to public pressure that emerged from the national and international outrage. Although his efforts stopped far short of reform, Fleury followed the usual route of elected officials following such high-profile acts of police malfeasance, first defending the police and its actions and then firing police commanders and a trusted secretary of security. Not only that, Fleury also granted his new secretary of security, Temer, "freedom to act"[31] in a way contrary to Fleury's own stated security preferences. Temer's second tenure as security secretary saw a precipitous drop in the number of police killings, a type of coercive practice that Fleury had previously defended vehemently. This suggests that it is possible the convergence of preferences would have led to a shift in Fleury's incentives and strategy, as occurred with centrist and center-right politicians Governor Eduardo Duhalde in Buenos Aires Province and President César Gaviria in Colombia, who saw short-term shifts in their approaches to police violence and police reform following the emergence of broad societal and political pressures.

Such broad societal condemnation, however, did not manifest in the case of the Carandiru massacre. The fragmented nature of societal views toward the 111 killings by police continue to this day, as indicated by an activist with Amparar – an association of family members of incarcerated individuals in São Paulo – who highlighted perspectives of both the social movements and families of victims who condemn the killings and the social sectors that continue to defend the police's actions:

The society applauded it. And you still hear, even today, 'there were no priests in Carandiru' – that no one was praying, that no one was an altar boy. 'They were criminals that deserved to die – in fact, they killed too few.' You still hear that even today. [Carandiru] had strong repercussions in Brazil, in the whole world. It was a

---

[31] "'Trauma do Carandiru é fruto do sistema autoritário,' diz Michel Temer," *IG São Paulo*, April 7, 2013, available at http://ultimosegundo.ig.com.br/brasil/sp/2013-04-07/trauma-do-carandiru-e-fruto-do-sistema-autoritario-diz-michel-temer.html.

huge tragedy in Brazil. Maybe they wouldn't do the same thing today because they know there are a lot of committed social movements.[32]

FAVELA NAVAL: SCANDAL, MARGINAL REFORMS, AND THE CONTINUITY OF AUTHORITARIAN COERCION (1997)

Governor Fleury was succeeded by Mário Covas, who, like Montoro, was a reformist leader with ties to the pro-democracy and human rights movement. Like Montoro, Covas also demonstrated a commitment to controlling police violence and corruption, creating a new institution intended to provide greater transparency among the state's police forces but which was nevertheless limited to a marginal reform. Similarly to his predecessor, Covas faced constrained policy options due to the police's structural power and the persistence of authoritarian coercion reinforced by societal contestation and demand-making. During his administration, however, Covas faced a shift in societal preferences from fragmentation to convergence in response to a high-profile incident of police abuse in a low-income community, which was widely broadcast on television and lead to broad-based outrage. Although the case of Favela Naval led to important responses by political leaders, their efforts stopped far short of structural police reforms. I argue this was the case due to the absence of a robust political opposition, as Covas's term represented the consolidation of power by his party, the Brazilian Social Democracy Party (PSDB), which has governed the state without interruption to this day.

Police Transparency without Reform: The Creation of the Ombudsman (1995)

Like his predecessor and co-partisan Governor Montoro, Governor Covas came to office with a commitment to reform the police but saw his policy options constrained to enacting marginal reforms. On his first day in office, Governor Covas enacted a proposal brought to him by human rights activists to reduce police violence and corruption, creating the Ouvidoria da Polícia or Police Ombudsman's Office (Decree 39.900/ 1995). The Police Ombudsman's Office was tasked with receiving complaints from the citizenry regarding abuses by Civil and Military Police officers, contributing to the investigation of such complaints, and

---

[32] Author interview with activist from Associação Amparar, São Paulo, September 4, 2017.

forwarding them to the relevant authorities, including the police's internal affairs unit (*Corregedoria*) or judicial authorities.

The *ouvidoria* (ombudsman) certainly sought to promote democratic coercion, bolstering external accountability by creating an external entity to collect and publicize data on police malfeasance. But, in accordance with the index of democratic police reforms introduced in Chapter 2, it remains a marginal reform, leaving police structures and rules unchanged and exercising no formal authority over the state's police forces. Moreover, since it was created through executive order rather than a law, it was not considered permanent and could be easily undone by the next governor. Like Montoro, Covas lacked broader support from other politicians, even those in his own party, which impeded his ability to institutionalize the Police Ombudsman's Office through a law.[33]

State legislators likely perceived little electoral incentive to pursue such reforms due to the absence of a broadly shared societal demand for police reform. Recall, for instance, the attitudes toward police violence reflected in the 1995 survey cited in Chapter 3 and reproduced in Figure 6.1. The survey suggests that societal preferences over police reform were highly fragmented at the time that Covas created the Ombudsman's Office with the explicit objective of reducing police violence. For instance, taking the attitudes toward police violence as a proxy for preferences over police reform, the survey showed that 44 percent of respondents believed that the Military Police was "more violent than it should be," 35 percent believed it was "violent to the right extent," and 19 percent expressed the view that the police force was "less violent than it should be."[34] Moreover, the survey also showed that the respondents were divided in how they viewed the Military Police, with 46 percent expressing "more trust than fear," while 52 percent said they felt "more fear than trust" in the PM.

In this context, political leaders would likely see little electoral incentive to enact police reforms. Covas, like Montoro, seemingly sought to avoid dividing public opinion and confronting the police through structural reform. The mobilizations and the persistent

---

[33] For instance, in a report summing up his first term as ombudsman, Benedito Mariano observed, "Perhaps, if the governor of São Paulo had been someone else (even from the same political party) the Police Ombudsman's Office would not have been created" (Ouvidoria da Polícia do Estado de São Paulo 2000, 4).

[34] "A imagem da polícia," survey of São Paulo residents conducted by the Datafolha Institute, dataset accessed via the CESOP database maintained by the University of Campinas (Unicamp), DAT/SP-RJ95.DEZ-00532.

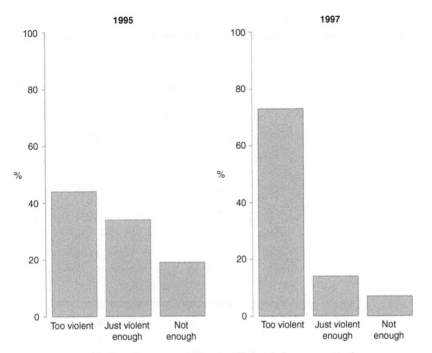

FIGURE 6.1 Shifts in societal opinions of police violence in São Paulo
Datafolha surveys "A imagem da polícia," 1995 and 1997

fragmentation following the Carandiru massacre perhaps also showed that there may have been insufficient societal appetite for challenging police reforms to curb police violence and that doing so might come at a cost. His efforts to reduce police violence and corruption were thus limited to a marginal reform that was susceptible to being undone by a future governor.

Authoritarian Coercion Will Be Televised: Favela Naval and Preference Convergence (1997)

Societal preferences and demand-making around policing shifted two years into Covas's term. One of the most widely known instances of police violence in São Paulo occurred in late March 1997, when television viewers were confronted with video footage of military police officers – including one that went by the nickname "Rambo" – engaging in extortion, beatings, torture, and even an execution in Favela Naval, a low-income community in the municipality of Diadema.[35] A retired lieutenant colonel who worked in Diadema at the time recounted in an interview how events unfolded from his perspective:

During the nights, military police officers would place two patrol cars at a location where they knew drug deals took place, and whoever entered that location, on foot or in a car, would suffer a series of [acts of] physical violence. They would be beaten, and smacked in the face. But someone who wanted drug trafficking to continue in that location asked someone to film all of that. And over the course of more than a month, someone who works in television filmed all that happened there, in detail. One of those videos was seen on television, on the Globo network ... The Globo network broadcast the images of the military police officers doing all of that.[36]

The societal reaction following this high-profile televised footage of police violence marked a key moment of preference convergence in the São Paulo State. Although the episode of police violence in Favela Naval differed from previous routine acts of police violence only in that it was captured on video and broadcast on television, it led to broadly shared outrage, despite the fact that its victims belong to typically criminalized populations (the "three Ps"). This convergence of attitudes and preferences reflected in the unequivocally critical reaction to Favela Naval was expressed through protests, public statements, surveys, and even in police officers' own homes.

The societal outrage that resulted from the Favela Naval incident was palpable among the sectors that are typically subjected to police abuses – such as the roughly 1,000 Favela Naval residents that attended a protest denouncing the violence[37] – and from sectors that are typically supportive of police, including an official statement of repudiation from the General Community Council of the Military Police, the police commander's civilian advisory board, which includes business leaders.[38] A survey conducted just days after the footage of police violence in Favela Naval was aired also revealed this convergence.[39] As was the case with Carandiru, the acts of

[35] Archived footage originally aired on the Globo network on March 31, 1997, is available at http://memoriaglobo.globo.com/programas/jornalismo/telejornais/jornal-nacional/favela-naval.htm.
[36] Author interview with retired lieutenant colonel of the Military Police of São Paulo, São Paulo, June 25, 2012.
[37] "Manifestantes protestam contra PMs e cercam delegacia," *Folha de São Paulo*, April 2, 1997.
[38] "Conselho da PM de SP repudia ação violenta de policiais," *Folha de São Paulo*, April 1, 1997.
[39] "A imagem da polícia," survey of São Paulo residents conducted by the Datafolha Institute on April 2, 1997, dataset accessed via the CESOP database maintained by the University of Campinas (Unicamp), DAT/SP97.ABR-00805.

police violence broadcast on television were widely known, with 91 percent of respondents expressing awareness of the "television footage showing Military Police officers assaulting people in the city of Diadema." The survey also showed that 73 percent believed Covas somewhat or completely responsible "for what happened in Diadema," and about 60 percent of respondents thought the secretary of security and general commander of the Military Police should be fired.

But the clearest evidence of the shift from fragmentation to convergence can be discerned in responses to questions that were previously asked in the 1995 survey cited earlier in the chapter. As can be observed from the right-hand side of Figure 6.1, societal preferences toward police violence converged. In this second wave of the survey, the proportion of *paulistanos* who viewed the police as too violent rose to 73 percent from 44 percent. Similarly, 74 percent of respondents now said they felt "more fear than trust" in the Military Police (up from 52 percent in 1995), while 24 percent said they felt more "trust than fear" (down from 46 percent). Indeed, many citizens who had previously been indifferent toward or even supportive of police violence had now joined the ranks of critics.

The broad societal outrage generated by the Favela Naval video footage was also felt strongly by the Military Police itself. Although many officers – including the retired lieutenant colonel already quoted – tried to justify the actions taken by police on a daily basis in Favela Naval ostensibly in the fight against drug trafficking, the societal reaction to the events that occurred in Favela Naval was powerful and left a lasting mark on many of the police officials I interviewed a decade and a half later. Col. Alves, quoted at the beginning of this chapter, recounted in that same meeting that, after the video aired, he received a call from his mother, who angrily demanded, "You tell me right now if you and your brother [also a police officer] engage in what I am seeing on television." Col. Arruda, quoted discussing police actions in Carandiru prison, compared how these events – and the societal reaction to them – were perceived from within the Military Police:

For the internal public, [Favela Naval] was much more shocking . . . With the Casa de Detenção, what's the internal understanding, then and even now? It was an enormous fatality, a sequence of fatalities. What is the understanding of Favela Naval? It was a shameful act, to the point that police officers went home and their families asked them, 'Is this how you work? Do you do this?' Children asked this of police officers.[40]

[40] Author interview with Colonel Luiz Eduardo Pesce de Arruda, commander of the Metropolitan Region of São Paulo, São Paulo, March 20, 2012.

Along with national and international scrutiny (Neves & Maia 2009), the widespread societal condemnation that had failed to materialize in response to the Carandiru massacre thus manifested in rather poignant ways in response to police actions in Favela Naval.

Police Resistance, Weak Political Competition, and the Continuity of Authoritarian Coercion

Following widespread societal condemnation of the Military Police, a robust debate emerged about the police and the need for reforms. For the first time since the Constituent Assembly, serious debates emerged in the national Congress about abolishing the Military Police, which is established as such in the federal constitution. According to the retired lieutenant colonel quoted earlier,

> there was great pressure for the elimination of the Military Police forces as a result of what was shown on television ... With Favela Naval, [people] watched and said, 'Wait, what's happening here?' The things everyone already knew was happening suddenly went on to take on national and global connotation, since this was shown all over the world, [and] there was a need to shift the focus of policing.[41]

Despite this recognition of the "need to shift the focus of policing," congressional debates and proposals for the unification of the two police forces and the creation of a civilian police force responsible for crime prevention[42] were met with police strikes and violence all over the country in June and July 1997 (Caldeira 2000, 180). Such proposals were swiftly abandoned, though other policy reforms regarding torture[43] and human abuses were adopted (Rifiotis 1999, 29). These federal policies, however, did not change police structures nor provide mechanisms for external oversight.

Within São Paulo State, Governor Mário Covas, who had previously proven to be a reformer with the creation of the Ouvidoria da Polícia, responded with largely symbolic actions. The day after the footage aired, Covas issued an apology "to the people of São Paulo" and dismissed two high-ranking police officials.[44] Ten days after the video of the Favela Naval

---

[41] Author interview with retired lieutenant colonel of the Military Police of São Paulo, São Paulo, June 25, 2012.

[42] Note the similarity between these proposals and those that were debated during the early 1980s and 2010s, discussed at the beginning of Chapter 2.

[43] At the national level, the Congress passed Law 9.455/1997, which defined torture as a crime.

[44] "Violência em Diadema afasta comandantes da PM," Folha de São Paulo, April 1, 1997.

incident was broadcast on television, Covas submitted a bill to the state's Legislative Assembly to strengthen the legal basis of the Ouvidoria da Polícia, institutionalizing its creation through law rather than executive order,[45] which was approved with near unanimous support in the legislature (Law 826/1997). While the institutionalization of the Ouvidoria da Polícia through a law was an important measure to ensure that it could not be instantly dismantled by the next governor, comprehensive structural reforms of the sort that occurred around the same time in Buenos Aires Province (Chapter 7) did not follow the Favela Naval scandal.

But the absence of structural police reforms in the wake of Favela Naval was not due to an absence of proposals. In the state's legislative assembly, for instance, bills introduced following the Favela Naval scandal sought to establish greater restrictions on police use of force,[46] collect and publicize data on "arbitrary actions against civil society" committed by police,[47] and establish mandatory human rights education for police.[48] The only bill that was approved by the legislature, however, was the governor's proposal to institutionalize the Police Ombudsman's Office. Within the executive branch, Benedito Mariano, police ombudsman since 1995, also offered structural reform proposals after Favela Naval, including a reform to the Military Police's disciplinary code.[49] According to Mariano, however,

> the government didn't want to move forward with those proposals. The one that had the most resistance from the police was the new disciplinary code [I proposed], because that messed with the internal culture of the Military Police ... The secretary [of security] made the mistake of sending the proposal to the Military Police commander, and of course when you send it to the police to opine, they're going to want to maintain the status quo.[50]

---

[45] "Ouvidoria da polícia pode ficar amparada por lei em São Paulo," *Folha de São Paulo*, April 11, 1997.

[46] Projeto de lei (Bill) 0274/1997, "Dispõe sobre o controle da utilização da força e dos meios letais, em situações perigosas e de confronto, por parte dos policiais," published May 29, 1997.

[47] Projeto de lei 0259/1997, "Dispõe sobre publicidade das ocorrências envolvendo policiais civis e militares em arbitrariedades contra a sociedade civil," published May 23, 1997.

[48] Projeto de lei 0162/1997, "Dispõe sobre a obrigatoriedade da inclusão da disciplina de Educação em Direitos Humanos, nos cursos de formação, treinamento e reciclagem dos integrantes dos quadros das Polícias Civil e Militar do Estado," published April 15, 1997.

[49] "Ouvidoria da polícia pode ficar amparada por lei em São Paulo," *Folha de São Paulo*, April 11, 1997.

[50] Author interview with Benedito Mariano, former *ouvidor*, São Paulo, September 14, 2017.

Thus, in the wake of a high-profile event that led to a palpable conver-gence of societal preferences, police reform was limited to legislation that reinforced a previous marginal reform. As Mariano's remarks suggest, this was due to the police's ability to leverage its structural power to constrain the policy agenda. But I argue the key reason police were able to keep certain policy options off the agenda is due to the absence of a robust political opposition that would pose an electoral threat to the governor and, consequently, an electoral counterweight to the police's structural power. In contrast to the precarious victory of Governor Fleury in the 1990 elections, Covas won decisively in 1994 (see Table 6.1). Covas defeated his opponent in a runoff election for governor in 1994 by more than 10 percentage points; the challenger's political party, the PDT (Partido Democrático Trabalhista, Democratic Labor Party), won only 3 percent of the votes for the state legislature. Meanwhile, the previously dominant political party in the state, the PMDB, was in retreat, with a very poor showing in the gubernatorial elections and only 24 percent of the vote in the legislative elections (see Table 6.2). Covas thus did not face much of a threat of replacement at the time from an opposition party that could have mobilized the widespread societal outrage that followed the Favela Naval case.

In the absence of such an electoral counterweight to the police's struc-tural power, Governor Covas could address societal and political pressure through symbolic actions and marginal reforms, without needing to incur the costs of alienating the state's police through difficult structural reforms. It is, of course, impossible to say with certainty that a robust political opposition would have changed the governor's incentives or strategies, leading him to pursue structural police reform. But the experi-ence of Buenos Aires Province's governor, Eduardo Duhalde, discussed in the next chapter offers an instructive contrast. Like Covas, Duhalde faced a massive scandal following an egregious act of police violence in early 1997 and initially adopted similar strategies to Covas, largely symbolic and short-term measures. But once Duhalde faced robust political compe-tition from an opposition party that won midterm legislative elections in late 1997, an ambitious structural police reform quickly followed.

The outcome of the Favela Naval scandal would come to define the approach to police reform taken by the Military Police of São Paulo State and the democratically elected leaders that ostensibly control it in the two decades that followed. What we've observed since then has been two parallel systems that, like the response to Favela Naval, avoid structural police reform: one of marginal reforms that seek to improve security provision or reduce police violence without changing police structures; and another in which police have broad autonomy to enact operational reforms while changing little else. I analyze elsewhere the range of operational reforms adopted by the Military Police in response to the broad outrage following the Favela Naval episode, including community policing (González n.d.), while some of the marginal reform measures were described by a security expert with the civil society organization Sou da Paz:

There's an important juncture that you must have heard of, which was in 1997 with the issue of Favela Naval ... From that point on there was a good moment [of reforms] that I can't quite say was of the Military Police, but it was a moment when there came to be a public security policy by the Secretariat [of Security], which created, for instance, Infocrim [a crime data system], the Office of Analysis and Planning to monitor statistics, the Commission of Police Lethality, the PROAR, a program for high-risk actions.[51]

While these are undoubtedly notable measures, they leave police structures largely intact, limiting the impact of any measure to promote democratic coercion. As a security official characterized it: "The police hasn't gone back to what it was before, during the military period, but a lot of that has come back, ok? ... What has changed in the police was due to its own initiative. What the police changed, it changed due to its own influence, not due to the influence of the [civilian] governments."[52]

CONCLUSION: HOW ORDINARY DEMOCRATIC POLITICS
UNDERMINED DEMOCRACY'S "NEW POLICE"

"When we talk about the 'old police,'" wrote a sociologist at the outset of democratic rule in Brazil, "we are referring to the abuse of power and violence, torture in the police stations, 'unexplained shootouts,' unlawful detentions, etc., always against the poorest and most vulnerable populations" (Benevides 1985, 26). Such practices were characteristic of the police under military rule, which is likely why André Franco Montoro, São Paulo's first democratically elected governor, called for reforms to

---

[51] Author interview with a security expert with the civil society organization Sou da Paz, São Paulo, May 15, 2012. PROAR stands for Programa de Acompanhamento a Policiais Militares Envolvidos em Ocorrências de Alto Risco (Program for the Accompaniment of Military Police Officers Involved in High-Risk Occurrences).
[52] Author interview with anonymous security official who requested that he not be identified, São Paulo, June 6, 2012.

create a *"nova polícia,"* a new police, by eradicating these practices (Mingardi 1992).

In Chapter 3 I presented ample evidence of the persistence of the authoritarian coercive practices of the "old police," long after the transition to democracy. As the cases examined in this chapter demonstrate, these authoritarian coercive practices and structures have endured in large part due to the ways in which fragmented societal preferences and patterns of political competition shape politicians' incentives to enact reform or maintain the status quo.

Indeed, the three cases analyzed in this chapter about the role of ordinary democratic politics as drivers of authoritarian coercion provide a useful lens for understanding what has happened in the decades since the events at Favela Naval shocked the conscience of a large majority of *paulistas* but failed to usher in structural police reforms. A similar outcome followed in the face of the "Crimes of May," when approximately 500 civilians were killed by uniformed police officers and death squads reportedly composed of police officers between May 12 and May 20, 2006 (Delgado, Dodge & Carvalho 2011); the high-profile repression of protests in 2013; and the ever-growing list of *chacinas*, multiple-victim killings reportedly as retaliation for the killing of a police officer, such as the *chacina* of Osasco in 2015, in which "18 people died and 6 were injured in attacks perpetrated within a three-hour period by armed individuals at 11 locations in the state of São Paulo";[53] or the sharp rise in police killings since 2014 (see Figure 3.2). The absence of structural reform, or even much vigorous public debate, in the face of these stark instances of authoritarian coercive practices is understandable once one considers how politicians perceive their electoral incentives in light of the enduring preference fragmentation over policing.

Instead, recent governors and other political leaders in the state have continued to tie their political fortunes to authoritarian coercion. An operation by the Civil Police in which ten alleged robbers were killed in a supposed shootout – in which police fired 139 bullets but not a single officer was shot – in the wealthy neighborhood of Morumbi was met with immediate praise by the governor rather than a promise to investigate.[54]

---

[53] "IACHR Condemns Killings in São Paulo, Brazil," Inter-American Commission on Human Rights press release, August 21, 2015, available at www.oas.org/en/iachr/med ia_center/PReleases/2015/092.asp.

[54] "Polícia e Alckmin elogiam ação que matou 10 no Morumbi: 'inteligência' 'eficiência de Deus,'" *Notícias UOL*, September 4, 2017, https://noticias.uol.com.br/cotidiano/ulti mas-noticias/2017/09/04/policia-e-alckmin-elogiam-acao-que-matou-10-no-morumbi-i nteligencia-e-eficiencia-de-deus.htm.

Governor João Doria, meanwhile, saw the promise that, under his administration, police would "shoot to kill" as his path to victory during the 2018 gubernatorial campaign.[55] And retired police officers turned politicians successfully won elected office with the slogan "a good criminal is a dead criminal."[56]

In adopting these discursive strategies, politicians are calculating their electoral incentives based on the ongoing fragmentation of societal preferences over policing. This profound fragmentation allows politicians to be selective in whose demands to prioritize, appealing to a fairly stable constituency that favors authoritarian coercion. The relative absence of robust political competition in the state, meanwhile, enables politicians to take symbolic or marginal police reform measures, while continuing to accommodate the police by granting it expansive autonomy.

The urgency of the problem of police violence alerted to by Governor Marin in 1982 (see Chapter 2), and the institutional conditions from which it results, have remained largely unchanged in more than three decades since the return to democratic rule. Also unchanged have been the political incentives and choices of consecutive governors, as Mariano, the first police ombudsman, noted in an interview: "This is a debate that even the progressive [political] parties have to undertake. In the period since the transition [to democracy], considering all state governors, we didn't have great advances in terms of structural reforms. Not from any administration. In some ways it continues to be a big taboo."[57]

---

[55] After then-candidate Dória made these statements, the commander of the Military Police was forced to affirm the police's commitment to "legality." See "Após declaração de Doria, comandante-geral diz que PM deve proteger vidas," *Notícias UOL*, October 2, 2018.

[56] "Ex-policiais da Rota eleitos em SP somam 77 mortes," *Estado de São Paulo*, October 8, 2012.

[57] Author interview with Benedito Mariano, former police ombudsman, São Paulo, September 14, 2017.

7

The Social and Political Drivers of Reform in Buenos Aires Province and Colombia

For the immense mass of humanity, the only authority they will encounter on a daily basis, and which for them represents all power, is the police. And there will be good or bad government depending on whether there is a good or bad police; an arbitrary or just government, depending on how the police operates.

Alberto Lleras Camargo, president of Colombia, 1958–1962

Citing the words of his predecessor, Colombian President César Gaviria convened a Consultative Commission representing a wide swath of Colombian political and social life to evaluate and generate proposals to fundamentally reform the National Police, insisting that their mandate was "none other than good government" (Presidencia de la República 1994). President Gaviria ordered the reform of the country's police force in 1993, after years of authoritarian coercive practices, growing public discontent and distrust toward the police, and organizational disarray caused by the demands of combating guerrilla groups and drug-trafficking organizations, threatened his efforts to reestablish the legitimacy of the Colombian state through what he called a *revolcón institucional* (institutional shake-up). In Buenos Aires Province, meanwhile, Governor Eduardo Duhalde closed out 1997 declaring the police to be in a state of emergency, enacting a civilian intervention of the organization, and calling for proposals to reform the police force he had called "the best police in the world" just three years earlier.[1]

---

[1] "La Bonaerense en diez años," *Clarín*, January 28, 2002.

In each of these cases, the respective executive had for years been overseeing a police force that routinely engaged in authoritarian coercive practices and had demonstrated itself to be largely incompetent at its primary task of protecting citizens from crime. Both leaders, however, also avoided reforming their police forces despite these urgent institutional deficiencies and incompatibility with democratic principles.

As I argued in Chapters 4 and 5, politicians' decision to maintain the status quo despite these conditions was the result of ordinary democratic politics. Political leaders in Buenos Aires Province and Colombia had long avoided needed police reforms because the fragmentation of societal preferences over policing and security made the electoral gains of police reform uncertain at best, while risking alienating a powerful institution. In the sections that follow, I demonstrate how institutional persistence gave way to comprehensive structural reform in Buenos Aires Province and Colombia following shifts in societal preferences from fragmentation to convergence and in the strength of the political opposition. These two factors changed the incentives of the governor and the president, providing an electoral counterweight to the structural power of police.

In Buenos Aires Province, a horrific and politically motivated police killing led to the convergence of societal preferences in early 1997. The scandal, however, failed to bring about reform until midterm elections later that year produced a change in the strength of the political opposition. In contrast to the case of São Paulo State (Chapter 6), which contemporaneously experienced widespread societal outrage in response to a shocking case of police violence but lacked a strong opposition, the emergence of a robust political opposition that posed a threat to his electoral prospects pushed the governor to pursue structural police reforms to promote democratic coercion in Buenos Aires Province. In Colombia, meanwhile, the emergence of a fairly robust political opposition on its own proved insufficient to bring about police reform, leading to the failure of a reform proposal in the Congress in late 1992. The proposal was revived just six months later, following the convergence of societal preferences in the form of a scandal.

The analysis that follows thus underscores how ordinary democratic politics can produce both the persistence of authoritarian coercion and reform efforts to promote democratic coercion. It employs comparative sequential analysis (Falleti & Mahoney 2015) to demonstrate how, even over a relatively short period, shifts in patterns of societal contestation and political competition shaped politicians' electoral calculations about the costs and benefits of enacting police reform. Despite the range of structural differences between Buenos Aires Province and Colombia, political leaders in both settings opted to maintain the status quo upon observing either fragmented preferences or a weak political opposition, concluding that police reform would be unlikely to yield electoral benefits, while potentially alienating an important bureaucracy. In both instances, their electoral incentives changed upon observing shifts in societal preferences and the strength of the political opposition. The same democratic processes that previously yielded institutional continuity – patterns of political competition and societal contestation and demand-making – inspired the first meaningful effort by democratically elected leaders to enact reforms intended to eradicate authoritarian coercive practices and structures that had endured for many years.

REFORMING THE "MALDITA POLICÍA" OF BUENOS AIRES PROVINCE (1997–1998)

Chapter 4 provided a detailed overview of the nature of authoritarian coercion exercised by the Police of Buenos Aires Province, as well as how the police's structural power and the fragmentation of societal preferences favored the persistence of authoritarian coercive practices and structures. The provincial police engaged in routine extrajudicial violence and predation of the citizenry, including an extensive illicit rent-extraction network, connivance with criminal actors, and widespread "*gatillo fácil*" killings and torture. Elected officials, meanwhile, did little to provide external oversight of police, with many instead reportedly benefiting directly from the system of *recaudación*, the illicit rents collected by the provincial police. In the face of rising crime and social unrest, meanwhile, societal demands and preferences over policing were fragmented, with citizens in low-income areas and their allies in human rights organizations mobilizing against police violence and more privileged sectors demanding greater police discretion and authority in light of rising crime and protest. In the context of such fragmentation of preferences, elected leaders likely saw little electoral gain in enacting police reform and little cost to pursuing continued accommodation of police.

The Buenos Aires case illustrates well the importance of electoral incentives in politicians' choices over continuity and reform. Sequential analysis may be especially helpful in identifying how the *joint occurrence* of the convergence of societal preferences and a robust political opposition shifts politicians' incentives in favor of reform. The introduction to Part II of the book lays out the causal sequence likely to bring about police reform: a high-profile act of police deviance, the convergence of societal preferences, and the change in incentives if the incumbent faces a robust political opposition. It was precisely this sequence of events that transpired following the murder of photojournalist José Luis Cabezas at the hands of the Police of Buenos Aires Province in early 1997. The high-profile killing was indeed followed by widespread societal mobilization, reflecting the convergence of preferences. Despite this ongoing mobilization, however, the governor did not decide to undertake police reform until after his party lost midterm legislative elections in late 1997.

Before turning to discussing the drivers and content of the sweeping reform adopted in Buenos Aires Province in an attempt to transform the notorious police force, however, it is worth briefly comparing the Cabezas case with earlier police killings in order to understand why reform is less likely when events deviate from the sequence described in Figure II.A. As the cases sketched out in the next section demonstrate, when either preference convergence or a robust political opposition emerge alone, politicians are likely to feel little electoral pressure to enact reform. Instead, they are likely to continue to accommodate police, thereby maintaining the status quo of authoritarian coercion.

Assessing Previous Scandals and Moments of Strong Opposition (1987–1993)

Chapter 4 made clear that rampant extrajudicial violence was a constant for the *Bonaerense* since the transition to democracy, in particular during the administration of Governor Eduardo Duhalde. Yet, through most of the 1980s and 1990s, police reform remained off the agenda, despite extralegal violence, widespread corruption, and considerable deficiencies in the face of rising crime. Brief sequential analysis of two high-profile instances of police violence that preceded the Cabezas case illustrates why this occurred. The first instance is the "Ingeniero Budge massacre," a prominent case of extrajudicial police violence that nevertheless did not result in the convergence of preferences, though it did take place in the context of robust political competition. The second instance is the disappearance of university student Miguel Bru at the hands of police, which led to broad societal outrage and mobilization but in a time of weak political competition. The absence of preference convergence in the first case and of political competition in the second shed light on why reform remained off the table for many years – and why the Cabezas case yielded a different outcome.

Ten years before Cabezas was killed, one of the most prominent cases of *gatillo fácil* (trigger-happy) killings – and the first to be characterized as such since the transition to democracy – came to light. The case known as the "massacre of Ingeniero Budge" occurred in May 1987 (see Chapter 4). According to CORREPI, a grassroots organization that advocates for victims of police violence, the case demonstrates "that repression did not end with the return to democracy, least of all in the most low-income neighborhoods and against working-class youth."[2] Three young men drinking beer on a street corner were killed by police officers, who then tried to claim they had engaged in a shootout.[3] Although the case of Ingeniero Budge was an emblematic case of police violence and mobilized a committed group of family, neighbors, and friends of the victims who pressured for justice over the course of seven years, the case did not become a scandal as defined in Chapter 2, since broader societal sectors did not express outrage or mobilize much beyond the local community of Ingeniero Budge.[4] Months after Ingeniero Budge, Luis Brunati was appointed minister of government, the entity that was charged with overseeing the police at the time. Brunati made concerted attempts to enact changes in order to diminish police corruption and violence. His efforts, however, yielded few actual changes. As discussed in Chapter 4, Brunati reported police threats and opposition, as well as interference by police-allied politicians to block his efforts. Importantly, however, Brunati noted that another obstacle to his efforts was the absence of societal mobilization: "I didn't have the benefit of having people out on the streets, of having society mobilized. I did have the understanding of society and the press. But I did not have a mobilized society [behind me]."[5]

Despite the sustained mobilization of the Ingeniero Budge community, the absence of broader mobilization meant politicians did not perceive a demand for police reform shared across societal sectors. The implication for politicians' electoral incentives is significant because 1987 was a rare moment of robust political competition in the province. Not only would

---

[2] Statement by CORREPI, "30 años de la Masacre de Budge: No hay olvido ni perdon," CORREPI Website, May 8, 2017, https://correpi.lahaine.org/30-anos-de-la-masacre-de/.
[3] "A 30 años de la Masacre de Budge," *Página/12*, May 8, 2017, available at www.pagina12 .com.ar/36463-a-30-anos-de-la-masacre-de-budge.
[4] "Protesta vecinal ante el juez por la muerte de los tres jóvenes," *Clarín*, May 13, 1987. See digital archive of the Comisión Provincial por la Memoria (Provincial Commission for Memory), which published materials on the Budge case and community mobilization originally compiled by the Intelligence Division of the provincial police (DIPPBA), available at www.comisionporlamemoria.org/investigacion/project/masacre-de-budge/.
[5] "La historia de un precursor," *Página/12*, April 11, 2004.

gubernatorial and legislative elections take place later that year, it was also a time of shifting partisan strength (see Figure 7.1). The incumbent party, the UCR (Unión Cívica Radical, Radical Civic Union), was weakened at the national level due to then-president Alfonsín's handling of the economy and (among some sectors) the laws intended to stop prosecutions of military and police officials involved in human rights violations during the dictatorship. Meanwhile, the main opposition party, the Peronist Party or PJ (Partido Justicialista), was bolstered heading into the 1987 elections, after smoothing over frictions that led it to present two separate lists during the preceding legislative elections. However, without a clear message of shared outrage from a diverse range of societal sectors, the incumbent UCR and the opposition Peronist Party likely saw little electoral gain in enacting police reform in 1987, despite the latter's traditional support from working-class and low-income sectors.[6]

Thus, although the Ingeniero Budge massacre became a high-profile instance of extrajudicial police violence, the continued fragmentation of societal preferences meant politicians faced little electoral counterweight to the structural power of the police. As discussed in Chapter 4, politicians instead accommodated the police, which continued to constrain the policy agenda by thwarting the reform attempts of Brunati. The result was the persistence of authoritarian coercive practices and structures.

A second case worth analyzing further in comparison with the murder of Cabezas occurred four years prior: the disappearance of Miguel Bru, also discussed in Chapter 4. Miguel Bru was a journalism student in the provincial capital, La Plata, who was detained and subsequently disappeared by police officers after denouncing an unlawful police search in his home.[7] It soon became apparent that police had engaged in a cover-up to conceal evidence that Bru disappeared while in police custody (Human Rights Watch & CELS 1998, 106). Bru's disappearance sparked memories of the estimated tens of thousands of individuals disappeared during the dictatorship and prompted broad mobilization, particularly by university students and human rights groups, including the Mothers of Plaza de Mayo. Protesters held frequent demonstrations in the capital, in front

---

[6] Although the PJ did not take on the Budge massacre as an electoral issue, individual Peronist provincial legislators did express demands for a thorough investigation of the case. See "Pedido de informes sobre la muerte de 3 jóvenes," May 13, 1987, accessed via digital archive of the Comisión Provincial por la Memoria (Provincial Commission for Memory).

[7] "Misteriosa desaparicion de un estudiante de periodismo," *Clarin*, September 23, 1993, 55.

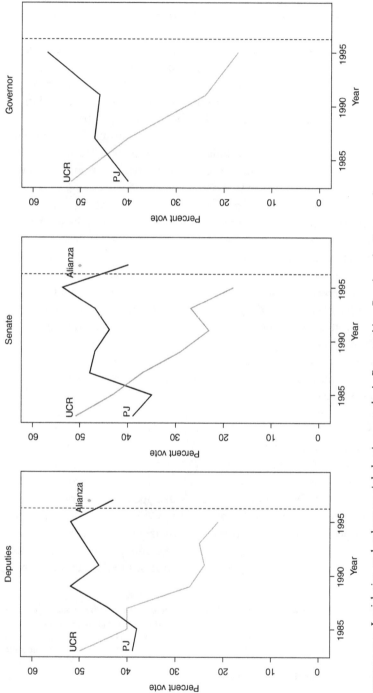

FIGURE 7.1 Legislative and gubernatorial elections results in Buenos Aires Province (1983–1999)
Data collected from the Department of Statistics, National Election Office, Argentine Ministry of the Interior

of Casa de Gobierno (the governor's mansion), eventually prompting Governor Duhalde to meet with Miguel Bru's mother and offer to create a special task force to investigate the case.[8]

The disappearance of Miguel Bru became a prominent case of police violence and shared many common characteristics to that of Cabezas – including the profession of the victims, widespread middle-class mobilization, frequent media attention, and a broader climate of social and institutional recognition of the provincial police's rampant violence and corruption[9] (see Chapter 4). But police reform did not follow the disappearance of Miguel Bru as it did in the case of Cabezas. I argue this is likely due to the absence of a crucial part of the causal sequence laid out in Figure II.A: a robust political opposition. Like the killing of Jose Luis Cabezas, Miguel Bru's disappearance occurred shortly before legislative elections. But while the 1997 legislative elections led to the emergence of a newly robust political opposition, the 1993 elections did not produce the same outcome. As Figure 7.1 shows, the Radical Party had been in decline since losing the 1987 elections, and, by 1993, no alternative political party presented an electoral threat to Peronist dominance. A referendum held in 1994, moreover, further demonstrated that the governor faced little electoral threat. After he put forth a referendum to ask the citizenry whether he could run for reelection, 61 percent voted to support his run for a second term.[10] Governor Duhalde thus faced little electoral pressure to reform the embattled provincial police.

As this brief overview of two high-profile cases of police violence demonstrates, neither a robust political opposition nor the convergence of societal preferences were sufficient on their own to serve as an electoral counterweight to the structural power of the provincial police and the strong incentives to engage in continued accommodation. Table 7.1 compares the relevant sequence of events across these three cases to underscore why the Cabezas case ultimately resulted in reform while the "massacre of Ingeniero Budge" and the disappearance of Miguel Bru did not. The following sections offer sequential analysis of events taking place over the course of 1997 to demonstrate how the joint occurrence of

---

[8] Author interview with Rosa Bru, mother of Miguel Bru, La Plata, August 23, 2017.

[9] Recall, for instance, the frequent media reports of *"gatillo facil"* police killings and disappearances and the extraordinary step by the provincial Supreme Court to investigate dozens of these cases in 1993, including that of Miguel Bru. See "La Suprema Corte bonaerense investiga a la Policía por 20 muertes y desapariciones," *Clarín*, October 25, 1993, 40.

[10] "Duhalde logró una victoria rotunda," *Clarín*, October 3, 1994.

TABLE 7.1 *Comparative sequential analysis of selected police violence cases*

Period	High-profile case	Convergence of preferences	Robust opposition	Reform
1987	Ing. Budge	No	Yes	No
1993	Bru	Yes	No	No
1997 (Jan–Oct)	Cabezas	Yes	No	No
1997 (Oct–Dec)	Cabezas	Yes	Yes	Yes

preference convergence and, subsequently, the emergence of a robust political opposition shift politicians' incentives in favor of reform.

Scandal and a Shared Demand for Reform (January–October 1997)

The notorious killing of photojournalist Jose Luis Cabezas by the *Bonaerense* is broadly recognized as the catalyst for the long-delayed reform of the provincial police. But while the widespread and prolonged mobilization that resulted from this egregious act of police violence demonstrated a shared societal demand for police reform, this convergence of societal preferences did not initially result in police reform. As I lay out in the discussion that follows, the first nine months after Cabezas's murder produced sustained mobilization and the case remained at the forefront of the public agenda, but available evidence suggests the governor and his long-dominant Peronist Party had little intention to enact police reform during the period that preceded midterm legislative elections.

José Luis Cabezas was a photojournalist who worked for the prominent news magazine *Noticias*. In January 1997, Cabezas was murdered, in a scene described as follows on the front page of the country's main newspaper, *Clarín*: "[He was found] handcuffed, with his hands behind his back, in his car, burned. A crime like this has no precedent since the restoration of democracy."[11] Cabezas was found with two bullet wounds, brutally beaten, and his body had been burned inside of his car, which had been left on the side of a road, just an hour and a half after leaving a party in the early hours of the morning on January 25, 1997. He had been working in Pinamar, a coastal town in Buenos Aires Province, where Argentine economic and political elites spend the summer months.

[11] *Clarín* front page, January 26, 1997.

The political significance of Cabezas's murder was readily apparent. As a report prepared by opposition members of the Bicameral Commission for Oversight and Follow-up of the Investigations of the Murder of José Luis Cabezas put it: "The crime, the place where it was carried out, the implications of the work done by José Luis and the magazine *Noticias* regarding the *Bonaerense* and the businessman Yabrán, placed, from the first moment, the political elite (*el poder*) under suspicion."[12] From the very first news reports, two possible linkages were made: to Alfredo Yabrán; and to the *Bonaerense* police.[13] Alfredo Yabrán was the executive of a shipping and mail company who had been denounced in 1996 by then-minister of the economy Domingo Cavallo as part of the "'mafias of power' that sought to pressure the government to favor the businesses of the postal executive and open the doors to drug trafficking."[14] Yabrán had famously declared, around that time, "Taking a photo of me is like shooting me in the forehead with a bullet."[15] In March 1996, Cabezas became the first journalist to photograph Yabrán, who ended up on the cover of *Noticias* as a result. Yabrán had close ties to President Carlos Menem and to many other politicians.[16] Meanwhile, Cabezas had also been involved in investigating the corruption of the *Bonaerense* in his work for the news magazine *Noticias*, which in August 1996 ran a famous cover story on the extent of corruption in the *Bonaerense* with a cover photo of then-chief of police Pedro Klodczyk taken by Cabezas.

For these reasons, the Cabezas case immediately became a scandal, with widespread mobilization and sustained media coverage underscoring the convergence of societal preferences in favor of police reform. In response to the killing, protests took place in Buenos Aires City and Buenos Aires Province "with a broad adherence of different groups representative of the society,"[17] including student groups, religious leaders,

---

[12] The report, "Evaluation of the Bicameral Commission for Oversight and Follow-up of the Investigations of the Murder of José Luis Cabezas," was given to me by one of its authors, former provincial senator Eduardo Sigal.

[13] Yabrán was formally accused in the case as the intellectual author of the crime in May 1998, but he died by suicide shortly thereafter. The head of his security team, three officers of the Buenos Aires provincial police, and four additional accomplices were ultimately convicted in the case (ARGRA & CELS 2003).

[14] "Brutal crimen en Pinamar," *Página/12*, January 26, 1997.

[15] "Vida y muerte de un cartero," *Página/12*, May 21, 1998.

[16] Just three days after the murder of Cabezas, the mayor of Pinamar came out to declare that "Yabrán had nothing to do with it," adding "Yabrán and I are united by friendship, by a neighborhood." See "Quién mató a Cabezas?," *Página/12*, January 28, 1997.

[17] CELS, *Annual Report on Human Rights in Argentina 1997*, 30.

major labor unions, the Federation of Chambers of Commerce, and traditional human rights organizations that emerged during the dictatorship (Abuelas de Plaza de Mayo, Serpaj, Madres de Plaza de Mayo, CELS, and so on).[18] Notably, the Cabezas case was one of the first instances in which traditional human rights groups focused on political violence targeting largely middle-class victims during the dictatorship, mobilized explicitly around police violence in democracy, alongside organizations such as CORREPI, whose work focuses on police violence targeting poor and working-class victims (Verdú 2009, 81). While thousands marched demanding "Justice for José Luis,"[19] reporting and analysis of the crime immediately laid blame on the police[20] and produced "a change in social perception – at least among some sectors of society – of police repression" (Verdú 2009, 81–82). Activists held protests on the twenty-fifth day of every month, and small fliers with a photo of Cabezas and the phrase "*No se olviden de Cabezas*" (Don't forget Cabezas) became ubiquitous, with diverse sectors of Argentine society – from soccer teams to prominent politicians – taking photographs with it.[21] Following sustained mobilization by journalists and human rights organizations, the Cabezas case remained in the news for years. Indeed, for years after the murder of Cabezas, news anchor Santo Biasatti ended his nightly broadcast saying, "*No se olviden de Cabezas.*"[22]

The extensive mobilization by journalists was itself an important indicator of the moment of the convergence brought about by the Cabezas case, in which a middle-class sector not typically active on issues of police violence joined the ranks of critics. As Carlos Rodríguez, a journalist with the newspaper *Página/12*, put it, the Cabezas case "had a lot more repercussion than any other case [of police killings], because it had a national impact that other cases did not have ... I think it was due to a number of things, primarily because he was a photojournalist and the press took that on as a cause."[23] Indeed, the personal characteristics of Cabezas, particularly the fact that he was a journalist, were highly significant. Marcela Perelman, security policy and institutional violence coordinator at the human rights NGO CELS, said in an interview, "We're

---

[18] "Con todo el calor de un mediodía porteño," *Página/12*, January 29, 1997.
[19] "La marcha por la justicia se desencontró con Menem," *Página/12*, January 30, 1997.
[20] CELS, *Annual Report on Human Rights in Argentina 1997*, 20.
[21] "No se olviden de Cabezas," *Clarín*, February 2, 1997.
[22] Author interview with journalist Carlos Rodríguez, Buenos Aires, September 16, 2011.
[23] Author interview with Carlos Rodríguez, Buenos Aires, September 16, 2011.

talking about a journalist ... In Argentina the tradition of journalism is very strong, and the legitimacy of journalism was very high back then."[24] The Cabezas case was thus one in which the victim belonged to a social class and enjoyed a social status not typical of victims of police violence, which led similarly situated journalists to lead the broader societal outrage. In particular, two associations of journalists, the Unión de Trabajadores de Prensa de Buenos Aires (UTPBA, Union of Press Workers in Buenos Aires) and primarily the Asociación de Reporteros Gráficos de la República Argentina (ARGRA, Association of Argentine Photojournalists), led the demands for justice and an end to impunity. The UTPBA and ARGRA called on their members to pressure political authorities to duly investigate and prosecute the case:

Each time authorities from any of the three branches of the national or provincial governments call us to cover an activity, we will request a minute of silence in remembrance of our murdered colleague and demand the investigation of the crime. In every professional contact with these authorities we will include questions about the advances and setbacks of the investigation and we will publicize their responses. We encourage every media outlet to include in their editions a permanent section that informs [the public] of the state of the investigation until the crime is resolved. Our efforts will be oriented not only toward the investigation of the crime, but also in the cases that José Luis Cabezas was working on, because if they were to be abandoned the crime will have been successful."[25]

Governor Duhalde's Initial Response: Continuity (January–October 1997)

Widespread societal mobilization kept up the pressure on the ongoing investigation,[26] which was, unsurprisingly, plagued with malfeasance.[27]

---

[24] Interview with Marcela Perelman, security policy and institutional violence coordinator, CELS, Buenos Aires, August 26, 2011.
[25] "Plan de trabajo para reclamar justicia," *Página/12*, January 29, 1997.
[26] Brinks (2008) finds in his studies of police killings in Argentina, Brazil, and Uruguay that societal mobilizations, even those much more limited than what occurred in the case of Cabezas, can move investigations forward and increase the rate of conviction.
[27] Police attempted to cover up or tamper with evidence, and there were several irregularities by the initial forensic investigation (e.g., they drove the car in which Cabezas was found to a nearby police station before conducting forensic analysis of the car, its tracks, the scene of the crime was not duly cordoned off; the first autopsy failed to indicate that Cabezas had been beaten and did not note a second bullet wound, etc.). The investigation was plagued by truly odd moments, such as the discovery that a key police informant in the case was then arrested and accused of taking part in Cabezas's killing. See Guillermo Oliver, Eduardo Sigal, and Alejandro Mosquera, 1997, "Evaluación de la Comisión

Duhalde responded to this broadly shared message with short-term measures, including the continuation of purges of allegedly corrupt officers (see Chapter 4). In response to the societal outcry during this initial stage, Duhalde spoke publicly about the case frequently and called for a thorough investigation; he even requested the help of the FBI[28] and offered a reward to anyone who came forward with information about the case. The Peronist Party created a bicameral commission in the provincial legislature to provide oversight of the investigations in the case; a similar "multi-partisan" commission was created at the national level by the minister of the interior.[29]

Nevertheless, many of the actions by Governor Duhalde and his Peronist Party in response to Cabezas's murder lost momentum after the first few months, and a range of evidence suggests that Governor Duhalde had no intention of enacting reform of the provincial police during this period. By the legislative elections in October 1997, nine months had passed since the killing of Cabezas. Yet broader reform remained off the agenda, even as the scandal remained in the news for months. The secretary of security at the time, Eduardo de Lázzari, despite recognizing that the Cabezas murder "unleashed a storm," said that his office continued its previous strategy, investigating corruption and institutional purges.[30] Even with this timid response to the Cabezas case, Duhalde removed the reformist Secretary de Lázzari in May 1997 in response to police pressure, replacing him with Carlos Brown, a long-time Peronist operative (Saín 2015, 143). The Peronist Party, meanwhile, at the national and provincial levels, rejected any broader claims or criticisms beyond the Cabezas case. Carlos Corach, the national minister of the interior, declared that the murder of Cabezas "was not a security problem ... It was an isolated case. It cannot be used to make conclusions about the system of security."[31]

The Cabezas case did not lead the governor or his party to address the police's nearly universally acknowledged deficiencies, despite the fact that, a year earlier, Duhalde declared his intention to carry out a "profound reform" of the provincial police, including the creation of

Bicameral de Control y Seguimiento de las Investigaciones del Asesinato de José Luis Cabezas" (copy furnished by the authors of the report). See also "Caso Cabezas: dudas y un nuevo procesado," *Clarín*, April 26, 1997.

[28] "Sálvenme de mis policías," *Página/12*, January 31, 1997.
[29] "La politización tan temida," *Página/12*, January 30, 1997.
[30] Author interview with Eduardo de Lázzari, La Plata, October 19, 2011.
[31] Author interview with Carlos Corach, Buenos Aires, October 27, 2011.

an internal affairs entity, decentralization, and citizen participation and oversight (Saín 2015, 131). Cabezas's murder could have been an opportunity for Duhalde to assuage widespread outrage by enacting the comprehensive structural reform plan he had previously announced, but he did not do so (Saín 2015, 141). One month before the elections, the opposition members of the legislative commission investigating the Cabezas case denounced in an internal report that fact that "more than three months after the appointment of the new Secretary of Security ... [we observe] no major changes in the police institution nor relevant advances relating to the case that concerns us."[32] The opposition legislators also denounced that the bicameral commission in the legislature had become lethargic as members of the PJ tried to impede its work.

Thus, a range of events in the first nine months following Cabezas's murder – Duhalde's decision to fire, rather than empower, his own reformist secretary of security; the failure to push for his own previous reform proposal; the stalled investigations by the bicameral commission his own party created in the legislature; and the denial of broader institutional problems within the police by Peronist politicians – suggest Duhalde and his Peronist Party had little intention of pursuing police reform. Despite prolonged and unprecedented societal mobilization following Cabezas's murder conveying broadly shared societal discontent with the police and a coherent demand for reform, on the eve of midterm legislative elections Duhalde likely concluded he would face little electoral cost in continuing to avoid police reform.

Midterm Elections and a Strengthened Opposition (October 1997)

Governor Duhalde likely believed he would not face electoral punishment at the polls because of the aforementioned dominance of his Peronist Party in the province over the preceding decade (see Figure 7.1). By the time of Cabezas's death in early 1997, the Peronist Party had come to occupy a solid majority in the Province of Buenos Aires, consolidated, in large part, through the efforts of Eduardo Duhalde. The UCR (Unión Cívica Radical, Radical Civil Union), meanwhile, went from governing the

---

[32] *"Evaluación de la Comisión Bicameral de Control y Seguimiento de las Investigaciones del asesinato de José Luis Cabezas."* A copy of the internal report was given to me by one of its authors in 2011.

province and dominating the legislature in the 1980s to holding about one-quarter of the vote and seat share by the mid-1990s. The elections held in 1995 saw a new party emerge out of smaller left and progressive parties, FREPASO (Frente País Solidario, Front for a Country in Solidarity), but it did not have much strength in Buenos Aires Province.

The relative weakness of these two opposition parties[33] likely led Duhalde to discount the strategic use of the Cabezas case by opposition legislators to make broader criticisms of his administration. Leading up to the October 1997 legislative elections, the opposition parties ramped up their criticism of Duhalde and the provincial police in connection with the Cabezas murder. In early October, the leader of the UCR issued a statement calling on Duhalde to give answers to voters about the Cabezas case and saying that "if it weren't for the administration [of Duhalde], the Cabezas murder would already be resolved."[34] Legislators from FREPASO, meanwhile, issued the aforementioned report evaluating the bicameral commission in September 1997. The report was filled with tacit and explicit criticisms of the government, and of the PJ members of the commission, accusing them of not being aggressive enough in the investigation. The report emphasized at various point that "we are not looking at isolated cases" and pointed to systemic issues in the police dating to the tenure of Pedro Klodczyk and, by implication, the governor who put him in charge.

By 1997, the national governing bodies of the UCR and FREPASO decided to form an alliance,[35] and they competed in various national and provincial contests as the Alianza por el Trabajo, Justicia, y la Educación (Alliance for Work, Justice, and Education, henceforth Alianza). Despite this new political formation, however, Duhalde likely saw little electoral threat in the 1997 midterm elections and instead sought to shore up his prospects for the upcoming presidential elections. For instance, Duhalde recognized fully the electoral risk that the Cabezas murder presented, but he did so with an eye toward the 1999 presidential contest more than anything else. Just over a week before the legislative elections, Hilda "Chiche" Duhalde, the governor's wife and head of the Peronist list in the coming legislative elections, spoke to reporters about Cabezas case

[33] Each of the two parties – UCR and FREPASO – had held no more than a quarter of legislative seats in the province during most of the preceding decade. Data were collected from the Department of Statistics, National Election Office, Ministry of the Interior.

[34] "Duhalde tendrá que dar muchas explicaciones a la sociedad," Union Cívica Radical, Dirección de Prensa, October 2, 1997.

[35] "Habrá alianza entre la UCR y el Frepaso," *La Nación*, August 3, 1997.

and her husband's presidential prospects, saying, "If the case is not resolved, he can't be president." Duhalde did not perceive the Cabezas case, nor the provincial opposition, as presenting the same threat at the provincial level, however, particularly as his approval ratings had increased.[36] The front page of the newspaper *Página/12* declared, two days before the election, "Everyone takes as given the victory of the Alianza at the national level but Buenos Aires remains unknown."[37] The PJ's own pollsters, meanwhile, predicted an electoral victory for the governor's party.[38]

With improved approval ratings, doubt about the opposition Alianza's prospects in Buenos Aires Province, and favorable internal polling, Duhalde had reason to go into the midterm elections expecting his party to win. But despite the uncertainty of the outcome on the eve of the elections, the results dealt an important blow to the governor. The Alianza defeated the Peronists in the 1997 legislative elections in the national congress, in eight provinces, and the national capital. The Alianza also won a majority of legislative seats in Buenos Aires Province, defeating the PJ for the first time in a decade (see Figure 7.1). The Alianza won 47 percent of the vote in the province's chamber of deputies to the Peronists' 43 percent – giving it a total of twenty-six out of forty-six seats up for grabs (compared to twenty for the PJ) – and nearly 50 percent of the vote for the senate against the Peronists' 40 percent (fourteen of twenty-three seats for the Alianza, nine for the PJ).[39]

The media declared that "the provincial PJ had its worst electoral performance since 1987" and that the outcome had "hurt the presidential ambitions of Eduardo Duhalde,"[40] a damaging assessment as the presidential campaign drew closer. In light of the Alianza's victories at the national level and throughout the country as well, Duhalde realized he was now faced with a robust political opposition. His presidential chances in the balance, Duhalde quickly changed his approach and started moving toward reforming the *Bonaerense*.[41]

---

[36] "Chiche condicionó la candidatura de Eduardo Duhalde," *Clarín*, October 15, 1997.
[37] *Página/12* front page, October 24, 1997.
[38] "Buenos Aires le dio a la Alianza dimensión nacional," *Clarín*, October 27, 1997.
[39] Data were collected from the Department of Statistics, National Election Office, Ministry of the Interior. Only half of all seats were up for election in 1997. See also "Totales Provinciales," *Hoy*, October 27, 1997, 17.
[40] "Buenos Aires le dio a la Alianza dimensión nacional," *Clarín*, October 27, 1997.
[41] Duhalde declared after the electoral loss: "I am the father of this defeat." See *Hoy* front page, October 27, 1997.

Convergence, Robust Opposition, and an Ambitious Reform
(October–December 1997)

Facing a newly robust political opposition in the legislature, and eying the presidency in 1999, Duhalde began his push for comprehensive police reform a month after his party's electoral defeat. The governor took a dramatic step, declaring a "state of emergency" within the police (again) – which facilitated a civilian intervention of the police and the early retirement of all police commanders – and soliciting reform proposals from civil society. As Alberto Binder, one of two criminal justice experts that designed the reform, glibly put it: "Duhalde was sort of desperately looking for a reform plan, and we had one."[42] The reform proposal drafted by Binder and Arslanian,[43] cognizant of the usual approach taken by Governor Duhalde and his predecessors to address police malfeasance, emphasized on the very first page that such an approach would not work:

There are no short-term solutions ... The various "emergency" solutions, such as changes in leadership, purges, etc., have not demonstrated effectiveness in this or other similar areas (such as the judiciary, for example). On the contrary, the [police] institution has an enormous capacity to reproduce personnel that perpetuate the state of corruption and inefficiency.[44]

The document called for a bold strategy, one that Duhalde was now willing to accept. Less than two months after losing the legislative elections to the Alianza, Duhalde signed off on an audacious reform plan. In December 1997, Duhalde signed a decree (4.506/1997) declaring the intervention of the provincial police and appointed a civilian to lead the intervention and the institution. In effect, the *Bonaerense* now had a civilian as its chief. The legislature then passed a law validating the intervention and creating a bicameral commission to oversee the reform process (Law 12.068/1998). Additionally, there was a particularly radical measure, described by the civilian designated to lead the intervention, Peronist legislator Luis Lugones:

---

[42] Author interview with Alberto Binder, Buenos Aires, September 27, 2011.

[43] Arslanian had previously served as a judge, including on the tribunal that judged the trial against the leaders of the military juntas, and as minister of justice at the national level under President Menem. Binder is a lawyer who had been working on criminal justice system reforms for many years.

[44] León Arslanian and Alberto Binder, 1997, "Plan de Reorganización General del Sistema de Seguridad e Investigación de los Delitos en la Provincia de Buenos Aires." Copy of the proposal was furnished by Eduardo Estévez, former Ministry of Security official. Boldface in original.

There was an idea that you had to make a definitive break ... an intervention that would reshape governance of the police from the root of the police structure, generate new structures and new conditions ... We decreed the intervention and put all of the police in a state of emergency in order to suspend institutional rules that limited certain decision-making regarding the operation of the police ... Concretely, we decided to send all police officials above a certain rank into retirement ... The top part of the [police] hierarchy was sent into retirement; that is, the commissioner generals, the commissioner majors, and the commissioner inspectors. Not because there was a direct [suspicion] that they had been linked to corruption, but instead as a general measure to try to generate conditions for a new opening and a new methodology of working within the police.[45]

This measure was not only an extraordinary attempt to create a rupture with past structures but also underscored the extent to which the governor now faced an electoral counterweight to the police's structural power. In contrast to secretaries of security in the mid-1990s who were unable to remove police leaders (see discussion of Piotti and De Lazzari's tenures in Chapter 4) due to intervention by local politicians and the governor himself, the drastic steps taken in the wake of Duhalde's electoral defeat represented a marked departure from the constraints police leaders were able to impose on available policy options and the usual incentives to engage in accommodation.

These drastic measures not only created a break with existing power structures: they also revealed a greater degree of division and contestation than had previously been visible within the provincial police. Indeed, such divisions were prevalent within the police force, as officers took on opposing views of the reform. Some viewed the reform "with the hope that it would change the [police's] way of thinking ... of giving everyone an opportunity [to ascend the ranks and be promoted], not simply to certain groups (*grupitos*) ... this law opened up a great hope (*ilusión*), the possibility of being able to reach positions we previously could not."[46] Others saw the process as a farce enabling the police to continue its extralegal practices, particularly the emergency measure enabling arbitrary firings (*Ley de Prescindibilidad*):

After twenty years the police decides it no longer needs you. You're dismissed, and not for cause, but because of *recaudación* (collection). If you were the head of a police precinct (*comisaría*) that never arrested a single person but you collected a certain amount for the power structure (*el poder*), you robbed for the crown, you

---

[45] Author interview with Luis Lugones, La Plata, September 14, 2011.

[46] Author interview with anonymous active-duty *comisario* of the Police of Buenos Aires Province 2, La Plata, October 18, 2011.

were never going to be dismissed. But if you were in a *comisaría* where every day you took criminals off the street, you were let go because you didn't collect (*porque no recaudabas*) ... It was a bitter pill to swallow, because it was not a reform that helped us. To the contrary, it harmed us. It didn't reform us, it deformed us."[47]

Irrespective of whether viewed positively or negatively, high-ranking officers who were young officers at the time of the reform described an atmosphere of "malaise" and "confusion." As one retired *comisario* put it, "predictability is a characteristic of institutions ... but that idea was lost with the reform ... there was not a clear idea of where we were headed ... you knew you were in an operating room and you could see they were operating on you, but you didn't know what they were taking out – you just knew you were in critical condition. It was traumatic."[48]

This internal chaos and disarray within the police force stood in sharp contrast to what civilian officials described as a broad political consensus in favor of reform. Luis Lugones, the chief of the civilian intervention, told me in an interview:

Before the intervention, we met with all the political parties with representation in the legislature ... When the law was sent to the legislature, [it] was approved unanimously in both chambers because there was this prior consensus that had brought together the leaders of each of the parties at the national level. That is, we spoke with the top political leaders of each of the parties, such that this was an institutionalized agreement.

Eduardo Sigal, a senator from the opposition, agreed that the various political parties succeeded in working together: "We were able to establish this as a state policy (*política de estado*). [We said] in light of the seriousness of the situation, let's try to establish common denominators. This was one of the few issues where we were able to work in a coordinated manner."[49]

As Lugones saw it, there was little choice within the provincial police but to cooperate with the civilian intervention he led and the reform process that followed. While some police officers, particularly those high-ranking officials that had been forced to retire, engaged in intimidation and fear tactics, Lugones recalled that "those officers that remained in activity – insofar as a political decision had been made and the degree of

---

[47] Author interview with anonymous retired *comisario* of the Police of Buenos Aires Province 2, Gonnet, Buenos Aires Province, October 18, 2011.

[48] Author interview with anonymous retired *comisario* of the Police of Buenos Aires Province 3, La Plata, October 27, 2011.

[49] Author interview with Eduardo Sigal, Buenos Aires, October 21, 2011.

importance and determination of this political decision, that is to say, the consensus by which these measures had been taken – felt trapped" and went along with the reform.

"The End of the *Maldita Policía*?": Toward Democratic Coercion

A decade and a half after the transition to democracy, Duhalde now faced an electoral counterweight to the police's structural power, obligating him to undertake the first earnest effort to reform the *"maldita policía"* in accordance with the principles of democratic rule.[50] In accordance with the index of democratic police reform outlined in Chapter 2, the reform legislation was explicitly designed to eradicate the provincial police's extensive authoritarian coercive practices and structures and to decidedly promote democratic coercion.

The architects of the reform designed the legislation so as to definitively break with the structures and practices that enabled the police to cultivate political power and deploy coercion in the interests of political leaders, instead shifting its orientation to protecting citizens from crime. Perhaps no measure evidenced the shift in political conditions and the existence of a counterweight to the police's structural power more than measures targeting the police's political and economic power structure. The most dramatic initiative was a structural reform that sought to refocus the police function to providing security rather than serving political interests, bolster adherence to the rule of law, and strengthen external accountability: the dissolution of the *Bonaerense* and, with it, the powerful role of the police chief. The *Bonaerense* was replaced with eighteen police departments, corresponding to the territorial jurisdictions of the judiciary, and overseen by the Ministry of Justice and Security (Law 12.155/1998, Art. 12). The combined set of measures – from the declaration of a state of emergency that enabled mass firings without due process to the civilian intervention and the dissolution of the *Bonaerense* – broke with what a police commander would subsequently call "the greatest concentration of power known in the police force, the command of Pedro Klodczyk."[51]

---

[50] The title of this subsection refers to the book *El Final de La Maldita Policía?* by Sigal, Binder & Annichiarico (1998).

[51] The statement was made in 2002 in an open letter from a then–departmental commander, Julio César Frutos, to then-president Eduardo Duhalde, who had criticized the police force he once oversaw as governor of Buenos Aires Province following the infamous massacre of protesters by the provincial police in Puente Pueyerredón. See "Carta abierta de un policía al Sr. Presidente," *La Nación*, July 2, 2002.

When asked why he took this drastic step of decentralizing the police in this way, reform architect and subsequent minister of justice and security Carlos León Arslanian responded that the purpose was "primarily to fundamentally democratize the police institution."[52]

The reform also included other operational and structural measures to improve the police force's capacity to provide security for citizens rather than serving the interests of political leaders. It did so by raising educational standards and improving training (Law 12.155, Book IV). It also achieved greater functional specialization and promoted effectiveness and efficiency by creating distinct institutional entities charged with security (patrolling and other preventive activities), investigation of crimes in assistance to the judiciary, and transit security (*seguridad vial*) (Law 12.155, Art. 2). This objective was also bolstered through an external control mechanism, the creation of the Institute for Criminal Policy and Security within the Ministry of Security. Run by civilian experts, the Institute intended to collect, systematize, and analyze criminal data, with the objective of using these analyses to inform policy. The institute was intended to build expertise with the goal of improving the police's, and the state's, administration of security, backed by the ministry's broader authority over the police.

The legislation also sought to increase citizen input in security policy through a marginal reform, the creation of Neighborhood Security Forums (Law 12.154/1998, Title III), characterizing such participation as a right (Art. 11). According to Arslanian, security minister and architect of the reform, "we wanted the citizenry ... to co-participate in decision-making as the beneficiaries of state action and public authority in the protection of their person and possessions."

The reform also targeted the entrenched and pervasive use of arbitrary or exceptional coercion by the provincial police, expressly looking to constrain the deployment of coercion within the bounds of the rule of law through operational and structural measures. The law laid out explicit and well-defined restrictions in the deployment of coercion (Law 12.155, Art. 7–8) and protections afforded to citizens in police interactions, including nondiscrimination (Art. 9–11, 28). It also dedicated a full section to "the fight against corruption, abuse of authority, and human rights violations in the exercise of the police function" (Law 12.155, Book III), including the creation of an internal affairs auditor (Art. 45) endowed with broad authority to investigate and sanction abuses. In an interview,

---

[52] Author interview with Carlos León Arslanian, Buenos Aires, September 12, 2011.

a *comisario* who was a young police official at the time of the reform claimed that his superiors came to realize the reform sought to put an end to arbitrary coercive practices: "They started to come to terms with it on their own. They knew they could no longer say, 'Well, we have the power [to do this] because we're the police.' They started to be more careful, and the police began to democratize."[53]

But the reform's priority was undoubtedly to put an end to the provincial police's enduring "self-governance" (*autogobierno*), through robust external control measures. According to Alberto Binder, one of the architects of the reform, "one of the fundamental concepts of the reform was to take away the police's autonomy and impose [civilian] governance over the police," identifying "two basic instruments of civilian governance of security": "civilians managing security policy from a ministry" and "community oversight."[54] The reform thus created a number of structures to reinforce civilian governance of security and external accountability of the police. First, the Secretariat of Security was elevated to the level of ministry (as the Ministry of Justice and Security at the time) and declared that the twenty or so police forces created by Law 12.155 responded directly to the minister of security, such that the highest authority of the police would in fact be a civilian. Second, the law created a structure for the province's civilian authorities, both from the executive and the legislative branches, to set broad security policy, through the Provincial Security Council (Law 12.154). This represented a stark contrast to the era of delegation of decision-making over security policy to the police. Third, the legislation endowed the Neighborhood Security Forums with a number of formal mechanisms for holding police accountable, including surveys evaluating police performance, the creation of local "crime maps" that the Ministry of Security would then utilize to assess whether police operations and resources corresponded to local needs, and a civilian structure within the Ministry of Security where members of the Forums could denounce corruption or poor police performance (González 2016).

The hard-fought reform enacted through broad social and political consensus in Buenos Aires Province sought, after a decade and a half since the transition to democracy, to expressly target the profound authoritarian coercive practices and structures of the *"maldita policía."* The case of the police of Buenos Aires Province is especially

---

[53] Author interview with anonymous active-duty *comisario* of the Police of Buenos Aires Province 2, La Plata, October 18, 2011.

[54] Author interview with Alberto Binder, Buenos Aires, September 27, 2011.

indicative of the ways in which democratic processes can both reproduce authoritarian coercion and bring about transformative efforts to
promote democratic coercion. After a long period in which fragmented
societal preferences and demands shaped politicians' electoral incentives
against police reform, robust political competition and broadly shared
societal outrage and mobilization ushered in an audacious democratic
police reform.

THE "INSTITUTIONAL SHAKE-UP" OF THE COLOMBIAN NATIONAL POLICE

Like the police of Buenos Aires Province, Colombia's National Police
similarly underwent a dramatic reform process after many years of
entrenched authoritarian coercive practices and structures. As detailed
in Chapter 5, the Colombian National Police faced a prolonged period of
institutional decay, with rampant corruption, widespread extrajudicial
violence, infiltration by drug cartels, and the deployment of coercion in
the service of political and private interests. Despite these grave deficiencies, the National Police was able to leverage its structural power – bolstered by its control over the drug war, the government's policy priority –
to evade civilian oversight and thwart reform efforts. Notably, even as
several state officials made urgent pronouncements about the police's dire
condition, and every other area of the Colombian state saw important
transformations through President Gaviria's "institutional shake-up,"
structural reform of the National Police remained conspicuously absent
from the agenda.

As I demonstrated in Chapter 5, the absence of police reform to
promote democratic coercion was not due to a lack of salience of security
issues or of the police's deficiencies, nor due to a crowded policy agenda.
Instead, the president and other politicians likely saw little electoral
advantage in enacting police reform in the context of fragmented societal
preferences and demands over security. Needing to ensure the police's
cooperation with the drug war, politicians instead accommodated the
police and maintained the status quo, likely expecting it to bring little
electoral cost.

As occurred in Buenos Aires Province, however, politicians quickly saw
their incentives change when they observed a shift in the strength of the
political opposition and an egregious scandal that led to a broadly shared
societal outrage and demand for reform. The sections that follow provide
sequential analysis of shifts in these conditions in order to explain marked

short-term changes in politicians' decision-making from choosing to maintain the status quo of authoritarian coercion to enacting dramatic reform to promote democratic coercion. Political competition – considered an important driver of institutional reform (Geddes 1994; Grzymala-Busse 2007; O'Neill 2005) – became increasingly robust during the administration of César Gaviria, after decades of distortion introduced by the National Front power-sharing pact between Liberals and Conservatives. Despite this strengthened competition, opposition parties – including from the left – did not use the National Police's grave deficiencies to attack President Gaviria, perhaps because they perceived fragmented societal preferences and were constrained by the police's structural power. These pressures led to the failure of a legislative bill to reform the National Police in September 1992, despite the police's prolonged institutional decay. Just six months later, however, widespread societal outrage following the rape and murder of a young girl in a police station was indicative of preference convergence and shared demands for reform. Seeing a shift in electoral incentives, politicians revived the bill that had languished in Congress months earlier, and they collaborated to design a transformative reform to promote democratic coercion.

The Colombian case underscores the importance of ordinary democratic politics as a determinant of institutional continuity and reform among police forces. A range of conditions that would seemingly militate against reform – a strong military, widespread violence, weak state capacity – all remained constant in the short time period between the failure of a reform bill in 1992 and its unanimous passage in the Congress in 1993. What shifted was the nature of societal contestation and demand-making and how politicians came to understand the electoral costs and benefits of police reform as a result.

A Strengthened Opposition amid Fragmented Societal Preferences (1990–1992)

Reform of the profoundly troubled Colombian National Police was not forthcoming during the first half of the Gaviria administration despite an increasingly robust opposition that could have used the highly dysfunctional police force as a way of attacking the incumbent and his party. The Colombian case illustrate the limits of political competition as a driver of reform, at least when it comes to the police, if societal preferences are fragmented (as discussed in Chapter 5).

The discussion that follows outlines the growing strength of the political opposition beginning with the 1990 presidential elections; it contrasts the willingness of the opposition to challenge the incumbent following the dramatic prison escape of drug kingpin Pablo Escobar in July 1992 with its reticence to similarly challenge the president regarding the dire deficiencies of the police, culminating in the failure of reform proposals months later.

Many observers view the political opposition during the administration of César Gaviria as largely weak; chief among them is former president César Gaviria. Recalling the role of the opposition during the first half of his term, Gaviria emphasized their fairly compliant participation in his agenda: "I couldn't say that I had initiatives that were not approved or that I had political opposition. There were sectors that started to be critical of [my] administration, [for example] the M-19, Dr. Álvaro Gómez's sector from Salvación Nacional (National Salvation), but this criticism was never obstructionist – we never had problems developing our legislative initiatives."[55] Gaviria's co-partisan, former Liberal senator Jose Blackburn, agreed, arguing, "It's not that everyone was with the [Gaviria] administration, but there wasn't really much opposition."[56] Scholarship on Colombian politics from this period supports Gaviria's and Blackburn's assessment of muted political competition. As O'Neill (2005) has noted, the Liberal Party had been dominant in the country since the 1960s, winning most presidential elections and majorities in both chambers of Congress by fairly comfortable margins (98). Moreover, although the National Front power-sharing pact ended officially in 1978, the two parties continued the practice of sharing government posts with the opposition through the Gaviria administration (O'Neill 2005, 96; Ungar Bleier 1995, 110). Gaviria, meanwhile, was seen as successfully exerting considerable pressure on members of Congress, across party lines, to get his initiatives passed through the legislature (Ungar Bleier 1995, 109).

But the very fact that the National Front pact and the political violence that produced it introduced significant distortions to Colombian democracy that truncated political competition makes even more remarkable the degree of political opposition that did emerge during Gaviria's administration (see Table 7.2). While the president's Liberal Party held a solid majority in the Congress – with 57 percent of the seats in the Senate and 53 percent in the Chamber of Deputies – it also confronted for the first time an increasingly robust opposition to both its right and its left. The

[55] Author interview with former president César Gaviria, Bogotá, July 11, 2013.
[56] Author interview with José Blackburn, Bogotá, July 15, 2013.

TABLE 7.2 *Colombian political party strength (1980s–1994)*

Political party	Presidential elections 1986	Presidential elections 1990	% Senate seats 1990	% Senate seats 1991	% deputies 1990	% deputies 1991	Constitutional Assembly 1991
Liberal Party	58%	48%	58%	57%	60%	53%	28%
Conservative Party	1	12	33	19	31	16	11
National Salvation Movement	36	24	–	5	–	7	27
M-19	5	12	–	9	–	9	16
Other	–	2	9	11	10	13	16

Note: New congressional elections were held in 1991 in accordance with the new Constitution
Georgetown University's Political Database of the Americas, Colombia: Elección Presidencial de 1990, Elecciones Presidenciales 1826–1990, Elecciones para Asamblea Constitucional de 1990, Elecciones legislativas de 1990 (Cámara de Representantes), Elecciones legislativas de 1990 (Cámara de Representantes). Inter-Parliamentary Union Election Archives, http://archive.ipu.org/parline-e/reports/arc/2067_91.htm.

size of the Conservative Party in Congress – 23 percen of deputies and 25 percent of senators – was modest at best.[57] But Gaviria also faced new opposition from the left via the M-19 Democratic Alliance, a demobilized former guerrilla group that not only won 27 percent of votes for the 1991 Constitutional Assembly (compared to the Liberal Party's 28 percent) but also increased its vote share in the preceding presidential elections and, following the 1991 legislative elections,[58] came to occupy nearly 10 percent of seats in both houses of Congress for the first time. Per Gaviria, the M-19 represented "an opposition that expressed itself but did not impede the legislative process."

By the start of 1993, the opposition was thus increasingly robust in vote/seat shares; but it was also unequivocally robust along three other indicators: decreased presidential approval rating; increased opposition to incumbent's legislative agenda; and proximity to the presidential elections the following year. The Conservative Party, for instance, began the 1993 legislative session by demanding that the country's inspector general investigate Gaviria.[59] Moreover, Gaviria's Liberal Party faced a relatively strong performance by a leftist party for the first time, which presented an increasingly strong opposition to Gaviria's policies. The M-19, for instance, led an effort in the Congress to declare dozens of Gaviria's executive orders illegal and to demand censure of Gaviria's minister of labor, with the support of dissident "independent Liberals" who opposed the president's economic agenda.[60] In addition to this growing opposition from the left and the right, Gaviria also had to contend with a growing split within his own Liberal Party along ideological lines in response to his neoliberal economic agenda. A sizable social-democratic current within the Liberal Party emerged as such a strong critic of the incumbent administration that observers speculated that the upcoming presidential elections could well have "two opposition candidates," including that of the president's own Liberal Party.[61]

The balance of power between the administration and the opposition shifted further in mid-1992, following a series of embarrassing conditions

---

[57] This measure includes the Conservative Party and its offshoot, the National Salvation Movement.

[58] The 1991 Constitution required new legislative elections due to changed composition of both houses of Congress.

[59] "Conservadores piden a la Procuraduría que investigue al presidente Gaviria," *El Espectador*, March 3, 1993.

[60] "ADM-19 abre oposición con censura a Min-Trabajo," *El Espectador*, March 10, 1993.

[61] "Foro Liberal con Sabor a Division," *El Tiempo*, March 27, 1993; "Dos candidatos de oposición," *El Espectador*, March 9, 1993.

for the president, including high inflation, electricity rationing, and the escape of drug kingpin Pablo Escobar from prison. Over the course of the preceding year, the president had seen a sharp decline in his approval rating, particularly when compared to his first year in office. During our conversation, former president Gaviria described facing "traumas in my administration, such as the rationing of electricity and Pablo Escobar's escape" and still remembered well (decades later) the fluctuations in his approval rating that resulted from these events.[62] Whereas in 1990 the president had a 70 percent approval rating,[63] a 1992 survey found that only 29 percent of respondents approved of his administration (Lemoine 1993, 265).

By 1992, Gaviria was thus flanked by a relatively robust opposition on both sides of the ideological spectrum as well as facing challenges from within his own party. The newly strengthened opposition, however, did not use the crisis facing the National Police to challenge the president. To Gaviria's left, the M-19 had an ambiguous position relative to police reform. On the one hand, while it engaged in frequent confrontations with police and endured egregious extrajudicial killings when it was still an armed movement,[64] it also voted against important police reforms during the Constitutional Assembly introduced by the leftist Patriotic Union representatives.[65] Moreover, Conservatives did not rally behind a reform bill introduced by a Conservative senator.[66] Tellingly, a dissident Liberal presidential candidate interviewed in early 1993 was highly critical of Gaviria's security policy, declaring he would "return security to the country," but did not discuss the need for police reform.[67]

A Selectively Robust Opposition and Failed Police Reform Efforts (1992)

The relative silence of the opposition on policing issues was underscored by two events in 1992. The first – the explosive legislative reaction to the escape of Pablo Escobar from prison in July 1992 – demonstrated the

---

[62] Author interview with former president César Gaviria, Bogotá, July 11, 2013.
[63] "Calificación: Apenas Regular," *El Tiempo*, August 7, 1992.
[64] "Millonaria condena a la policía," *El Tiempo*, February 21, 1992; "Corte reabrió investigación a 33 policías por ejecución extrajudicial de milicianos del M-19," *El Espectador*, December 12, 2014.
[65] "La Asamblea Constituyente no tocó a las fuerzas armadas," *El Tiempo*, May 31, 1991; "Se conservó integridad de FFMM," *El Tiempo*, July 2, 1991.
[66] "Proponen proyecto para reorganizar la Policía," *El Colombiano*, March 3, 1992; "Debate sobre la Policía," *El Nuevo Siglo*, November 4, 1992.
[67] "Empezaría por devolverle la seguridad al país: Lemos," *El Tiempo*, January 25, 1993.

willingness of Gaviria's political opponents to challenge him, while the second – the failure of a police reform bill in September 1992 – highlighted their hesitation to do so when it came to the National Police.

The escape of Medellín Cartel leader Pablo Escobar from Envigado prison in July 1992 was a damaging blow to the presidency of César Gaviria. The surrender of Escobar to the Colombian justice system a year earlier, in July 1991, was an important validation of the administration's policy for fighting the war against drug cartels.[68] His escape, therefore, had the opposite effect. The event generated a great deal of outrage in society and in the Congress, and it was a staple of media coverage for many months. The opposition was emboldened by the event, calling frequent hearings in the Congress to investigate the escape and thoroughly chastise administration officials.[69] Minister of Defense Rafael Pardo described the "political storm" as follows:

> The climate was explosive. In the halls of Congress the resignation of the President was openly discussed as a possibility, and that of the ministers was taken as given ... The session was very intense ... After nearly five hours, tensions had calmed and the climate of confrontation with the government had been reduced. Nevertheless, there was no shortage of positions that disagreed with the Executive and that remembered, among other things, that the government had promoted in the new Constitution the early closure and dissolution of the Congress. In addition to demanding political responsibility [for Escobar's escape], many saw in this opportunity the possibility of getting back at the government for what they considered a low blow to the political class. (Pardo Rueda 1996, 441)

The Senate created a special commission to investigate Escobar's escape and the prison from which he fled, holding regular hearings over the course of three months, with sessions transmitted live on television. The investigation by the special commission, although politically damaging for the Gaviria administration, was considered by some observers a positive exercise in accountability that helped improve the image of the Congress.[70] Legislators, even those from the Liberal Party, openly discussed a motion to censure the ministers responsible and asked for Defense Minister Pardo's resignation (Pardo Rueda 1996, 442). In

---

[68] The policy of "surrender to justice" (*sometimiento a la justicia*) as a means of dealing with the drug cartels within the domestic justice system, rather than extraditing drug traffickers to the United States, was a cornerstone of Gaviria's administration (see Chapter 5).

[69] It should be noted that the National Police was not the target of the wave of criticism of Escobar's escape from jail. Prisons were under the control of the Ministry of Justice, and the particular prison where Escobar was held was under the supervision of the Army.

[70] See Maria Isabel Rueda, "Archivo Secreto," *Semana*, November 23, 1992.

a further embarrassing episode, in December 1992, Escobar and dozens of his men, armed with machine guns, put up roadblocks and even personally inspected vehicles: "The effect [of this event] was tremendous and the criticism was immediate ... The image of invulnerability of the cartel emerged once again and in the inverse sense the prestige of the Bloque de Búsqueda (Search Bloc) and the Public Force diminished" (Pardo Rueda 1996, 455).[71]

As a Colombian news magazine put it, the public and political spectacle around Pablo Escobar's escape from Envigado prison "produced internal commotion, shook the government, sent a number of generals to retirement, struck blows to ministers, scandalized the public and mobilized political forces in a way that had not been seen in a long time."[72] In an interview, the president's security advisor agreed with this view:

The escape was a tragedy. It was a very politically complicated moment for the government. At that time the government was at a complicated political juncture. We were in the period in which ... for the first time in Colombia we had blackouts. There were enormous restrictions on electricity. The economy was not doing well. In other words, we were in a moment in which, following a great reformist impulse and optimism that the government had brought, with the slogan "welcome to the future, there will be a future," [there were] the constitutional reform, the reforms on a number of dimensions, economic growth, Pablo Escobar's turning himself in, and the idea that narcoterrorism had ended. It was after 1992 that [Gaviria] starts to have problems: the blackouts, then comes the escape of Escobar, and that lasted a while. It was a very difficult moment for the government, and it was used politically by people who said that the policy of "submission to justice" (*sometimiento a la justicia*) had been a failure and that that was a problem that directly went up to the president of the Republic.[73]

The escape of drug kingpin Pablo Escobar from prison was indeed a major blow to President Gaviria, whose approval rating "descended vertiginously since [Escobar's] escape" (Palacios 1995, 345). During the first two years of his administration Gaviria faced negligible opposition to his highly transformative agenda. Congressional reaction to Escobar's escape from jail – and the missteps by state officials that facilitated it – represented the first strong pushback this president received from the Congress. In light of the National Front pact between the two historic parties, the

---

[71] The Bloque de Búsqueda, or "search task force," was an elite team of police officers who were conducting the search for Escobar; the Public Force as defined in the 1991 Constitution consists of the National Police and the three branches of the military.
[72] "Un hombre impasible," *Semana*, September 7, 1992.
[73] Author interview with Camilo Granada, Bogotá, July 17, 2013.

political agreements to share government posts, the semi-permanent condition of state of exception throughout the 1980s (during which the executive effectively ruled by decree), and the pro-reform consensus that emerged at the beginning of Gaviria's term, there had long been little institutional space from which to exercise opposition in Colombia. The mobilization of the scandal (Sherman 1978) by Gaviria's political opponents in response to Pablo Escobar's escape is therefore highly significant.

But just as notable as the firestorm that erupted over Escobar's escape is the relative quiet of the political opposition regarding another area of the state's security apparatus that had long been in disarray: the National Police. For the newly empowered opposition, the undeniable crisis facing the National Police was not seen as an additional issue on which to challenge the president. But this relative silence on police reform was not due to a lack of policy options. The fate of two police reform bills introduced in 1992 is illustrative. Conservative Senator Fabio Valencia Cossio introduced a reform bill in March 1992 – a year before an egregious scandal of police violence against a little girl would serve as the catalyst of long-needed reforms. The senator's proposed bill included significant structural changes, including specialized bodies, improved technical capacity, and new civilian oversight entities.[74]

The Gaviria administration, however, considered the proposed bill too far-reaching and "inconvenient for the stability of the institution" (Pardo Rueda 1996, 342). In September 1992, therefore, the government countered Senator Valencia Cossio's proposal with its own bill (Bill 43/1992) to reform the National Police's Organic Law, which attempted to codify some of the legal changes required by the new Constitution.[75] The bill, however, was, according to former minister Pardo, "of limited reach and advanced little along the parliamentary path" (Pardo Rueda 1996, 342). Former senator José Blackburn, who would later sponsor a successful police reform bill the following year, said in an interview he did not have any recollection of this initial bill.[76]

Although a congressional committee held hearings on police reform in November 1992,[77] the bill that was ultimately voted out of committee in

[74] "Proponen proyecto para reorganizar la Policía," El Colombiano, March 3, 1992; "Debate sobre la Policía," El Nuevo Siglo, November 4, 1992.
[75] Gaceta del Congreso 51, September 4, 1992.
[76] Author interview with José Blackburn, Bogotá, July 15, 2013.
[77] "Debate sobre la Policía," El Nuevo Siglo, November 4, 1992; "Policía debe pasar a Mingobierno," El Tiempo, November 12, 1992.

December 1992 resembled neither proposal. The approved measure changed all of four articles to the existing police statute, including one regarding human and economic resources and another that added two members of Congress to the Superior Council of the National Police.[78] Senator Valencia Cossio's proposal, as well as the Gaviria's administration own bill, were both shelved.

The failure of these two police reform bills demonstrates how police constrain available policy options and shape the agenda, even in the context of a political opposition that could have strategically used the National Police's profound deficiencies to attack the president, just as they did following Escobar's escape. Then–defense minister Rafael Pardo said the reluctance to move the bill forward was "because of the Colombian police itself. The police would say that it was taking corrective measures, and the Congress would not challenge the opinions of the institutions of the Public Force [National Police and armed forces], so there was not an environment that would justify the bill. So the reform [bill] that was making its way [through Congress] very slowly was a reform [bill] to avoid having to reform" (*una reforma para no reformar*).[79] It is also evident, however, that the president and the defense minister did not put their political weight behind the bill. The failure of the 1992 police reform bill stands in sharp contrast to Gaviria's "institutional shake-up" and the considerable pressure he exerted on legislators to ensure the passage of his initiatives (Ungar Bleier 1995, 109).

But the failure of Gaviria's political opponents to rally behind Senator Valencia Cossio's proposal and to use the police's broader institutional disarray to attack the incumbent also speaks to the weak incentives for politicians to push for police reform in the context of fragmented societal preferences and demands. The crisis facing the National Police was no less serious than that caused by Pablo Escobar's escape: the entity charged with exercising the state's monopoly of violence routinely used its coercive authority to engage in predation, extrajudicial killings, massacres, torture, and disappearances against the citizenry, and it faced extensive infiltration from the drug cartels it was supposed to combat. But in the context of the constraints posed by the police's structural power, politicians – in both the government and opposition – saw little electoral gain in the face of citizens' conflicting demands and contestation.

---

[78] "Aprobado Estatuto de la Policía," *El Espectador*, December 16, 1992.
[79] Author interview with Rafael Pardo Rueda, Bogotá, October 12, 2012.

Scandal and a Shared Demand for Reform (1993)

Politicians' incentives changed months later when, in early 1993, a notorious instance of police violence generated widespread societal outrage. On February 28, 1993, Sandra Janneth Guzman Aranda and her daughter, Sandra Catalina Vásquez Guzman, entered the Third Station of the National Police in downtown Bogotá in search of the girl's father, a police officer who worked at that station. While the mother spoke to other officers asking for her estranged husband's whereabouts, the young girl wandered around the police station in search of her father. Soon after,[80] Sandra Catalina was found in agonizing pain in the station bathroom, having been brutally raped and strangled with a string.[81] She died as she was being transferred to a local hospital. The Prosecutor's Office began its investigation that same day, and a special police commission was formed to investigate the case.

To discern the effect of the scandal on politicians' strategies, one need only examine what occurred before and after the case became broadly known. Available evidence suggests that neither the president, the Liberal Party, nor the leadership of the National Police initially considered enacting police reforms in response to the case. On March 1, the day after Sandra Catalina's death, legislators and Gaviria's administration announced a shared legislative agenda for the remainder of the term. Though expansive in its coverage of a range of policy areas, that agenda did not include reforming the National Police.[82] The National Police, meanwhile, sought to minimize the significance of the case and the blame placed on the institution. Police leaders sought to blame the girl's father, including the Bogotá police commander, Oscar Eduardo Peláez Carmona, who issued a statement the day after the murder claiming that the girl's father was responsible for the crime – despite the fact that all 350 police officers present in the station at the time were still under investigation – and other officials claimed that the girl had not been raped.[83] Officer Vasquez was arrested and imprisoned for more than three months, erroneously suspected of raping and murdering his own daughter.

---

[80] The actual period of time between when Sandra Catalina wandered off and when she was found is unclear. The first reports claim it took ten minutes, but subsequent reports say twenty, thirty, and even forty.

[81] "Asesinada una niña dentro de cuartel policial," *El Tiempo*, March 1, 1993.

[82] "Gran acuerdo sobre agenda legislativa," *El Tiempo*, March 2, 1993.

[83] "Dios sabe que soy inocente: Vásquez," *El Tiempo*, March 2, 1993.

"No se sabe quién mató a Sandra Catalina," *El Tiempo*, March 2, 1993.

"Los indicios señalan al padre," *El Tiempo*, March 3, 1993.

Despite this initial indifference to the case, the societal and political reaction quickly changed politicians' incentives in favor of reform. Within a month of Sandra Catalina's murder, President Gaviria had convened two commissions – one made up of political and societal leaders and another composed of police officers of all ranks – to propose measures to reform the National Police. Within six months, both chambers of Congress had passed a piece of legislation they had previously ignored "with near unanimous support."[84] How can we account for this rapid shift in strategy by the incumbent and his party – both from late 1992 to early 1993 and from March 1 to March 31?

We must look, I argue, to the shift in societal preferences over reform. "If a person is not safe inside a police station, then where?" said Sandra Janneth Guzman, the child's mother.[85] It is perhaps due to the symbolism of the case that Sandra Catalina's murder "infuriated Colombian public opinion ... [and] prompted a national debate about the role of the police and the creation of a commission about its reform," in a country where more than 1,500 children were murdered in 1992 alone (Amnesty International 1994a, 14). Reacting to the rape and murder of Sandra Catalina in a police station, the highly respected veteran journalist Enrique Santos Calderón (the brother of future president Juan Manuel Santos) wrote an opinion piece titled "Sandra Catalina Concerns Us All":

It will be said that in a country that has beaten all the records on the subject of violence and death, nothing surprises or perturbs. But the case of Sandra Catalina Vásquez is the most demoralizing and indignant thing that could occur in a society that still hopes to conserve basic values.[86]

Santos's article was credited with galvanizing criticism of the police over the case, with media reports on the case having died down after the first few days.[87] Nevertheless, the case would subsequently receive a great deal of media coverage, with prominent individuals, including the president of

---

[84] Author interview with Rafael Pardo Rueda, Bogotá, October 12, 2012.

[85] "No se sabe quién mató a Sandra Catalina," *El Tiempo*, March 2, 1993.

[86] Enrique Santos Calderón, "Sandra Catalina nos concierne a todos," *El Tiempo*, March 7, 1993.

[87] Interestingly, a subsequent article about the case that Santos wrote two years later – expressing indignation about the fact that the investigation had been shelved and that the murder of Sandra Catalina would be left in impunity – was said to be responsible for the reopening of the case. See "Recuerdan a Sandra Catalina," *El Tiempo*, March 12, 1995, and "Confesó el policía que mató a Sandra Catalina," *El Tiempo*, October 14, 1995.

the National Federation of Commerce and the Bogotá Chamber of Commerce, called for police reform.[88]

Politicians, both in the executive and the legislative branches, heard the outcry from society and were compelled to take action. The president and the minister of defense felt a great deal of pressure to respond to the killing, particularly following a tone-deaf statement by General Miguel Antonio Gómez Padilla, then director of the National Police, who, "exasperated by pressure from journalists, declared that the citizenry couldn't expect such a quick discovery of the person responsible for the crime, for if the murder of [Liberal Party Leader Jorge Eliecer] Gaitán hadn't been solved in forty years, the same should be expected from this case" (Pardo Rueda 1996, 341).[89] Gómez Padilla was harshly criticized for this statement, including in a hearing in the Bogotá city legislature, where a legislator retorted that Gaitán had not been not killed in a police station.[90] Accordingly, many demanded that the director general of the National Police resign.

The case was the subject of impassioned debate in the Congress. In March 1993, the Congress held two sessions of debate, during which legislators called upon the ministers of defense and of justice to testify about the progress of the investigation to find the perpetrator, thereby keeping the case on the public agenda.[91] Legislators from across the political spectrum shared the view during hearings that "society and the legislative branch can no longer tolerate the problems that exist within the Police." One dissident Liberal senator even issued harsh criticism of the administration's failed reform bill from the previous year – a criticism he did not express at the time: "The bill's text reveals that the administration lacks awareness of the seriousness of the problem. There is nothing here related to [the need for] civilian and moral education of the police, nor to the establishment of a system of internal oversight or promoting more efficient and honest officers."[92]

---

[88] "FENALCO urge reforma a policía," *El Tiempo*, March 27, 1993; "Jornada contra la violencia," *El Espectador*, March 17, 1993.

[89] Gómez Padilla's successor as director general, Rosso José Serrano, was more sensitive to the impact of this crime on public opinion. Shortly after taking on the top job in the National Police, Serrano said that the "atrocious crime of Sandra Catalina would not remain unpunished and that he would not rest until the perpetrator was found." See "El Culpable," *Semana*, November 13, 1995.

[90] "Policía anuncia primer informe," *El Tiempo*, March 24, 1993.

[91] "Continúa el debate," *El Tiempo*, March 22, 1993.

[92] "La Policía debe ser totalmente reestructurada," *El Nuevo Siglo*, March 19, 1993.

Camilo Granada, then presidential advisor on national security and defense, said this societal and political reaction to the case pushed the administration to take action:

That was the event that generated, that crystallized, all societal concerns regarding the role of the police, of the distrust of the institution, and in terms of the [lack of] oversight that existed over the police. This generated an enormous debate ... It was a scandal. It opened the doors to allow a broad reform process and posed a political obligation on the government to do another reform. We were able to do a comprehensive, complete, strong reform that would change the dynamic of the police.[93]

The killing of Sandra Catalina continued to have social, political, and legal significance for decades. In March 2012, the Consejo de Estado, Colombia's highest court on administrative matters, ruled that the National Police was responsible for Sandra Catalina's death and owed damages to her family – it ordered the police to issue an official public apology to the girl's family;[94] to publicize the verdict in all police stations in the country; and to indemnify her father for falsely accusing him of the crime of raping and murdering his own daughter.[95] In February 2013, on the twenty-year anniversary of her murder, a plaque commemorating her life was installed in a small park outside the police station where she was killed.[96]

The Emergence of an Electoral Counterweight and a "Shake-Up" of the National Police

The heinous crime helped create an electoral counterweight to the structural power of the National Police, which had long succeeded in blocking reforms. The broadly shared outrage it generated occurred in the context of a newly empowered political opposition that saw the case as an opportunity to attack the incumbent and his party a year before presidential elections. In contrast to the police reform bill that had been

---

[93] Author interview with Camilo Granada, presidential advisor on national security and defense, Bogotá, July 17, 2013.

[94] The National Police issued an official public apology to the girl's family on April 2012. "Policía pidió perdón por asesinato de niña en una estación," *El Tiempo*, April 10, 2012.

[95] Consejo de Estado, Sala de lo Contencioso Administrativo, Sección Tercera, Subsección C, Verdict No. 25000-23-26-000-1997-04813-01 (20880), February 15, 2012.

[96] During my fieldwork, many people in my age group, who would thus be of the same age group as Sandra Catalina, told me they remember hearing about the case and watching reports about it on the news when they were children.

introduced in the Congress in late 1992 and was effectively dead on arrival, the widespread societal outrage in the face of the murder of Sandra Catalina demonstrated to both incumbent and opposition politicians that, in contrast to the usual fragmented preferences and conflicting demands, there was an electoral gain to be had from pursuing police reform.

Much like Governor Duhalde's dramatic declaration of a state of emergency and a civilian intervention of the Police of Buenos Aires Province, the social and political fallout from the rape and murder of Sandra Catalina initiated a process of profound examination and consensus-building about the fate of the National Police. What followed was an ambitious plan to overhaul the National Police, including educational and training requirements, functional specialization, organizational structure, ranks and hierarchies, operational decentralization, and subordination to civilian authorities, among others. President Gaviria and Defense Minister Pardo initiated the reform process through two commissions. The Consultative Commission to Reform the National Police (created by Decree 591/1993 on March 30) was an external commission composed of civil society experts and prominent political and social representatives, including senators and deputies, academics, union and professional association meetings, governors, and mayors. The Internal Commission for Institutional Modernization, meanwhile, was made up of police agents and officers of all ranks and from all regions of the country. When President Gaviria inaugurated the Consultative Commission and Minister Pardo the Internal Commission, the two made it clear that all aspects of the police structure should be evaluated and debated (Presidencia de la República 1994).

Then–defense minister Rafael Pardo recalled in his memoirs how he made it clear in a meeting with thousands of agents and officers that police reform was unavoidable: "I put before them the crude diagnosis of the Police and outlined the plan to be followed: the citizenry not only did not trust but instead feared the police, the Congress wanted a broad reform and the government was willing to lead it ... The president gave priority in his administration to a new law to reform the Police" (Pardo Rueda, 1996, 342). The police heard his message. In a meeting to inaugurate an internal commission convened by the president to propose reforms, Gómez Padilla, the director general of the National Police, said to his fellow officers, "Due to the emergence of an alarming level of criticism and dissatisfaction about police service in some sectors of the country, it is urgently necessary that we adopt corrective actions."[97] Perhaps realizing that, faced with such external pressure and a newly strengthened opposition, the government could no longer maintain its deferential position, the National Police accepted the reforms. In an interview, Pardo reflected, "This public opinion climate put the police in a very favorable attitude in terms of reform ... I think the key was to take very rapidly this negative event and say, 'We need a profound reform here,' and no one could oppose that idea."[98]

The two reform commissions had just forty days to complete their work and issue recommendations for reform. The Consultative Commission traveled the country and heard directly from citizens about the police's abuses and failure to offer protection from rising violence. The commission's final report offered a troubling diagnosis of the dire conditions of the National Police (Presidencia de la República 1994), and its key recommendations were used to revise Legislative Bill 43, the administration's legislative bill that had been shelved the previous year. This time, however, the Gaviria administration requested the Congress to give "urgent treatment" to the bill, and the president is quoted as saying at the time of debate that "in light of the crisis facing the National Police and the low levels of credibility in front of society, a deep restructuring of this body is required."[99] The bicameral legislative commission that emitted the final bill emphasized the National Police's "crisis," arguing it had "lost its identity before the public and has been wayward in fulfilling its constitutional mission."[100]

The revised bill incorporating the Consultative Commission's recommendations for reforming the police's Organic Law was reintroduced in the Congress in June 1993 and was approved in August. According to Pardo, "there had already been a good climate in the Congress previously [to the bill's introduction] and in the Congress it was a very fast process. It came out of the Congress in two months, which is a record; and it was passed with near unanimous support." The government, in sharp contrast to how it responded to a bill introduced nearly a year before, committed to putting its full weight behind the bill to ensure its passage (Pardo Rueda 1996, 341). Former senator Blackburn also noted that both Liberal and opposition legislators got behind the new bill: "We

---

[97] Speech of General Miguel Antonio Gómez Padilla, director general of the Colombian National Police, at the installation of the Internal Commission, Bogotá, March 27, 1993.

[98] Author interview with Rafael Pardo Rueda, Bogotá, October 16, 2012.

[99] *Gaceta del Congreso* 180, June 8, 1993, 8.

[100] *Gaceta del Congreso* 178, June 7, 1993, 2.

worked together in the commission to move the bill forward ... There
was not strong opposition."

In a similar moment of political and social consensus to what we observed
in Buenos Aires Province, political and civil society leaders came together to
usher in an ambitious overhaul of an embattled police force they now all
considered to be in crisis. But, as with the *Bonaerense*, the Colombian
National Police had long engaged in authoritarian coercive practices and
faced extensive institutional deterioration. A full year before the rape and
murder of Sandra Catalina galvanized broad demands for police reform, the
country's inspector general had already sounded the alarm regarding the
grave accusations of malfeasance facing the police ranging from common
crimes to massacres, declaring the status quo "a problem for the country as
a whole, which has to acknowledge that [the Police] is one of the most
important institutions for democracy and the Republic."[101] But while these
conditions "had been a constant during many years" (Pardo Rueda 1996,
343), as former defense minister Pardo put it, it was not until a scandal and
a strengthened political opposition shifted politicians' electoral incentives
that the president and his party took concerted action to eradicate
entrenched authoritarian coercive practices and structures.

Toward Democratic Coercion in a Time of War

Like the reform of the Police of Buenos Aires Province, the reform of the
National Police, codified through Law 62/1993, scores "High" in the index
of democratic police reform presented in Chapter 2. It was a concerted
effort to promote democratic coercion, even in the context of multiple wars
that produced extraordinary levels of violence and enabled authoritarian
coercion for many years (see Chapter 5). As occurred in Buenos Aires
Province, the architects of the reform in Colombia sought to redesign the
institutional structure in order to introduce greater professionalization,
decentralization, and specialization to meet the country's specific security
needs rather than serving political and private interests; to demilitarize its
rank structure and training and strengthen adherence to the rule of law; and
to install a series of formal mechanisms to bolster civilian oversight and
external accountability.[102]

---

[101] "Pide aligerar proceso de depuración," *El Mundo*, February 29, 1992, 12A.
[102] There were also numerous efforts to improve the living conditions of police officers
themselves. The reform created the Institute for the Social Security and Welfare of the
Police, within in the Ministry of Defense, which was charged with developing and

A key focus of Law 62/1993 was to ensure that the primary function of coercion was to provide security for the citizenry, moving the police away from National Security Doctrine, which calls for the protection of the political order or regime from "internal enemies" (Camacho 1994; Leal Buitrago 1994). The reform thus included a number of structural measures intended to improve the police's capacity to protect citizens from crime. The law created a highly specialized bureaucracy, with new functional and operational divisions (Art. 18), including urban, rural (for areas with less than 50,000 inhabitants), judicial police and investigation, and specialized forces (antinarcotics, antikidnapping, etc.). The significance of this correspondence between the police's main responsibilities and its official structure lies in its potential to ensure greater specialization and improved capacity. Recall that, for many experts, one of the main shortcomings of the police was the lack of specialization and deficiencies in urban policing. For many contemporary observers, the demands of battling cartels and armed guerrilla groups led the police "to neglect the everyday needs of the citizenry, such as street crime, controlling public spaces, or the regulation of coexistence (*convivencia*)" (Casas Dupuy 2005, 24). Along these lines, the reform also created a series of marginal participatory institutions enabling police and security officials to receive citizen input on local security conditions but without formal authority over the police (González 2019a).

The reform also included key operational and structural measures to improve educational standards, training, and career trajectories for officers, particularly those at the lower ranks. The poor educational and training standards of the police was considered one of the most crucial aspects of the reform for the Consultative Commission (Camacho 1993, 7). Law 62 increased the minimum educational requirement for entry to a high school diploma and also established a minimum training period of eighteen months for agents (Art. 35).[103] The reform also mandated an extension of the period of training and education for all ranks, including required courses for promotion, as well as the incorporation of human rights, community relations, and professional ethics, all of which

---

implementing programs to improve health, education, housing, and other living and work conditions of police officers (Art. 33). Law 62 was emphatic about the need to provide housing subsidies to police officers as well as build new housing for them on public land. A subsequent presidential decree (352/1994) specified further provisions.

[103] Recall that the pressure of increasing the number of agents on the ground led to the incorporation of agents after only six months of training.

were emphasized by the Consultative Commission for their absence in the pre-reform curriculum.

Another priority of the reform was also to strengthen the National Police's adherence to the rule of law. As discussed at length in Chapter 5, the demands of the drug war and the extraordinary violence targeting police in the context of the armed conflict led the police to adopt greater militarization and to expand recruitment at the expense of standards and oversight. Both conditions bolstered the National Police's reliance on exceptional coercion and deepened its institutional crisis. The reform therefore sought to enforce explicit differentiation from the military and reinforce the civilian legal order (Leal Buitrago 1994, 183). It ended what Defense Minister Pardo called the "de facto subordination" of the police to the armed forces, particularly the Army, in the context of the armed conflict (Art. 30). The reform process also included efforts to rein in a security apparatus seen as out of control. It sought to achieve greater balance within the police by increasing the number of mid-ranking non-commissioned police officers, since one of the roots of the police's deterioration was the large number of rank and file officers without adequate supervision (Llorente 1997, 17).

The reform also created new operational and structural institutions to ensure the police's conduct adhered to the constraints established by the rule of law and to bolster external accountability, including a new Code of Police Ethics, an Internal Audit Office created within the Office of the Director General to oversee financial operations, and a Diagnostic and Self-Evaluation Office to oversee police investigations, promote greater efficiency, and coordinate with the new Commissioner's Office (Casas Dupuy 2005, 19).

The reform legislation also instituted a number of external control measures that sought to strengthen the police's security provision function, adherence to the rule of law, and external accountability. A key institutional change enshrined in Law 62 that bolstered the civilian legal order was the reinforcement of the constitutional principle that mayors and governors were the "first police authority" in their respective jurisdictions. Law 62 "put teeth" on this constitutionally mandated relationship (Llorente 1997, 36), thereby advancing three central objectives of the reform: the decentralization of security policy; bringing police closer to society; and loosening the institutional linkage to the military by tying police structure to civilian political-administrative units rather than military territorial divisions. But most crucially this relationship to civilian leaders was intended to establish the rule of law as the basis for coercion. The law not only reestablished the police's relationship to civilian authorities in determining the deployment of coercion: it also included a number of measures that strengthened external oversight of an institution that had long enjoyed expansive autonomy. Regarding the subordination of police to municipal and departmental authorities, for instance, the law incorporated key mechanisms to ensure police compliance. The law established an obligation for municipal and departmental police commanders to abide by the orders of the corresponding political authorities (Art. 12). It further laid out additional obligations vis-à-vis mayors and governors, including the provision of daily reports of security conditions in the respective jurisdiction, regular accounting of police operations and results, and the presentation of a security plan to the executive (Art. 17). The law also included mechanisms to enforce the authority of mayors and governors over the police, including issuing periodic evaluations of the local police commander's performance and the ability to initiate disciplinary action against police officers with the Inspector General's Office (Art. 16).

In addition to the subordination of police to mayors and governors, the reform enacted in 1993 also created other important external control mechanisms to ensure civilians could hold police accountable. The most significant of these was the creation of the National Council for Police and Citizen Security, a civilian administrative body replacing the National Security Council, a militarized and defense-focused body (Camacho 1993, 9), as the maximum authority on policing matters (Art. 14–15). But by far the strongest instrument of external accountability was the creation of a novel institutional avenue for police oversight and accountability, the Office of the National Police Commissioner. The commissioner was to have two main sets of functions: exercise oversight of the disciplinary system (including compliance with internal police regulations) and police operations; and serve as a channel for citizen complaints (as well as complaints by public officials). The commissioner was also charged with evaluating and diagnosing problems within the National Police, proposing public policies, and submitting periodic reforms to Congress. The commissioner was established as the maximum authority in internal oversight and disciplinary control (Art. 24). Crucially, the law mandated that the commissioner must be a civilian and meet the same qualifications as a Supreme Court justice (Art. 22).

The law thus sought to explicitly target the sources of the National Police's authoritarian coercive practices, including its profound militarization and adherence to the antiquated National Security Doctrine, autonomy from civilian authorities, alienation from the citizenry, and poor education, training, standards, and bureaucratic capacity.

ORDINARY DEMOCRATIC POLITICS AND THE VIABILITY OF POLICE REFORM

This book has provided ample evidence of the remarkable persistence of police forces and the seemingly insurmountable political challenge of enacting reforms. Political leaders eschewed police reform even as other state institutions were overhauled during democratic transitions (Chapters 3 and 4) and "institutional shake-ups" (Chapter 5). They opted to maintain the status quo even when public trust in police dropped to single digits in surveys and thousands marched in the streets to repudiate police violence, as occurred in Buenos Aires Province (Chapter 4). In Colombia, as thousands of officers were expelled for corruption and malfeasance and the country's administrative court issued dozens of verdicts holding the state responsible for police massacres, executions, tortures, and other crimes, the president called the police "a source of pride for the country" and shelved his own administration's reform proposal (Chapter 5). In São Paulo State, successive governors have long evaded structural police reform to promote democratic coercion, despite repeated egregious acts of police violence, including the Carandiru massacre, Favela Naval, and the massacres of May 2006, with one external oversight official calling such reforms a "big taboo" (Chapter 6). Beyond the cases studied in this book, scholars have provided compelling accounts of obstacles to police reform in Mexico (Davis 2006; Müller 2017; Sabet 2012), the State of Bahia (Durazo Hermann 2017), Rio de Janeiro and Buenos Aires (Hinton 2006), Venezuela (Ungar 2002), and Chile (Fuentes 2005). Scholars and other observers have also demonstrated the cyclical nature of police reforms (Macaulay 2012), in which long-sought reforms confront police pressure and popular backlash and are quickly rolled back shortly after enacted (Eaton 2008; Ruiz Vasquez, Illera Correal, & Manrique 2006; Saín, 2015), only to see the emergence of similar demands for reform years later.

Why, then, does police reform appear to be singularly "elusive" (Ungar 2002), both unlikely to be enacted and, once enacted, difficult to sustain?

While the cases analyzed throughout this book indeed underscore the extent to which police constitute a "hard case" for reform, the present chapter has elucidated the conditions under which police reform intended to promoted democratic coercion becomes possible. In doing so, this sequential analysis of two distinct instances of successful enactment of reform can provide important insight to help address fundamental questions about the possibility and viability of police reform.

The comparative sequential analysis of the ambitious police reforms enacted in Colombia and Buenos Aires Province sheds light on our understanding of the obstacles to and drivers of reform, demonstrating that politicians' choices between maintaining the status quo of authoritarian coercive institutions and enacting unprecedented, far-reaching police reform to promote democratic coercion are both functions of societal preferences over reform and political competition. Across the three cases analyzed in this book, politicians opted to maintain the status quo when they perceived that societal preferences over police reform were fragmented; they chose to enact reform when they perceived preference convergence and faced a robust political opposition.

Elucidating the relationship between reform outcomes and ordinary democratic politics is important because it adds considerable nuance to accounts found in the literature. In accounting for the near absence of police reforms, or the swift dismantling of reforms after they are enacted, scholars have cited structural factors such as federalism (Eaton 2008) and regime type (Davis 2006) as conditions that may hinder coordination or disincentivize cooperation, as well as conditions such as high levels of violence that reduce capacity and support for institutional reforms (Call 2003). Other scholars have similarly cited entrenched political conditions, such as "political culture" and weak parties (Hinton 2006), clientelism (Durazo Hermann 2017; Müller 2017), and executive control of police (Sabet 2012; Ungar 2002) as obstacles to enduring structural police reform. Still other scholars highlight the role of police resistance, putting pressure on politicians and allies to successfully block reforms or to weaken them once they are enacted (Fuentes 2005; Saín 2002, 2015; Ungar 2002).

While these conditions are certainly important for understanding the challenges of enacting police reforms, they fall short of explaining change over time. Many of these factors cited by scholars – federalism, corruption and patronage, executive dominance, police resistance – are largely fixed or change gradually over long periods of time. Yet the cases analyzed in this chapter demonstrate that underlying the decision to maintain the status quo or to enact reform is a dynamic process that can produce radically different outcomes in the short term. Through careful sequential analysis of cases where reform was successfully enacted, we are able to shed light on factors that also act as enduring obstacles to reform and threaten reforms even after they are enacted.

First, the preceding analysis underscores that the institutional persistence and reform of police forces likely result not from static, structural conditions often cited in the literature but rather from short-term shifts in the electoral incentives of political leaders. The Police of Buenos Aires Province and Colombia's National Police are embedded in institutional contexts that are, in many ways, structural opposites. Colombia is a unitary country, while Buenos Aires Province is a subnational unit in a federal country. Buenos Aires Province, and Argentina broadly, endured multiple periods of authoritarian rule throughout the twentieth century, while Colombia was governed by military dictatorship only briefly. Colombia had a strong military with considerable formal and informal authority over the police, while Argentina's military had been weakened and stripped of prerogatives over the country's police forces since the transition to democracy. With a protracted armed conflict and an ongoing battle with drug cartels, Colombia faced some of the highest levels of violence in the world; Buenos Aires Province faced comparably low levels of crime and violence by regional standards, despite important increases in the post-transition period. These structural conditions would seemingly exert different pressures on politicians' choices between continuity and reform, yielding different police reform outcomes across the two cases.

Yet, despite these profound structural differences, the police forces of Colombia and Buenos Aires Province underwent remarkably similar reforms in the 1990s. In both cases, political leaders sought to enact reforms to shift the focus of coercion to protecting citizens from crime and violence, bolster adherence to the rule of law, and strengthen external accountability. As the case studies presented here demonstrate, however, these leaders undertook these ambitious reforms to promote democratic coercion not long after explicitly choosing to maintain the status quo of authoritarian coercive practices and structures. Both President Gaviria and Governor Duhalde opted to forgo police reform proposals developed by their own administrations, only to radically change course shortly thereafter. In both instances, political leaders made different policy choices in response to shifts in the fragmentation of societal preferences and the strength of the political opposition, laying bare how these two dynamic conditions shape politicians' calculations of the electoral advantage of police reform, even in the short term.

Second, the case studies also elucidate and add nuance to our understanding of police pressure – or more broadly what I refer to as the police's structural power – as an obstacle to reform. Rather than blocking reform altogether and exercising what Latin American scholars call *autogobierno* (self-governance), as much of the literature suggests (Casas Dupuy, 2005; Ruiz Vasquez et al. 2006; Saín 2002, 2015), police forces leverage their structural power to raise the threshold for reform. The cases of the Police of Buenos Aires Province and the Colombian National Police demonstrate that police forces indeed exercise considerable structural power over political leaders – effectively constraining policy options and maintaining comprehensive police reform off the agenda. Yet they also demonstrate how the joint occurrence of the convergence of societal preferences and robust political competition acts as an electoral counterweight, compelling even reticent politicians to enact reforms.

Third, and most significantly, the case studies clarify the central role of democratic processes in shaping the outcome of institutional persistence or reform among police forces. When considering the effects of ordinary democratic politics on politicians' incentives to enact police reform, scholars have often reached opposing conclusions. Bailey and Dammert (2005), for instance, view citizen outcry and pressure over rising crime as a key driver of police reform (2), while work by other scholars suggests that popular concern and mobilization over crime can lead to demands to expand police discretion to engage in repression rather than constrain it through reform (Caldeira 2002; Eaton 2008). Policing scholars have also shown that partisan competition, particularly across different levels of government, can act as an obstacle to reform (Davis 2006; Eaton 2008; Hinton 2006), in contrast to scholarship on broader institutional reform (Geddes 1994; Grzymala-Busse 2007). Despite reaching divergent conclusions, however, these scholars present theoretical frameworks that largely view democratic processes as fixed and unidirectional in their impact on politicians' decisions to reform or maintain the status quo.

Yet, teasing out the dynamic relationship between everyday democratic politics – such as societal contestation and political competition – and the persistence and reform of police institutions is essential. The three police forces examined in this book exhibited profound institutional deficiencies that pose grave challenges for democratic governance – deploying coercion in the interest of political leaders and private actors, failing to provide effective protection from crime and violence, routinely participating in criminal activity, engaging in systematic extrajudicial violence against the citizenry, and evading external oversight and accountability. Yet these conditions persisted for years and even decades with little intervention by civilian officials. In the context of both democratization and rising crime and violence, the long persistence of such authoritarian coercive practices and structures in the face of growing societal pressure for improved security may appear to be a failure of democratic processes to respond to citizens' demands. As the analysis presented in Part I of this book makes clear, however, political leaders did not ignore citizens' demands in choosing to maintain this status quo of authoritarian coercion. Instead, politicians observed that societal preferences and demands regarding police reform were divided, often reflecting existing cleavages along lines of race, class, and geography. In the face of such fragmentation of preferences, political leaders likely concluded that the electoral advantages of police reform were uncertain at best. As demonstrated in this chapter, however, such calculations can shift rapidly in response to preference convergence and a robust opposition.

Both the persistence of authoritarian coercion and the enactment of reform are thus exercises in democratic responsiveness. The fact that institutional continuity and change among police forces both result from ordinary democratic politics points to the central role of preference fragmentation in shaping politicians' incentives and choice over police reform. The cases analyzed here demonstrate that the possibility of police reform may well rest on shared societal demands expressed across standard social and political cleavages, as occurred temporarily in all three cases.

Yet the shared societal demands and political pressures that can shift politicians' incentives in favor of police reform remain relatively rare, even in the context of unpopular, corrupt, violent, and ineffective police forces. Patterns of societal demand-making and contestation in São Paulo State since the transition to democracy are illustrative of this point. In the decades since democratization, there have been few instances akin to the convergence seen in response to police violence in Favela Naval, an episode that was repudiated by both business leaders and favela residents and led three-quarters of survey respondents to view police as too violent (Chapter 6). Instead, political leaders have perceived enduring fragmentation in citizens' demands and preferences over policing, divided along familiar cleavages of race, class, and geography. Indeed, Governor Montoro's decision to roll back his police reform efforts in response to fragmented societal demands is perhaps the clearest illustration of how the persistence of police forces' authoritarian structures and practices can emerge as acts of democratic responsiveness.

Viewing police reform as the result of dynamic political and social drivers rather than static structural conditions has important implications for our understanding of police reform. First, the remarkable persistence of authoritarian coercion is sustained by patterns of societal contestation and demand-making. Accordingly, what appears as the failure of democratic governments in the region to effectively perform the state's central task and respond to citizens' demand for improved security is actually the result of ordinary democratic politics.

Second, if ordinary democratic politics can pose a challenge to the *onset* of reform, we must also ask whether it poses a risk to the *durability* of reforms as well. While such analysis is beyond the scope of this book, research by other scholars suggests this may well be the case. In both Buenos Aires Province and Colombia, the hard-fought and far-reaching reforms described in this chapter faced a swift backlash, and important components of the reforms were dismantled shortly after being enacted (Casas Dupuy, 2005; Ruiz Vasquez et al. 2006; Saín 2002, 2015). Particularly in the case of Buenos Aires Province, shifts in electoral incentives and societal preferences led political leaders to abandon support for reform as swiftly as they had previously changed course in favor of it.

Shortly after the passage of a law to reform the Colombian National Police, signs of fragmentation became palpable. Despite being the product of consensus among political and societal leaders – including business leaders – strong criticisms of the reform emerged from "professionals, industrialists, businessmen, criminal justice lawyers, etc.," who believed the legislation, which they said emerged from a "demagogic climate," granted too much authority to civilians.[104] Moreover, the National Police's esteem in the eyes of public opinion saw a marked improvement following the announcement that it had killed notorious drug kingpin Pablo Escobar. A survey conducted days after his death in December 1993 found that – in contrast to the 20 percent of respondents that expressed trust in police earlier that year (see Table 5.1) – 47% of respondents now expressed trust in the National Police.[105] Meanwhile, President Gaviria's successor, Ernesto Samper, became increasingly constrained by the National Police's structural power, as the police's leader Rosso Jose

---

[104] "El Elogio de la Locura: La Reestructuración de la Policía Nacional," *El Tiempo*, September 3, 1993.
[105] Survey of urban centers conducted in Colombia in December 1993 by the local firm Centro Nacional de Consultoría and sponsored by the United States Information Agency. Survey data accessed via the Latin American Databank housed at the Roper Center Public Opinion Archives at the University of Connecticut.

Serrano became "the darling son of anti-drug authorities" in the United States, serving as an "interlocutor" between President Samper and the Clinton administration at a time when the latter shunned Colombian diplomats as a result of a scandal over drug money in the Samper campaign.[106] Samper likely saw little advantage in sustaining a contested police reform in the face of rising fragmentation. At the same time, he likely needed to maintain a mutually beneficial relationship with the police in light of his decline in public opinion – and in the esteem of the US government – and the police's considerable gains. Samper thus began pushing for laws and decrees that dismantled key parts of the reform, famously declaring, "Let's let the police regulate itself."[107]

In Buenos Aires Province, "counter-reform" also began with a famous phrase, by then–gubernatorial candidate Carlos Ruckauf, who declared during the 1999 campaign that the solution to insecurity was to "hit the thieves with bullets" (*hay que meter bala a los ladrones*).[108] His running mate, Felipe Solá – who would ironically go on to implement the second wave of police reforms in 2004 – doubled down: "The only way to defend society is with bullets."[109] Solá responded in an interview that, in making these remarks, he was simply going along with a campaign strategy that had been "a personal determination of the candidate [Ruckauf]" but which ultimately sought "to give a supposedly more effective response to the insecurity that was prevalent at the time."[110]

By 1999, societal divisions regarding security policy were once again palpable in reaction to an increase in crime rates in Buenos Aires Province (Saín 2015). Societal opinion at the time was clearly divided, with different conceptions about the distribution of protection and repression. A public opinion poll taken shortly after Ruckauf's infamous statement found that 55 percent of respondents agreed, strongly agreed, or somewhat agreed that criminals should be shot (Brinks 2008, 119). The October 1999 gubernatorial elections also became a referendum on reform and rival visions of how protection and repression ought to be distributed – accordingly, the results showed a divided public. Ruckauf, who in his famous remarks also called for massive police operations in "all the *villas*" to shoot "criminals," won 48 percent of the vote; Graciela

---

[106] "Con los soles a la espalda," *Semana*, July 17, 2000.
[107] "Entra en liquidación la oficina del comisionado," *El Tiempo*, September 14, 1996.
[108] "La seguridad desató un debate en el duhaldismo," *Clarín*, August 5, 1999.
[109] "Una reforma al borde del abismo," *Página/12*, August 5, 1999.
[110] Author interview with Felipe Solá, Buenos Aires, November 1, 2011.

Fernández Meijide, of the opposition party/coalition Alianza, who called for limits on the police,[111] won 41 percent.[112] Upon taking office, Ruckauf began dismantling the reform, appointing an anti-reform military officer as minister of security,[113] refusing to implement many aspects of the reform, and adopting measures that human rights NGO CELS argued "explicitly rejected principles of the rule of law" – including a decree that offered police officers substantial raises for "*actos de arrojo*" (bold or intrepid acts) (CELS 2001, chapter 2). The apparent effects of Ruckauf's rhetoric in favor of police killings became palpable immediately: according to CELS, civilians killed by police in the Greater Buenos Aires region rose to 210 in 1999 and to 196 in 2000, from 114 in 1998.

The police forces of Colombia and Buenos Aires Province underwent historic reforms forged through genuine exercises intended to build consensus. Presumably the point of such exercises was precisely to ensure the continuity of the reform, even after the term of the officials who initially enacted it had ended. Yet, in both settings, the "counterreform" processes began within a year or two of the initial reform's passage. While the analysis presented here has been only cursory, it suggests that politicians saw a shift in their electoral incentives in the face of societal preference fragmentation, leading them to dismantle reforms that had been pushed through by their predecessors from their own political parties.

Democratization has thus presented Latin American governments and societies with a paradox regarding the use of coercion. Sharp increases in crime and violence following transitions to democracy created an imperative for elected leaders to provide effective solutions. As the case studies analyzed in this book demonstrate, however, democratic governments seeking to respond to societal demands frequently failed in their efforts to build state capacity in the provision of security. What we've observed throughout Latin America, and beyond, has been the persistence of coercive institutions that have both failed to satisfy citizens' demands for greater protection and exercised their authority in decidedly undemocratic ways. Patterns of coercion in many Latin American democracies have been characterized by widespread extralegal use of lethal force,

---

[111] "Graciela mano de seda," *Página/12*, August 9, 1999.
[112] "Ruckauf gobernará en Buenos Aires," *La Nación*, October 25, 1999.
[113] Aldo Rico was a former military officer who had led *carapintada* (painted face, referring to the practice of the soldiers who participated) military uprisings against the trials of officers for human rights violations during the 1980s.

discriminatory application of the law, rampant corruption, and complicity with crime.

At the root of these seemingly intractable structures and practices is the simple fact that the solutions to security challenges, institutional deficiencies, and even authoritarian coercive practices are often highly contested. The implication of this framework is that undemocratic coercive institutions may persist not because politicians are unresponsive to societal demands for security but rather because contestation among different societal groups means that reforming defective police institutions may not be electorally advantageous.

In light of the role of democratic processes as catalysts of and obstacles to police reform, it is therefore essential to interrogate the endurance of preference fragmentation and how such fragmented preferences and demands are channeled through democratic processes to yield outcomes that favor the status quo of authoritarian coercion. I now turn to this question in the book's final chapter.

8

Conclusion

Inequality and the Dissonance of Policing and Democracy

While driving around together, a community leader in a low-income, largely black favela in São Paulo expressed to me his displeasure after observing that police cars were placed along a major road rather than within the community or its commercial areas. He discussed the issue with the local police commander, who informed us that the governor requested that police cars be distributed in this way, after having received complaints from residents of a neighboring wealthy, mostly white municipality that they suffered robberies when driving through this community on their way out of São Paulo. The governor's order regarding the distribution of protection and repression not only reinforced existing patterns of inequality across race, class, and geography; it also served his electoral interests. While the low-income community was a stronghold of the leftist Workers Party and former president Lula, the governor had received upwards of 60 percent of the vote in the adjacent municipality.[1]

This anecdote is illustrative of the tensions between policing and democracy in the unequal societies found throughout Latin America. On the one hand, this episode evidences how political decisions about the distribution of protection and repression (re)produce stratified citizenship, wherein access to fundamental rights of citizenship – security and protection from state repression – is determined by existing social hierarchies and power structures (González 2017). On the other hand, it underscores how this outcome, despite contravening democratic principles, is actually the result of ordinary democratic politics. The governor's actions were driven by electoral incentives, leading him to provide a desired state

---

[1] Electoral data from Superior Electoral Tribunal 2010 (tse.jus.br) Electoral Statistics.

service to the constituents who had previously supported him and whose votes he sought in the next elections.

This account underscores the key tension explored throughout this book, the contradictions that often emerge between procedural dimensions of democracy – such as elections and "democratic innovations" (Smith 2009) such as participatory institutions – and substantive dimensions of democracy, such as the rule of law and citizens' rights. It is fitting to conclude, therefore, by disaggregating democracy in order to probe these contradictions further, considering how *procedural* aspects of democracy undermine the possibility of *substantively* democratic outcomes in the exercise of the state's coercive authority. As I argue in this chapter, this tension requires us to reflect on how inequality shapes what I call the *input* of democracy, the societal contestation and demand-making that are channeled through democratic processes, ultimately resulting in coercive practices and institutions that I have characterized throughout this book as authoritarian.

DISAGGREGATING DEMOCRACY: SUBSTANTIVE OUTCOMES, PROCESS, AND INPUT

Upon taking office as the first democratically elected president following the demise of the most brutal of the Southern Cone dictatorial regimes, Argentine president Raúl Alfonsín triumphantly declared, "With democracy you don't just vote; you also eat, educate, and cure."[2] Yet, the initial "euphoria" (Valenzuela 2004, 5; Wiarda & Skelley 2005, 213) about the promise of democracy that accompanied transitions in the region did not materialize in the case of security. As Chapters 3 and 4 demonstrated, the so-called third wave of democratization (Huntington 1991) in countries such as Argentina and Brazil brought dramatic transformation in crime and violence, bringing not only historic increases in crime rates but also significant shifts in the nature of violence. Latin America's "violent democracies" (Arias & Goldstein 2010) have been characterized by a multiplicity of armed groups acting outside the bounds of the law, including, more often than not, the state's own security forces.

The cases analyzed in this book attest to the continuity of repertoires of extrajudicial violence in Latin America's democracies. In Buenos Aires Province, modalities of violence that developed under

---

[2] "Con la democracia se come, se cura y se educa," *Clarín*, December 16, 2018.

authoritarian rule – from arbitrary detention and torture to *"gatillo fácil"* killings and disappearances – were routinely practiced by police long after the transition to democracy. In São Paulo State, police not only maintained extralegal violent practices consolidated under the dictatorship, including extrajudicial executions and death squads, but also broadly expanded their use. Colombia's National Police, meanwhile, regularly carried out similar practices, intensified by the pressures of the armed conflict and an expanding war on drug cartels. As the Colombian case demonstrates, moreover, such practices are not merely a holdover from previous authoritarian periods. Meanwhile, across the three cases, this rampant extrajudicial violence largely targeted the most marginalized segments of the population, with little intervention by elected authorities and civilian institutions to constrain these extralegal coercive practices.

Latin America's democracies have thus not only prevented the emergence or persistence of extensive extrajudicial violence but also proven incapable of effectively curbing it. This book's key finding is that, far from constituting a failure of democratic processes, politicians' decisions to either maintain the status quo in the face of alarming rates of extrajudicial violence by police or to undertake police reform are both the result of ordinary democratic politics – a function of how the degree of fragmentation of societal preferences and the nature of political competition shape their electoral incentives.

The often-contradictory relationship between democracy and enduring state violence has been explored by a number of scholars working in the Global South (Bonner, Seri & Kubal 2018), from analyses of the prevalence of police violence in Venezuela (Hanson 2015) and India (Wahl 2018) as a counterintuitive result of human rights–based police training to ethnographic analysis relating South Africa's much-lauded rights-based constitution to widespread citizen demands for extrajudicial killings (Smith 2019). This more recent literature follows earlier scholarship on the limitations of Latin America's new democratic governments to adequately protect citizens from violence by state and non-state actors (Holston & Caldeira 1998; Leeds 1996; O'Donnell 1993). Yet, even as scholars have consistently demonstrated that democratic institutions may not only fail to prevent but instead reinforce the types of extrajudicial violence employed by the authoritarian regimes that preceded them, few scholars have unpacked the mechanisms underlying these seemingly contradictory outcomes.

Dimensions and Tensions of Democracy

In order to account for the tensions inherent in the remarkable persistence of Buenos Aires's "damned police" and São Paulo's "police that kills" even as democracy took hold in Argentina and Brazil, respectively, we must explore the parallel tensions inherent in democratic theory.

Democracy is a multidimensional concept, with scholars continually engaged in debate about how it ought to be defined and measured. The dominant approaches to understanding democracy are procedural theories, which largely emphasize the central role of elections. The most common definition of democracy, developed by Schumpeter (1942), views democracy as a "method," an "institutional arrangement for arriving at political decisions in which individuals acquire the power to decide by means of a competitive struggle for the people's vote" (269). Many contemporary political scientists share this preference for a "minimal" definition of democracy as "just a system in which rulers are selected by competitive elections," arguing that elections are far from trivial in what they achieve – enabling political conflicts to be resolved peacefully (Przeworski 1999, 23). Other scholars have proposed a more expansive election-based definition, a "procedural minimum" (Collier & Levitsky 1997, 434) set of conditions needed to ensure contestation and participation (or "inclusiveness") in elections, including free, fair, frequent elections; the right to vote and the right to run for office; and freedom of expression, information, and association (Dahl 1982, 10–11). Still other scholars, even as they expand definitions of democracy beyond elections, nonetheless focus on procedural dimensions. Pateman (1970), for instance, argues that the "educative impact of the participatory process" outside of elections is self-reinforcing and constitutive of democracy (42). Pateman and other scholars of participatory democracy call for more "opportunities for individuals to participate in decision-making in their everyday lives as well as in the wider political system. It is about democratizing democracy" (Pateman 2012, 10).

From this procedural perspective of democracy – whether focused on elections or non-electoral participatory processes – the emergence and persistence of police forces that routinely act outside the bounds of the law and violate citizens' rights without intervention by elected officials and civilian institutions may be perfectly consistent with democracy. Though they may be normatively troubling, these practices and structures persist due to politicians' electoral incentives based on the preferences expressed by citizens and the strength of the political opposition. Thus,

Buenos Aires's governor Eduardo Duhalde avoided reforming his belea-guered police force until his party faced electoral defeat in midterm elections (Chapter 4), and consecutive governors in São Paulo likely felt little urgency to reform the state's highly violent police, given the demands for police repression expressed by citizens in the CONSEGs, a robust participatory institution (Chapter 3).

Yet, because "purely procedural rules need not generate wise or virtu-ous outcomes" (Przeworski 2016, 7), other scholars have argued that democracy must adhere to, and be assessed in accordance with, certain substantive principles and, in some instances, outcomes. For this group of scholars, the definition of democracy ought to contemplate principles of "liberal democracy," including civilian control of the military, horizontal accountability, equality under the law, nondiscrimination in the judiciary, protection for ethnic, religious, and cultural minorities, and the rule of law (Diamond 1999, 11–12).[3] Other scholars argue further that, in addition to formal procedures and principles, democracies must also be evaluated by outcomes, including the extent to which they promote social rights and redistribution – or "economic integration through the expansion of social citizenship," as Heller (2000, 490) puts it – and "structure the power dimensions of human interaction so as to ameliorate domination in walks of life" (Shapiro 2006, 5). Heller (2000), for instance, argues that "while the distinction between process and outcome is heuristically useful, in the context of the developing world there are compelling reasons not to treat these attributes of democracy in analytical isolation" (489). According to this set of scholars, procedural democracy cannot be decoupled from these substantive principles and outcomes.[4]

From the perspective of theorists who favor more comprehensive def-initions of democracy – which encompass equality, transparency, accountability, and the rule of law – the police forces studied in this book pose a profound challenge. If, as Diamond (1999) argues, "the rule of law protects citizens from unjustified detention, exile, terror, torture, and undue interference in their personal lives not only by the

---

[3] See also O'Donnell (1998, 2004), Schmitter (1999), and Schedler (1999). Linz and Stepan (1996) argue further that the rule of law is a requirement for democratic consolidation (17).

[4] Scholars preferring minimal or procedural definitions warn against broader definitions of democracy, in which "almost all normatively desirable aspects of political, and sometimes even of social and economic, life are credited as intrinsic to democracy: representation, accountability, equality, participation, justice, dignity, rationality, security, freedom ... The list goes on" (Przeworski 1999, 23).

state but also by organized nonstate or antistate forces" (12), the coercive practices of the police forces examined in this book run counter to the rule of law and related substantive principles of this conceptualization of democracy. Moreover, since these practices are largely suffered by the most disadvantaged social groups (Brinks 2008), they reinforce – and indeed exacerbate – social and political inequality and "domination," undermining substantive dimensions of democracy.

While adjudicating between these different conceptions of democracy is beyond the scope of this book, the purpose of this discussion is simply to elucidate the problem that policing poses for democracy, in theory and in practice. The repertoires and distribution of protection and repression in the cases analyzed in this book – and, indeed, in many other democracies – are antithetical to what some scholars view as the substantive principles and outcomes of democracy. At the same time, these practices are often reinforced by the electoral and participatory processes other scholars have identified as constitutive of democracy.

Disaggregating Democracy and the Distortions of Inequality

This book's analysis of three police forces lays bare a tension between procedural and substantive dimensions of democracy. In order to elucidate this tension, it is important to disaggregate democracy and consider how these two dimensions may come to be at odds with one another. Such contradictions are by no means limited to issues of policing and security. Indeed, they have become increasingly important as an object of inquiry of political science research, which has come to focus on the potential for democratic processes to produce outcomes that run counter to substantive definitions of democracy. Scholars such as Achen and Bartels (2016) have demonstrated how ordinary democratic politics may actually undermine government responsiveness, while Gilens (2014) examines how democratic processes can reproduce societal inequalities, with important implications for representation. These recent studies follow classic models of democratic politics in which contestation between different sets of organized interests representing existing social cleavages yields systematically unequal outcomes biased toward more powerful actors and groups (Bachrach & Baratz 1962).

As these scholars suggest, the key to understanding these contradictions lies in elucidating the distorting effects of inequality on democratic processes, yielding outcomes that contradict substantive dimensions of democracy. The analysis presented throughout this book draws on this central insight to explore the tensions that policing and coercion pose for democracy, often constituting an authoritarian enclave (Chapter 1).

This book's central finding is that the persistence of authoritarian policing in democracy often results from ordinary democratic processes, with ample evidence demonstrating that politicians' choices between maintaining the status quo of violent, corrupt, and ineffective police and enacting structural police reforms are a function of the degree of fragmentation of societal preferences and patterns of political competition. But even as politicians' decision-making over the distribution of protection and repression results from ordinary contestation between different groups of citizens, politicians' choices over policing inevitably reflect societal inequalities and power structures.

Key to understanding how this quintessentially democratic relationship results in authoritarian policing practices and structures are the distortions introduced by inequality to each dimension of democracy (see Figure 8.1). It is therefore essential to consider how the *input* of democracy – citizens' preferences and demands – is channeled through democratic *processes* such as elections and participatory institutions to produce *substantive outcomes* that are antithetical to democratic principles.

Under procedural models of democracy, we would indeed expect citizens to engage in contestation to express demands, which are then channeled through democratic processes such as elections, yielding policy outcomes that reflect those demands. The nature of societal contestation and demand-making over policing and security is central to shaping politicians' calculations about the electoral benefits of reforming the police. In accordance with the expectations of procedural democracy – and as the cases examined in this book demonstrate – such reform is more likely to occur when politicians observe the convergence of societal preferences and demands (and face robust political opposition).

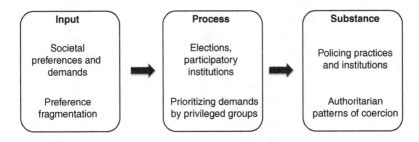

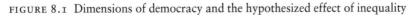

FIGURE 8.1 Dimensions of democracy and the hypothesized effect of inequality

The problem for would-be reformers, however, is how inequality distorts this otherwise democratic process. As the case studies suggest, such convergence is unlikely to occur in contexts where social inequality is high. In such contexts, the distribution of protection and repression occurs along prominent social cleavages and inequalities, such that different societal groups may come to have vastly different experiences with the state's coercive apparatus, in turn leading to fragmented understandings and preferences toward policing and security. As with policy feedback effects scholars have identified for other bureaucracies (Soss 1999), citizens' differentiated experiences with police may well lead to divergent views and preferences regarding police. The *input* that is channeled through democratic processes, therefore, is an enduring fragmentation corresponding to existing patterns of inequality.

Inequality introduces additional distortions to how those societal preferences and demands are channeled through democratic processes. Rather than "ameliorating domination" (Shapiro 2006), elections and participatory institutions alike may shape politicians' incentives in ways that favor the preferences and demands of more privileged sectors of society (Galdeano Cruz 2009; Luna 2014; Lupien 2018). This is especially the case for policing and security, since police can successfully leverage their structural power to constrain policy options and raise the threshold for reform. Facing this constrained policy space, politicians are unlikely to risk alienating a key bureaucracy whose cooperation they need unless they observe the convergence of preferences, wherein privileged sectors join the usual critics of police in demanding reform (González 2019b). Because these sectors – what Fuentes (2005) calls the "pro-order" coalition – are more likely to favor greater police discretion and authority, however, political leaders are more likely to maintain the status quo rather than enacting police reform to curb violence and other extralegal practices.

What emerges from this exercise of ordinary democratic politics is often the persistence of a set of policing practices and structures that resemble coercion in authoritarian regimes: coercion in the service of the interests of political leaders exercised arbitrarily and not subject to external accountability (Chapter 1). As Chapters 3–5 demonstrate, the brunt of this authoritarian coercion in democracy is largely borne by disadvantaged sectors of society, with the distribution of protection and repression reflecting patterns of inequality in society, thereby reproducing stratified citizenship (González 2017). The continuity of these politicized, unaccountable, and extrajudicial coercive practices and structures thus runs counter to substantive dimensions of democracy, such as the rule of law, accountability, and citizens' rights.

In the sections that follow I provide an overview of the book's primary theoretical insights and findings, beginning with a review of the framework that conceptualizes the substantive outcome of interest, the persistence of authoritarian coercion in democracy. I then review some of the key findings of the case studies that elucidate how this authoritarian coercion is reinforced by democratic processes. Finally, I focus on the fragmentation of societal preferences – one of the key drivers shaping politicians' decisions to maintain the status quo and, thereby, the persistence of authoritarian coercion – and how it emerges as a result of entrenched social inequalities.

SUBSTANTIVE OUTCOME: POLICE INSTITUTIONS AS AUTHORITARIAN ENCLAVES IN DEMOCRACIES

One of the central arguments of this book is that the famously troubled police forces found throughout Latin America's democracies paradoxically resemble the coercive patterns of security forces in authoritarian regimes. In making this argument, I introduced a classification of coercion, defining a continuum between authoritarian and democratic coercion along three dimensions: the primary purpose for which coercion is deployed; the extent to which the deployment of coercion adheres to the rule of law; and the extent to which the deployment of coercion is subject to external accountability. Drawing on a small but robust literature on coercive institutions in authoritarian regimes (Greitens 2016; Kalmanowiecki 2000; Policzer 2009; Taylor 2011), I define authoritarian coercion as coercion exercised to serve the interests of political leaders, deployed exceptionally or arbitrarily, and subject to weak, if any, external accountability. Drawing on democratic theorists, meanwhile, I define democratic coercion as coercion that is exercised primarily to protect citizens from crime, adheres to the rule of law, and is subject to robust external accountability. This theoretical framework thus decouples coercion from regime type, allowing us to examine the prevalence of authoritarian coercion in otherwise democratic regimes.

The case studies underscore the pervasiveness of authoritarian coercive practices and structures in countries otherwise characterized as democratic. Police in Buenos Aires Province epitomized the classic role of coercive institutions under authoritarian regimes, exercising coercion in the service of the interests of political leaders to keep them in power rather than with the objective of protecting citizens from rising crime and violence. The *Bonaerense* not only spied on the governor's political opponents but also operated an extensive network of rent extraction from licit and illicit economic activity, much of which was allegedly funneled to politicians and political parties. In exchange for the police's cooperation with their political objectives, politicians granted the police considerable autonomy to not only engage in this widespread predation against the citizenry but also carry out routine extrajudicial violence, including extrajudicial killings, torture, and disappearances.

Such practices also characterized São Paulo's Military Police, whose coercive practices and structures similarly diverged from the rule of law. As discussed extensively in Chapter 3, the three decades since the transition to democracy have been defined by exceptional modes of coercion, with the state's Military Police engaging in widespread extrajudicial killings and massacres, whether while on duty or through police-linked death squads. As homicide rates remained largely stable in the 2010s, police killings rose dramatically, coming to constitute, as discussed in Chapter 3, the equivalent of one-quarter of the state's homicides. Moreover, the highly racialized nature of these killings – a pattern that has remained consistent for decades (Mariano 2018; Ouvidoria da Polícia do Estado de São Paulo 2000; Sinhoretto, Silvestre & Schlitter 2014) – suggests that being subjected to lethal violence by the state is not merely determined by the law. This rampant and arbitrary violence, however, is rarely subjected to external accountability, with little oversight by the executive and legislative branches and few convictions in civilian courts (Brinks 2008).

Similar conditions held in Colombia, where the National Police's profound institutional crisis and the escalation of the war against drug cartels in the 1980s led to rampant state violence against civilians, with hundreds of extrajudicial killings and "social cleansing" murders, torture, disappearances, and other grave human rights violations. Although a number of civilian officials, particularly the Inspector General's Office, sounded the alarm that the National Police was in dire need of reform, the president and the Congress took little action to reform the police, even as other areas of the state saw important transformations. Instead politicians engaged the National Police in accommodation, granting it considerable autonomy in the face of rapid institutional deterioration, in exchange for cooperation with the government's policy priority – the drug war – and the police force's close relationship to the United States.

Across the three cases, these police forces maintained coercive practices and structures that invariably contradict substantive democratic principles and outcomes. Police routinely exercise the state's monopoly of coercion in ways that fall well outside the scope of the rule of law, not only facing little constraint in exerting extralegal violence and predation on citizens but often doing so in the interest of political leaders and private actors. Through such actions, these police forces posed a key challenge to other principles central to liberal democracy, such as accountability, transparency, and citizens' rights, including equality under the law and due process. Along these lines, the authoritarian coercive practices of the police forces studied in this book also pose a problem for proponents of substantive democracy, since the violations of citizens' rights discussed here are disproportionately suffered by more disadvantaged sectors of society, reinforcing social inequality.

Despite these tensions with substantive democratic principles and outcomes, democratic governments in Latin America and beyond have done relatively little to curb authoritarian coercive practices and structures within their police forces. The relative absence of structural reforms to address these challenges is notable due to the high salience of policing and security issues in the region, which not only reached historically high crime rates in recent decades but also has the highest homicide rates in the world. Despite the strong societal demand for improved security, however, most Latin American governments have done relatively little to improve state capacity in the provision of security. The reform of the Police of Buenos Aires Province, for instance, occurred fifteen years after the transition to democracy and was only the second structural police reform effort in the twentieth century (Barreneche & Galeano 2008). Such reform has yet to occur in nearly four decades of democratic rule in São Paulo State. Even democratic leaders have thus opted to maintain the status quo with regard to police institutions, even in the face of widespread corruption, violence, and other extralegal practices constitutive of authoritarian coercion.

Political scientist Adam Przeworski posited that "the big puzzle during the past two centuries has been the compatibility of democracy ... with social and economic inequality" (Przeworski 2016, 3), a question that has indeed remained central to political science (Scheve & Stasavage 2017). A similar puzzle lies at the heart of this book, which has examined the apparent enduring compatibility of democracy with authoritarian coercion. As with the "compatibility" that defies theories predicting democracy will produce policies to reduce inequality – whether for normative reasons (Heller 2000) or due to the presumed redistributive preferences of the disadvantaged (Meltzer & Richard 1981) – democracy has also come up short in addressing authoritarian coercion. In undertaking the exercise of disaggregating democracy, however, this "compatibility" becomes less of a "puzzle," as it is made clear the persistence of authoritarian coercion in contradiction with substantive democratic principles is actually sustained by democratic processes.

PROCESS: FRAGMENTED PREFERENCES, INEQUALITY, AND DEMOCRATIC PROCESSES

While Latin American police forces are typically depicted as rogue and uncontrollable – whether due to incompetence or malfeasance (Chevigny 1995; Dutil & Ragendorfer 1997; Saín 2015; Schmid 1996; Ungar 2002) – the cases analyzed throughout this book demonstrate that both the persistence of violent, corrupt, and ineffective police forces exerting authoritarian coercion *and* concerted police reform efforts to promote democratic coercion may represent exercises in democratic responsiveness. Indeed, the decision to enact reform or maintain the status quo on policing when preferences are aligned along patterns of social stratification is largely shaped by how democratic processes channel the preferences and demands of different societal groups and how politicians determine whose demands to prioritize.

As laid out in the empirical chapters, democratic processes are central to these choices. Politicians choosing between these outcomes assess the costs and benefits of each by looking to the degree of fragmentation of societal preferences over policing and security and patterns of political competition. The three police forces examined in this book – Colombia's National Police, the Police of Buenos Aires Province, and the Military Police of São Paulo State – exhibited remarkable institutional persistence for years and even decades, despite ample evidence of widespread extrajudicial violence, corruption, and ineffectiveness in curbing rising crime. As the case studies show, this institutional continuity did not result from the lack of salience of policing and security, nor from a lack of state capacity to enact costly institutional reforms. Recall, for instance, the absence of police reform from Colombian president César Gaviria's otherwise ambitious and transformative "institutional shake-up" reform agenda. Instead, politicians observing fragmented societal preferences and demands over policing and security – irrespective of political competition – likely concluded that police reform would be electorally disadvantageous. The experience of São Paulo State's former governor Franco Montoro – who came to office after two decades of authoritarian rule by vowing to "return to the rule of law" only to give up on police reform efforts in the face of resistance from police and business and other social groups – is illustrative of this point. Across the cases, institutional persistence emerged from the contestation and electoral calculations that constitute ordinary democratic politics.

Yet the case studies also suggest that politicians' incentives shift when they perceive the convergence of societal preferences over reform and face robust political competition. In contrast to the fragmented preferences and demands conveyed through societal contestation – in which views are divided among substantial segments of the population, such that divisions mirror social cleavages (such as race, class, and geography) – convergence reflects shared views and demands across these cleavages. Under such convergence, which typically occurs during scandals, groups that are usually critical of police mobilize and previously supportive or neutral societal sectors (typically the middle class) move into the ranks of critics. When politicians observed these conditions and faced a political opposition that posed an electoral threat, politicians undertook comprehensive structural reforms intended to address enduring and entrenched corruption, violence, and other deficiencies among the police forces they ostensibly control.

The cases analyzed in this book underscore how democratic processes can both bring about social and political demand-making in favor of concerted police reform efforts or can maintain the status quo. The contrast in outcomes between the police of Buenos Aires Province and the Military Police of São Paulo State following high-profile police violence scandals highlights the central role democratic processes can play in reinforcing institutional continuity *and* in bringing about ambitious comprehensive police reforms, even in the face of staunch police resistance. In both instances, low-income citizens and middle-class and business sectors alike mobilized in repudiation of heinous acts of police violence in early 1997 – the killing of a journalist in Buenos Aires Province and televised acts of extortion and extrajudicial violence in a favela in São Paulo State. Initially, however, neither resulted in structural police reforms. Conditions changed in Buenos Aires Province following midterm elections in which the governor's political party lost the majority in the legislature for the first time in a decade. After stalling on delivering promised police reforms for years, the governor initiated a dramatic and ambitious reform process in earnest about a month after his party's electoral defeat (Chapter 7). In São Paulo, meanwhile, the governor likely faced little electoral incentive to enact difficult police reforms, as his political party, the PSDB, faced weak political opposition and has remained dominant in the state for decades (Chapter 6).

Yet if democratic processes, particularly elections, can bring about reform, why does police reform remain relatively rare in democracies? The Colombian and Buenos Aires cases demonstrate how electoral pressures – shared societal outrage and robust political competition – may eventually push even reluctant politicians toward police reform. But the cases analyzed in this book also demonstrate that, when societal preferences over policing are fragmented, democratic processes may instead promote institutional continuity, reinforcing the persistence of violent, corrupt, and ineffective police forces.

Reformist government officials across the cases reflected on the effects of fragmentation, shedding light on the crucial challenge posed by the "conflicting visions"[5] of policing within their societies, as a former advisor to Colombia's Ministry of Defense put it. Indeed, as Colombia's former inspector general Carlos Gustavo Arrieta lamented, "Colombian civil society is extremely erratic in its opinion when it comes to condemning human rights violations [by police]."[6] Arslanian, the former minister of security of Buenos Aires Province who implemented far-reaching police reforms, used similar language to describe the challenge posed by conflicting views – which he characterized as "an erratic demand, frankly erratic" – between those who believe "that the efficacy of the fight against crime depends on the extent of power and discretion that governments grant to police" and others who felt "that we could not have such a corrupt, punitive, [and] feared police force, in light of daily events in which young people disappeared or were killed, shot and killed in the back, varied forms of executions in democracy"[7] (see Chapter 4). In the context of these divisions, electoral pressures militate against reform. Moreover, as Arrieta and Arslanian would learn, hard-fought reforms – if they come to be enacted – become difficult to sustain in the face of such fragmentation.

Perhaps the starkest illustration of what can occur when the conflicting views described by these officials are channeled through democratic processes was what we observed in the case of São Paulo State following the massacre of 111 prisoners by the Military Police in 1992 (Chapter 6). Public opinion surveys and street protests showed "the public in general ... split between supporters and critics of police action" (Caldeira 2000, 176–177), with hundreds protesting the massacre and

---

[5] Author interview with María Victoria Llorente, Bogotá, September 19, 2012.
[6] Procuraduría General de la Nación, *Informe sobre Derechos Humanos 1993–1994*, 15.
[7] Author interview with Carlos León Arslanian, Buenos Aires, September 9, 2011.

similarly large demonstrations in support of the police commanders involved in the massacre.[8] The massacre and its aftermath took place during a highly contested municipal election in which the governor had incentives to sweep the massacre under the rug.[9] In the context of one of the only periods since Brazil's democratic transition in which the State of São Paulo saw robust political competition (see Table 6.1), the enduring fragmentation of societal preferences likely led the governor to conclude that structural police reforms would not be electorally advantageous. Even in the face of an egregious act of extrajudicial police violence, the governor chose to maintain the status quo, favoring the preferences of more privileged sectors.

But elections were not the only democratic process through which fragmented societal preferences were channeled in a way that reinforced the persistence of authoritarian policing in line with patterns of social stratification. As discussed in Chapter 3, São Paulo State created the Community Security Councils (CONSEGs), in which ordinary residents participated in monthly meetings with local police commanders to identify security problems and recommend solutions. Yet, the CONSEGs, too, function as a clear example of how inequality distorts democratic processes. Through participant observation in dozens of CONSEG meetings around the city of São Paulo, I observed countless instances in which residents demanded legally dubious police repression of marginalized social groups. Local business owners in downtown districts, for instance, routinely asked for street vendors and people experiencing homelessness located around commercial areas to be removed. Recall, moreover, the account of a human rights lawyer who supports families of victims of police violence in a low-income community, who explained how human rights defenders and other critics of police violence are silenced in the CONSEGs and have refrained from further participation. Thus, despite constituting a vibrant institution of participatory democracy, the CONSEGs routinely became spaces for demands for repression against vulnerable populations (Galdeano Cruz 2009; González 2017), sometimes in ways that even police leaders acknowledged would contravene the law and democratic principles (see Chapter 3).

---

[8] See "Banho de sangue no Carandiru deixa 111 mortos," *Folha de São Paulo*, January 15, 2014, available online at http://f5.folha.uol.com.br/saiunonp/2014/01/1393908-banho-de-sangue-no-carandiru-deixa-111-mortos.shtml.

[9] "Cadáveres sob a urna," *Veja*, October 14, 1992.

These findings are consistent with other studies on public preferences over criminal justice, which find broad public support for punitive and repressive crime and security policies (Ahnen 2007; Caldeira 2002; Huber & Gordon 2004; Jacobs & Kleban 2003; Mingardi 1992), similarly suggesting a high threshold for police reform, as democratic processes yield policies that reflect those preferences. Even scholars who theorize about divergent civil society preferences over policing and security view these preferences as fixed, accounting for variation in reform outcomes as a function of shifts in power from one coalition to another (Fuentes 2005).

As I demonstrate throughout the book, however, societal preferences over policing and security are subject to change. Notwithstanding the fragmentation of preferences common under the status quo, scandals can bring about a convergence of preferences, with social groups that are typically supportive of or neutral on policing joining the ranks of critics and articulating demands for reform. Recall the mass protests taking place in Buenos Aires by business groups and unions alongside the usual human rights activists following the killing of the journalist (Chapter 7) or the shift in the segment of the population that considered that the police were too violent from 44 percent to 73 percent following the televised acts of police violence in São Paulo (see Chapter 6).

The question remains: if the distribution of societal opinion toward policing is subject to change, and the convergence of preferences (along with political competition) can lead even reluctant political leaders to enact police reform, why don't we observe such preference convergence more often?

What I demonstrate throughout this book is that the fragmentation in societal preferences over policing is often rooted in social cleavages along race, class, and geography, leading to enduring divisions in pattern of societal contestation and demand-making on issues of policing and security. But while there is considerable division in what different societal groups demand and want the police to do, these groups have different levels of power to have those demands acted upon by the state.

The absence of an emerging societal consensus in the form of preference convergence means there is little electoral counterweight to the structural power of the police, favoring the status quo. Thus, when fragmented societal preferences are channeled through democratic processes, such as elections and participatory democracy, they prioritize the demands of more powerful social groups and undermine demands for reform, thereby reinforcing the practices and structures of corrupt, violent, and deficient police forces. The resulting state practices and structures thus reinforce and are reinforced by patterns of societal inequality, as the next section discusses further.

Inequality pervades policing practices. As Egon Bittner, a veteran scholar of policing, put it, "police surveillance is inherently discriminatory. That is, all things being equal, some persons feel the sting of police scrutiny merely because of their station in life. Insofar as this is felt, police work has divisive effects in society" (Bittner 1970, 45). Indeed, police violence throughout Latin America is concentrated among the most vulnerable sectors of society, similar to what Bittner observed in the case of the United States. In his exhaustive comparative analysis of police killings in Argentina, Brazil, and Uruguay, Brinks (2008) demonstrates that police violence disproportionately targets individuals who are Afro-descendant, poor, and from low-income and informal urban peripheries. More recently, a report by the police ombudsman (*ouvidoria*) in São Paulo State, Brazil, showed that approximately 70 percent of young people killed by the police throughout the state in 2017 were black and 75 percent had only an elementary school education (Mariano 2018). The report also determined that there had been "excesses" in 74 percent of cases of lethal police violence.

But the "divisive effects" of policing are reflected not only in these outcomes and in the process by which patterns of social stratification determine whose demands for protection state officials prioritize. These divisions and inequalities are also central to the process of demand formation. Although many scholars have documented an enduring societal demand for police repression and resistance to reform measures to curb police authority (Caldeira 2000, 2002; Chevigny 1995; Krause 2014; Mingardi 1992), the cases examined in this book demonstrate the need for greater nuance.

Far from constituting what is often characterized as a "popular demand," citizens' preferences over policing and security are a site of fragmentation and contestation, wherein relatively privileged citizens facing crime and violence articulate demands for protection via the repression of citizens disadvantaged by race, class, and geography.

These stratified patterns of demand-making emerged in stark ways in the context of Latin America's "triple transition" during the 1980s, in which three contemporaneous processes transformed the state and the lives of ordinary citizens alike: democracy; neoliberal policies in the wake of profound economic crises; and dramatic increases in crime and violence. These transformations had opposing effects on efforts to reform police to promote democratic coercion. The transition to democracy created pressure to reform police forces that had constituted part of the repressive apparatus of the preceding authoritarian regime. But increased crime, economic strife, and social unrest strengthened views favoring greater police authority, particularly among more privileged social sectors.

In the face of this fragmentation of preferences over policing and security, politicians had little electoral incentive to enact police reform, particularly as more privileged sectors of society favored greater police discretion and authority to address rising crime and social unrest. These conditions defined the politics and fate of police reform efforts in São Paulo in the 1980s (see Chapter 6). São Paulo's first democratic elections after two decades of military dictatorship took place in the context of what the governor called "the biggest economic crisis experienced by Brazil in the last half-century, a crisis that has manifested in a particularly adverse form in our state."[10] But while Montoro won the 1982 elections with broad popular support for his campaign slogan to "return to the rule of law," rising crime rates and social protest divided the public's opinion of his initial reform attempts. At the same time that Montoro was installing pro–human rights officials at the helm of the Secretariat of Security and the Civil Police in preparation for police reforms, he also contended with widespread social unrest due to economic crisis. Protests at times turned to rioting and looting in commercial districts (Galdeano Cruz 2009, 32), and, during one infamous demonstration against unemployment, a large crowd marched to the Palácio dos Bandeirantes, the governor's mansion, and threatened to break down its gates (Montoro 2000, 174).

What emerged in response was the usual fragmentation of societal demands. Business leaders rejected Montoro's reformist policies in the face of rising crime and protest, even threatening to call upon the Army to intervene (Mingardi 1992, 115). Government officials received daily visits from citizens demanding that the governor return the deadly ROTA police unit – created under the dictatorship – to patrol the streets (Caldeira 2000, 171). But at the same time, groups such as the Unified Black Movement

---

[10] Democratic Government of the State of São Paulo, Budget Proposal 1984, accessed in the library of the Secretariat of Planning in 2012.

(Movimento Negro Unificado) denounced continued police abuses in the city's mostly black, mostly poor periphery (Chapter 6). In the face of this fragmentation, Montoro had little electoral counterweight to the police's structural power, leading him to abandon his efforts to reduce police corruption and violence during his first year in office. Despite his reformist intentions, Montoro's policy ultimately favored the preferences of more privileged *paulistas*. As a result, police killings – largely targeting the "three Ps" (*preto, pobre e periférico* – black, poor, and from the periphery) – rose considerably during the rest of his term (see Figure 3.2).

Fragmentation of preferences along lines of social stratification also characterized citizens' preferences and demands toward policing in Buenos Aires Province in the years following the transition to democracy. Beginning in the early 1990s, as Argentina's economic crisis caused by hyperinflation led to a wave of social unrest, "the feeling of insecurity" came to occupy a primary spot on the public agenda (Kessler 2009b). Crime rates rose during this period, and a clear link was established in the public discourse between insecurity and the economic and social crisis afflicting the country (Kessler 2009b, 77–78). Indeed, a 1998 survey showed that 65 percent of respondents attributed the increase in crime to unemployment and poverty (Fraga 1998).

As discussed in Chapter 4, Buenos Aires Province saw intense contestation and mobilization divided between those demanding expanded police authority – and even extrajudicial violence – in the face of rising crime and growing social unrest and those denouncing police violence against marginalized citizens. Recall, for instance, the mass protests in the well-to-do municipality of Pilar in defense of local police commander Luis Patti – who was accused of participating in torture, disappearances, and killings during the military dictatorship – after he was indicted by a judge in 1990 on charges of using torture against two robbery suspects (Americas Watch & CELS 1991, 22). At the same time, a growing social movement of the families of mostly low-income victims of police killings became constituted around the *conurbano* region of the province (Verdú 2009), protesting egregious acts of police violence, such as the disappearance of Miguel Bru and the torture and death of Sergio Durán (see Chapter 4). In the face of contestation by different social groups favoring different approaches to policing, the governor and his ruling party opted to maintain the status quo, reinforcing the higher levels of police discretion and authority favored by the province's more well-to-do citizens.

In the context of rising poverty, unemployment, and inequality, citizens' security demands came to reflect social stratification. Such divisions did not only take place in post-transition countries such as Argentina and Brazil. Similar fragmentation occurred in Colombia, as political leaders contended with both protests and petitions from low-income communities like Medellin's La Iguaná[11] and Bogotá's Ciudad Bolivar[12] decrying police abuses and demands from business leaders to expand police authority (Chapter 5).[13]

Importantly, these patterns of stratification are also reflected in experiences with police and patterns of demand-making even in low-income communities. As the Brazilian human rights lawyer cited in Chapter 3 noted, there is a significant distinction between those who live in favelas and those who live in the "*asfalto*" (more well-to-do areas, literally asphalt or paved roads) in their relationships with the police, even when both are located in the same low-income urban periphery. It is worth revisiting his reflection: "In the periphery there is a bit of a division," he observed. "People who live here in the peripheries, as they're heading to work or university, have been subjected to robberies ... so that's why this group from the *asfalto* sees the police as a solution ... So in the periphery we have people, even people I know, that say, 'Criminals have to be killed. They have to be killed – it's him or you'" (see Chapter 3).

This enduring fragmentation, rooted in existing patterns of social stratification, underlies the persistence of these police forces' decidedly authoritarian coercive practices and institutions, long after they were widely recognized to be in crisis. Recall that the Buenos Aires Police had reached single-digit approval ratings well before the killing of the journalist and provincial elections forced the governor to finally push for reform (Chapter 4).

Despite the seeming consensus in the literature of the punitive preferences of the masses and the "popular demand" for *mano dura* (iron fist) policies and vigilantism, this book has provided evidence of considerable fragmentation and contestation in citizens' preferences and demands over policing and security. Rather than reflecting a popular consensus, the substantive outcome of persistent authoritarian policing emerges because of how democratic processes come to privilege the demands of more privileged sectors of society, and high levels of inequality sustain enduring fragmentation of preferences, leaving politicians with little electoral incentive to reform authoritarian police forces.

---

[11] "Denuncian atropellos policiales," *El Mundo*, June 11, 1992, 6A.
[12] "Ciudad Bolívar: Cara ...," *El Tiempo*, September 20, 1992.
[13] "Volver a la justicia de antes: Carlos Lemos," *El Tiempo*, February 21, 1992, 9A.

AUTHORITARIAN COERCION BY DEMOCRATIC MEANS: THE ELECTION OF JAIR BOLSONARO IN BRAZIL

Few events exemplify the argument made throughout this book better than the election of Jair Bolsonaro as president of Brazil in 2018, a clear instance of a democratic process yielding a substantive outcome favoring authoritarian coercion. It is worth briefly considering how patterns of inequality shaped citizens' preferences and their decision to vote for Bolsonaro, with the electoral process privileging the voices of those who favored authoritarian coercive practices and institutions.

A former army captain and congressman, Bolsonaro's electoral campaign and prior legislative career represented an unequivocal endorsement of authoritarian coercion. Bolsonaro repeatedly advocated for coercive practices and structures that fall well outside the rule of law. He has long been a staunch defender of the previous authoritarian regime, infamously declaring his support for torture and arguing that it was necessary to "do the work that the military regime did not do, kill some 30 thousand."[14] Moreover, Bolsonaro's support for authoritarian coercion was not limited to the previous dictatorship. Instead, he openly announced his preference for and intention to promote widespread extrajudicial killings by police, vowing to remove existing legal constraints on the use of lethal force and external accountability mechanisms. Over the course of the presidential campaign, for instance, Bolsonaro declared that he would apply the legal figure of *excludente de ilicitude* to police killings, such that they would automatically be legally considered self-defense.[15] Bolsonaro went further, affirming that "if someone says I want to give carte blanche to the Military Police to kill, I'd respond: yes I do want that. A police officer that doesn't shoot anyone and gets shot at is not a police officer."[16]

Bolsonaro's explicit agenda of authoritarian coercion was reinforced by democratic processes, with Bolsonaro winning the presidency in

---

[14] João Paulo Charleaux, "O que Bolsonaro não sabe sobre tortura, execução, ditatura e guerra," *Nexo Jornal*, October 15, 2018, available at www.nexojornal.com.br/expres so/2017/10/14/O-que-Bolsonaro-n%C3%A3o-sabe-sobre-tortura-execu%C3%A7%C 3%A3o-ditadura-e-guerra; www1.folha.uol.com.br/poder/2018/06/nos-anos-90-bolsonaro-defendeu-novo-golpe-militar-e-guerra.shtml.

[15] Anita Abdalla, "O plano de Bolsonaro sobre 'excludentes de ilicitude,'" *Nexo Jornal*, October 1, 2018, www.nexojornal.com.br/expresso/2018/10/01/O-plano-de-Bolsonaro-sobre-%E2%80%98excludentes-de-ilicitude%E2%80%99.

[16] "Bolsonaro diz que quer dar 'carta branca' para PM matar em serviço," *UOL*, December 14, 2017, https://noticias.uol.com.br/politica/ultimas-noticias/2017/12/14/bol sonaro-diz-que-quer-dar-carta-branca-para-pm-matar-em-servico.htm.

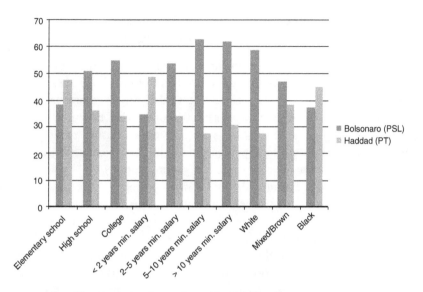

FIGURE 8.2 Vote intention in 2018 presidential runoff
Datafolha surveys, October 2018. Data for White, Mixed/Brown, Black from
survey PO3976 (October 10); all other data from PO3979 (October 26–27)

October 28, 2018, with 55 percent of the vote in the presidential runoff
election. But rather than representing a "popular demand" for authoritarian coercion, Bolsonaro's election reflected considerable fragmentation, with preferences largely (though not entirely) defined by existing
patterns of social stratification. An analysis of municipal voting results,
for instance, demonstrated that Bolsonaro won 94 percent of the wealthi-
est municipalities, while his Workers' Party (PT, Partido dos
Trabalhadores) opponent Fernando Haddad won in 90 percent of the
poorest municipalities. Bolsonaro also won majorities of the vote in
municipalities where white Brazilians made up majorities of the population, while Haddad won in municipalities where black Brazilians made up
a majority.[17]

These disparities in Bolsonaro's support are also reflected at the individual level. Surveys conducted by the Brazilian survey firm Datafolha in
October 2018 asked respondents which of the two candidates they
intended to vote for in the presidential runoff (see Figure 8.2). Although

[17] "Bolsonaro divide o Brasil: Arrasa nas cidades mais brancas e mais ricas," *El País Brasil*,
October 30, 2018, https://brasil.elpais.com/brasil/2018/10/29/actualidad/1540828734_
083649.html.

Bolsonaro enjoyed broad-based support, a clear pattern emerges. Respondents with only an elementary school education, those earning less than two minimum salaries, and those that identify as black (*preto*) were more likely to favor the PT candidate, Haddad, than Bolsonaro. Majorities of almost every other socioeconomic group, and individuals who identify as white, favored Bolsonaro. Yet, the segment of the population most likely to suffer extrajudicial police violence, those who are black and poor (recall the "three Ps": *pobre, preto e periférico*), were far more likely to reject Bolsonaro's agenda of authoritarian coercion.

In this cursory analysis of the outcome of Brazil's presidential contest, the objective is not to definitively prove that a majority of voters opted for Bolsonaro *because* of his authoritarian coercion agenda, nor that poor and black Brazilians opted for Bolsonaro's opponent for the same reason rather than other factors – such as the PT's traditional support base in the Northeast. What this limited overview of Bolsonaro's electoral victory seeks to demonstrate is simply that, once channeled through the democratic process of majoritarian elections, the fragmented and stratified preferences reflected in the vote totals resulted in the victory of a candidate who openly announced his intention to enact an agenda of authoritarian coercion. This contradiction of democracy, in which democratic processes can result in substantive outcomes that contravene democratic principles, was foreshadowed by Bolsonaro himself, who once predicted, "If one day the military comes to power, it will be through the vote."[18]

---

[18] "Nos anos 90, Bolsonaro defendeu novo golpe militar e guerra," *Folha de São Paulo*, June 3, 2018, www1.folha.uol.com.br/poder/2018/06/nos-anos-90-bolsonaro-defendeu-novo-golpe-militar-e-guerra.shtml.

References

Abregú, Martín. 1993. "Contra las apologías del 'homicidio uniforme': La violencia policial en Argentina." *Nueva Sociedad* 123: 68–83.

Achen, Christopher, and Larry Bartels. 2016. *Democracy for Realists: Why Elections Do Not Produce Responsive Government.* Princeton, NJ: Princeton University Press.

Acuña, Carlos, and Catalina Smulovitz. 1991. *Ni Olvido Ni Perdón? Derechos Humanos y Tensiones Cívico-Militares En La Transición Argentina.* Buenos Aires: Centro de Estudios de Estado y Sociedad.

Adorno, Sérgio. 2002. "Exclusão socioeconômica e violência urbana." *Sociologias* 4(8): 84–135.

2013. "Democracy in Progress in Contemporary Brazil: Corruption, Organized Crime, Violence and New Paths to the Rule of Law." *International Journal of Criminology and Sociology* 2(0): 409–425.

Adorno, Sérgio, and Nancy Cárdia. 1998. "Dilemas do controle democrático da violência: Execuções sumárias e grupos de extermínio." In *Violências Em Tempo de Globalização,* edited by J. V. T. dos Santos, 66–90. São Paulo: Hucitec.

Agamben, Giorgio. 2005. *State of Exception.* Chicago, IL: University of Chicago Press.

Agüero, Felipe, and Jeffrey Stark. 1998. *Fault Lines of Democracy in Post-Transition Latin America.* Miami, FL: North-South Center Press.

Ahnen, Ronald E. 2007. "The Politics of Police Violence in Democratic Brazil." *Latin American Politics & Society* 49(1): 141–164.

Alpert, Geoffrey, and Roger Dunham. 2004. *Understanding Police Use of Force: Officers, Suspects, and Reciprocity.* Cambridge: Cambridge University Press.

Alves, Jaime Amparo. 2014. "From Necropolis to Blackpolis: Necropolitical Governance and Black Spatial Praxis in São Paulo, Brazil." *Antipode* 46(2): 323–339.

Amengual, Matthew. 2014. "Pathways to Enforcement: Labor Inspectors Leveraging Linkages with Society in Argentina." *Industrial and Labor Relations Review* 67(1): 1–33.

Americas Watch. 1987. *Police Abuse in Brazil: Summary Executions and Torture in São Paulo and Rio de Janeiro*. New York: Americas Watch Committee.

1993. "Urban Police Violence in Brazil: Torture and Police Killings in São Paulo and Rio de Janeiro after Five Years." *News From Americas Watch* 5(5): 1–30.

Americas Watch and CELS. 1991. *Police Violence in Argentina: Torture and Police Killings in Buenos Aires*. Buenos Aires: Human Rights Watch.

Amnesty International. 1994a. *Colombia: Niños y nenores víctimas de la violencia política AMR 23/51/94*. Spain: Editorial Amnistía International.

1994b. *Political Violence in Colombia: Myth and Reality*. Spain: Editorial Amnistía International.

Andrews, Kenneth T. 2001. "Social Movements and Policy Implementation: The Mississippi Civil Rights Movement and the War on Poverty, 1965 to 1971." *American Sociological Review* 66(1): 71–95.

ARGRA and CELS. 2003. *Informe sobre el juicio oral y público por el homicidio del reportero gráfico*. Buenos Aires: AGRA and CELS.

Arias, Enrique Desmond, and Daniel Goldstein (eds.). 2010. *Violent Democracies in Latin America*. Durham, NC: Duke University Press.

Arjona, Ana. 2019. "Subnational Units, the Locus of Choice, and Concept Formation." In *Inside Countries: Subnational Research in Comparative Politics*, edited by Agustina Giraudy, Eduardo Moncada, and Richard Snyder, 214–242. Cambridge: Cambridge University Press.

Bachrach, Peter, and Morton Baratz. 1962. "Peter Bachrach & Morton Baratz, 'Two Faces of Power.'" *American Political Science Review* 56(4): 947–952.

Bailey, John, and Lucía Dammert. 2005. *Public Security and Police Reform in the Americas*. Pittsburgh, PA: University of Pittsburgh Press.

Balán, Manuel. 2011. "Competition by Denunciation: The Political Dynamics of Corruption Scandals in Argentina and Chile." *Comparative Politics* 43(4): 459–478.

Barcellos, Caco. 1992. *Rota 66: A História Da Polícia Que Mata*. São Paulo: RECORD.

Barreneche, Osvaldo. 2007. "La reforma policial del peronismo en la provincia de Buenos Aires, 1946–1951." *Desarrollo Económico* 47(186): 225–248.

Barreneche, Osvaldo, and Diego Galeano. 2008. "Notas sobre las reformas policiales en la Argentina, siglos XIX y XX." *Cuadernos de Seguridad* 8: 73–112.

Barros, Geová da Silva. 2008. "Filtragem racial: A cor na seleção do suspeito." *Revista Brasileira de Segurança Pública* 2(3): 134–155.

Bayley, David. 1975. "The Police and Political Development in Europe." In *The Formation of National States in Western Europe*, edited by Charles Tilly and Gabriel Ardant, 328–379. Princeton, NJ: Princeton University Press.

1985. *Patterns of Policing: A Comparative International Analysis*. New Brunswick, NJ: Rutgers University Press.

2006. *Changing the Guard: Developing Democratic Police Abroad*. New York: Oxford University Press.

Beetham, David. 2015. "Authoritarianism and Democracy: Beyond Regime Types." Symposium "Reconceptualizing Authoritarianism." *Comparative*

Democratization Newsletter 13(2): 2, https://pure.uva.nl/ws/files/2648663/
170808_APSA_CD_June_2015.pdf.

Benevides, Maria Victoria. 1985. "Violência policial e democracia podem conviver?" *Lua Nova: Revista de Cultura e Política* 1(4): 25–26.

Bittner, Egon. 1970. *The Functions of the Police in Modern Society: A Review of Background Factors, Current Practices, and Possible Role Models*. Chevy Chase, MD: National Institute of Mental Health, Center for Studies of Crime and Delinquency.

Bonner, Michelle. 2018. "Media and Punitive Populism in Argentina and Chile." *Bulletin of Latin American Research* 37(3): 275–90.

Bonner, Michelle, Guillermina Seri, and Mary Kubal (eds.). 2018. *Police Abuse in Contemporary Democracies*. London: Palgrave Macmillan.

Brinks, Daniel. 2008. *The Judicial Response to Policing Killings in Latin America: Inequality and the Rule of Law*. Cambridge: Cambridge University Press.

Brownlee, Jason. 2010. "Authoritarianism after 1989." *Harvard International Review* (February).

Brysk, Alison. 2012. "National Insecurity and the Citizenship Gap." In *Shifting Frontiers of Citizenship: The Latin American Experience*, edited by Mario Sznajder, Luis Roniger, and Carlos Forment, 459–474. Boston, MA: Brill.

Buitrago, Francisco Leal. 2003. "La doctrina de seguridad nacional: Materialización de la guerra fría en América del Sur." *Revista de Estudios Sociales* 15: 74–87.

Caldeira, Teresa. 2000. *City of Walls: Crime, Segregation, and Citizenship in São Paulo*. Berkeley: University of California Press.

2002. "The Paradox of Police Violence in Democratic Brazil." *Ethnography* 3 (3): 235–263.

Caldeira, Teresa, and James Holston. 1999. "Democracy and Violence in Brazil." *Comparative Studies in Society and History* 41(4): 691–729.

Call, Charles T. 2003. "Democratisation, War, and State-Building: Constructing the Rule of Law in El Salvador." *Journal of Latin American Studies* 35: 827–862.

Camacho, Alvaro. 1993. "La reforma de la policía: Realidades inmediatas y objetivos estratégicos." *Análisis Político* 19: 50–62.

1994. "La reforma de la policía Colombiana: Esperanzas o frustraciones?" *Nueva Sociedad* 129: 27–40.

Câmara dos Deputados. 2009. Franco Montoro – Perfis Parlamentares 54. Brasília.

Canes-Wrone, Brandice. 2010. *Who Leads Whom? Presidents, Policy, and the Public*. Chicago, IL: University of Chicago Press.

Cao, Liqun. 2011. "Visible Minorities and Confidence in the Police." *Canadian Journal of Criminology and Criminal Justice/La Revue canadienne de criminologie et de justice pénale* 53(1): 1–26.

Cárdia, Nancy. 1999. *Pesquisa sobre atitudes, normas culturais e valores em relação a violência em 10 capitais brasileiras*. Brasília: Ministério da Justiça, Secretaria Nacional dos Direitos Humanos.

2002. "The Impact of Exposure to Violence in São Paulo: Accepting Violence or Continuing Horror?" In *Citizens of Fear: Urban Violence in Latin America*, edited by Susana Rotker and Katherine Goldman, 152–185. New Brunswick, NJ: Rutgers University Press.

Cárdia, Nancy, and Sueli Schiffer. 2002. "Violência e desigualdade social." *Ciência e Cultura (SBPC)* 54(1): 25–31.

Carpenter, Daniel, and G. Sin. 2007. "Policy Tragedy and the Emergence of Regulation: The Food, Drug, and Cosmetic Act of 1938." *Studies in American Political Development* 21(Fall): 149–180.

Carreras, Miguel. 2013. "The Impact of Criminal Violence on Regime Legitimacy in Latin America." *Latin American Research Review* 48(3): 85–107.

Casas Dupuy, Pablo. 2005. "Reformas y contrarrefomas en la policía Colombiana." In *Seguridad Urbana y Policía En Colombia*, 1–80. Bogotá: Fundación Seguridad y Democracia.

CELS. 1994. *Informe sobre la situación de los derechos humanos en Argentina*. Buenos Aires: CELS.

1997. *Informe sobre la situación de los derechos humanos en Argentina*. Buenos Aires: CELS.

1998. *Informe sobre la situación de los derechos humanos en Argentina*. Buenos Aires: CELS.

2001. *Informe sobre la situación de los derechos humanos en Argentina*. Buenos Aires: CELS.

2003. *El estado frente a La protesta social 1996–2002*. Buenos Aires: Siglo XXI Editores.

Cerruti, Pedro. 2011. "El surgimiento de la 'inseguridad' como problema público político en la Argentina post-dictatorial (The Emergence of 'Insecurity' as a Public Political Problem in Post-Dictatorial Argentina)." *Revista Oficios Terrestres* 1(27): 1–30.

Chevigny, Paul. 1995. *Edge of the Knife: Police Violence in the Americas*. New York: New Press.

1999. "Defining the Role of the Police in Latin America." In *The (Un)Rule of Law and the Underprivileged in Latin America*, 49–70. Notre Dame, IN: University of Notre Dame Press.

Collier, David, and Steven Levitsky. 1997. "Democracy with Adjectives: Conceptual Innovation in Comparative Research." *World Politics* 49(3): 430–451.

Comisión de Estudios sobre la Violencia. 1987. *Colombia: Violencia y democracia*. Bogotá: Instituto de Estudios Políticos y Relaciones Internacionales, Universidad Nacional de Colombia.

CONADEP. 1984. *Nunca más: Informe de la comisión nacional sobre la desaparición de personas*. Buenos Aires: EUDEBA.

Cox, Gary, and Scott Morgenstern. 2001. "Latin America's Reactive Assemblies and Proactive Presidents." *Comparative Politics* 33(2): 171–189.

Cruz, José Miguel. 2003. "Violencia y democratización en Centroamérica: El impacto del crimen en la legitimidad de los regímenes de posguerra." *América latina hoy: Revista de ciencias sociales* 35: 19–59.

2015. "Police Misconduct and Political Legitimacy in Central America." *Journal of Latin American Studies* 47(2): 251–283.

Culpepper, Pepper D. 2015. "Structural Power and Political Science in the Post-Crisis Era." *Business and Politics* 17(3): 391–409.

Dahl, Robert. 1961. *Who Governs? Democracy and Power in an American City.* New Haven, CT: Yale University Press.

 1971. *Polyarchy: Participation and Opposition.* New Haven, CT: Yale University Press.

 1982. *Dilemmas of Pluralist Democracy: Autonomy Vs. Control.* New Haven, CT: Yale University Press.

Dammert, Lucia, and Mary Fran T. Malone. 2003. "Fear of Crime or Fear of Life? Public Insecurities in Chile." *Bulletin of Latin American Research* 22(1): 79–101.

Davenport, Christian, Sarah A. Soule, and David A. Armstrong. 2011. "Protesting While Black? The Differential Policing of American Activism, 1960 to 1990." *American Sociological Review* 76(1): 152–178.

Davis, Diane. 2006. "Undermining the Rule of Law: Democratization and the Dark Side of Police Reform in Mexico." *Latin American Politics and Society* 48(1): 55–86.

Davis, Diane, and Anthony W. Pereira. 2003. *Irregular Armed Forces and Their Role in Politics and State Formation.* Cambridge: Cambridge University Press.

Delgado, Fernando Ribeiro, Raquel Elias Ferreira Dodge, and Sandra Carvalho. 2011. *São Paulo sob achaque: Corrupção, crime organizado e violência institucional em Maio de 2006.* São Paulo: Internationla Human Rights Clinic at Harvard Law School and Justiça Global.

Dewey, Matías. 2012. "The Making of Hybrid Stateness: Sources of Police Performance in the Conurbano." *Revista de Ciencia Política* 32(3): 659–672.

Diamint, Rut (ed.). 1999. *Control civil y fuerzas armadas en las nuevas democracias Latinoamericanas.* Buenos Aires: Nuevohacer, Grupo Editor Latinoamericano.

 2003. "The Military." In *Constructing Democratic Governance in Latin America*, edited by Jorge Domínguez and Michael Shifter, 43–73. Baltimore, MD: Johns Hopkins University Press.

Diamond, Larry. 1999. *Developing Democracy: Toward Consolidation.* Baltimore, MD: Johns Hopkins University Press.

Durazo Hermann, Julián. 2017. "Clientelism and State Violence in Subnational Democratic Consolidation in Bahia, Brazil." In *Violence in Latin America and the Caribbean: Subnational Structures, Institutions, and Clientelistic Networks*, edited by Tina Hilgers and Laura Macdonald, 211–229. Cambridge: Cambridge University Press.

Dutil, Carlos, and Ricardo Ragendorfer. 1997. *La Bonaerense: Historia criminal de la policía de la provincia de Buenos Aires.* Buenos Aires: Editorial Planeta.

Eaton, Kent. 2008. "Federalism, Parties, and Civil Society in Argentina's Public Security Crisis." *Latin American Research Review* 43(3): 5–32.

Eckhouse, Laurel. 2019. "Race, Party, and Representation in Criminal Justice Politics." *Journal of Politics* 81(3): 1143–1152.

Falleti, Tulia. 2010. "Infiltrating the State: The Evolution of Health Care Reforms in Brazil, 1964–1988." In *Explaining Institutional Change: Ambiguity,*

Agency, and Power, edited by James Mahoney and Kathleen Thelen, 38–62. Cambridge: Cambridge University Press.

Falleti, Tulia, and James Mahoney. 2015. "The Comparative Sequential Method." In *Advances in Comparative-Historical Analysis*, edited by James Mahoney and Kathleen Thelen, 211–239. Cambridge: Cambridge University Press.

Feltran, Gabriel de Santis. 2008. "Fronteiras de tensão: Um estudo sobre política e violência nas periferias de São Paulo." Universidade Estadual de Campinas.

Fernandez Roich, Cynthia. 2017. *Media and Crime in Argentina: Punitive Discourse during the 1990s*. London: Palgrave Macmillan.

Forero Hidalgo, Jymy, and Frank Molano Camargo. 2015. "El paro cívico de Octubre de 1993 en Ciudad Bolívar (Bogotá): La formación de un campo de protesta urbana." *Anuario Colombiano de Historia Social y de la Cultura* 42 (1): 115–143.

Forman, James Jr. 2017. *Locking Up Our Own: Crime and Punishment in Black America*. New York: Farrar, Straus and Giroux.

Fortner, Michael Javen. 2015. *Black Silent Majority: The Rockefeller Drug Laws and the Politics of Punishment*. Cambridge, MA: Harvard University Press.

Fórum Brasileiro de Segurança Pública. 2015. *Anuário Brasileiro de segurança pública*. São Paulo: Fórum Brasileiro de Segurança Pública.

Fox, Jonathan. 1992. *The Politics of Food in Mexico: State Power and Social Mobilization*. Ithaca, NY: Cornell University Press.

2015. "Social Accountability: What Does the Evidence Really Say?" *World Development* 72: 346–361.

Fraga, Rosendo. 1998. *La seguridad pública*. Buenos Aires: Editorial Centro de Estudios Union para la Nueva Mayoría.

Franco Agudelo, Saúl. 1997. "Violencia y salud en Colombia." *Revista Panamericana de Salud Publica/Pan American Journal of Public Health* 1 (2): 93–103.

Fruhling, Hugo. 2009. *Violencia y policía en América Latina*. Quito, Ecuador: FLACSO.

Fuentes, Claudio. 2005. *Contesting the Iron Fist: Advocacy Networks and Police Violence in Democratic Argentina and Chile*. New York: Routledge.

Fung, Archon. 2004. *Empowered Participation: Reinventing Urban Democracy*. Princeton, NJ: Princeton University Press.

Gabaldón, Luis Gerardo, and Andrés Antillano. 2007. *La Policía Venezolana: Desarrollo institucional y perspectivas de reforma al inicio del tercer Milenio*. Caracas: Comisión Nacional para la Reforma Policial.

Galdeano Cruz, Ana Paula. 2009. "Para Falar Em Nome Da Segurança: O Que Pensam, Querem e Fazem Os Representantes Dos Conselhos Comunitários de Segurança." Universidade de Campinas.

Garay, Candelaria. 2017. *Social Policy Expansion in Latin America*. Cambridge: Cambridge University Press.

Geddes, Barbara. 1994. *Politician's Dilemma: Building State Capacity in Latin America*. Berkeley: University of California Press.

Gibson, Edward L. 2013. *Boundary Control: Subnational Authoritarianism in Federal Democracies*. Cambridge: Cambridge University Press.

Gilens, Martin. 2014. *Affluence and Influence: Economic Inequality and Political Power in America*. Princeton, NJ: Princeton University Press.

Gilens, Martin, and Benjamin Page. 2014. "Testing Theories of American Politics: Elites, Interest Groups, and Average Citizens." *Perspectives on Politics* 12(3): 564–581.

Giraudy, Agustina. 2015. *Democrats and Autocrats: Pathways of Subnational Undemocratic Regime*. New York: Oxford University Press.

Glasius, Marlies. 2018. "What Authoritarianism Is … and Is Not: A Practice Perspective." *International Affairs* 94(3): 515–533.

Goldsmith, Andrew. 2000. "Police Accountability Reform in Colombia: The Civilian Oversight Experiment." In *Civilian Oversight of Policing: Governance, Democracy, and Human Rights*, edited by Andrew Goldsmith and Colleen Hart, 167–194. Portland, OR: Hart Publishing.

Goldstein, Herman. 1977. *Policing a Free Society*. Cambridge, MA: Ballinger Publishing Company.

González, Gustavo. 2007. "Reforma policial y política: Un complejo entramado de compromisos, resistencias, y condiciones de posibilidad." *Urvio: Revista Latinoamericana de Seguridad Ciudadana* (2): 154–163.

González, Yanilda. 2016. "Varieties of Participatory Security: Assessing Community Participation in Policing in Latin America." *Public Administration and Development* 36: 132–143.

2017. "'What Citizens Can See of the State': Police and the Construction of Democratic Citizenship in Latin America." *Theoretical Criminology* 21(4): 494–511.

2019a. "Participation as a Safety Valve: Police Reform through Participatory Security in Latin America." *Latin American Politics & Society* 61(2): 68–92.

2019b. "The Social Origins of Institutional Weakness and Change." *World Politics* 71(1): 44–87.

n.d. "Reforming to Avoid Reform: Strategic Policy Substitution and the Reform Gap in Policing." Working Paper.

Greif, Avner, and David Laitin. 2004. "A Theory of Endogenous Institutional Change." *American Political Science Review* 98(4): 633–652.

Greitens, Sheena Chestnut. 2013. "*Coercive Institutions and State Violence under Authoritarianism.*" Cambridge, MA: Harvard University Press.

2016. *Dictators and Their Secret Police: Coercive Institutions and State Violence*. Cambridge: Cambridge University Press.

Grzymala-Busse, Anna. 2007. *Rebuilding Leviathan: Party Competition and State Exploitation in Post-Communist Democracies*. New York: Cambridge University Press.

Hanson, Rebecca. 2015. "Policing the Protests in Post-Chávez Venezuela: How Human Rights Legitimize Coercion." Hot Spots, *Fieldsights*, February 5. https://culanth.org/fieldsights/policing-the-protests-in-post-ch%C3%A1ve z-venezuela-how-human-rights-legitimize-coercion.

Heilmann, Sebastian. 2008. "Policy Experimentation in China's Economic Rise." *Studies in Comparative International Development* 43(1): 1–26.

Heller, Patrick. 2000. "Degrees of Democracy: Some Comparative Lessons from India." *World Politics* 52(July): 484–519.

Hill, Kim Quaile, and Angela Hinton-Anderson. 1995. "Pathways of Representation: A Causal Analysis of Public Opinion–Policy Linkages." *American Journal of Political Science* 39(4): 924–935.

Hinton, Mercedes. 2006. *The State on the Streets: Police and Politics in Argentina and Brazil.* Boulder, CO: Lynne Rienner Publishers.

Hite, Katherine, and Paola Cesarini. 2004. *Authoritarian Legacies and Democracy in Latin America and Southern Europe.* Notre Dame, IN: University of Notre Dame Press.

Hobbes, Thomas. [1651] 1996. *Leviathan*, edited by J. C. Gaskin. Oxford: Oxford University Press.

Holland, Alisha C. 2015. "The Distributive Politics of Enforcement." *American Journal of Political Science* 59(2): 357–371.

Holmes, Stephen. 2003. "Lineages of the Rule of Law." In *Democracy and the Rule of Law*, edited by Adam Przeworski and José María Maravall, 19–61. Cambridge: Cambridge University Press.

Holston, James, and Teresa Caldeira. 1998. "Democracy, Law, and Violence: Disjunctions of Brazilian Citizenship." In *Fault Lines of Democracy in Post-Transition Latin America*, edited by Felipe Aguero and Jeffrey Stark, 263–296. Miami, FL: North-South Center Press/University of Miami.

Huber, Gregory A., and Sanford C. Gordon. 2004. "Accountability and Coercion: Is Justice Blind When It Runs for Office?" *Americal Journal of Political Science* 48(2): 247–263.

Huggins, Martha Knisely (ed.). 1991. *Vigilantism and the State in Modern Latin America: Essays on Extralegal Violence.* New York: Praeger.

Human Rights Watch. 1994. *Generation under Fire: Children and Violence in Colombia.* New York: Human Rights Watch.

2009. *Lethal Force: Police Violence and Public Security in Rio de Janeiro and São Paulo.* New York: Human Rights Watch.

Human Rights Watch and CELS. 1998. *La inseguridad policial: Violencia de las fuerzas de seguridad en la Argentina.* Buenos Aires: EUDEBA.

Hunter, Wendy. 1997. *Eroding Military Influence in Brazil: Politicians against Soldiers.* Chapel Hill: University of North Carolina Press.

2006. *State and Soldier in Latin America: Redefining the Military's Role in Argentina, Brazil, and Chile.* Washington, DC: United States Institute of Peace.

Huntington, Samuel P. 1991. *The Third Wave: Democratization in the Late 20th Century.* Norman: University of Oklahoma Press.

Jacobs, David, and Richard Kleban. 2003. "Political Institutions, Minorities, and Punishment: A Pooled Cross-National Analysis of Imprisonment Rates." *Social Forces* 80(2): 725–755.

Kääriäinen, Juha. 2008. "Why Do the Finns Trust the Police?" *Journal of Scandinavian Studies in Criminology and Crime Prevention* 9(2): 141–159.

Kalmanowiecki, Laura. 2000. "Origins and Applications of Political Policing in Argentina." *Latin American Perspectives* 27(2): 36–56.

Kessler, Gabriel. 2009a. *El eentimiento de inseguridad: Sociología del temor al delito.* Buenos Aires: Siglo XXI Editores.

2009b. *El Sentimiento de Inseguridad.* Buenos Aires: Siglo XXI.

Krause, Krystin. 2014. "Supporting the Iron Fist: Crime News, Public Opinion, and Authoritarian Crime Control in Guatemala." *Latin American Politics & Society* 56(1): 98–119.

Laniyonu, Ayobami. 2018. "The Political Consequences of Policing: Evidence from New York City." *Political Behavior* 41(2): 527–558.

Lawson, Chappell. 2002. *Building the Fourth Estate: Democratization and the Rise of a Free Press in Mexico*. Berkeley: University of California Press.

Lax, Jeffrey R., and Justin H. Phillips. 2009. "Gay Rights in the States: Public Opinion and Policy Responsiveness." *American Political Science Review* 103 (3): 367–386.

Leal Buitrago, Francisco. 1994. *El oficio de la guerra: La seguridad nacional en Colombia*. Bogotá: Tercer Mundo Editores.

  1995. *En busca de la estabilidad perdida: Actores políticos y sociales en los años noventa*. Bogotá: Tercer Mundo Editores.

Leeds, E. 1996. "Cocaine and Parallel Polities in the Brazilian Urban Periphery: Constraints on Local-Level Democratization." *Latin American Research Review* 31(3): 47–83.

Lemoine, Carlos. 1986. *Como conseguir el voto de los Colombianos*. Bogotá: Editorial Oveja Negra.

  1993. *Las fuerzas de La opinión*. Bogotá: Centro Nacional de Consultoría.

  1997. *Iberoamérica habla*. Bogotá: CIMA.

Levitsky, Steven, and María Victoria Murillo. 2014. "Building Institutions on Weak Foundations: Lessons from Latin America." In *Reflections on Uneven Democracies: The Legacy of Guillermo O'Donnell*, edited by Daniel Brinks, Marcelo Leiras, and Scott Mainwaring, 189–213. Baltimore, MD: Johns Hopkins University Press.

Levitsky, Steven, and Daniel Ziblatt. 2018. *How Democracies Die*. New York: Crown.

Light, Matthew. 2016. "Varieties of Police Reform in Electoral Authoritarian Regimes: Armenia in Comparative Post-Soviet Perspective." Working Paper.

Lindblom, Charles. 1977. *Politics and Markets: The World's Political Economic Systems*. New York: Basic Books.

Linz, Juan J. 2000. *Totalitarian and Authoritarian Regimes*. Boulder, CO: Lynne Rienner Publishers.

Linz, Juan J., and Alfred C. Stepan. 1996. "Toward Consolidated Democracies." *Journal of Democracy* 7(2): 14–33.

Lipset, Martin Seymour. 1959. "Some Social Requisites of Democracy: Economic Development and Political Legitimacy." *American Political Science Review* 53: 69–105.

Lipsky, Michael. 2010. *Street-Level Bureaucracy: Dilemmas of the Individual in Public Services*. New York: Russell Sage Foundation.

Llorente, Maria Victoria. 1997. *Perfil de la policía Colombiana*. Bogotá, Colombia.

  2005. "Demilitarization in Times of War? Police Reform in Colombia." In *Public Security and Police Reform in the Americas*, edited by Lucía Dammert and John Bailey, 111–132. Pittsburgh: University of Pittsburgh Press.

Loewenstein, Karl. 1937. "Militant Democracy and Fundamental Rights I." *American Political Science Review* 31: 417–432.

Lukes, Steven. 1974. *Power: A Radical View*. London: Palgrave Macmillan.

Luna, Juan Pablo. 2014. *Segmented Representation: Political Party Strategies in Unequal Democracies*. New York: Oxford University Press.

Lupien, Pascal. 2018. "Participatory Democracy and Ethnic Minorities: Opening Inclusive New Spaces or Reproducing Inequalities?" *Democratization* 25(7): 1251–1269.

Macaulay, Fiona. 2012. "Cycles of Police Reform in Latin America." In *Policing in Africa*, edited by David J. Francis, 165–190. New York: Palgrave Macmillan.

Mahoney, James. 2000. "Path Dependence in Historical Sociology." *Theory and Society* 29(4): 507–548.

Mahoney, James, and Kathleen Thelen (eds.). 2009. *Explaining Institutional Change: Ambiguity, Agency, and Power*. Cambridge: Cambridge University Press.

Mann, Michael. 1984. "The Autonomous Power of the State: Its Origins, Mechanisms, and Results." *European Journal of Sociology* 25(2): 185–213.

Maravall, José María, and Adam Przeworski (eds.). 2003. *Democracy and the Rule of Law*. Cambridge: Cambridge University Press.

Mariano, Benedito Domingos. 2018. *Pesquisa sobre o uso da força letal por policiais de São Paulo e vitimização policial em 2017*. São Paulo: Ouvidoria da Polícia do Estado de São Paulo.

Marshall, T. H. 1950. *Citizenship and Social Class and Other Essays*. London: Cambridge University Press.

Mayka, Lindsay. 2019. *Building Participatory Institutions in Latin America*. Cambridge: Cambridge University Press.

Meltzer, Allan H., and Scott F. Richard. 1981. "A Rational Theory of the Size of Government." *Journal of Political Economy* 89(5): 914–927.

de Mesquita Neto, Paulo. 2011. *Ensaios sobre segurança cidadã*. São Paulo: Quartier Latin.

Mickey, Robert. 2015. *Paths Out of Dixie: The Democratization of Authoritarian Enclaves in America's Deep South, 1944–1972*. Princeton, NJ: Princeton University Press.

Miller, Lisa L. 2016. *The Myth of Mob Rule: Violent Crime and Democratic Politics*. New York: Oxford University Press.

Mingardi, Guaracy. 1992. *Tiras, gansos, e trutas: Cotidiano e reforma na Polícia Civil*. São Paulo: Editora Página Aberta.

Moncada, Eduardo. 2009. "Toward Democratic Policing in Colombia? Institutional Accountability through Lateral Reform." *Comparative Politics* 41(4): 431–450.

2016. *Cities, Business and the Politics of Urban Violence in Latin America*. Stanford, CA: Stanford University Press.

Montoro, André Franco. 2000. *Memórias em linha reta*. São Paulo: SENAC SP.

Movimento Mães de Maio. 2019. *Memorial dos nossos filhos vivos: As vítimas invisíveis da democracia*. São Paulo: Nós por Nós Editora.

Müller, Markus-Michael. 2017. "The Clientelist Bases of Police Violence in Mexico City." In *Violence in Latin America and the Caribbean:*

Subnational Structures, Institutions, and Clientelistic Networks, edited by Tina Hilgers and Laura Macdonald, 59–74. Cambridge: Cambridge University Press.

Najdowski, Cynthia J., Bette L. Bottoms, and Phillip Goff. 2015. "Stereotype Threat and Racial Differences in Citizens' Experiences of Police Encounters." *Law and Human Behavior* 39(5): 463–477.

Neild, Rachel. 2001. "Democratic Police Reform in War-Torn Societies." *Conflict, Security and Development* 1(1): 21–43.

Neves, Braulio B., and Rousiley C. M. Maia. 2009. "Astonishing Images: TV News and Accountability Processes." *Brazilian Journalism Research* 5(1): 77–99.

Nogueira, Rose. 2007. *Crimes de Maio*. São Paulo: Conselho Estadual de Defesa dos Direitos da Pessoa Humana, Secretaria da Justiça e Cidadania do Estado de São Paulo.

North, Douglass. 1990. *Institutions, Institutional Change, and Economic Performance*. Cambridge: Cambridge University Press.

Nunes Dias, Camila. 2011. "Da dulverização ao monopólio da violência: Expansão e consolidação do Primeiro Comando Da Capital (PCC) no sistema carcerário paulista." University of São Paulo.

O'Donnell, Guillermo. 1993. "On the State, Democratization and Some Conceptual Problems." *World Development* 21(8): 1355–1369.

  1998. "Horizontal Accountability in New Democracies." *Journal of Democracy* 9(3): 112–126.

  2004. "Why the Rule of Law Matters." *Journal of Democracy* 15(4): 32–46.

O'Neill, Kathleen. 2005. *Decentralizing the State: Elections, Parties, and Local Power in the Andes*. New York: Cambridge University Press.

Oates, Wallace. 1999. "An Essay on Fiscal Federalism." *Journal of Economic Literature* 37(3): 1120–1149.

Ortiz, David G., Daniel J. Myers, N. Eugene Walls, and Maria-Elena D. Diaz. 2005. "Where Do We Stand with Newspaper Data?" *Mobilization: An International Journal* 10(3): 397–419.

Ouvidoria da Polícia do Estado de São Paulo. 2000. *Relatório anual de prestação de contas da Ouvidoria da Polícia – 2000*. São Paulo: Ouvidoria da Polícia do Estado de São Paulo.

Page, Benjamin, and Robert Shapiro. 1983. "Effects of Public Opinion on Policy." *American Political Science Review* 77(1): 175–190.

Palacios, Marco. 1995. *Entre la legitimidad y la violencia: Colombia 1875–1994*. Bogotá: Grupo Editorial Norma.

Pardo Rueda, Rafael. 1996. *De primera mano: Colombia 1986–1994, entre conflictos y esperanzas*. Bogotá: Cerec Norma.

Paschel, Tianna. 2010. "The Right to Difference: Explaining Colombia's Shift from Color Blindness to the Law of Black Communities." *American Journal of Sociology* 116(3): 729–769.

  2016. *Becoming Black Political Subjects: Movements and Ethno-Racial Rights in Colombia and Brazil*. Princeton, NJ: Princeton University Press.

Pateman, Carole. 1970. *Participation and Democratic Theory*. Cambridge: Cambridge University Press.

2012. "Participatory Democracy Revisited." *Perspectives on Politics* 10(1): 7–19.

Pekny, Ana Carolina, Fabiana Bento, and Stephanie Morin. 2017. *Linha de Frente: Vitimização e Letalidade Policial Na Cidade de São Paulo.* São Paulo: Instituto Sou da Paz.

Peregrino Fernández, Rodolfo. 1983. *Autocrítica policial.* Buenos Aires: El Cid Editor/Fundación para la Democracia en Argentina.

Pereira, Anthony. 2005. *Political (In)Justice: Authoritarianism and the Rule of Law in Brazil, Chile, and Argentina.* Pittsburgh, PA: University of Pittsburgh Press.

Pereira, Anthony, and Mark Ungar. 2004. "The Persistence of the Mano Dura: Authoritarian Legacies and Policing in Brazil and the Southern Cone." In *Authoritarian Legacies and Democracy in Latin America and Southern Europe*, edited by Katherine Hite and Paola Cesarini, 263–304. Notre Dame, IN: University of Notre Dame Press.

Pérez, Orlando J. 2003. "Democratic Legitimacy and Public Insecurity: Crime and Democracy in El Salvador and Guatemala." *Political Science Quarterly* 118 (4): 627–644.

2009. "Crime and Support for Coups in Latin America." *AmericasBarometer Insights* 32: 1–8.

Peruzzotti, Enrique, and Catalina Smulovitz. 2000. "Societal Accountability in Latin America." *Journal of Democracy* 11(4): 147–158.

(eds.). 2006. *Enforcing the Rule of Law: Social Accountability in the New Latin American Democracies.* Pittsburgh, PA: University of Pittsburgh Press.

Pinheiro, Paulo Sérgio. 1982. "Polícia e crise política: O caso das Polícias Militares." In *A Violencia Brasileira*, edited by Maria Célia Paoli, Maria Victoria Benevides, Paulo Sérgio Pinheiro, and Roberto da Matta, 57–92. São Paulo: Editora Brasiliense S.A.

1992. "Preface." In Guaracy Mingardi, *Tiras Gansos e Trutas: Cotidiano e Reforma Na Polícia Civil*, xv–xx. São Paulo: Editora Página Aberta.

1994. "The Legacy of Authoritarianism in Democratic Brazil." In Stuart S. Nagel, *Latin American Development and Public Policy*, 237–253. New York: St. Martin's Press.

Pinheiro, Paulo Sérgio, Eduardo Izumino, and Maria Fernandes. 1991. "Violência Fatal: Conflitos Policiais Em São Paulo (81–89)." *Revista USP* (9): 95–112.

Pion-Berlin, David. 1988. "The National Security Doctrine, Military Threat Perception, and the 'Dirty War' in Argentina." *Comparative Political Studies* 21(3): 382–407.

1997. *Through Corridors of Power: Institutions and Civil–Military Relations in Argentina.* University Park, PA: Penn State University Press.

Pita, María Victoria. 2010. *Formas de morir y formas de vivir: El activismo contra la violencia policial.* Buenos Aires: Editores del Puerto.

Policzer, Pablo. 2009. *The Rise and Fall of Repression in Chile.* Notre Dame, IN: University of Notre Dame Press.

Power, Timothy J., and César Zucco. 2009. "Estimating Ideology of Brazilian Legislative Parties, 1990–2005." *Latin American Research Review* 44(1): 218–246.

Presidencia de la República. 1994. *La nueva policía para Colombia*. Bogotá: Consejería Presidencial para la Defensa y la Seguridad Nacional.

Prowse, Gwen, Vesla M. Weaver, and Tracey L. Meares. 2019. "The State from Below: Distorted Responsiveness in Policed Communities." *Urban Affairs Review*, doi:107808741984483.

Przeworski, Adam. 1999. "Minimalist Conception of Democracy: A Defense." In *Democracy's Value*, edited by Ian Shapiro and Casiano Hacker-Cordón, 23–55. Cambridge: Cambridge University Press.

2016. "Democracy: A Never-Ending Quest." *Annual Review of Political Science* 19: 1–12.

Quintero Ramírez, Oscar. 2002. "Sociología e historia del movimiento estudiantil por la Asamblea Constituyente de 1991." *Revista Colombiana de Sociología* VII(418): 125–151.

Ralph, Laurence. 2020. *The Torture Letters: Reckoning with Police Violence*. Chicago, IL: University of Chicago Press.

Reiner, Robert. 1998. "Policing, Protest, and Disorder in Britain." In *Policing Protest: The Control of Mass Demonstrations in Western Democracies*, edited by Donatella della Porta and Herbert Reiter, 35–48. Minneapolis: University of Minnesota Press.

Restrepo Riaza, William, et al. 1994a. "La imagen social de la policía en Medellín." *Estudios Políticos* 5: 47–67.

1994b. "Policía y Sociedad." *Estudios Políticos* 5: 27–43.

Rich, Jessica. 2019. *State-Sponsored Activism: Bureaucrats and Social Movements in Democratic Brazil*. Cambridge: Cambridge University Press.

Rifiotis, Theophilos. 1999. "Violência policial e imprensa: O caso da Favela Naval." *São Paulo em Perspectiva* 13(4): 28–41.

Rivers, Douglas, and Nancy Rose. 1985. "Passing the President's Program: Public Opinion and Presidential Influence in Congress." *American Journal of Political Science* 29(2): 183–196.

Rojas, Carlos Eduardo. 1996. *La violencia llamada limpieza social*. Bogotá: CINEP.

Rotker, Susana (ed.). 2002. *Citizens of Fear: Urban Violence in Latin America*. New Brunswick, NJ: Rutgers University Press.

Ruiz Vasquez, Juan Carlos, Olga Illera Correal, and Viviana Manrique. 2006. *La tenue línea de la tranquilidad: Estudio comparado sobre seguridad ciudadana y policía*. Bogotá: Editorial Universidad del Rosario.

Sabet, Daniel. 2012. *Police Reform in Mexico: Informal Politics and the Challenge of Institutional Change*. Stanford, CA: Stanford University Press.

Saín, Marcelo Fabián. 2002. *Seguridad, democracia y reforma del sistema policial en la Argentina*. Buenos Aires: Fondo de Cultura Económica.

2004. "Un estado fallido ante las nuevas problemáticas delictivas: El caso Argentino." Universidad de Belgrano, Buenos Aires.

2006. "Police, Politics, and Society in the Province of Buenos Aires." In *Broken Promises? The Argentine Crisis and Argentine Democracy*, edited by E. Epstein and D. Pion-Berlin, 51–70. Lanham, MD: Lexington Books.

2015. *El péndulo: Reforma y contrarreforma en la policía de la provincia de Buenos Aires*. Buenos Aires: Editorial Octubre.

Sances, Michael W., and Hye Young You. 2017. "Who Pays for Government? Descriptive Representation and Exploitative Revenue Sources." *Journal of Politics* 79(3): 1090–1094.

Savage, Stephen P. 2007. *Police Reform: Forces for Change.* Oxford: Oxford University Press.

Schedler, Andreas. 1999. "Conceptualizing Accountability." In *The Self-Restraining State: Power and Accountability in New Democracies*, edited by Andreas Schedler, Larry Diamond, and Marc Plattner, 13–28. Boulder, CO: Lynne Rienner Publishers.

Scheve, Kenneth, and David Stasavage. 2017. "Wealth Inequality and Democracy." *Annual Review of Political Science* 20: 451–468.

Schmid, Robert. 1996. "La corrupción en la policía preventiva del Distrito Federal de México." In *Justicia en la calle: Ensayos sobre la policía en América Latina*, edited by Peter Waldmann, 301–320. Buenos Aires: Konrad Adenauer Stiftung-CIEDLA.

Schmitter, Philippe. 1999. "The Limits of Horizontal Accountability." In *The Self-Restraining State: Power and Accountability in New Democracies*, edited by Andreas Schedler, Larry Diamond, and Marc Plattner, 59–63. Boulder, CO: Lynne Rienner Publishers.

Schmitter, Philippe, and Terry Lynn Karl. 1991. "What Democracy Is ... And Is Not." *Journal of Democracy* 2(3): 75–88.

Schumpeter, Joseph. 1942. *Capitalism, Socialism, and Democracy*, 2nd ed. New York: Harper & Brothers.

Schuster, Federico, et al. 2006. *Transformaciones de La protesta social en Argentina 1989–2003.* Buenos Aires: Instituto de Investigaciones Gino Germani, Facultad de Ciencias Sociales, UBA.

Secretaria Municipal de Promoção da Igualdade Racial. 2015. *Igualdade racial em São Paulo: Avanços e Desafios.* São Paulo: Prefeitura de São Paulo.

Shapiro, Ian. 2006. *The State of Democratic Theory.* Princeton, NJ: Princeton University Press.

Sherman, Lawrence. 1978. *Scandal and Reform: Controlling Police Corruption.* Berkeley: University of California Press.

Sigal, Eduardo, Alberto Binder, and Ciro Annichiarico. 1998. *El final de la maldita policía?* Buenos Aires: Fundación Acción para la Comunidad.

Sinhoretto, Jacqueline. 2009. "Linchamentos: Insegurança e Revolta Popular." *Revista Brasileira de Segurança Pública* 3(4): 72–92.

Sinhoretto, Jacqueline, Giane Silvestre, and Maria Carolina Schlitter. 2014. *Desigualdade racial e segurança pública em São Paulo: Letalidade policial e prisões em flagrante.* São Carlos: Universidade Federal de São Carlos.

Skogan, Wesley G. 2006. "Asymmetry in the Impact of Encounters with Police." *Policing and Society* 16(2): 99–126.

Smith, Graham. 2009. *Democratic Innovations: Designing Institutions for Citizen Participation.* Cambridge: Cambridge University Press.

Smith, Nicholas Rush. 2015. "Rejecting Rights: Vigilantism and Violence in Post-Apartheid South Africa." *African Affairs* 114(456): 341–360.

2019. *Contradictions of Democracy: Vigilantism and Rights in Post-Apartheid South Africa.* New York: Oxford University Press.

Soifer, Hillel. 2015. *State Building in Latin America*. Cambridge: Cambridge University Press.

Soss, Joe. 1999. "Lessons of Welfare: Policy Design, Political Learning, and Political Action." *American Political Science Review* 93(2): 363–380.

Soss, Joe, and Vesla Weaver. 2017. "Police Are Our Government: Politics, Political Science, and the Policing of Race–Class Subjugated Communities." *Annual Review of Political Science* 20: 565–591.

Stanley, William. 1995. "International Tutelage and Domestic Political Will: Building a New Civilian Police Force in El Salvador." *Studies in Comparative International Development* 30(1): 30–58.

Stepan, Alfred. 1988. *Rethinking Military Politics: Brazil and the Southern Cone*. Princeton, NJ: Princeton University Press.

Storino dos Santos, Fabio. 2008. "Um Partido, Três Agendas? Política de Segurança Pública No Estado de São Paulo (1995–2006)." Dissertation. Fundação Getúlio Vargas.

Tanner, Murray Scot. 2000. "Review: Will the State Bring You Back In? Policing and Democratization." *Comparative Politics* 33(1): 101–124.

Taylor, Brian D. 2011. *State Building in Putin's Russia: Policing and Coercion after Communism*. Cambridge: Cambridge University Press.

Tilly, Charles. 1985. "War Making and State Making as Organized Crime." In *Bringing the State Back In*, edited by Peter Evans, Dietrich Rueschemeyer, and Theda Skocpol, 169–191. Cambridge: Cambridge University Press.

    1993. *Coercion, Capital and European States: AD 990–1992*. Cambridge, MA: Wiley-Blackwell.

Torres Forero, César Agusto. 2007. *De las aulas a las urnas: La Universidad Del Rosario, la Séptima Papeleta, y la Constituyente de 1991*. Bogotá: Editorial Universidad del Rosario.

Ungar Bleier, Elisabeth. 1995. "El Congreso en la nueva realidad: Modernización o retroceso?" In *En busca de la estabilidad perdida: Actores políicos y sociales en los años noventa*, edited by Francisco Leal Buitrago, 93–134. Bogotá: TM Editores.

Ungar, Mark. 2002. *Elusive Reform: Democracy and the Rule of Law in Latin America*. Boulder, CO: Lynne Rienner Publishers.

UNODC. 2013. *UNODC Global Study on Homicide 2013*. Vienna: UNODC.

Uribe de Hincapié, Maria Teresa. 1995. "Crisis política y gobernabilidad en Colombia 1980–1995." *Estudios Políticos* 7–8: 39–59.

Valenzuela, Arturo. 2004. "Latin American Presidencies Interrupted." *Journal of Democracy* 15(4): 5–19.

Varella, Drauzio. 1999. *Estação Carandiru*. São Paulo: Companhia das Letras.

Verbitsky, Horacio. 1995. *El vuelo*. Buenos Aires: Editorial Planeta Argentina S. A.I.C.

Verdú, María del Carmen. 2009. *Represión en democracia*. Buenos Aires: Editorial Herramienta.

Wade, Peter. 1995. *Blackness and Race Mixture: The Dynamics of Racial Identity in Colombia*. Baltimore, MD: Johns Hopkins University Press.

Wahl, Rachel. 2018. *Just Violence: Torture and Human Rights in the Eyes of the Police*. Stanford, CA: Stanford University Press.

Waylen, Georgina. 2007. *Engendering Transitions: Women's Mobilization, Institutions, and Gender Outcomes*. Oxford: Oxford University Press.

Weber, Max. 2009. *From Max Weber: Essays in Sociology*, edited by H. H. Gerth and C. W. Mills. New York: Routledge.

Weitzer, Ronald, and Steven Tuch. 2004. "Race and Perceptions of Police Misconduct." *Social Problems* 51(3): 305–25.

2005. "Racially Biased Policing: Determinants of Citizen Perceptions." *Social Forces* 83(3): 1009–1030.Weyland, Kurt. 2008. "Toward a New Theory of Institutional Change." *World Politics* 60(2): 281–314.

Wiarda, Howard J., and Esther M. Skelley. 2005. *Dilemmas of Democracy in Latin America: Crises and Opportunity*. Lanham, MD: Rowman & Littlefield.

Wilkinson, Steven I. 2004. *Votes and Violence: Electoral Competition and Ethnic Riots in India*. Cambridge: Cambridge University Press.

Willis, Graham Denyer. 2015. *The Killing Consensus: Police, Organized Crime, and the Regulation of Life and Death in Urban Brazil*. Berkeley: University of California Press.

Wilson, James Q. 1978. *Varieties of Police Behavior: The Management of Law and Order in Eight Communities*. Cambridge, MA: Harvard University Press.

1989. *Bureaucracy: What Government Agencies Do and Why They Do It*. New York: Basic Books.

Yashar, Deborah. 2012. "Institutions and Citizenship: Reflections on the Illicit." In *Shifting Frontiers of Citizenship: The Latin American Experience*, edited by Mario Sznajder, Carlos A. Forment, and Laurence Whitehead, 431–458. Boston, MA: Brill.

2019. *Homicidal Ecologies: Illicit Economies and Complicit States in Latin America*. Cambridge: Cambridge University Press.

Zechmeister, Elizabeth (ed.). 2014. *The Political Culture of Democracy in the Americas, 2014: Democratic Governance across 10 Years of the AmericasBarometer*. Nashville, TN: USAID – Latin American Public Opinion Project, Vanderbilt University.

Index

A page in italics indicates a table or figure. A page followed by an n indicates a footnote.

Herbert Kitschelt, Zdenka Mansfeldova, Radek Markowski, and Gabor Toka, *Post-Communist Party Systems*

David Knoke, Franz Urban Pappi, Jeffrey Broadbent, and Yutaka Tsujinaka, eds., *Comparing Policy Networks*

Ken Kollman, *Perils of Centralization: Lessons from Church, State, and Corporation*

Allan Kornberg and Harold D. Clarke, *Citizens and Community: Political Support in a Representative Democracy*

Amie Kreppel, *The European Parliament and the Supranational Party System*

David D. Laitin, *Language Repertoires and State Construction in Africa*

Fabrice E. Lehoucq and Ivan Molina, *Stuffing the Ballot Box: Fraud, Electoral Reform, and Democratization in Costa Rica*

Benjamin Lessing *Making Peace in Drug Wars: Crackdowns and Cartels in Latin America*

Janet I. Lewis *How Insurgency Begins: Rebel Group Formation in Uganda and Beyond*

Mark Irving Lichbach and Alan S. Zuckerman, eds., *Comparative Politics: Rationality, Culture, and Structure, 2nd edition*

Evan Lieberman, *Race and Regionalism in the Politics of Taxation in Brazil and South Africa*

Richard M. Locke, *The Promise and Limits of Private Power: Promoting Labor Standards in a Global Economy*

Julia Lynch, *Age in the Welfare State: The Origins of Social Spending on Pensioners, Workers, and Children*

Pauline Jones Luong, *Institutional Change and Political Continuity in Post-Soviet Central Asia*

Pauline Jones Luong and Erika Weinthal, *Oil is Not a Curse: Ownership Structure and Institutions in Soviet Successor States*

Doug McAdam, John McCarthy, and Mayer Zald, eds., *Comparative Perspectives on Social Movements*

Gwyneth H. McClendon and Rachel Beatty Riedl, *From Pews to Politics in Africa: Religious Sermons and Political Behavior*

Lauren M. MacLean, *Informal Institutions and Citizenship in Rural Africa: Risk and Reciprocity in Ghana and Côte d'Ivoire*

Beatriz Magaloni, *Voting for Autocracy: Hegemonic Party Survival and its Demise in Mexico*

James Mahoney, *Colonialism and Postcolonial Development: Spanish America in Comparative Perspective*

James Mahoney and Dietrich Rueschemeyer, eds., *Historical Analysis and the Social Sciences*

Scott Mainwaring and Matthew Soberg Shugart, eds., *Presidentialism and Democracy in Latin America*

Melanie Manion, *Information for Autocrats: Representation in Chinese Local Congresses*

Isabela Mares, *From Open Secrets to Secret Voting: Democratic Electoral Reforms and Voter Autonomy*

Daniel Treisman, *The Architecture of Government: Rethinking Political Decentralization*

Guillermo Trejo, *Popular Movements in Autocracies: Religion, Repression, and Indigenous Collective Action in Mexico*

Guillermo Trejo and Sandra Ley, *Votes, Drugs, and Violence: The Political Logic of Criminal Wars in Mexico*

Rory Truex, *Making Autocracy Work: Representation and Responsiveness in Modern China*

Lily Lee Tsai, *Accountability without Democracy: How Solidary Groups Provide Public Goods in Rural China*

Joshua Tucker, *Regional Economic Voting: Russia, Poland, Hungary, Slovakia and the Czech Republic, 1990–1999*

Ashutosh Varshney, *Democracy, Development, and the Countryside*

Yuhua Wang, *Tying the Autocrat's Hand: The Rise of The Rule of Law in China*

Jeremy M. Weinstein, *Inside Rebellion: The Politics of Insurgent Violence*

Stephen I. Wilkinson, *Votes and Violence: Electoral Competition and Ethnic Riots in India*

Andreas Wimmer, *Waves of War: Nationalism, State Formation, and Ethnic Exclusion in the Modern World*

Jason Wittenberg, *Crucibles of Political Loyalty: Church Institutions and Electoral Continuity in Hungary*

Elisabeth J. Wood, *Forging Democracy from Below: Insurgent Transitions in South Africa and El Salvador*

Elisabeth J. Wood, *Insurgent Collective Action and Civil War in El Salvador*

Deborah J. Yashar, *Homicidal Ecologies: Illicit Economies and Complicit States in Latin America*

Daniel Ziblatt, *Conservative Parties and the Birth of Democracy*